THE GENERALS

★★★★

ALSO BY WINSTON GROOM

Nonfiction

Conversations with the Enemy (1982, with Duncan Spencer)

Shrouds of Glory (1995)

The Crimson Tide (2002)

A Storm in Flanders (2002)

1942 (2004)

Patriotic Fire (2006)

Vicksburg, 1863 (2009)

Kearny's March (2011)

Shiloh, 1862 (2012)

The Aviators (2013)

Fiction

Better Times Than These (1978)

As Summers Die (1980)

Only (1984)

Forrest Gump (1986)

Gone the Sun (1988)

Gump and Co. (1995)

Such a Pretty, Pretty Girl (1998)

THE GENERALS

★ ★ ★ ★

PATTON, MACARTHUR, MARSHALL,
AND THE WINNING OF WORLD WAR II

WINSTON GROOM

 NATIONAL GEOGRAPHIC

WASHINGTON, D.C.

Published by National Geographic Partners, LLC

Library of Congress Cataloging-in-Publication Data
Groom, Winston, 1944-
  The generals : Patton, MacArthur, Marshall, and the winning of World War II / Winston Groom. -- 1st edition.
    pages cm
  Includes bibliographical references and index.
  ISBN 978-1-4262-1549-0 (hardcover : alk. paper)
  1. World War, 1939-1945--United States--Biography. 2. Patton, George S. (George Smith), 1885-1945. 3. MacArthur, Douglas, 1880-1964. 4. Marshall, George C. (George Catlett), 1880-1959. 5. Generals--United States--Biography. I. Title. II. Title: Patton, MacArthur, Marshall, and the winning of World War II.
  D736.G69 2015
  940.54)12730922--dc23
                              2015021562

Since 1888, the National Geographic Society has funded more than 12,000 research, exploration, and preservation projects around the world. National Geographic Partners distributes a portion of the funds it receives from your purchase to National Geographic Society to support programs including the conservation of animals and their habitats.

National Geographic Partners, LLC
1145 17th Street NW
Washington, DC 20036-4688 USA

Become a member of National Geographic and activate your benefits today at natgeo.com/jointoday.

For information about special discounts for bulk purchases, please contact
National Geographic Books Special Sales: ngspecsales@ngs.org

For rights or permissions inquiries, please contact National Geographic Books
Subsidiary Rights: ngbookrights@ngs.org

Interior design: Melissa Farris / Katie Olsen

Printed in the United States of America

16/QGF-RRDML/3

To Susan Helmsing,
who has lived with this book
nearly as long as I have, with all love.

So as through a glass and darkly
The age long strife I see
Where I fought in many guises
Many names—but always me.

★ ★ ★ ★

—George S. Patton Jr.,
a firm believer in reincarnation

CONTENTS

★ ★ ★ ★

AUTHOR'S NOTE

U.S. Army generals do not wear insignia of the division in which they serve, such as infantry, armor, artillery, signal corps, and so on. They are supposed to be masters of all the branches—"branch immaterial," as the saying goes.

There are five ranks for generals in the U.S. Army. A single-star *brigadier general,* in theory, leads a brigade composed of men in squads of a dozen or more. These are arranged with four squads to a platoon, which come four platoons to a company—four to as many as eight of which make up a battalion—several or more of which form a brigade of four thousand to six thousand men. A two-star *major general* commands a division, which is composed of several brigades. A three-star *lieutenant general* commands an army corps, which is composed of several divisions. A four-star *general of the army* commands an army consisting of several corps, and a five-star *general of the armies* commands more than one army, such as General Dwight D. Eisenhower did in the European theater in World War II.

This sounds cut-and-dried, but it isn't, because of the way ranks are made; however, as a rule it's the way it's supposed to work.

★ ★ ★ ★

PREFACE

Generals are a breed apart in the U.S. military. It's not simply a matter of higher rank; to wear the stars of a general in the American army is to belong to one of the most exclusive clubs on earth. Throughout the pages of history generals in war have often passed into outsize legend. Americans have seen fit to elect twelve generals to the U.S. presidency, but even before there was a United States of America generals ruled the earth.

Take for example Alexander the Great, who was born in 356 B.C. in Macedonia (ancient Greece). He was tutored as a youth by Aristotle and educated in the manner of all royal Macedonian boys to read, ride, fight, hunt, contemplate, paint, and play the harp. When he was ten, according to the Macedonian philosopher and historian Plutarch, Alexander's father informed him, "My boy, you must find a kingdom big enough for your ambitions. Macedon is too small for you."

At the age of twenty, after the assassination of his father, he succeeded to the throne and took command of the Macedonian army. Then he set out to conquer the world.

With a force of 6,000 cavalry and 50,000 foot soldiers, and a fleet of 120 ships crewed by 40,000 sailors, in 334 B.C. Alexander crossed the Hellespont into Asia, which was then ruled by the Persian Empire of

King Darius III. Once on Asian soil, he threw a spear into the ground and claimed it for himself "as a gift from the gods."

After liberating half a dozen cities along the Ionian coast, Alexander marched inland to Phrygia in Anatolia (Turkey) where he came upon the famous Gordian Knot that had been tied by the legendary King Gordias—who had decreed that anyone able to undo the knot would become "the king of Asia." Alexander hacked the thing apart with his sword and marched on to Syria where he encountered Darius and his vast army.

Slipping through the Pass of Jonah, Alexander placed his men in a terrain of mountains and rivers that gave him a tactical advantage over Darius's vastly superior forces, said to number 100,000. After Darius's cavalry broke itself on a stout Greek phalanx, Alexander personally led a charge that frightened King Darius to the extent that he ran off leaving his wife and entire family to the tender mercies of the Greeks. His army likewise fled, giving Alexander possession of Syria, where, we are told, he massacred the men of military age and sold the women into slavery.

He next marched through Jerusalem to Gaza where he was forced to conduct a siege at an Egyptian fortress. Although he was wounded in the shoulder by a spear, Alexander again won the battle, massacred the men, sold the women, and marched on into Egypt where he founded the soon-to-be prosperous city of Alexandria.

He continued to pursue Darius through Mesopotamia (Iraq) and Persia (Iran), overrunning every army in his path, acquiring a herd of a thousand of Darius's war elephants, until he eventually reached present-day Bangladesh. There, with Darius dead and the Persian Empire under his command, Alexander's army mutinied, refusing to continue after years of constant battles. The men were homesick, their spokesman said. That was the farthest extent of Alexander's conquests, and in 323 B.C., he died a painful death at the age of thirty-two, in the palace of Nebuchadrezzar in Babylon, possibly from poisoned wine.

In his time, Alexander became the world's foremost warrior, having disposed of all competitors and expanded his empire's territory manifold. Nearly two thousand years later, however, the role of the general has evolved. Modern American generals no longer fight wars of conquest; their success is not based solely on ground gained or lost, but instead on how quickly they can obtain victory and turn war into peace, which presents a professional contradiction for a soldier's job is to fight.

Still, there are striking similarities between modern and ancient battlefields, allowing many of Alexander's lessons in leadership, strategy, and tactics to still be taught in the military academies and colleges today. Indeed, over the course of human history, the general's mission might have changed, but the core values and responsibilities have remained the same. As gods among men, they not only decide who lives and who dies but how the rest of us live. We are, and always will be, mere players on their stage.

★ ★ ★ ★

THE THREE OFFICERS AT ISSUE HERE were born not into the previous century but into the one before that. As a young boy, Douglas MacArthur withstood attacks by hostile Indians as his army officer father, a hero of the Civil War, traveled from post to post in the Old West. George Patton, who became the richest man in the army, was fifteen years old before the first automobiles appeared in his California hometown. George Marshall was a teenager attending the Virginia Military Institute when the entire cadet corps signed a document offering their services to the U.S. Army, which was fighting in the Spanish-American War of 1898.

Each, too, was extraordinary in his own way. Patton had to overcome a learning disability; Marshall was in the beginning a poor student; MacArthur, "who learned to ride and shoot before he learned to read and write," lived in the shadow of his army general father, who had been awarded the Medal of Honor. These three rose steadily through the officers' ranks, were hammered into sturdy metal in the crucible of World War I, and arrived at the top just as World War II was about to begin. They soon proved to be outstanding, whether in the field—as were MacArthur and Patton—or managing the vast planning and logistics, which Marshall did as chief of staff.

By the time MacArthur, Patton, and Marshall reached the rank of general, armies had become too large to lead from the fighting front and the military had long since abandoned the practice of putting its top leaders in harm's way. While Patton and MacArthur took pains to place themselves in the front lines, it is still difficult to compare them with earlier great chieftains of history such as Hannibal, Alexander, or Scipio, all of whom led their troops into battle and fought alongside their men.

Along with Marshall, Patton and MacArthur are more comfortably identified with the Napoleonic era. It would be easy to feature George Patton as Napoleon storming through Europe at the head of great armies; MacArthur could be likened to the Iron Duke, Wellington, directing his hordes against the French menace, and Marshall might be compared to the great Prussian military strategist Carl von Clausewitz, who fell into a state of melancholy after Napoleon's defeat at Waterloo because he no longer had any opportunity to distinguish himself on the battlefield.

Like their predecessors, all three generals also became famous after returning home from war. Excellent motion pictures were made of Patton's and MacArthur's careers in World War II, starring George C. Scott and Gregory Peck, respectively. They were accurate portrayals and filmed with such strong characterizations that it is hard to imagine these vivid field generals on the screen as being anything or anyone other than the movie stars who played them.

The specter of George Marshall, on the other hand, has faded since he was an eternal newsreel headliner as the army's chief of staff, secretary of state, and secretary of defense. Few people fully realize the efforts he expended trying to rein in the likes of Patton and MacArthur, both of whom often behaved as though they were a thing unto themselves. But as long as there was a fight, Marshall kept them in it, never losing sight of the fact that a war had to be won and Patton and MacArthur gave their country the best chances to accomplish that.

★ ★ ★ ★

UNLIKE BEING A CEO of a major corporation, the very essence of a general, or any professional soldier for that matter, is a contradiction. For their entire career they are trained to fight and kill and conquer and yet, the more effective they are, the quicker they return to peace and the problems that peace often presents—dynamic changes in power, uncertainty, unrest.

As we will see in the following pages, peacetime is not always kind to generals and they do not necessarily do well outside their task of generaling. Perhaps that is because during war they become as close to gods on earth as we are ever likely to see.

Patton and MacArthur were the shrewdest, most aggressive, battle-wise, and successful generals in the field. They were also—including Marshall—among the most colorful, interesting, and, at times, exasperating characters to come out of the Second World War. Their stories are linked as closely as any other set of generals in history and when they died they passed into legend, long linked with their names.

PART I

BEGINNINGS

FIRST CAPTAIN, VMI

For George Marshall's entire army career he'd longed to be a combat officer, but it was not to be. He possessed an uncanny genius for organization and leadership that perennially led him to staff duty. Staff officers solve problems, large or small, day or night, all night long if necessary.

They concern themselves with sticky questions, ones that often involve weighty matters, such as who should or should not be in command and where important military resources should be used. It could even involve a simple thing like trimming a tree while trying to place an artillery battery on an obscure Caribbean island, and therein lies a tale.

Marshall had been sworn in during a 3 a.m. emergency meeting at the War Department on September 1, 1939, a day that by coincidence carried more ominous portent than any U.S. Army chief of staff has had to contend with before or after. It was the day Germany invaded Poland, starting World War II. Soon after, the U.S. War Department began to try and convince the Dutch to place a battery of U.S.-made 155mm howitzers on the islands of Aruba and Curaçao, which were in Dutch possession. Because of their proximity to oil-rich Venezuela, these islands contained the world's largest oil refineries, run by the state petroleum company Royal Dutch Shell. U.S. forces, alarmed by the imminence of war, feared this valuable resource could be cut off, as was certainly threatened when Hitler's armies conquered and occupied Holland, and German submarines and even a large German raider ship had been sighted in the area. This might be seen as a small factor in the larger scheme of things, but Marshall was never one to avoid details. No good staff man could afford to.

It was on a Sunday in early 1942 when Marshall was looking forward to a leisurely afternoon at Dodona, his elegantly restored nineteenth-century manor house and gardens in Leesburg, Virginia, about half an hour's drive from the War Department in the capital.

Mrs. Marshall, however, had different plans. There was a large tree on the lawn that had been nagging at her for months. Some of its limbs were growing the wrong way, stunting growth on the other branches, and needed to be cut.

Casual help, such as yardmen, was impossible to get because of the war, "so she took me out there on this Sunday afternoon and sicced me on this tree," said Marshall, who was sixty-one years old at the time, "and I climbed up there with a saw and started on the limbs."

It was a grueling climb, Marshall recalled, but no sooner had he begun sawing than there came a telephone call from the War Department, chief of staff's office. Dutifully, he climbed down to receive it and, sure enough, a German raider had been spotted prowling ominously off the Venezuelan coast, "and they were afraid," Marshall said, "it was after these Dutch oil refineries."

Marshall told the officer on the phone to fly up that same afternoon to Hyde Park, New York, where President Franklin Roosevelt was spending the weekend, and see if he would authorize a message to Queen Wilhelmina of the Netherlands* requesting her to give immediate permission for the United States to set up artillery batteries on the islands.

Then Marshall reascended his tree. "Climbing up was the hardest thing and I didn't even have on sneakers," Marshall remembered. But he

---

* The queen and her government escaped The Hague before the Germans arrived and set up a government in exile in London.

had only just resumed his sawing when the phone rang again. It was the same officer he had told to fly to Hyde Park to consult with Roosevelt, who had several questions about what he was to tell the president.

That having been dealt with, "I went back up the tree," Marshall said, when the phone rang once more. This time it was President Roosevelt himself, who had some questions of his own. "So I climbed down out of the tree and went back to the house and got on the telephone and explained the situation and recommended the action I thought ought to be taken," Marshall said. "Then I went back to my peaceful occupation up the tree," though by this time he was "a little run down."

He was not there long, however, when President Roosevelt "thought of something further, and I had to come down out of the tree again." This time—following his fourth descension of the tree—he gave up, changed his clothes, got into his car, and drove to the office.[1]

This, and situations like it, are the enduring fate of the staff man. It takes a personality of inordinate composure and equanimity to handle the constant vicissitudes of making decisions that have consequences both grave and great, even while you're up a tree.

The outcome of the story was rewarding, however. Roosevelt okayed Marshall's message to Queen Wilhelmina, who herself okayed the establishment of U.S. artillery batteries on Aruba and Curaçao. The batteries arrived and got set up, Marshall said, the very evening before a German submarine surfaced and opened fire on the large refinery on Aruba. But the response from the American 155mm batteries was enough to drive it away, and the refineries continued to supply oil to the United States and other Allies.

Incidentally, Marshall said, he once told the story of the artillery batteries and the tree to England's King George while having dinner with Winston Churchill in the bombproof cellar of number 10 Downing Street. It "struck the king as very funny," Marshall said, and on those frequent occasions when the two men were again found in each other's company, King George would always ask Marshall to retell the ordeal of the tree for the amusement of other guests.

GEORGE CATLETT MARSHALL JR. was born on New Year's Eve, 1880. He was ushered into the so-called Gilded Age, the Gay Nineties, "la belle époque" of citizens riding around on bicycles with enormous front wheels and of barbershop quartets; when men wore mustaches instead of beards and parted their hair in the middle, and women wore floor-sweeping dresses with bustles and twisted the hair on their heads into buns.

The great American Civil War had been over now for a quarter century, and many of the old animosities between North and South had mostly faded. By then the United States was the most prosperous nation in the world, producing vast amounts of iron, steel, and other manufactured goods and commodities, including a huge trade surplus of food grown on farms in the Midwest. This was the America of muscle, of strong trade, of Irish, Welsh, and continental European immigrants teeming into the country to work for the railroads, steel mills, and shipyards. They worked for men like young George Marshall's father, who was involved in the iron and steel industry, but lest we get ahead of ourselves, let's take time now to visit the vestiges of the Marshall clan. In America at least, it traces as far back as the year 1650, when an Irish Anglican cavalier named Captain John Marshall landed at Jamestown, Virginia, to escape the tyranny of Oliver Cromwell and his Roundheads.

These worthies included a namesake—the eminent Chief Justice of the United States John Marshall—as well as, down through the ages, a productive gaggle of Revolutionary War heroes, lawyers, preachers, planters, doctors, congressmen, surveyors, ambassadors, military officers, and others a cut above average. Somewhere around the end of the eighteenth century the Marshall line abandoned Virginia for the fertile and lightly settled lands across the Appalachians in Kentucky—just as it became the fifteenth state in the Union.

There, in the port town of Augusta on the Ohio River, they prospered in mercantile trade, the law, and politics, constructing, in due time, a substantial three-story, sixteen-room brick residence that came close to being a mansion. When the Civil War came to a divided Kentucky in 1862, George Catlett Marshall Sr. was a sixteen-year-old member of the

Augusta Home Guard, sworn to uphold the Union cause, while his two older brothers were away serving in the Confederate Army.

On September 27, 1862, a Saturday, forces under the Rebel general Basil Duke appeared on a hill south of Augusta. Duke used his artillery to disperse two Federal gunboats, and then marched his 450 cavalrymen down the town's main street. The commander of the outnumbered Home Guard, which consisted of only one hundred men and no artillery, raised a white flag. Scattered in houses and buildings, most of the guard did not see it and opened fire on the Southern soldiers.

In the ensuing fight some seventeen Confederates and seven Home Guardsmen were killed, and a number on both sides wounded. The Home Guard eventually surrendered and it became but one of hundreds of such skirmishes that marked the backwaters of the war in the Border States, where brothers truly fought brothers and the calamity was profound. Years later Marshall remembered that General Duke himself, a Kentuckian, was also a relative, and family lore had it that after the fighting was over he came to the door of the Marshall home to see if everyone was all right.

When the war ended Marshall Sr. was nineteen and engaged to Laura Emily Bradford, daughter of the town doctor who had commanded (and surrendered) the august Home Guard to General Duke. Young Marshall, seeking his fortune as a merchant, had, it seems, begun at the wrong time. Railroads were quickly surpassing riverboats in carrying the nation's trade, and Augusta was fast declining as a center of commerce. Through a relative, he got wind of a clerkship at an ironworks in a small town in Pennsylvania called Dunbar, which was in the shadow of the Alleghenies about forty miles south of Pittsburgh.

Once at the Dunbar Iron Company, Marshall Sr. had no intention of making a career out of being a clerk. The earth of western Pennsylvania was already yielding great fortunes for hearty go-getters such as John D. Rockefeller and his Standard Oil Company and the iron and steel works of Andrew Carnegie and his partner Henry Clay Frick. After the Civil War there was a rapid expansion of railroads, metal ship hulls, iron bridges, and girder-built constructions that allowed the building of structures many stories high instead of just three or four. In turn, there became an insatiable demand for forged metals and the processes that created them.

One such process produced coke, a pure-burning fuel with a high carbon content derived from cooking coal in an oven at high temperatures until it forms a hard, gray, porous solid block of ash. The coke was then used to fuel the thousands of "beehive" coke ovens* that dotted the countryside of Pittsburgh and its environs, for the furnaces of Carnegie and others ran night and day. Marshall Sr. had been at the Dunbar Ironworks a little more than a year when he teamed with a young bookkeeper from Alabama named Arthur W. Bliss to form a company that manufactured the firebricks with which to build beehive ovens. By 1872 it was reported that "Bliss, Marshall & Company was producing seven thousand brick a day—the beginning of a solid business with wealth perhaps ahead."[2]

Meanwhile, Marshall returned to Augusta to marry his fiancée, Laura Bradford, in a society wedding reported in the Cincinnati newspapers. The following year she gave birth to a child and the Marshalls moved from Dunbar. They settled eight miles south in Uniontown, a small city of thirty-five hundred, which sat on the enormous Connellsville vein of coal and was bisected by a watercourse with the unappealing name Coal Lick Run. Founded in 1776, Uniontown had been a stagecoach stop on the old National Road that ran across the mountains. Its history dates back to the French and Indian War and George Washington's surrender of Fort Necessity to the French.

In due time Marshall and Bliss branched into the coke-producing business, operating their own coke ovens as well as selling lump coal from a mining operation. Not even the depression of 1873 could stop them, and by the middle of that decade Bliss and Marshall expanded dramatically, buying a mining company as well as coalfields. In 1880, the year George Jr. was born, his father was named company president.

....

* So called because they were shaped like beehives.

Marshall Sr. was a gregarious and friendly personality in Uniontown, where he joined the Masons and the Democratic Party, despite the fact that Democrats were a decided minority in Pennsylvania. He was proud of his family's history, especially its connection, however tenuous, with Justice John Marshall (a distant cousin). He was scandalized when young George, given a copy of the family genealogy, discovered (and went about telling anyone who would listen) that a Marshall ancestor in the early eighteenth century had married the pirate Blackbeard—the infamous Edward Teach who was beheaded by the British in 1718.

Growing up, the young boy made frequent trips back to the family place in Augusta, Kentucky, where there was a flock of cousins to play with and hideouts and haunts along the tall bluffs of the Ohio that one writer described as "reminiscent of stretches of the Rhine."[3] Here, where the Marshalls had lived for generations, they were gentry, but back in Uniontown the Marshalls were not readily accepted by some of the older families "that dated back almost to George Washington's day." There remained in northern states such as Pennsylvania—as it did in the South—vestiges of the old sectional animosities and mistrust. As Marshall recalled long afterward, "Father came up from the South; Mother came up from the South," and so, "for a long time," it was mostly the newer residents of Uniontown whom the Marshalls associated with.

But it was the picturesque Uniontown that was formative in the boy's life, where he spent his childhood hunting quail and grouse in the mountains with his father and fishing for bass and pike on rock-ledged icy rivers. At night his mother would read to the family, by fireside in the cooler months and outside on the wide veranda in summer—mainly, Marshall remembered, the Sir Walter Scott romances such as *Ivanhoe*. Later, when her eyesight began to fail, she had to hand over the reading duties to George's father, who favored all the James Fenimore Cooper stories and a long saga by Arthur Conan Doyle called *The Refugees*.

At Miss Thompson's School, and away from his literary parents, young George Jr. was a mostly indifferent student, except on Sunday school picnics where they would churn ice cream. In winter there was skating on frozen ponds, sledding, and sleigh rides bundled in straw, and at Christmas a large tree in the dining room lit by candles on its branches just before daylight. On the Fourth of July George took out "several cigar boxes full of firecrackers and rockets." His nickname was "Flicker," because of his sandy hair.

Alongside his brother and sister, George would sit by the fireside while his father read, opening hickory nuts with a hammer "for mother's very famous hickory nut cake." "I always liked our fires," he said, "because we had what was called cannel coal and it made a soft, delightful home-like flame . . . and it was very agreeable to sit in front of. Later on," he remembered, "when natural gas was piped in, the fireplace lost a great deal of its charm."

As he grew older the boy became a keen entrepreneur. At the age of ten, with his friend Andy Thompson, he opened a greenhouse and florist shop, selling flowers to the schoolgirls for a penny—until, that is, the girls discovered that they were not actually growing the flowers themselves, but combing the countryside around Uniontown for them. The girls insisted that they shouldn't be charged for things that were free and the business collapsed. Next the pair set up shop in the basement of the Marshalls' house selling homemade corn silk cigars and root beer—until the elder Marshall discovered that the enterprise involved selling *his own* root beer, which he had put into the cellar to age. The illicit funds gleaned from this enterprise were spent at the corner drugstore on penny thrillers and licorice sticks.

After this, the two began a clandestine venture raising fighting chickens—clandestine because cockfighting was illegal in most of the United States. They raised Red Bantams with eggs ordered from Georgia and had an older friend enter them into the fights. But later, when they went to the pits to see their birds fight, the affair was raided by the sheriff and the two barely escaped capture and arrest.

Once he and Andy scooped out a canal on Coal Lick Creek that ran behind George's house and filled it with "The Great Pacific Fleet," made of matchbox battleships with matchstick masts, after the same powerful naval squadron Admiral George Dewey would later command when it sank the Spanish fleet in Manila harbor during the Spanish-American War. Soon this became the exhibit of the neighborhood.

So the boy's life was idyllic, more or less, in a *Tom Sawyer*ish way.

In his teens George was athletically inclined but, in his own words, "not very talented." He played football and baseball with his school's teams, developed unsuccessful crushes on several girls, and remained lackadaisical in his scholarship. He grew to be more than six feet tall and gangly, but with a handsome face, probing eyes, and a rather stern countenance except on those infrequent occasions when he smiled, which gave him a warm and comforting expression.

In 1890 the Marshalls' world changed dramatically. To consolidate operations, Marshall Sr. and his partners had decided to sell most of their coke and coal holdings to Henry Clay Frick, who was busy creating a monopoly in that part of Pennsylvania. Against the advice of his wife, Marshall Sr. put practically all the proceeds of his part of the sale—approximately $150,000*—into a resort land company in Virginia's Shenandoah Valley. When it went sour later that year with the crash of 1890 and the ensuing depression, not only did Marshall lose his investment, as president of the company he had obligated himself for all its debts and he lost his savings as well. Ultimately Marshall Sr. was forced into bankruptcy and the family very suddenly went from comfortable affluence to having practically no money at all.

The boy's mother had been left some rental properties in Philadelphia and lots in Augusta that contributed a relatively small amount to the family income, and his father still retained an interest in several smaller businesses connected with the coal and iron industries. But financially it was a strain. George suddenly found himself in public school instead of the fashionable Miss Thompson's. Fifty years later he put it bluntly: "The years of my boyhood, from the 1890 crash until I went away to school, were very limited financially, and only my mother's modest income from

---

* Approximately $5 million in today's money.

some property she still held in Pittsburgh saved the situation . . . We had to economize very bitterly."[4]

But it was far more than money his mother brought to the boy. Character often springs from diverse, hidden sources, and if you believe in such things as ancestry and breeding that might account for some of it—yet as the years passed there was much, much more. It had become increasingly evident, says Marshall's biographer William Frye, that young George Marshall "had his mother's reserve, her great dignity, her steadiness, the same profound moral integrity, tempered perhaps by some of his father's easy manner and that indefinable quality that gentlefolk call presence."[5]

America in the 1890s was characterized by the financial crash at the beginning of the decade and the subsequent depression and recovery; industrial labor upheavals; and the Spanish-American War of 1898. As we have seen, the financial crash created a great burden on Marshall's teenage years, though he seemed stoic about it, remarking later, "Every boy in a democracy should attend, at least for a period of time, a public school."

The labor troubles were just then turning deadly, with bitter strikes in the mining and railroad industries; beatings and killings were frequent and often the army, state militia, or National Guard was called upon to keep labor unions at bay. In the previous decade there had been an estimated twenty-four thousand strikes and lockouts; with all the coal mining around Uniontown, Marshall was smack in the midst of the ugliness. In fact, one of his father's business partners was assassinated by the Molly McGuires, a violent secret society that used murder, arson, and kidnapping to intimidate mine and mill owners and other capitalists. The senior Marshall was likewise on the Mollies' "black list," according to George, but somehow escaped harm. As for George himself, he was once struck in the head by a lump of coal thrown by an angry striking miner. Later in life, Marshall noted that miners rarely joined the army, since they considered U.S. soldiers as a kind of enemy.

In those times youngsters often went to college at the age of sixteen, sometimes earlier. Both George's brother, Stuart, five years older, and his sister, Marie, four years older, were away at school, money having been put aside for this by the elder Marshall before the crash and his financial ruin. George wasn't so lucky. He wanted to attend West Point both because he fancied a military career and because it was free. Unfortunately, his district's congressman was a Republican—as were both of Pennsylvania's senators—and Marshall Sr.'s prominent affiliation with the Democratic Party spoiled that notion. The next best thing was the Virginia Military Institute, where brother Stuart was in his senior year and where generations of the Virginia Marshalls had received their education.

What made George most keen to attend VMI was a conversation he surreptitiously overheard between his mother and his brother, who had been home on leave from the institute. Because of George's mediocre grades in high school, Stuart urged his mother *not* to send him to VMI for fear of disgracing the family name. The incident had such a profound effect on Marshall that he remembered it vividly in his later years, saying that it motivated him more "than all the instructors, parental pressure, or anything else," and "had a psychological effect" on his entire career.

Passing the entrance exam to VMI was dictated in large measure on whether or not the school's superintendent, General Scott Shipp, liked the applicant. Shipp, known as a straitlaced but kindly man, had been at VMI for nearly forty years. As commandant during the Civil War, he had led the school's corps of cadets, and he was wounded in its celebrated charge against the Union line during the Battle of New Market in 1864. Fortunately for George, the Marshall name in Virginia lay very high in the estimation of General Shipp, and the fact that George's brother had excelled at VMI also prepared the road for his acceptance. For reasons that remain inexplicable, George took easily to the harsh military life of the academy; in fact, he thrived in it.

When, in September 1897, he arrived at the imposing and austere-looking campus in Lexington, Virginia, in the shadows of the Blue Ridge Mountains, sixteen-year-old cadet George Catlett Marshall Jr. (reporting three days late after having contracted typhoid fever) was in awe. "I will never forget," he said years later, "walking down the long approach avenue to the barracks and hearing the bugle sound the assembly and seeing the adjutant and the sergeant major strut out to form the line on which the battalion would form. They were wonderful figures to me."

Discipline at VMI was as strict or stricter than it was at West Point. Hazing of the freshmen cadets (known as "rats") was severe as upperclassmen "braced" their young charges, shouting harshly in their faces. They were compelled to haul buckets of water from an outside tap up stairs to the upperclassmen's quarters. Inspections of rooms and personages were rigorous and demerits distributed freely for any offense; these would be marched off on the parade grounds—one per hour—before the cadet was allowed freedom on Saturday afternoons to go into the town of Lexington. During the first few weeks of the hazing, which were the worst, Marshall suffered an injury that might well have been very serious, if not fatal. On the parade ground he was forced to squat over an unsheathed bayonet sticking out of the ground as a foolish and irresponsible endurance test. Probably weakened by the typhoid, he slipped, lacerating his buttock on the weapon. The wound caused him to miss formation for several days, but it would have been far more dangerous by a matter of an inch or so.

Marshall came in for special hazing because of his Pennsylvania Yankee accent. VMI remained a strong Southern institution, the Civil War barely thirty years past. In Marshall's first year, the final building to be restored after Northern general David Hunter burned VMI nearly to the ground in 1864 was Jackson Memorial Hall, named after the legendary Confederate general Thomas J. "Stonewall" Jackson, who had been brought there for burial following the Battle of Chancellorsville. Each year in May the names of the cadets who had been slain during the Battle of New Market were read aloud at formation. Moreover, the walls of barracks that had not been completely destroyed bore the blemishes of Hunter's cannonballs during the 1864 incident. Older residents, and not a few VMI cadets, felt themselves well up at the frequent playing of "Dixie."

Next door in Lexington was Washington and Lee College, of which Robert E. Lee had been president. Following his death in 1870, his body was entombed in what had been renamed Lee Chapel. Marshall was surprised, and on occasion shocked, that the South seemed utterly unrepentant following the war. In those days, the school often presented speakers at morning assembly such as the former Rebel general Jubal A. Early who, Marshall later noted, gave a speech defending the Confederacy "that seemed almost treasonous!"

If Marshall found the hazing annoying he at least took it passively. "I think I was more philosophical about this sort of thing than a great many boys," he said long afterward. "It was part of the business and the only thing was to accept it as best you could." Fortunately for Marshall, he lucked into a roommate his first year named Leonard Nicholson, scion of the New Orleans *Times-Picayune.* Nicholson became his closest friend and remained with him until graduation. He was a man of great charm and good humor, as well as generosity when Marshall needed it most. (George's allowance from home was $5 a month, and Nicholson more than once made up the shortfalls.) Even so, with such little money, Marshall avoided dances and other social functions during his first two years at VMI. He remained a marginal student, somewhere in the middle of his class, but in military studies and on the drill field his performance was such that at the final formation in the spring of 1898 it was announced that he would be first corporal the following term.

About that same time the United States declared war on Spain. The issue was Cuba, where a civil war had been raging for nearly three years because of the despotic behavior of its new Spanish governor Valeriano Weyler. There had long been talk in the United States of annexing Cuba from Spain; southerners had their eye on it for half a century before the American Civil War. In February 1898 the battleship *Maine,* stationed in the Havana harbor to protect U.S. interests, exploded and sank killing 260 of her 374-man crew. The American press nearly became unhinged—especially the so-called yellow journalism newspapers of William Randolph Hearst and Joseph Pulitzer. They blamed Spain for the incident, saying the ship had been deliberately blown up by a Spanish mine.* When the United States called for Spain's immediate removal and self-government for the Cuban Isles, Spain of course refused. In April 1898 both houses of the U.S. Congress declared war on Spain.

Within a week Dewey's Asiatic Squadron had destroyed the entire Spanish fleet in the Philippines, and the United States claimed that huge piece of island territory. The VMI corps of cadets voted to a man to sign a document offering its services to the U.S. Army.

Shortly after subduing the Spanish officials and military forces in Manila, the United States attempted to establish an administration for the islands until some kind of Philippine government could be organized.† But soon a serious insurrection broke out that taxed the United States' resources and willpower over this problem-child territory eight thousand miles from its shores.‡

By the end of his sophomore year at VMI, Marshall had not only put on weight that enhanced his looks but also improved his grades, bringing himself to the mid-third of his class. He decided to major in civil engineering. At the final formation that spring his name was announced as the first in the new promotion to first sergeants for the upcoming school term. Back in Uniontown, he was stirred by the triumphant return of the local National Guard company that had been fighting the Spanish in Cuba and the *insurrectos* in the Philippines. He later remembered that this martial spectacle galvanized his "choice of profession."

....

* What exactly happened to the *Maine* remains a subject of controversy. Shortly after the incident a U.S. Navy board concluded that a mine had caused the explosion. Later investigations by private interests suggested that the forward coal bunker had blown up from an excess of coal dust. In any event, in 1912, following a three-year effort, U.S. Army engineers raised the ship and removed scores of bodies, which were sent for burial in Arlington National Cemetery. The *Maine* was then towed out to sea and scuttled to make an offshore fishing reef.

† Spanish officials, hoping to save face, had secretly arranged with the U.S. Army to surrender after a sham battle was staged.

‡ The Philippines remained in an almost constant state of insurrection from that time until after World War II when it was granted independence.

That summer he served as a rodman on a surveying crew, and when classes resumed in the fall he went out for the VMI football team. He became a standout left tackle and made the first squad, immortalizing himself with a fifty-yard touchdown run in a victory over next-door rival Washington and Lee.[6] It was a seminal year for George Catlett Marshall Jr. for two reasons: he was named first captain, VMI's highest military honor, and he fell in love.

She was Elizabeth Carter Coles, known as Lily, who lived with her mother in her grandfather's house, which was almost adjacent to the entrance—or "limit gates"—of VMI. Marshall was drawn by her piano playing, which wafted out of an open window as he passed by one evening. He stopped and listened, remembering years later that she was "the finest amateur pianist I have ever heard." The next evening Marshall returned with several classmates; the night after that he was invited inside.

If it wasn't love at first sight it was something close to it: two or three weeks later they were "steadies," and they were engaged for the last year and a half Marshall was in school. She was a beauty of some renown, and also four years older than Marshall, who, though he was but nineteen years old at the time, cut a fine tall handsome figure in his first captain's uniform. Lily came from fine old Virginia stock; one of her Pendleton ancestors was a signer of the Declaration of Independence and governor of Virginia. Another had harbored Thomas Jefferson from the British on his plantation during the Revolution.

Unfortunately Lily's social activities were strictly limited by a bad constitution. She was unable to exert herself, even to dance.* But they found time together riding in her carriage, a stanhope trap, or sitting in her parlor. Even though it was thoroughly un–first captaincy behavior on his part, Marshall frequently went AWOL to see her late at night, sneaking off campus after lights-out—a practice known as "running the block." "It was a dismissal offense," Marshall recalled, "but I was very much in love and willing to take the chance."

---

* Her condition, Marshall said, was a heart defect called mitral regurgitation.

He came out fifth in his class in civil engineering, later remembering that by that time "ambition had set in." At graduation, he was initiated into the Kappa Alpha fraternity, as VMI cadets are not allowed to join fraternities while in school. Then, armed with a college degree, he set out to find a way to get a commission in the U.S. Army, and to select a date to marry Elizabeth Carter Coles.

★ ★ ★ ★

MARSHALL'S QUEST FOR A LIEUTENANT'S commission in the army was an exercise in persistence and tenacity, traits that had been nurtured at VMI, along with self-control, discipline, honesty, and leadership— the ability to control men. His parents at first resisted the notion of a military career for their son. The army in those days was not held in very high regard, notwithstanding the celebrated victory over Spain. Pay was low for junior officers, promotions slow, and the duty was often onerous. Since the nation's inception, Americans have opposed having a large standing army. Instead they have opted for a small professional army whose ranks could quickly be swelled by volunteers (or in some cases the draft) in times of crisis. Therefore there were few openings for junior officers' positions, most of them going to graduates of West Point.

In time, Marshall's father came around and his mother also reluctantly accepted the idea of an army officer for a son. The elder Marshall, with his tenacious personality, then began to assemble a series of political contacts, beginning with General Shipp at VMI and leading all the way up to Elihu Root, the secretary of war, and ultimately to President William McKinley himself, a Republican. Thus on an April day in 1901, young George Marshall found himself in the waiting room next to President McKinley's office on the second floor of the White House "without an appointment of any kind," having been told by "an old colored man" (the head usher) that he would never get in.

After watching more than a dozen people enter the president's office, Marshall saw his chance. When a man and his young daughter arrived and the usher escorted them in to see McKinley, Marshall "attached [him-] self to the tail of this procession and gained the President's office," adding that "the old colored man frowned at me on his way out but I stood pat."

Marshall stated his case as succinctly as possible while the president listened politely and then he took his leave. Marshall later credited this presidential encounter with his being invited to take the army's entrance examination for officers, which his principal biographer Forrest Pogue disputes. Whatever the case, he passed the exam and, on January 4, 1902, when he had just turned twenty-one, orders were issued commissioning George C. Marshall as a second lieutenant in the U.S. Army with a date of rank from February 2, 1901. His orders further stated that in five days he was to report to Fort Myer, Virginia, and thence to Columbus barracks, Ohio. There he was to assume command of a detachment of recruits and take them by train to San Francisco, where they would board a ship for the Philippines. But, first, he had to get married.

The day after passing his exam, Marshall arrived in Lexington where the wedding was to be held in the bride's home. The ceremony was performed by an Episcopal priest before Marshall's parents, brother and sister, and his best friend from boyhood, Andy Thompson, with whom he had raised the fighting chickens back in Uniontown. Lily, dressed in white, was attended by her mother and sister and a number of friends from Lexington. It was reported that as the wedding guests mingled and chatted she turned to the tall, handsome newly commissioned second lieutenant and said, "Come on, George, let's get married."[7]

They boarded the train to Washington the following day to spend a week's honeymoon at the fashionable new Willard Hotel a few blocks from the White House, which was followed by the sorrow of parting for his two-year tour of duty across eight thousand miles of ocean. On April 12, 1902, Marshall embarked on the troop transport *Kilpatrick,* bound for Manila.

While the Philippine insurrection would not be declared officially over for another three months, by the time Marshall's transport arrived the uprising had been largely put down, with its leaders agreeing to take the American loyalty oath. Still, Marshall arrived in the Philippines in the midst of a deadly cholera epidemic and was assigned as a platoon leader with G Company of the 30th Infantry Regiment of the regular army, stationed on the island of Mindoro.* While in transit there, the interisland steamer *Isla de Negros,* on which he was a passenger, was caught in a terrifying typhoon that nearly wrecked the ship when the captain deserted the bridge for his stateroom and Marshall and another army officer had to take control of the vessel, not only steering it away from dangerous rocks but forcing the engine room crew back to their posts at pistol point.

Safely on land, his company was posted to the town of Calapan, which Marshall found inhabited mainly by women and children. Most of the men were living out in the hills as guerrilla fighters who, he said, "would shoot into the town from time to time." The regiment was commanded by a colonel who had lost an arm in the Civil War and, Marshall remembered, was composed mostly of former Indian fighters, "about the wildest crowd I've ever seen, before or since."

The sole entertainment in town for the officers was a trio of girls—sisters—one of whom played the harp, and "they played and sang sweetly" in the mornings. Through all his life since, the horror still raised a shiver in Marshall about the cholera attack reaching Calapan. "It broke out in almost a day," he said, right after he had heard the girls sing. "We had no warning of it there. We thought we were safe. It broke out and the three sisters—I helped bury them all by three o'clock that afternoon."

The men were immediately confined to quarters. Everything had to be boiled. The fingernails had to be cleaned, Marshall said. The hands and mess kits had to be washed in hot water. "You had to enforce these things very carefully or they would skimp them," Marshall said. "A very little skimping would cost you your life." They set up a cholera camp by a spring about two miles outside of town. Marshall went there sometimes as officer of the day. The first time he went up, "I found the soldiers peacefully eating their supper on a pile of coffins. Later there weren't

---

* Marshall himself estimated there were about five thousand cholera deaths a day.

any coffins. The deaths came too rapidly," and the victims then had to be buried wrapped only in a sheet and laid in trenches.

Cholera is a bacterial disease with dreadful symptoms. Marshall remembered its victims lying on metal cots, "with their knees almost under their chins and generally shrieking with the agonies of their convulsions. I don't recall, myself, anybody recovering at that time."*

By July 4 the epidemic had run its course. Theodore Roosevelt, who had become president after the assassination of President McKinley, officially declared that the insurrection in the Philippines was over. But this was news to large numbers of *insurrectos* who roamed the mountains, as well as to the hostile Moros, and so the army began sending out patrols to rein in these guerrillas. Marshall was ordered to lead a twenty-six-man detachment to the very southern tip of Mindoro, where he often set up the patrols. In the process he encountered one of the strange primitive tribes that inhabited the Philippines—who frequently greeted unexpected visitors with a flurry of poisoned arrows and blowgun darts. They were Batanganis, a light-skinned race identified with the legend that one woman of the tribe was so beautiful that any white man who saw her once would never return from Mindoro.[8]

At one point Marshall and his detachment were given the onerous duty of guarding a prison island in Laguna Bay inhabited by "the dregs of the army . . . the toughest crowd of men I've ever seen. You had to count them twice every night." On one occasion Marshall saw one of these men attack another with a meat cleaver and nearly cut his head off.

But army life is one of contrasts, and he soon found himself posted to the quaint town of Santa Mesa just outside Manila. There he could go to the Army-Navy Club, dine al fresco in the delightful courtyard, and access the club's riding stables, which was where Marshall developed his lifelong devotion to horseback riding. In the evening there was always a concert on the Luneta where, Marshall said, "everybody in Manila in our social order" would go, paying visits to one another from carriage to carriage

---

* A reported 109,461 people died in the Philippines during the cholera plague.

while the music played. Frequently there were "insurrection" scares, in which a bugler would blow the clarion call to quarters at all hours of the night on unreliable evidence that a new revolution was at hand.

★ ★ ★ ★

IN 1903 MARSHALL RETURNED to the United States and his company was posted to Fort Reno in the remote wilds of the Oklahoma Territory. It was garrison duty and fairly routine: close order drill, inspections, reports, spit-and-polish. At last Lily joined him, ending his enforced bachelorhood of nearly two years. Marshall rather enjoyed the routine, noting that the hunting and fishing on the Cheyenne and Arapaho Indian reservations were "superb" year-round—quail, ducks, channel catfish in the Canadian River, small game, and deer.

"One morning Mrs. Marshall and I were early for breakfast, and we heard the quail calling in a little sumac grove near us," he remembered fifty years later. "I went out there and in about thirty minutes I came back for breakfast and I had twelve quail [the legal limit]. Actually I think I had fifteen, but I don't want to claim that."

In the summer of 1905 Marshall was ordered to what he called "the hardest service I ever had in the army." This involved a surveying trip in which he was to map two thousand square miles of the remote south Texas desert between the Rio Grande and the Devil's River.

First off, he was improperly provisioned. The detachment Marshall led consisted of a wagon, a team of eight mules and a muleskinner, twenty pack mules and a packer, an assistant packer, and a sergeant who was fond of alcohol. As there was no place to resupply in the desert, Marshall would have to husband every morsel of food for both man and beast as they made their way—fifteen or twenty miles a day—over the scorched rocky desert. July was the hardest month, he said, when the thermometer would rise to 130 degrees.

About halfway through the month they were down to nothing to eat but bacon and canned meat—the onions, potatoes, and other fresh vegetables having been exhausted. At times they were out of water for nearly a day. By the end of the month they had come to the settlement of Langtry where they were able to obtain some provisions, but the sergeant predictably took to drink and scandalized the town.* In the end of August, Marshall returned to Fort Clark, Texas, to turn in the animals and wagon, the mapping mission being completed. There he met Captain Malin Craig, whose cavalry troop had lent him his horses, but Marshall recalled being so shabby-looking—"I was burnt almost black and had on an old panama hat which a mule had bitten the top out of—that Craig didn't think I could be an officer, and talked only to my sergeant. He wouldn't even look at me."

In 1906 Marshall was assigned a coveted post to the army's Infantry and Cavalry School at Fort Leavenworth, Kansas. This was a period in which forces within the army and without were trying to change the service's reputation as a hidebound megalith that—martinet-like—resisted all efforts to modernize it. The agent of much of this change was the secretary of war, Elihu Root, who reopened the then dormant Infantry and Cavalry School at Fort Leavenworth, renaming it in 1907 the Army School of the Line, a one-year course whose top graduates would be eligible to attend the Army Staff College.

Root likewise began a reorganization of the army's staff system. He was convinced that in modern warfare officers needed the highest quality of training and that a military education did not end at West Point (or the Virginia Military Institute, for that matter), but must be continuously evolving. He also concluded that the present staff structure in Washington was an administrative nightmare. The commanding general had virtually no power over the adjutant general or the dozen other bureaucrats who fought with and needled one another. To correct this, Root established the office of chief of staff and gave this officer almost unlimited (save for himself) jurisdiction over every aspect of the army down to and including the precise color of socks that a soldier could wear and what the army would pay for them. Many of the older officers

----

* Langtry was named for the odious Judge Roy Bean's favorite singer, Lillie Langtry.

objected to this system, but it proved to work well, with modifications, from that day to this.

★ ★ ★ ★

MARSHALL FOUND THE COURSEWORK at Leavenworth highly challenging but from the first remained in the top 5 percent of his class. All the discipline and dedication that had been instilled in him at VMI began to pay off and, a year later, when the course had ended, he graduated first in his class and was headed for the prestigious Army Staff College.

Many of the problems there were theoretical and intellectual, designed to inculcate the officers to think on their own, and quickly, in fluid, developing military situations. They delved heavily in the voluminous Official Records of the War of the Rebellion, or OR, in order to reconstruct Civil War battles, some of which they then reenacted on paper to see what could be learned from them. Then they turned to practical matters. A great staff ride was prepared to help understand the complexity of the Battle of Gettysburg. Several dozen officers from the Leavenworth college rode horses along the path that Lee's army took down the Shenandoah Valley en route to its terrific encounter with the Union Army in Pennsylvania, stopping along the way for lectures at other famous battle sites.

In their study of topography and military art (mapmaking) the student officers assessed tactical situations around Metz during the Franco-Prussian War (1870–71) using German maps and reports because that was all that was available. They reviewed this material so thoroughly, in fact, that when these students became high-ranking officers in World War I they were utterly familiar with the topography around the town of Metz, a scene of heavy battle action by the American army in France, as Marshall himself recalled: "I found myself [in 1918] familiar with the names of practically every village because they were all on this Griepenkerl map . . . and were right in the track of these great moves we were making towards the Meuse-Argonne front. I think that of the twenty-nine combat division commanders that got into action in France, some twenty-six or twenty-seven were graduates of Leavenworth during the period [when he was there]."

Aside from the tactical knowledge gained at the school, Marshall remembered that he also took away a sense of "thoroughness" that he might have lacked before, and which "stood me in good stead through all the clamor, excitement, [and] lack of time during the war, particularly in the Meuse-Argonne battle."

After he graduated, Marshall was invited to become an instructor at the Leavenworth school, and he accepted. Lily had come to be with him most of the time, and with her bad heart she seemed to like the stability of the post. Marshall was still a lieutenant, albeit a first lieutenant, and he had spent much of his spare time riding, hunting, and playing tennis and golf. While there hadn't been much in the way of social life as a student, now that he was on staff, that world seemed to open up. Much of this was Lily's doing, for she was a woman of much charm, gaiety, and wit who often organized small dinner parties at the couple's duplex quarters that were surrounded by "a generous green lawn shaded by noble elms and oaks."[9]

(Leavenworth was a venerable old post built at the convergence of the Oregon and Santa Fe Trails, down which sixty years earlier General Stephen W. Kearny had marched his Army of the West to wrest the Santa Fe and California Territories from Mexico during the Mexican War. Later, it became the staging point for many of the expeditions of the Indian wars. But now it was alive with an "enthusiastic intellectual renaissance" striving hard to grasp solutions to the ever more complex military problems of the day.)

During his four years as a teacher, Marshall associated with some of the brightest minds in the army and developed not only an unusually effective ability to impart knowledge, but also a reverence from his students that was long remembered. Once, for instance, on a grueling hot summer mapmaking field exercise that involved many hours in the saddle, Marshall's students were flabbergasted when at last they returned to their rendezvous to find Marshall waiting there with cases of cold beer for all.

Fifty years later, M. W. Clement, president of the Pennsylvania Railroad, who in the summer of 1908 had been a lieutenant with the Pennsylvania National Guard, told Marshall's biographer Forrest Pogue that Marshall "had the ability to make everybody understand," which must certainly rank among the highest compliments a teacher can accrue.[10]

★ ★ ★ ★

IN 1909 MARSHALL SR. DIED. In the two decades since he'd lost his fortune he had redeemed himself from near poverty but the family's living standards had never approached the level as before. Marshall's brother and sister had both married and his parents had left their comfortable house in the West End of Uniontown and moved into an apartment building in town known as "the skyscraper."

When Marshall returned to his old neighborhood, the sights that greeted him were poignant and affecting. His family home had been pulled down, the lot leveled with landfill and a movie house built on the site. The fill now clogged Coal Lick Run where he'd launched his matchbox battleship fleet as a boy. His lone nostalgic encounter came when the aged dog of a boyhood friend who'd long since died recognized him by his scent and "just went crazy." It was, in Marshall's words, "the most flattering thing that happened to me on that short visit home."

Soon after the visit home, First Lieutenant and Mrs. Marshall went abroad. They had to do it on "a shoestring," but over the course of four months in 1910 they managed to cover six countries "while I was on half pay," Marshall said. They saw Paris, the château country, Austria, Florence, Rome, and Algiers—visiting ruins, palaces, and so forth—and finally made it to London and then County Surrey, where Arthur Conan Doyle had set the Sir Nigel stories that Marshall heard his father read by the fireside as a child. At one point he rented a bicycle at the military town of Aldershot, thirty-seven miles southwest of London, and followed the British army on its maneuvers. It was to be the last glimmer of the old Europe and its belle époque. "In 1914," Marshall said, "it blew up. The lights went out, and it never was the same again."

★ ★ ★ ★

IN 1912 AND STATESIDE AGAIN, Marshall was posted with the Fourth Infantry Regiment at San Antonio near the Mexican border where there had been trouble from the ongoing revolutions. Marshall was assigned to lead a signal outfit that received what was said to be the first wireless message sent on U.S. Army maneuvers. It came from the commander of the cavalry who, in reporting his position to headquarters, radioed: "I am just west of the manure pile."

After a year on detached duty instructing various state National Guard units, Marshall was sent back to the Philippines. In August 1913 he and Lily arrived in Manila where he joined the 13th Infantry Regiment stationed at Fort McKinley. Marshall found that the Islamist Moros in the southern islands were still in rebellion, but the main military concern now was of a possible Japanese invasion owing to a rise in Japanese imperialism following their stunning victory over the Russians in the Russo-Japanese War in 1905.

U.S. relations with Japan had become strained by anti-Japanese immigration legislation and Asian-hostile newspapers in California.* The situation was deemed critical enough that defensive emplacements with heavy artillery were being constructed with a mind to repel invaders from the beaches and harbors. A grand series of maneuvers had also been organized to test the strength of the defenses of the main island of Luzon.† The maneuver to test Luzon's defenses against an invading force was composed of a nearly 5,000-man "White Force" (the invaders)

---

* These were the infamous "Yellow Peril" headlines, much of them from the Hearst press.

† Maneuvers, or "war games," are the method the army uses to test its own effectiveness. Like a full-contact scrimmage in football, they are designed to be as realistic as possible.

and a more than 3,000-man "Brown Force" (the defenders). The Whites were to make an amphibious landing and the Browns were to defend Manila against capture.

First, Marshall was assigned as adjutant and chief of staff to the White Force commander, but when the regular chief of staff became ill with malaria George Marshall got his job. The White Force commander, it seems, a soon-to-retire colonel, had been found incompetent by the inspector general; he was told by the commanding general to retire immediately or to let Marshall run the maneuver.* Marshall himself privately objected to this solution on grounds that the next in command was even worse, but an accommodation was reached in which Lieutenant George C. Marshall himself was put in command of the White Force, and neither the first nor the second in command could interfere with any orders he issued.

Each side was briefed on what was expected of them, but the details remained to be worked out and the date of the opening of the maneuver was kept secret by the commanding general. Thus, on the morning of January 22, Marshall was summoned by headquarters from the field "in a soaking wet flannel shirt" and told that the maneuver was on.

The situation was outlined for both White and Brown Forces. Marshall's job was to get the 4,842-man army, with all its guns and wagons and eighteen hundred horses and mules—scattered all over Luzon—pulled together and loaded onto boats to rendezvous at Batangas at the far southern tip of Luzon. From there, they were to attack seventy-five miles up the peninsula and try to capture Manila.

Marshall immediately realized the difficulties before him, not the least of which was the army's parochial command system. He was a mere lieutenant ordering around superior officers who, though they had been told to obey him, often did so with the most grudging and hidebound alacrity. On the other hand, the opposing Brown Force was commanded

* It seems that the colonel drank. As Marshall put it, "He was a courtly gentleman, a very nice fellow. He carried a zinc-lined suitcase with him . . . and every time we would stop . . . he would refresh himself against the Philippine heat."

by two full colonels who could make anyone beneath their rank hop. It would be a trying experience.

When Marshall found that he would need to have stalls made on boats for the animals, he was informed he didn't even have permission to see the department quartermaster, who had refused his request. Marshall threatened to go to the commanding general, adding tactfully, "to ask him what I should do now."

By January 29 the White Force had landed at Batangas and was making its way up toward Manila, overcoming Brown Forces along the way. At one point Lieutenant Henry H. "Hap" Arnold* came upon his friend Lieutenant Marshall lying on his back in a stand of snaky-looking brush, surrounded by staff, unit commanders, and maneuver umpires. He was staring fervently at a map tacked to a tree above his head and dictating the order for the final assault on Manila.

It was a long and complex order, but when he stopped speaking ten or fifteen minutes later "the group around him was awed."[11] Off the top of his head, Marshall had dictated the most complete, comprehensible, and tactically perfect order possible without notes or other references— an episode that eventually passed into one of the enduring Marshall legends.† Having witnessed this, Hap Arnold predicted to his wife that Marshall "would one day become chief of staff of the Army."[12]

Indeed, Marshall's White Force prevailed, outflanking the Browns and marching triumphantly into Manila. Marshall received extraordinary praise from the maneuver's umpires—so much that on January 1, 1916, he was selected to be aide-de-camp to General Hunter Liggett, who had arrived to command an infantry brigade.‡

----

* Arnold would go on to command the U.S. Army Air Forces in World War II.

† This was the "Standard Field Order" recently developed at Fort Leavenworth, whose various paragraphs Marshall had memorized, having only to "fill in the blanks" with pertinent information.

‡ Liggett in 1917 would rise to become second in command of the American Expeditionary Forces in France.

The officer in charge of training and maneuvers in the Philippine Department advanced the opinion in his report on the exercise that Lieutenant George Marshall "was the best leader of large bodies of troops in the entire American Army without regard of age, rank, or previous experience," and several days later, at a luncheon given for his staff, the department commander, Major General J. Franklin Bell, stated that he regarded Lieutenant Marshall as "the greatest potential wartime leader in the Army."[13]

The general's effusive compliments notwithstanding, Marshall was set to be severely tested. The slaughter that had become the Great War in Europe—indeed the war throughout the world—had been grinding out corpses for nearly two years. In May 1915 a German submarine off the Irish coast sank the British liner *Lusitania,* once the largest ship in the world, drowning some 1,200 souls, including 128 Americans.

The ensuing uproar in the United States prompted the Germans to abstain for a time from unrestricted naval warfare, but in January 1917, as Germany's situation became increasingly desperate, the kaiser once again declared that all ships in British waters, armed or unarmed, were fair game. Three months later the United States declared war on Germany.

Chapter Two

MASTER OF THE SWORD

The attack in a corner of northeastern France was stalled and Colonel George S. Patton of the American Expeditionary Forces went forward from his command post, on foot, in a heavy fog, to see what was the matter with his tanks. As he—along with an entourage of several officers and half a dozen enlisted men for runners (also hauling a detachment of carrier pigeons)—neared the front lines, the racket of the battle became terrific. Later, at least twenty-five German machine-gun nests that were firing on the American soldiers had been identified (and destroyed), their bullets constant little winks of flame that stabbed through the shrouding gloom, while larger flashes marked the explosions of enemy artillery shells that were now booming and ranging in.

Earlier, more than 2,800 large guns had lashed for three hours at the German front lines, which appeared to the American fighter ace Eddie Rickenbacker, tooling along above the fray in his French-built Spad, like a giant switchboard "which emanated thousands of electric flashes as invisible hands manipulated the plugs," and a U.S. major general compared the racket to "the collision of a million express trains."[1] For his part Patton, said to be the richest officer in the U.S. Army, later wrote home that the noise blended into a sound not unlike a lawn mower—the one without a muffler—that had once cut the grass back at his family's estate in California.

The date was September 26, 1918, the first day of the Big Push by the U.S. Army in World War I, a clash that would go down in history as the Battle of the Argonne Forest—the bloodiest battle ever fought by U.S. armed forces before or since. By the time it was over, 26,277 American soldiers would be dead and 95,786 wounded.

Patton's tanks were supporting the U.S. 28th and 35th Infantry Divisions, about 27,000-strong, both of them green National Guard outfits from Pennsylvania and Kansas–Missouri, respectively—including future president Harry S. Truman's artillery battery with the 35th. Their role in the offensive was to move in a northerly direction through the Argonne Forest and the narrow valley of the Aire River past the towns of Varennes and Cheppy toward Charpentry, about ten miles distant—the first day's objective.

The Meuse-Argonne Campaign, the planning of which was carried out by Colonel George C. Marshall, involved first secretly replacing hundreds of thousands of French troops at the front with American divisions in what was then considered a "quiet" part of the line (despite being in the Verdun sector where in 1916 a million soldiers had fallen in battle).

The day before the offensive was to open, Patton reconnoitered the area where his tanks were to go, dressed in the blue uniform and helmet of a French soldier so as not to give away the deception and wrote this to his wife that evening: "I will have two battalions and a group of French tanks in the show . . . We go up a stinking river valley which will not be at all a comfortable place in a few hours," he said, referring to the upcoming artillery barrage.

★ ★ ★ ★

As PATTON AND HIS ENTOURAGE reached the scene of the foul-up, about three hundred yards from Germany's infamous Hindenburg Line that ran through the village of Cheppy, the fog lifted and it became immediately apparent to Patton what had gone wrong. One of his lead tanks had become stuck on the precipice of a long, deep, wide trench. It was an old German combat trench, but it made an excellent tank trap because none could cross it without falling inside. It required the tankers to dig furiously and then level out a cut or breach on either side of the trench so that the tanks would not simply drop into the pit but could also crawl out of it.

Men had been sent to do this, but when Patton found them cowering at the bottom of the trench he did not hesitate to resolve the situation. Here, during the next few hours, according to biographer Carlo D'Este, "the legend of George S. Patton the warrior was born."

He appeared on the parapet of the excavation, pointedly exposing himself to the "intense enemy gunfire that came from the front, flanks, and sometimes from the rear," according to the official report, and looked down. Earlier the men in the trench had begun hacking at the walls but each time a shell burst nearby or machine-gun bullets kicked up dust, they jumped back inside for cover.

The situation was developing into a catastrophe. More tanks had begun to arrive and a colossal armored traffic jam was in the making. Worse, as the fog lifted, German spotters got the range and enemy artillery began furiously shelling these valuable targets.

"To hell with them, they can't hit me!" Patton roared, ordering the soldiers out of the trench to resume work. (Later he wrote to his wife that he "had probably killed one of them" who refused to obey by hitting him over the head with a shovel.) Patton stormed over to a company of stalled American tanks waiting for the obstacle to be cleared and personally began removing shovels and picks that were strapped to their sides. With enemy bullets pinging and ricocheting off the tanks, he ordered the Americans out of their vehicles to assist in the excavation and continued to march atop the parapet of the trench as soldiers with shovels were being shot down on all sides, exhorting the men and ridiculing the Germans' marksmanship with a flood of horrible profanity.

Colonel Patton, who only a year earlier had been Lieutenant Patton, was the commanding officer of the First U.S. Tank Brigade, consisting of approximately 140 tanks. They were French-built machines, so-called light tanks that Patton, an old cavalryman, preferred to the much larger, heavier (and less maneuverable) armored vehicles being built in England.

Patton's tanks were made by Renault, the French automobile company. A 50-hp engine could propel them about 4.5 miles per hour, and their revolving turret was armed with either a 37mm cannon or a 9mm machine gun. The two-man crew consisted of a driver, who sat below, and the gunner/tank commander (the only one who could actually see out) who gave steering directions to the driver by kicking him in the back, head, or shoulders.

★ ★ ★ ★

WHEN THE ENEMY TRENCH was at last made fit for passing Patton ordered his tanks forward, telling them to silence the German machine guns. Then he went back to the reverse slope of another small hill where more than a hundred American soldiers had been shrinking against the enemy fire when the fog lifted, having become separated or lost from their units. As the armored vehicles began to clear the crest of the low rise ahead Patton told these fugitives to form up and follow him behind the tanks. "Let's go get them," he shouted. "Who's with me," and he began walking forward, cursing and waving his walking stick over his head.*

Most of the men rose up enthusiastically and took off after Patton, but when they, too, cleared the crest of the hill they were met with a furious hail of enemy machine-gun fire that killed and wounded many, and everyone flung himself to the ground. The fire came from nearly every direction; the Germans, it seems, not wanting to tangle with the tanks, had gone to ground and let them pass by unmolested—and the infantry as well—before opening up. Many of the Americans were thus shot in the back and lay in sad, promiscuous heaps upon the ground.

---

* Patton used the walking stick, or cane, to bang on the sides of his tanks during maneuvers to let them know it was him outside.

Patton later wrote to his father that he had been trembling with fear and at that point "felt a great desire to run" when amid all the firing an apparition suddenly appeared before him in the clouds above the German lines, he said—a kind of panorama of his heroic ancestors who had died in American wars from the Revolution to the Civil War. They spoke to him in soothing tones, which calmed him, Patton wrote, and, saying aloud to himself, "It is time for another Patton to die," he rose up and again shouted for volunteers to go forward into "what I honestly believed was certain death."

"Six men went with me," he said, "five were killed and I was wounded, so I was not much in error."

Patton and his little entourage, including his orderly Private First Class Joseph Angelo, plunged into the maelstrom headlong, but every dozen steps or so one of the soldiers would fall to the ground after being struck by German bullets, until at last there was only Patton and Angelo moving in the ghastly and dangerous landscape "like Don Quixote and his faithful servant Sancho Panza," according to biographer Martin Blumenson.

At one point Angelo said to his boss, "We are alone."

"Come on anyway," Patton replied, but a few seconds later he was struck in the thigh by a bullet and soon collapsed to the ground.

What was Patton thinking, marching into such danger? It certainly wasn't what his headquarters superiors expected of him; in fact, they would have been horrified, if not furious—Patton was the commander of the First U.S. Tank Brigade.

It was nearly inconceivable that a field officer of Patton's stature would expose himself in such a reckless manner but it was neither the first time nor the last. His explanation for it, gleaned from letters he wrote over time to his wife, father, and other family members, seems to indicate some abstract and almost perverse need to prove his nerve or bravery under fire. That he had led the five men with him to their deaths seems not to have occurred to him. What was more important to Patton was to demonstrate to himself that he was not a coward, but fearless and/ or bulletproof.

Having now disproved the latter, Patton and Angelo lay in a shallow shell hole as bullets and shrapnel skimmed overhead and kicked up dust in the drying mud. Angelo sliced open Patton's trousers and saw that a German machine-gun bullet had entered his left thigh and come out his buttock near the rectum, "leaving a hole the size of a teacup."[2] The orderly dressed the wound with his own first aid kit and also one he took off a dead soldier lying near.

By then the Germans had maneuvered into a railroad cut about fifty yards distant, where they set up a machine gun. They were so close that Patton and Angelo could hear them talking. Sometime within a half hour Patton's sergeant, who had been frantically looking for his commander, came scrambling and panting into the shallow shell depression, where he further attended to the wound. Patton then ordered him to find Major Serano Brett and tell him he was now in command of the brigade, but also said that no attempt to remove him should be made until the enemy machine guns ahead were silenced.

An hour passed, possibly more, and Patton remained half in shock but conscious during the ordeal with the enemy machine guns constantly sweeping the battlefield. At one point Patton told Angelo to go out and find his tankers and tell them where the German guns were located. As more U.S. soldiers came up Patton's tanks began maneuvering with the infantry to knock out the German emplacements. When another company of Patton's tanks came up, he once again told Angelo to go out and tell them about the enemy emplacements. Meantime, word got back to the communications squad and a pigeon was released with a message that Patton had been wounded.[3] During this time, Patton said, "One of my tanks [sat] guarding me like a watchdog."[4]

Finally, at about 1 p.m., tanks and infantry managed to silence most of the enemy guns so that Patton could be rescued. He gave his last order sending a lieutenant in search of Major Brett, who had not yet been located. Then he was placed on a stretcher and evacuated to an aid station two miles to the rear, an experience, Patton said, that "was not at all pleasant."

For his actions that day—personally breaking up the tank logjam under fire, and directing the attack on the machine guns after being badly wounded—Colonel George S. Patton, age thirty-two, received the Distinguished Service Cross, America's second highest award for valor.

★ ★ ★ ★

GEORGE SMITH PATTON JR. was born November 11, 1885, at Lake Vineyard, his family's 1,300-acre winery and citrus estate in what is now Pasadena, California, in the shadows of the 10,000-foot San Gabriel Mountains. Like George Marshall, Patton came from a long line of illustrious ancestors who settled in Virginia in the 1700s after arriving from the British Isles.

His great-grandfather Robert Patton immigrated to America from Scotland in 1750 and became a successful merchant in international trade. He settled in Culpeper, Virginia, then moved to Fredericksburg and married Anne Gordon Mercer, daughter of Dr. (Brigadier General) Hugh Mercer, a close friend of George Washington's who was mortally wounded at the Battle of Princeton during the Revolution—"the first of the Patton ancestors to combine erudition and valor in his bloodstream."[5] (Bayoneted and left to die by the British, General Mercer told an aide who rushed up to carry him away to instead follow the Continental Army, saying, "It needs your services more than I do.")

Their son John Mercer Patton, one of seven children, was in turn a physician, lawyer, and U.S. congressman, and for a time governor of Virginia. He married Margaret French Williams and fathered twelve children, including seven sons all of whom but one* became Confederate officers during the Civil War.

A story some historians use to point out the strain of obstinacy in the Patton family stems from an incident that took place in the first decade of the nineteenth century. John Mercer Patton threatened in a letter to his father "to kill himself by cutting his throat" because his father insisted that he go to medical school at the University of Pennsylvania instead

---

* He was Robert Patton, the eldest, a former navy officer and alcoholic who died of excessive drink.

of studying law. Several days later came the reply: a package containing "a freshly honed straight razor and a note that said: 'Go ahead. Your devoted father.'" In the end he became both a doctor and a lawyer and famously wound up writing the Virginia Legal Code.[6]

Four of his sons, including Patton's grandfather the first George Smith Patton, graduated from the Virginia Military Institute. He was second in his class, which was also filled with various ancestors of George C. Marshall, and afterward studied law with his father before marrying the wealthy Susan Thornton Glassell, whose family claimed to descend from George Washington's great-grandfather, as well as from several of the English barons who forced King John to sign the Magna Carta. The union of George S. Patton and Susan Glassell produced nine children including, in 1856, Patton's father, George Smith Patton.

This George Smith Patton cut a rakish, elegant, romantic figure in antebellum Virginia society, well known for his wit, wisdom, and repartee. A fervent believer in secession, by the eve of Fort Sumter George S. Patton had become the commander of H Company of the 22nd Virginia Regiment, and he and many of his brothers, sisters, and cousins moved into the magnificent Patton ancestral home, Spring Farm, in Culpeper, where they prepared for war.

The matriarch of the Patton family and owner of Spring Farm was the widow of John Mercer Patton, the former Margaret French Williams, who had a hatred of Yankees that was almost obscene. (During the war she is said to have cried upon learning of the wounding of one of her sons but afterward said it was only because she had no more sons to send to the fight.) After the war had ended, the story goes that she was riding from church one Sunday with a former Confederate colonel and inquired if he had said "Amen" when the minister prayed for the president of the United States. When the answer was affirmative, she lashed him across the face with her buggy whip.[7]

To say that the Civil War was unkind to the Patton family is a vast understatement. Waller Tazewell Patton was the first of the Patton boys to die. A VMI graduate and lawyer, "Taz" was badly wounded at Second Manassas but recuperated in time for the Battle of Gettysburg where, as the colonel commanding the Seventh Virginia Infantry, he was shot through the mouth at the stone wall during Pickett's Charge. He lived long enough to write a note to his mother reaffirming his love for her, and "my God and my Country," before dying on July 23, 1863, at the age of twenty-nine. The two youngest brothers, Hugh Mercer and James French Patton, were both lieutenants and both wounded but survived.

May 15, 1864, became a kind of Patton watershed in the Civil War when no fewer than four Pattons, including some attending VMI, clashed with the Union Army in the Shenandoah Valley at the Battle of New Market. The VMI cadet corps—mostly fifteen- and sixteen-year-olds—were called out to fight for the Confederacy.

Colonel George S. Patton, Patton's grandfather, now commanding a brigade, managed to extract his cousin Colonel George Hugh Smith's 62nd Virginia Regiment from a Union trap, then turned to face and repel a Federal cavalry attack on his flank.

Although the Battle of New Market was a Rebel victory, this particular Patton's luck ran out on September 19, 1864, at the Battle of Opequon, also known as the Third (last) Battle of Winchester, when Federals under Philip Sheridan attacked and crushed the army of General Jubal A. Early.

That spring the Patton family had been forced to move owing to the presence of Federal armies in northern Virginia; they chose the home of John Mercer Patton, the Meadows, in Albemarle County in central Virginia, near Charlottesville. There, Susan Patton received a letter from her husband, George, saying he would be on a train with the army of General Early whose tracks passed nearby the Meadows' garden.

His son George Smith Patton, then a boy of eight, poignantly recalled his father in a memoir dictated the year of his own death in 1927: "He got off and stayed with us for several hours . . . then the last train with flat cars loaded with artillery stopped for him. I remember seeing a soldier on a car giving him a hand to get aboard and as the train moved out he was leaning against a gun and waved us goodbye. I never saw him again."[8]

By then George S. Patton had become the commander of "Patton's Brigade" and his promotion to brigadier general was approved by the

Confederate Congress.* Patton's men were in the thick of the fighting and as usual he was in their midst when the fatal bullet struck him. He lingered alive for a few days at the home of Mary Williams, a cousin by marriage, before expiring on September 25 at the age of thirty-one.†

★ ★ ★ ★

SEVEN MONTHS LATER THE WAR WAS OVER and the Pattons were thrown into the direst poverty. With no income and all the family savings gone, they had almost starved during the winter of 1864. Susan Patton had gone to Goochland, north of Richmond, to care for her blind father who, like most Virginians, had lost everything to the Confederate cause. All livestock had been driven away by the depredations of the Yankee general George Stoneman and his cavalry.

The state was utterly devastated; railroads, bridges, waterways, and other infrastructure were wrecked. Administrative offices such as the postal system had collapsed and Richmond had burned to the ground. Land had gone fallow; fences were trampled down, fields were choked with weeds, homes were in a state of decay. Tens of thousands of Virginia's men were dead or maimed and with emancipation there was no one to work the fields. Four years of war had left people destitute; trade had virtually ceased during the conflict and remained stagnant afterward. Confederate money and bonds were worthless and most families had sold off what gold, silver, or furniture they had to buy food or other necessities. The stench of death and privation lay heavily across the state.

---

* Because the official orders remained to be cut before his death, the promotion was not awarded.

† A decade later Colonel George S. Patton and his brother Colonel Waller Tazewell Patton were disinterred and reburied together, covered by a Confederate flag, in a midnight ceremony attended by many old Confederate soldiers, illegally in their uniforms, as well as his son George S. Patton II, then in the uniform of a VMI cadet.

The Patton family next moved in with other Pattons, who were trying to maintain a corn patch and truck farm in a river bottom, but there was little or no future in Virginia for now, if ever. Then Susan Patton received a letter from her brother Andrew Glassell, an attorney who had made his way to California before the war. It contained money for their passage to that mysterious and faraway place.

They pooled what little they had and sold it, save for Susan's dead husband's "sword, saddle, gold watch, and bible," and boarded a steamer for Panama, where they crossed the fever-plagued isthmus and boarded a ship for Los Angeles. As George Patton's sister put it nearly 150 years later, "There was nothing left for them in the ruins of their politics and their plantations—and their way of life."[9]

They must have been an extraordinary-looking party, the Pattons: the beautiful thirty-one-year-old widow and her four children, her blind father, as well as her brother the gallant Commander William Glassell, who was dying of tuberculosis contracted in a Union prison camp after being captured during the Battle of Charleston Harbor. Nevertheless, they arrived in California just before Christmas 1866, to a warm welcome from not only Andrew Glassell and his large family but also other Patton cousins, including Williamses who had also immigrated to the new American frontier.

For Susan Patton, Los Angeles was a rude, un-American kind of place, only sixteen years free of Mexican rule, populated mostly by Mexicans, Indians—some of them hostile—and a clique of Spanish landholders right out of the age of Zorro. With its strange Mediterranean climate and barren hills, California was the antithesis of the verdant fertile farmland of her native Virginia, but Susan eventually acclimated and started a small school for girls until, as her granddaughter put it, "Up from Mexico came the knight in shining armor—and that he was to anyone who ever knew him."[10]

He was Colonel George Hugh Smith, first cousin, beloved friend, and VMI classmate of the late George S. Patton. A native Philadelphian whose family had resettled in Virginia, Smith had secretly been in love with Susan for years and for that reason had remained a bachelor. A lawyer by trade, he refused to take the loyalty oath when the war ended and went to Mexico where he engaged in cotton growing and surveying for a living, before ultimately returning to the United States via California.*

Smith joined Andrew Glassell's law firm and began a courtship of Susan that resulted in their marriage in 1870. He adopted her four children and brought them up as his own. According to his step-granddaughter he was much beloved and regaled the children with heroic stories of their dead father. By all appearances they led a happy, successful, if not wealthy life until 1883 when Susan died of cancer at the age of forty-eight.

By that time her son twenty-seven-year-old George Smith Patton II was a well-established lawyer and political figure in Los Angeles. Like his father before him he had attended VMI, which offered free appointments to the sons of alumni who had fallen in the Civil War. He became an outstanding student, first in his senior year and the ranking cadet officer in the class of 1877. It was said that when he went out riding one day in White Sulphur Springs in his cadet uniform, a former Confederate general mistook him for his father.[11]

Back in Los Angeles he studied law with his stepfather and uncle and passed the bar exam and joined the firm, which also placed him among the most eligible young bachelors in town. In 1884, a year after his mother's death, he fell in love and married twenty-three-year-old Ruth Wilson, daughter of the fabled Benjamin Davis "Don Benito" Wilson, a former mountain man out of Tennessee who had become one of the wealthiest landowners in California.

Don Benito's story is a book in itself, as he rode, trapped, explored, and fought Indians with the likes of Kit Carson, John C. Frémont, and Jedediah Smith. He was "a tenacious warrior who feared neither man nor beast," slaying grizzly bears and Indians alike who crossed his

....

* A number of Confederate officers and soldiers went to Mexico or to Central or South American countries after the war. Most returned but some stayed, most famously in Brazil, where there remains today a large colony of the descendants of Southern Confederates who successfully colonized there.

"frightful temper." He also married well, taking for his bride, in 1844, Ramona Yorba, the sixteen-year-old daughter of one of the wealthiest estate holders in Southern California.[12]

That marriage was cut short by Ramona's tragic death at the age of twenty-one, but in 1853 Wilson married Margaret Short Hereford, an Alabama-born widow of a doctor, who gave him two children. One of them, Ruth, married George Smith Patton and became the mother of George Smith Patton Jr.—the subject of this story—and the other, Annie, "a lifelong spinster," became Patton's beloved Aunt Nannie.[13]

★ ★ ★ ★

DON BENITO WILSON HAD BEEN instrumental in the California revolution, conversion to U.S. territory, and eventual statehood in 1850. In 1851 he was elected mayor of Los Angeles and was later a two-term California state senator. At one point he held more than fourteen thousand acres in and around Los Angeles County, including a sheep ranch that is today the campus of UCLA. But it was Lake Vineyard, Wilson's residence amidst thirteen hundred acres of well-tended grapevines and fruit orchards, that he cherished above all else.* The home was of the large "raised hacienda" style with steep front steps, a slate roof, and a long, wide veranda surrounded by fruit and flower trees as well as towering pines and eucalyptus.

Don Benito had also gained a reputation as one of California's leading horticulturists. In 1873 his combined harvest produced 75,000 gallons of wine and 5,000 gallons of brandy. Some 600,000 oranges and 75,000 lemons were produced and it was estimated that at least as many remained on the trees unharvested. A decade later the San Gabriel Wine Company had become one of the largest in the world, capable of turning out 1.5 million gallons a year. In any event, from the mid-nineteenth century on, the Wilsons were high on the list of frontier aristocracy in the state of California.

---

* Today it is the site of the widely respected Caltech.

Don Benito passed away in 1878, so young George Smith Patton Jr., born seven years later, never got to know his legendary mountain-man grandfather. Still, Patton Jr. was regaled with enough heroic stories from Hugh Smith about his gallant Confederate grandfather to put notions of a military career into his head at an early age. Among Hugh Smith's friends was John Singleton Mosby, a member of the prewar Virginia gentry who had served as a major under the Confederate cavalry leader J.E.B. Stuart until, in 1863, he was promoted to colonel and founded the 43rd Virginia Regiment of partisan rangers, in which he spent the rest of the war infamously harassing Union forces in Virginia with tactics that bordered on terrorism. (Once he captured a Union general by entering his tent at night, waking him with a slap of saber on his bare behind, and roaring, "Have you heard of Mosby?" When the response was affirmative, he again roared, "I am Mosby!")

Mosby had come to California as an attorney for the Southern Pacific Railroad company and had business with the Glassell-Smith-Patton law firm. He and the young "Georgie" Patton, as he was known, would play on the lawns of Lake Vineyard for hours, reenacting Civil War battles with Georgie playing Robert E. Lee atop his Shetland pony Peach Blossom and Mosby playing himself.

On chilly nights, by the great fireside at Lake Vineyard, George Patton Sr. would read to the children from classics such as Pope's translation of the *Iliad* and the *Odyssey,* which Georgie came to know almost by heart, as he did the Bible, which was also read daily. Moreover, Papa Patton frequently read aloud from Plutarch's *Lives,* Caesar's *Commentaries,* biographies of Napoleon and Alexander the Great, the poetry of the English Romantics, and Shakespeare.[14]

His father did not believe in formal education for young children, but thought they would be better rounded by roaming in the wilds and at the same time fed a steady diet of works by the great writers, such as Kipling, who was frequently recited to Georgie and his sister, Anne (also known as Nita), by another family friend, retired major Arthur Thompson, formerly of His Majesty's Royal Lancers, who had served in battle at the notorious Khyber Pass on the North West Frontier of India.

The Patton children's early tutor was their Aunt Nannie, Ruth's sister, who soon revealed a terrible secret: Georgie was "slow to learn," in reading, writing, and mathematics, and showed few signs of improvement. What is known now through medical examination of his correspondence is that Patton was dyslexic, a condition then unknown, and even today much misunderstood. The most apparent affliction of dyslexia is an inability to spell, reversing some letters or spelling phonetically, and a confusion of numbers in math. Patton got by with a terrific effort at memorizing things, but his poor spelling plagued him all his life. He once joked about it as a grown-up saying to someone who had questioned his spelling, "Well, any idiot can spell a word the same way every time. But it takes imagination to spell it many different ways as I do." Once he famously told his troops, "I have trouble with the AB and—what do you call that other letter?"[15]

As Patton biographer D'Este points out, dyslexia brings with it a wide variety of other difficult symptoms that include self-contempt, impulsiveness, mood swings, obsessiveness, and hyperactivity. At one time or another, D'Este says, "virtually every symptom of dyslexia described above applied to Patton. During his plebe year at West Point he would write to his future wife Beatrice Banning Ayer, 'I am either very lazy or very stupid, or both, because it is beastly hard for me to learn and as a natural result I hate to study.'"[16]

All of that notwithstanding, Nannie also captivated Georgie and his sister by reading to them from exciting and powerful works such as *Beowulf,* Tennyson's *Idylls of the King,* Washington Irving's *The Alhambra,* and John Bunyan's *The Pilgrim's Progress,* in addition to *Ivanhoe* and other heroic tales by Sir Walter Scott—and this was not to mention children's adventure books such as *Lee in Virginia.* Patton liked to tell a story, perhaps apocryphal, about himself. When he was young he used to kneel and pray with his mother, who kept pictures of God and Jesus on the wall by her bedside. It wasn't until he was a teenager that he found out they were actually etchings of Robert E. Lee and Stonewall Jackson.[17]

Aunt Nannie (Annie Wilson) was three years older than Georgie's mother, and since their early childhood she had established herself as something of an eccentric. In part by virtue of being the eldest she was able to dominate Ruth in ways large and small. Growing up at Lake Vineyard the girls had been privately tutored in languages, literature, and the piano. While Ruth seemed to thrive in the placid, bucolic atmosphere, Nannie felt restive. According to her distant nephew Robert H. Patton, she feared staying at the ranch would turn her into "a cross, unloved, unloving old maid." Earlier she had told her diary that she would not marry since "the kind of man I would marry, and could love, I am afraid would never care for me." She went on to predict that rather than settle for the love of someone "less worthy," she would instead adore "my ideal" from afar, "and never have him care a bit for me."[18]

It has been someplace noted that the deadliest trap is the one you set for yourself, which seems precisely the case with Nannie Wilson when George S. Patton Sr. came calling on her sister Ruth. Nannie found him fascinating, highly intelligent, witty, and extremely handsome ("a splendid talker, he is so smart and well read"). She could not see how he could possibly fall for her little sister who was not nearly so well read and pretty as herself. So she hovered on the periphery, not as a tiger stalking prey but more like an aloof observer wanting to be part of the party but content to wait outside.

Not as a wholly "detached" observer, however. When on December 10, 1884, Ruth wed George Patton and the couple prepared to board the train for their honeymoon in New Orleans, who should they find waiting on the platform, baggage packed, but sister Nannie, intending to accompany them on the trip.

Talked out of proceeding, that night as she sat to write in the diary she'd kept every day since childhood, Nannie recalled an entry of seven years previous: "My youth is slipping by fast and I am beginning to feel old already . . . Oh I wonder if I shall always go on this same way!" Then she closed the book without writing a word and never resumed it. As her distant nephew would observe a hundred years later, "Nannie was well on her way toward becoming a very strange woman."[19]

Nannie would be a looming presence in the Pattons' lives over the years, especially from the moment little Georgie was born, when she immediately assumed the role of surrogate mother. He was a large "almost painfully beautiful" child, Nannie said, "curly golden hair, big blue eyes, a lovely nose and sensitive tender mouth."

★ ★ ★ ★

THROUGHOUT HIS YOUTH GEORGIE PATTON's pursuits revolved around horses, guns, and the military—especially the latter, when he would dress up in a blue uniform and march around the house and grounds brandishing a homemade wooden sword. On the blade he had prophetically carved "Lt. Gen. G.S. Patton." He learned to ride (his mother was an excellent horsewoman) on the same McClellan saddle that his grandfather had been killed on, and even reckoned that a dark stain around its pommel was actually his grandfather's blood. At about the age of ten his father gave him an English saddle and two blooded horses, Marmion and Galahad, whom he sometimes slept next to in the Lake Vineyard stables.[20]

When he was old enough to lift the .22 rifle that his father bought him, he used it to prove his marksmanship by knocking oranges off of fence posts. Around that same time he got a sixteen-gauge double-hammer shotgun for shooting quail, and when he reached age twelve his father scrambled to come up with enough cash to buy him a twelve-gauge hammerless Lefever, one of the best-built and most expensive American shotguns of the day. When it came to engraving its hard leather case Georgie later wrote he made his father "leave the Jr. off so that he could use it if he wanted to."

Money, in fact, had become a problematic subject at Lake Vineyard as the nineteenth century came to a close. Following the death of Don Benito Wilson, management of his estate, including the properties, vineries, and citrus groves, fell to his son-in-law the sybaritic James de Barthe Shoub, while Wilson's stepson George Patton Sr. continued his practice in the law.[21]

But Shoub turned out to be a profligate spendthrift and idler who squandered his own property and the great winery through inept speculation and nearly threw the Wilson/Patton fortune into bankruptcy as well. Patton Sr. found it necessary to leave the practice of law and his post at the Los Angeles district attorney's office to see to affairs at Lake Vineyard and the other vast Wilson properties, which were intermittently plagued with agricultural diseases and drought. While the Pattons were far from indigent, they were at times "land poor," and cash was not easy to come by. "Papa never economized so far as his family were concerned," George Jr. wrote in 1927, "but would get nothing for himself."[22]

That never stopped them, however, from living the lives of American aristocrats. The Pattons' cousins the Bannings were a wealthy clan who made their fortune first in stagecoach and freight transportation and later in shipping. They owned, among other things, most of Santa Catalina Island off the coast of Southern California. The Pattons had a "cottage" there, and during the long summers the Patton children played with the Bannings as well as with the Ayer children, who were also distant relatives—the scions of a great New England textile fortune.

Georgie had learned to swim at the age of eight in the waters of the Greenbriar at White Sulphur Springs in (now West) Virginia on a trip "back east" with his father. But on Catalina he sharpened his swimming skills to an extent that would one day win him a place on the 1912 U.S. Olympic team. In Catalina's rocky hills Georgie and other youngsters were taken by his father to hunt mountain goats that were in danger of overrunning the island. On his first hunt he shot and killed five of these. When Georgie was thirteen, Papa Patton had a sailboat built for him, which led to his enduring fascination with sailing and boats.

The two of them often sailed around the island, stopping to hunt, fish, and camp for the night in some of the many craggy coves. Patton later recorded in a lengthy paper entitled "My Father as I Knew Him and of Him from Memory and Legend" that "[Papa] hated both hunting and sea fishing but he went even when I was a grown man."

With such constant attention being lavished upon him, one might be tempted to conclude that Patton had been spoiled. That he was doted on is without question, but from Patton's letters and writings he seems to have appreciated the affection for what it was and returned it in full measure. He was precocious to be sure, and hogged the limelight even with all of his self-deprecation.

His father, while not particularly stern, was acutely tuned to instruct young Georgie in the manner of an aristocratic Virginia gentleman, which he was, or had been. He missed no occasion to point out his son's shortcomings, such as the time when at age eleven Georgie returned from a mountain goat hunt. The other children had each killed one but Georgie boasted that he had "killed several," after which his father took him aside, saying, "Son it would have been more like a sportsman not to have mentioned the extra goats."

★ ★ ★ ★

IN 1897, WHEN HE WAS ELEVEN, Georgie's parents decided to send him to the Classical School for Boys, a private institution in Pasadena run by the Clark brothers. The subjects taught were arithmetic, algebra, geometry, English, grammar, composition, declamation, as well as the languages and literature in Greek, Latin, French, and German.

But the curriculum leaned most heavily on the teaching of history. As Martin Blumenson, editor of *The Patton Papers,* explains it: "They taught history [as a] long conflict and clash between the personal ambitions of men—Persians, Romans and Greeks for the most part—who made good or bad decisions, who lived properly and righteously, or improperly and meanly; men who contributed to their nation's welfare and progress or who betrayed human hopes by reason of base motivation or weak character." It was in this realm of history that Georgie Patton flourished.

Despite his atrocious spelling and punctuation, Georgie even at his young age would avidly analyze the battles of the ancient world, dissecting the strategies of Alexander the Great or the Greeks at Marathon, or probe the tactics of Sir Walter Scott's Black Knight versus the Normans.

The brothers Clark emphasized character, patriotism, and self-sacrifice just as Papa Patton always had. Georgie took these virtues to heart from an early age, making such notations in his schoolboy notebook as: "John Alden was a weak character and timid as is shown by his not having told Standish at first that he was in love with Priscilla," or, "[On Themistocles] He was egotistical and had a right to be. He was unscrupiolos in ataining his ends and did not hesitate to decieve his best friends," adding perceptively that "Cimon['s] ideals were greater than Themistocles but he was not."[23]

Georgie also found time for pithy asides unconnected—or at least ancillary—to his lessons, such as, "The common people of ancient times were very ignorant, as is the case with many in modern times also."

Or, "A pair of the least fly-catcher, the bird which says chebec, chebec, and is a small edition of the peewee one season built their nest where I had them for many hours each day under my observation."

In the summer of 1902, eight of the Banning-Patton-Ayer children had formed a company of players they called the Eight Cousins and staged a play, *Undine,* for their families and their guests. Beatrice Banning Ayer, one of Georgie's distant cousins by marriage, played the guileless Undine, a water spirit; Georgie played Kuhlborn, her terrifying uncle. It was love at first sight for them both.

★ ★ ★ ★

IT HAD LONG BEEN DECIDED by Georgie Patton that he would become a great soldier in the footsteps of his slain grandfather and other family heroes whose exploits his father regularly touted. The U.S. Military Academy at West Point was the obvious path to becoming an officer in the regular army, but there were pitfalls from the beginning—not the least of which was the fact that Papa Patton was a prominent Democrat.

A congressman could appoint a candidate to West Point but was entitled under the rules to have only one cadet from his district at the academy at any given time. Unfortunately, the Pattons' local congressman had already appointed a cadet the previous year. The best bet for Georgie then became California's Senator Thomas R. Bard, who could appoint a cadet from the state at large. Bard, however, was a Republican and it thus fell on the senior Patton to pull out every stop in persuading this political rival to nominate his son to West Point.

Letters of recommendation from the most eminent Californians inundated Bard's office, nearly all of them stressing Patton's martial ancestry: "If 'blood tells' in boys as it does in colts, you will always be proud of having nominated [him]," wrote a prominent Los Angeles doctor.

Georgie's uncle George H. Smith informed the senator, "If inheritance counts, the young man ought to have all the qualifications required in a soldier."

"If blood counts for anything, he certainly comes of fighting stock . . ." wrote a well-known Los Angeles judge.

In return, Senator Bard acknowledged that Patton Jr. "possesses a strain of blood which ought to result in a successful army career," but nevertheless insisted that Georgie "present himself for examination in competition with other applicants for my recommendation."

Here was the rub: Papa Patton was well aware of his son's deficiencies in certain academic areas—in particular mathematics, languages, and of course his abysmal spelling. They cast around for prep schools but finally decided on VMI, where generations of Pattons had been educated. The school prided itself on having a curriculum similar to West Point's, and a military program even more strenuous than that at the celebrated military academy. A year at VMI seemed to be the logical entrée for prepping for West Point. Thus, in the autumn of 1903, seventeen-year-old Georgie Patton once and for all dropped the "ie" from his nickname and entered the forbidding, gray fortress-like facade of the Virginia Military Institute in Lexington, Virginia.

★ ★ ★ ★

CADET PATTON TOOK TO the harsh military routine as if it were a normal way of life. Unlike many of his classmates, he seemed to thrive on the starkness, austerity, and hazing—and like George Marshall he accepted his place as a "rat" with magnanimity if not actual appreciativeness.

He was delighted, for instance, to learn when being fitted for his uniform that the tailor was the same man who had fitted not only his father but also his grandfather, fifty years on. Upon taking his measurements, the tailor looked in his book and informed George Patton Jr. that he was exactly the same uniform size as both of those stellar VMI graduates.[24]

Cadet Patton was genial, but not particularly close with his class-mates. He was, in fact, a kind of snob in the way that only people who have spent any time in Virginia can appreciate. If there is anything approaching a self-acknowledged American version of aristocracy it will be found among the so-called First Families of Virginia—more so (in their estimation) even than among descendants of the *Mayflower.* From the time he began to talk and listen it was stressed to George Patton Jr. that his ancestors were among the top of these FFVs, as they have come to be known. In truth, the Patton ancestors, with a few notable exceptions, were not ranked particularly high in the pecking order of the landed Virginia gentry, but the fact that his grandfather had died for it certainly raised them a notch or two.

In letters home to his father, Patton expressed dismay when he discovered that certain of his fellow students were not "gentlemen," in the sense that he grew up understanding the term. Their values, he noted, as well as their manners, were different. While he nevertheless treated them as equals, he knew the distinction and did not hesitate to say so in private.

In his academic courses he struggled as he always had but persevered with hard study and ranked in the top third of his class. He went out for the football team and, like George Marshall before him, accepted a bid to join the KA fraternity in secret, since it was not permitted for cadets to be members. Beatrice wrote him to join her family at Thanksgiving dinner in Boston, but cadets were not allowed off campus; instead he spent Thanksgiving at the home of the VMI commandant then, after-ward, ate figs while sitting on the grave of Stonewall Jackson.

The romance with Beatrice was humming right along, but why a young woman from Boston with such immense wealth and high social standing would have fallen for a California boy and expatriated south-erner who claimed he wanted to become a soldier has become a topic for conversation from then until now. For Christmas she sent him a fox head tie pin and inquired as to how "Kuhlborn" was doing, receiving this in reply: "As to Kuhlborns self there is little to say except that owing to his immortal nature he lived through football season and did not break even a single bon[e] and that he is now devoting more time than he should to making a polo team (for above all things he is desirous of an early and glorious death)."[25]

Robert H. Patton, who naturally has had extraordinary access to Patton family lore, attributes his grandmother's infatuation with George Patton to a "quirky streak" and asserts that she was drawn to the kind of "self-mockery and drama" contained in his reply to her letter.*

Patton managed to get through his year at VMI with respectable grades and an excellent military rating and on May 24, 1904, he was at last accepted into West Point, which prompted a remarkable letter from his father, "to my boy," telling him, in part: "From that day eighteen years ago when you first saw the light of this world you have been a comfort and a joy to me—and now that we have come to a new point of departure I feel neither regret, nor fear, nor doubt." The letter goes on to caution him about selfishness and self-seeking, predicts the First World War or something like it, and prophesies that "Providence shall throw upon you the great responsibility by which you may quit yourself like a man. If you do this it matters not whether you achieve the fleeting applause of the unthinking multitude or not. You will have fulfilled your destiny—and played nobly your part in the drama of life."[26]

West Point, however, was far more of an ordeal for Patton than VMI. He considered the latter school harsher in its military discipline and again bemoaned the dearth of "gentlemen" among his classmates. But the academic work at West Point was harder, especially in mathematics and science and of course his old bugaboo English. He went through the daily

----

* Robert Patton notes in his excellent book *The Pattons* a most un-bluestocking side of Beatrice, such as the time when, on a cruise along the Nile at the age of eleven, she "bribed their Egyptian boatman with ten dollars to bring her to a local tattoo parlor where she hoped to receive a tattoo just like the boatman's: a full-rigged ship across the chest." Frustrated in this attempt, she then surreptitiously snapped the big toe off a two-thousand-year-old mummy during a tour of a recently discovered ancient tomb and kept it in a jelly jar for a souvenir.

grind but no amount of extra preparation could overcome his dyslexic tendency to transpose letters, revert to phonetics, or confuse numbers. It is almost heartbreaking when he asks his father in a letter, "Is my spelling still as bad as it was? I hope not for I heare WP is getting strict about that."*

He went out for the football and fencing teams with little success in either, a worrisome burden on his ego and mushrooming ambition. He had already set his sights at becoming cadet adjutant by his senior year, second in rank only to first captain. "I have lived 19 years but . . . amount to very little more than when I was a baby," he told his father as Thanksgiving approached. "I am fare in every thing but good in nothing. It seems to be that for a person to amount to some thing they should be good in at least one thing. I some times fear that I am one of these darned dreamers . . . who is always going to succeed but never does," adding that if that were the case "it would have been far more merciful if I had died ten years ago than to be forced to live—a failure."[27]

At least on paper the romance with Beatrice was going well but it had to have been hard on Patton that she was coming out in Boston's winter debutant season while he was cooped up a plebe at West Point with no off-post leave privileges. He wrote her, "Really the fact that you liked my flowers well enough to wear them [at your coming out party] gives me a great deal more pleasure than they could possibly have given you, so instead of your thanking me I should be grateful to you."

Patton at last got to see her on March 4, 1905, when the West Point cadet corps marched in the inaugural parade of President Theodore Roosevelt. That evening he got to dance with Beatrice at the inaugural ball. "I had the finest time in the world," he told her. He invited her in June to the graduation dance at the academy, but that turned out not to be necessary. On June 3, during a track meet, he was in the lead but tripped over the seventh hurdle and finished last and on that same day was "turned out" (failed) in his French class. The next week he failed

----

* Spelling continued to be a frustration for Patton, as is evident in his diaries and correspondence. His misspellings have been maintained in quotes and excerpts throughout this book.

math and was "turned back" academically, a full year. It was the unkindest blow. He would have to start all over again.

★ ★ ★ ★

ALTHOUGH BEING "TURNED BACK" was a tremendous disappointment, it undoubtedly saved George Patton's career. By the end of October, of 155 cadets in the class of 1909, he stood 14 in mathematics, 37 in English, number 1 in drill regulations, and had accumulated but one demerit. He achieved this by dint of terrific study and a prodigious memory so that, especially in math, he managed to memorize by rote the solutions to entire problems. On the football team he played third string but broke a bone in his arm that finished him for the season. When promotions were announced that spring he was named second corporal for the upcoming year, meaning that only one cadet in his class had scored higher in military science and conduct.

The next year was more of the same. Patton passed all of his subjects at about the middle of his class except for military bearing at which he excelled, when he entered his junior year as cadet sergeant major, the highest-ranked military office for the second class. Beatrice remained a romantic figure in his life and being an upperclassman he was now afforded more opportunity to see her on holidays. He went out for the 1907 football season and made the team but never got into a game.

He wrote in a notebook he kept: "Characteristics of a cavalry leader 1. Indomitable courage 2. Quick perception of right moment to attack 3. Capacity of inspiring confidence in troops," adding, "always work like Hell at all things and all times." In something at least prophetic and at best a minor miracle, when promotion time rolled around Patton was selected adjutant of the West Point Cadet Corps for his senior year, the position he'd aspired to ever since he'd been a first year plebe. Once more he went out for the football team but early on again broke a small bone in his arm, which put him out of action for the season.

Except for his tribulations on the football field, by that time Patton at last had become the athlete he always wanted to be. He was an accomplished swordsman on the fencing team, especially with the broadsword, as well as a stellar rider/jumper on the equestrian team. Not only that, but at the Annual West Point Field Day he also broke the school record in the 220-yard low hurdles, won the 159-yard high hurdles, and was second in the 220-yard dash.

By then he was revealing his deepest thoughts in his letters to Beatrice, many of them philosophical musings on war, peace, battle, and dreams of battle. At one point he told her, "Perhaps I said things though true that sound rather strange. But I am rather strange too, I fear."

In January 1909 he asked her to marry him; or rather, he asked her father's permission to ask her, which was given hesitantly, but magnanimously, considering that Frederick Ayer was eighty-six years old and could not but be dismayed at the prospect of his youngest daughter going off to who knows where with a lowly second lieutenant in the army. Even Ayer could not help being impressed, however, when upon a sparkling Sunday morning with the family gathered on the terrace of Avalon in Prides Crossing, who should come ascending the twenty-six stone steps to the spectacular mansion overlooking the crashing waves of the Atlantic on the rocks below, riding on a large white charger, but Lieutenant George S. Patton Jr. When he reached the terrace, he clattered up toward Beatrice, who was seated in a chair, and proceeded to have the horse bow in front of her, doffing his cap in a sweeping flourish. Ayer told him this in a letter: "All right. You let me worry about making the money, and you worry about getting the glory."[28]

As far as career choice Patton, who rode as though he was born in the saddle, had concluded that "cavalry as mounted infantry is the arm of the future," in the army, and chose that branch above all others—not the least because his academic record was such as to exclude him from the more elite branches, such as engineers.

Blumenson writes that, judging from remarks about him in the West Point magazine, his class *Furlough Book,* and the West Point yearbook, Patton's classmates regarded Patton "with some ambivalent emotions. They accepted him generally with affection and admiration for his sincerity, candor, and fairness. They smiled in condescension over his naïve earnestness and enthusiasm. They believed that he tried too hard, had too much spirit, and they were uncomfortable with his excessive concern for future glory."

Upon graduation Patton had hoped to be posted to Fort Myer, Virginia, right across the Potomac from Washington, D.C., with the 15th Cavalry. Instead he was relegated to Fort Sheridan, Illinois, a rather bleak outpost near Chicago, where a part of the 15th was stationed. His duties were menial but typical for a new second lieutenant: guard duty, stable duty, and duty at the post stockade, rifle and pistol practice (at which he attained the grade of "expert"), and occasional maneuvers. He was scheduled to marry Beatrice at the end of May and worried over the quarters they had been assigned on the post. He went into Chicago to shop for furnishings—chairs, sofas, lamps, and carpets.

In the first week of March 1910, a little of the Patton legend was put on show when his horse threw a conniption fit while he was drilling a formation of his troops. The horse suddenly began bucking fiercely and threw the surprised Patton off, but he immediately got back on. The animal began to buck again, reared, and fell down on the ground. But Patton stayed on, "[standing] across him" after he had gotten his leg out from under the animal, so that when Patton got the horse up he would be in the saddle. As the horse arose, however, it suddenly jerked its head back cracking Patton in the face and opening a nasty cut above his eye that "bled like a stuck pig."

Instead of going to the infirmary, for the next twenty minutes Patton continued drilling the men with the blood "running down [his] sleeve." No one there could help but take note of the young lieutenant with blood all over his face and uniform, patiently drilling the troops when by all rights he should have had the cut looked after. It was good, tough stuff, the stuff of which legends are made, and those cavalry troopers saw that the story got around.

The wedding on May 26, 1910, was one of the most graceful occasions of Boston's social season, being concluded at St. John's Episcopal Church in Beverly Farms. There the bride and groom—in his elegant army dress blue uniform—emerged beneath a phalanx of crossed swords held high by Patton's West Point classmates, who also wore full dress. The reception was held at Avalon, with special trains bringing guests from Boston. It featured a full orchestra that played on the terrace.

Beatrice's wedding dress had been her mother's of white handmade lace and trimmed in orange blossoms from Lake Vineyard "brought on the train by the Pattons in a box of wet cotton."[29] She cut the enormous wedding cake with her husband's sword, which was followed by army cheers and a rendition of "The Star-Spangled Banner" by the orchestra. The next day, the couple entrained for New York and the bridal suite on the SS *Deutschland* that would carry them to a monthlong honeymoon in England, where Patton poked around Cornwall, home to the legendary King Arthur—"People talk of him as if he were still here," he said.

★ ★ ★ ★

THE FIRST DAYS AT FORT SHERIDAN could not have been easy for Beatrice, who was reared in an excess of luxury. But between her drive to make a good wife and the marital bliss right off a honeymoon she seemed cheerful and happy in her letters home. Patton slowly but steadily advanced in the estimation of his military superiors, working his way to commanding officer of a machine-gun platoon and acting commanding officer of his cavalry troop. He began to salivate with news of trouble along the Mexican border—the current revolution was possibly in danger of spilling over into the United States. "There may be no war," Patton wrote Aunt Nannie, adding, "God forbid such an eventuality."

With assistance from the Patton and Ayer families he purchased a string of polo ponies, an expensive automobile,* as well as several fine thoroughbreds for both flat racing and steeplechases, which he could board at the Fort Sheridan stables for free. He wrote Aunt Nannie: "We had a polo match Saturday and I won a cup a foot high. It is very pretty." At night he began translating articles from French military journals into

---

* A five-passenger Stevens-Duryea listed at $1,750—about $45,000 in today's money.

English, taught himself how to type, and started writing military papers for distribution within the army—the first one entitled "Saddle Drill." A recurring theme in these papers was to "attack, push forward, attack again until the end," which would one day become a Patton trademark.[30]

In March 1911 Beatrice gave birth to a girl, Beatrice Smith (later changed to Ayer) Patton, of whom George soon wrote to Aunt Nannie at the end of the month, "The accursed infant has black hair is very ugly and is said by some dastardly people to resemble me which it does not because it is ugly." Again he added: "The Mexican trouble seems dormant for the moment but . . . it is not for long. We shall cross the border yet. I feel sure of it."

Some of Patton's biographers seem to take his remarks about the baby being ugly as made seriously instead of playfully, but that hardly seems the case. From this it has been extrapolated that Patton was terribly jealous of the baby for having "intruded" on his marriage with Beatrice—but hard evidence of this is difficult to come by. Once, a neighbor, the wife of a colonel, came to Beatrice to ask if things were all right in her marriage because her husband had informed her that Lieutenant Patton that day was observed "standing on the rifle butts in between the targets" on the rifle range during a firing exercise. It has been intimated that this behavior demonstrated that Patton was despondent, even suicidal, over the arrival of the child, but that hardly seems the case either.

The way he explained it later to Beatrice was that he was standing up between the targets during the shooting to see what the sound of bullets whizzing past him would feel like. He was merely testing his courage under fire, he explained, and the targets were large, so that it would have been a fluke for a rifleman to miss one entirely. It was a very Patton thing to do.

★ ★ ★ ★

IN DECEMBER 1911 Patton at last received the assignment he had originally wanted—a position with the other branch of the 15th Cavalry Regiment that was at Fort Myer, Virginia.

Fort Myer is the most elite post in the U.S. Army, in no small measure because of its proximity to Washington, D.C., and the political emoluments dangling there. Land that once belonged to George Washington and that was later bequeathed to Robert E. Lee's wife, Fort Myer has stood next to Arlington National Cemetery since the Civil War. It was home to the oldest regiment in the army (the Third U.S. Infantry Regiment: "The Old Guard") as well as the official residence of the army chief of staff, the U.S. Army Band, the Honor Guards of all three services, and Black Jack, the riderless horse used in state funeral processions.

Because of the high caliber of its polo team, Fort Myer featured the best horsemanship in the country by officers from some of the nation's best families. Washington was a relatively small town at that time, and the officers of Fort Myer were much in demand as escorts to royalty and to national presidents and their families. They often attended balls in various exclusive clubs in Washington, Georgetown, Chevy Chase, and the Maryland and Virginia Hunt Country. More important, they were often in direct contact with such big-name figures as the secretary of war, army chief of staff, War Department staff, U.S. senators and congressmen—all of the movers and shakers that could be useful to a young officer such as George Patton, who was clearly on the make. Washington, as Blumenson describes it, was "where, in the interest of advancing his [Patton's] prospects, he could exercise his fatal charm on those who counted and those who made the decisions."

Patton arrived at Fort Myer with all the trappings of an aristocratic army officer of the day: a stable of fine horses, expensive dogs, and shotguns. If anyone had any doubts, George Patton soon demonstrated that he was no poseur by starring on the Fort Myer polo team and riding in various foxhunts, steeplechases, and hell-for-leather point-to-point races in the Virginia piedmont country. With both the Patton and the Ayer heritages hovering over them, George and Beatrice quickly made friends among the horsey set as well as among the doyens of Washington's high society who inhabited the fashionable parts of the city and its suburbs.

The new officers' quarters were a great improvement over the shabby facilities that George and Beatrice shared at Fort Sheridan, and they were able to employ a maid and a chauffeur. One day Patton was out riding on one of the many equestrian trails in and around the post when he had the good luck to encounter Secretary of War Henry L. Stimson, who was enjoying his daily ride. The two joined and in no time Patton's youthful charm had won him a lifelong friend who would prove invaluable later in his career, during World War II, when his very presence in the army was in jeopardy.

★ ★ ★ ★

In March 1912 two interesting things occurred in Patton's career. First, he was assigned to be quartermaster for the First Squadron, 15th Cavalry Regiment. That might not seem an assignment that a man like George Patton would enjoy, but in his case it came as a compliment as it was in order for him to have more free time to practice and play polo. Second, and far more important, he was being talked about to represent the army, and the United States, in the upcoming Fifth Olympiad to be held in Stockholm, Sweden, in July.

There was an event known as the modern pentathlon that—astonishing as it may seem—encompassed all of Patton's best skills (which few others in the United States possessed collectively). In the ancient Olympics the pentathlon was conceived as a martial event that consisted of spear throwing, wrestling, and the like. But the modern version, conceived as a test for a young officer carrying a message through hostile territory, featured these five sports: fencing, swimming 300 meters, horseback steeplechase 5,000 meters, pistol shooting 25 meters, and distance running 4,000 meters. Patton was good at all of them: he'd learned distance swimming and shooting on Catalina Island, had been on the track and fencing teams at West Point, and was, of course, a first-rate rider.

In May an invitation was offered and Patton accepted, thus becoming the first army officer to represent the United States in the modern pentathlon. There were no other American competitors nor, in that era, were there Olympic trials, and athletes trained on their own hook.

In Patton's case, according to his daughter, "He started his serious training in May 1912 and it was hard on everyone. He went on a diet of raw steak and salad; according to Ma, he was unfit for human consumption."[31]

Patton put himself through a brutal training regimen in the five weeks he had before sailing to Europe, and when on June 14 the entire Patton family boarded the SS *Finland,* which carried most of the American Olympic competitors,* he used its training facilities, including a canvas pool on deck for swimming practice.

There were forty-two contestants in the pentathlon, including eight Swedish officers. Pistol competition was first and Patton had scored a near perfect 197 out of a possible 200 in practice the day before. He was right on target to repeat it when, "surprisingly, even inexplicably," two of his bullets missed the target entirely and he came out number 21 of his forty-two fellow shooters.†

Despite this dreadful beginning, next day at the Royal Tennis Club he finished third in fencing, handing the ultimate victor, a Frenchman, his only defeat. By then there were only twenty-nine competitors, the rest having dropped out.

The steeplechase began at 11 a.m. July 11, with riders starting at five-minute intervals on a course marked with flags a little over three miles in length with twenty-five major jumps and fifty smaller "obstacles" (ditches, logs, low fences, etc.). Patton and two Swedish riders were judged with "perfect" performances, but the Swedes finished ahead in time and Patton came in third.

The foot race was held two days later with the remaining competitors, now down to fifteen, lined up in front of the Royal Boxes. The contestants would run separately at one-minute intervals along a roughly two-and-a-half-mile course that began on the regulation track but quickly left the stadium into heavy woods, across rocks and steep precipices, and

---

* Including the great American Indian athlete Jim Thorpe.

† Some biographers, as well as the eight Swedes in the competition, insisted the bullets must have passed through previous holes, which is possible, but rules were rules.

into a forest with a swamp six inches deep in mud before finishing back in front of the Royal Boxes. For Patton it was the most grueling ordeal of the event. At the end he was fifty yards ahead of the closest Swedish competitor when, according to the *Los Angeles Times,* "He stopped almost to a walk as the Swede brushed by, and when [Patton] finished he dropped into a faint."[32] He had finished third.

In the final competition next day, swimming, he placed sixth. Overall, Patton's standing in the Fifth Olympiad's modern pentathlon was 5, a very credible showing, made somewhat bittersweet by the knowledge that in each event he had been near the top—except in pistol shooting where he was twenty-one of forty-two, and that is what cost him a possible win.

After the Olympics, Papa Patton took the family on a leisurely tour of Germany where they visited Berlin, Dresden, and Nuremberg, indulging themselves in delicate German candies, desserts, and other confections, which Patton had denied himself all through his training. Yet despite all the first-class accommodations and antique scenery Patton had other things on his mind.

In particular, he was determined to improve his swordsmanship and had discovered through inquiries at the Olympic games that the best swordsman in Europe—nay, the world—was a Monsieur l'Adjutant Clery, master of arms and instructor of fencing at the famous cavalry school at Saumur, France. He was the longtime European champion with the foil, the dueling sword, and the saber.

Patton immediately departed the family tour and journeyed to Saumur where he set up a rigorous schedule of personal instruction by M. Clery in the dueling sword and the saber for two weeks, after which time he rejoined the family for the transatlantic crossing. Upon his return, Patton presented a noteworthy report to the U.S. Adjutant General in which he observed that the French cavalry's practice of fighting with the sticking point of the saber was both superior and safer than with the slicing edge, as American cavalry did. "It is argued that Americans being a country of axmen the edge comes more natural but from what I saw and what I was told . . . [it is] *La pointe . . . toujours la pointe.* It gives the advantage of reaching the enemy at least a yard sooner than ours does, of presenting only a third of the (friendly) human as target, and of instilling the desire to speed up and hit hard."

In the days to come this newfound understanding of swordsmanship was to mean a good deal to George Patton's career.*

★ ★ ★ ★

UPON HIS RETURN TO FORT MYER Patton indulged himself in equestrian pursuits—flat racing, foxhunting, steeplechase—and buying more and better horses. In early 1912 he was detached to the Office of the Chief of Staff General Leonard Wood, where he often served as an aide to Secretary of War Stimson. At the request of superior officers he also prepared military papers such as a lengthy assessment of the latest in the eternal series of wars in the Balkans, which he compared with various campaigns of the ancient Greeks and Romans.

At the same time he waited almost breathlessly for some explosion that would bring the United States into the conflict in Mexico, and in his spare time he focused on improvement of swordsmanship for U.S. troops. He wrote to Aunt Nannie about an article he had produced for the *Army & Navy Journal:* "It is about the sabre and I hope it does some good in educating these [troops] to get over thinking they are all occupied in a carpet-beating contest every time they get hold of a sword." In a cavalry charge, Patton continued, "the point will always beat the edge. It gets there first."

The article so impressed Secretary of War Stimson that he ordered the Springfield Armory to manufacture twenty thousand cavalry sabers matching precisely the model Patton designed and showed in his paper. These would become known as "Patton Sabers," enhancing the already burgeoning career of the young second lieutenant.

In June 1913, doubtless at his own behest, Patton was ordered to return to Saumur for advanced instruction in swordsmanship with an

----

* In 1912 the cavalry saber was still considered a potent weapon in the arsenal of small arms throughout the armies of the world.

eye toward earning the title Master of the Sword. This in turn would lead to Patton's opening the army's first course of instruction in swordsmanship at the Mounted Service (Cavalry) School at Fort Riley, Kansas. Thus far, Patton was doing all the right things to ensure advancement in the army.

At the end of summer, when he was finished with Saumur and M. Clery, and brandishing his new title Master of the Sword, Patton and Beatrice, who had accompanied him, took a tour by motorcar across Brittany to Saint-Malo and across the ominous hedgerows of Normandy to Caen. To Beatrice's astonishment, George told her he had fought there before, "in an earlier life," when the Roman legions came to conquer two thousand years ago, and that he would fight there again. Three decades later George S. Patton would renew his acquaintance with these hedgerows on a much less genial basis.[33]

At Fort Riley Patton became the U.S. Army's first Master of the Sword. He went through two years of advanced instruction at the Mounted Service School as well as instructing students himself in swordsmanship. Realizing that captains and majors attending his classes might resent being taught by a low-ranking second lieutenant, he opened his discourse this way: "Now gentlemen, I know many of you outrank me and how hard it must be to take instruction from a man you must regard as a little damp behind the ears. But gentlemen, I am about to demonstrate to you that I am an expert in the sword, if in nothing else, for at least fifteen years, and in that respect I am your senior."[34]

He then opened a package on the table before him and produced the two little wooden swords he and his sister Nita had played with at Lake Vineyard, brandishing them in the air to gales of laughter by his class.

Patton satisfactorily completed the Mounted Service School's first course of instruction in the summer of 1914—the same summer that a Serbian nationalist assassinated Austria's Archduke Franz Ferdinand and his wife in Sarajevo, touching off World War I—and was selected to attend the second course, another feather in his cap.

Then, on February 28, 1915, at Lake Vineyard, Beatrice gave birth to Ruth Ellen Patton. While it wasn't the boy Patton had hoped for, he telegraphed her from Fort Riley "D-E-L-I-G-H-T-E-D." At the same time he unsuccessfully went through back channels seeking a leave of absence to get into the European war on the side of the French, being told by General Wood: "Don't think of attempting anything of the kind . . . We don't want to waste youngsters of your sort in the service of foreign nations."

Not to be done in, Patton managed to pull enough strings to get himself reassigned to the Eighth U.S. Cavalry at Fort Bliss, near El Paso, on the Mexican border. This was a wild, untamed land of violent men, some of them wanted, and volatile relations with various Mexican armies operating just across the border. It came as close to war as possible without actually being in one, and Patton felt right at home, a man convinced that his moment had come—or at least was coming.

The United States had been moving toward war with Mexico for several years and, as tensions heightened, the War Department began organizing a force of some five thousand troops to guard the border from Texas to Arizona, commanded by Brigadier General John J. "Black Jack" Pershing. He was a hard-charging, no-nonsense general who had received his nickname after commanding the all-black Buffalo Soldiers of the Tenth U.S. Cavalry.

Patton's job was to patrol with two cavalry troops a hundred-mile stretch between the remote outposts on the Texas end of the border that lay within the bleak 5,000-foot Sierra Blanca Mountains. There at a town called Mineral Wells he met and befriended some of the rowdiest men of the West. ("I get along with them well as I usually do with that sort of people.") One was a man named Dave Allison, "a very quiet-looking man with white hair and a sweet face. He alone killed all the Orasco bunch [a notorious bandit gang] five of them about a month ago, and he kills several Mexicans each month. He shot Orasco and his men each in the head at sixty yards. He seems much taken with me and is going hunting with me."

In between his hunting (deer, ducks, foxes, rabbits, and antelope), Patton chased down several false alarms of bandit gangs or Pancho Villa's army—each instance causing him to become almost beside himself at the lost opportunity for putting his saber fighting theory into practice against actual humans. ("We were all disgusted at not finding the Mexicans. It was fine to see how pleased the men were at the prospect of a fight. I had great hopes of seeing how my sabers would work but better luck next time.")

At some point, during this period in Mineral Wells, Patton had an embarrassing incident with his pistol that nearly unmanned him. The Colt Model 11 .45 semiautomatic had become the standard sidearm of the U.S. Army. But unlike a revolver, which is fairly simple, the automatic can be tricky sometimes, as Patton found when it went off unexpectedly. He had been wearing it "in his trouser fly—like all the local gunmen did . . . and that in sitting down or moving around he had somehow triggered it off and it had shot a hole right through his trouser leg and into the floor." Being a man of action, Patton immediately switched to a Colt .45 Model 78 single-action ivory-handled revolver, which remained his sidearm of choice from then on.[35]

At Christmas 1915 Beatrice came out to Fort Bliss when Patton's duties afforded him no leave and went to Mineral Wells, where she moved into the only house in town for rent. She roughed it, even with the babies along with their nurse. She and Patton hunted together, riding thirty miles one day along the Rio Grande and sleeping under the stars. ("We got thirteen duck most of them mallard and B. killed two of them besides a quail and a pluver [plover] so she had a fine time.")

During this period of his career, Patton seemed to lead a charmed life. His attractive twenty-nine-year-old unmarried sister Nita came to Fort Bliss with Beatrice. She was "a tall, blond Amazon with enormous capabilities of love and loyalty and great good sense." At a dance on the post she was introduced to General Pershing who had recently lost his wife and three daughters in a tragic fire in his quarters in San Francisco. The two were instantly attracted to each other.[36] Eventually they would become lovers, which of course put Lieutenant Patton in Pershing's spotlight as well.

By early 1916 Pancho Villa had turned murderous against Americans after President Woodrow Wilson refused to sell him guns and ammunition. His people kidnapped sixteen American mining engineers off a train and burned them alive. They murdered and mutilated an American ranch manager and kidnapped and raped his wife. Gathering strength as it moved north toward the border, Villa's army left in its wake a horror of looting, hanging, burning, and raping, before at last it staged an attack on the sleepy border town of Columbus, New Mexico, about a hundred miles west of El Paso, killing eighteen Americans. At last Wilson ordered Pershing to organize a punitive expedition into Mexico to run Pancho Villa to ground.

Patton was thrilled almost beyond words until it was announced that his Eighth Cavalry Regiment was not going on the expedition. This, he said, was because Pershing insisted his officers and men maintain a state of good physical fitness, and the colonel commanding the Eighth was rotund. "There should be a law killing fat colonels on sight," Patton wrote sourly to his father.[37]

Immediately he applied to Pershing to be taken on his staff, but the general had all the aides he was authorized. Patton managed to talk his way into going anyway, essentially because Pershing liked his company—and there was, of course, sister Nita too.

Patton at once made himself indispensable—carrying messages, seeing after the clerks, the mess, logistics, newspaper reporters, the animals, automobiles, and anything else that needed tending, including Pershing's hankering for engaging conversation on the trail. There were more than five thousand cavalrymen on the hunt for Pancho Villa, most on horseback but some in motorcars, as well as six flying machines for dispatch and reconnaissance—the first use of American aircraft on an actual combat mission.*

Pershing's party took the train from El Paso to Columbus and started to track down Villa from there. It was Patton's opinion that finding and

---

* These were Curtiss JN-2 "Jennies," all of which crashed within the first month—two in the first week.

punishing Villa was not going to be easy. His men had fought well at Columbus and the Mexican terrain was hard on U.S. troops. There were few roads, no maps, and no water for the first hundred miles, Patton told his father. "They can't beat us, but they will kill a lot of us. Not me," he added.

The punitive expedition was doomed to failure from the start; Pancho Villa simply had too many places to hide in the vast canyons of the Sierra Madre. Bands of Villistas would frequently ambush American convoys or pick off lone soldiers, then vanish into the murky wastes of the mountains. On March 30, 1916, the Seventh Cavalry killed about thirty Villistas in a gunfight near Guerrero, but other than that it was maddening between the boredom and the bugs, snakes, rats, tarantulas, nighttime cold, sleet, rain, and snow, daytime heat, dust, and high winds ("the windiest place in the world," Patton said)—they were on the edge of the Great Chihuahuan Desert at 4,000 feet of altitude with Mexicans taking potshots at them all the time.

Patton was constantly nagging Pershing to let him ride out on search missions; one of these, in early May, led to a famous incident that got Patton headlines in newspapers across America. Patton was part of a party from the 13th Cavalry that raided the San Miguel Ranch in search of Villa's top lieutenant, General Julio Cárdenas. They did not find Cárdenas but they did find his wife, baby, and, nearby, his uncle who, Patton wrote in his diary, "was a very brave man and nearly died before he would tell me anything."

A week later, Patton was sent by Pershing to the town of Rubio to purchase corn for the headquarters staff's horses. After doing so he decided on his own to return to the scene of the previous raid to see if he could catch General Cárdenas unawares. He had at his disposal ten armed men from the Eighth Infantry and two armed guides in three open touring cars.

Patton gathered the men around him and explained his plan, which was to surround the *rancho* where they had previously found Cárdenas's wife and child so that no one could leave without being seen. The raid was carried out at straight-up noon on May 14, and resembled, according to one historian, "a Mexican-American version of the gunfight at the OK Corral."

Patton approached the *rancho* from the front on a low rise from which his automobile could not be seen from the compound until he was relatively near it. Then as he topped the rise he gunned the motor and before anyone inside the *rancho* could react he and his men were out brandishing weapons. Outside the house were four men skinning a cow, who did not stop, even with the guns, but kept at their task as if nothing were happening.

As he rounded the corner of the walled patio, Patton was startled to see "three armed men [dash] out on horseback." Patton hollered "Halt," but instead the three shot at him, the bullets hitting the wall about a foot over his head and spattering him with adobe chips. One of the armed horsemen rode right in front of Patton, who was about to shoot him with his pistol but suddenly remembered something Dave Allison (the old lawman in Mineral Wells who had gunned down the Orasco gang) had told him: "Always shoot the horse of an escaping man." Patton did this and the horse fell with a broken hip; when the rider rose with his pistol, Patton and others of his party shot him "and he crumpled up."

The second man was on the verge of escaping when he was brought down in a hail of rifle bullets from the Americans, including Patton. The third man, witnessing this, had reentered the patio and was trying to escape on foot when he was spied by one of Patton's men and brought down at a distance of nearly three hundred yards. Wounded, he was approached by one of the guides and drew his pistol and fired but missed, then the guide "blew out his brains."

During all of this activity the four men skinning the cow had continued resolutely at their task. They stopped, however, long enough to identify for Patton the corpses of General Cárdenas and his aide, a colonel in Villa's army, and a private.

They slung the bloody corpses over the hoods of the motorcars and strapped them down like grisly hunting trophies. When they returned triumphantly to Pershing's headquarters, the general let Patton retain Cárdenas's fancy silver mounted saddle and saber, and the newspaper reporters went into a frenzy over finally having a story worthy of the name. Across the country, headlines lauded Patton as a hero, including the *New York Times,* which blared: "Dramatic Fight At Ranch—Lieut. Patton and Ten Men Killed Three Bandits—Peons Kept Skinning a Beef." He wrote Beatrice, "I have at last succeeded in getting into a fight . . . I have always expected to be scared but was not nor was I excited. I was afraid they would get away."

A few days afterward, outside his tent, he shot two rattlesnakes with his pistol and was teased for not killing them with his saber. He told Beatrice that it was improper to use a saber while on foot, and added, "You are probably wondering if my conscience hurts me for killing a man, it does not. I feel about it just as I did when I got my first sword fish, surprised at my luck."

On May 23, after seven years of service, he was at last promoted to first lieutenant. Not long after, Papa Patton had decided to run for the Senate as a Democrat from California, while at the same time campaigning for President Wilson. Patton despised Wilson as "that unspeakable ass," without "the backbone of a jellyfish," who had left the army unprepared for a major war that he was sure the United States would be drawn into in Europe despite Wilson's denials.

★ ★ ★ ★

THE PUNITIVE EXPEDITION against the elusive Villa seemed to take on a life of its own, with mountains of supplies arriving in Dublán and daily cavalry patrols returning empty-handed. Boredom set in and Patton began reflecting that he was thirty-two years old with no prospects in sight for the greatness he expected to achieve. He worried about losing his hair and kept trying on his cadet uniform to see if it still fit. His father lost the Senate race, which depressed Patton even more—he had thought that having a father in the Senate would be good for his career.

Pershing, meanwhile, pursued Nita with ever growing ardor. In early 1917 he traveled to Lake Vineyard to ask Papa Patton for her hand, but was met outwardly with "grave doubts" over the twenty-seven-year difference in their ages. What Patton Sr. kept to himself was that he did not think Pershing "was good enough" for his daughter because, among other things, Pershing's father had been a brakeman on the railroad.[38]

Both Mrs. Patton and Nita were "set on it," however, and Pershing left with the understanding that he and Nita would be married soon. There the matter stood until, on April 6, 1917, the United States entered World War I, precipitating the dispatch of more than two million American soldiers into what was at the time the most terrible conflagration in world history—and the bittersweet end of the hopes of marriage between Nita Patton and General John J. Pershing.

CHAPTER THREE

★ ★ ★ ★

THE CHAMPION OF VERA CRUZ

By the end of March 1918 the Germans were attacking ferociously all along the northern part of the nearly five-hundred-mile Western Front, in some instances pushing the Allied armies back for scores of miles in hopes of winning the war before the Americans could arrive in force. Then, in July, a final frenzy of 800,000 Germans lunged out of their trenches along a seventy-mile front from Reims to Arras in northeastern France in a desperate attempt to overrun the Allied lines, capture Paris and the vital Channel ports, and force the Allies to sue for peace.

The chief of staff of the famous U.S. 42nd "Rainbow" Division was one of the most remarkable and gifted officers ever to grace the U.S. Army. He was Douglas MacArthur, a strikingly handsome thirty-eight-year-old colonel considered by many to be one of the bravest officers of his day; in the scant six months since Americans had been in the war he had already won the Distinguished Service Cross and three silver stars. His commanding officer said of him: "MacArthur is the bloodiest fighting man in this army. I'm afraid we are going to lose him sometime."

The Rainbow Division was among the first American fighting units to arrive in Europe. So far it had bloodied itself down to nearly half its original fighting strength of 27,000 men, creating commensurate German losses along the way. "I cannot fight them if I cannot see them," was the way MacArthur put it to a general who was reluctant to let him go to the front.

Since mid-February 1918 the 42nd Division had been almost constantly in combat, at first under the command of the French army then, beginning in June, under direction of the American commander in chief, General John J. Pershing. Its infantry regiments had distinguished themselves in a long series of battles to break the so-called Hindenburg Line, a position heavily fortified by the Germans. At battles such as La Croix Rouge Ferme (Red Cross Farm), they engaged the enemy hand to hand and pushed him to the banks of the Ourcq River.

To knock out the deadly German machine-gun nests, MacArthur, who spent much of his youth on the Great Plains where his father was an army officer during the Indian wars, reverted to the Indian tactic of sneaking his men forward in twos and threes and crawling on their hands to surprise the enemy with the bayonet and hand grenade, instead of ordering an upright charge. "It was savage and there was no quarter asked or given," according to MacArthur. "It seemed to be endless. Bitterly, brutally . . . a point would be taken, and then would come a sudden fire from some unexpected direction and the deadly counterattack. Positions changed hands time and again. There was neither rest nor mercy."[1]

The village of Sergy, for example, had been won and lost eleven times in a single day until by dusk on July 29 the Americans of the 42nd had wiped out the Germans to the last man and were left in control of its grisly smoking ruins.

MacArthur was an astonishing contradiction in the army and in his life—dedicated, innovative, courteous, charming, and, as already noted, brilliant, absolutely fearless, and "unquestionably . . . the most gifted man-at-arms this nation has produced." He was also arrogant, eccentric, abrasive, flamboyant, imperious, and the most "baffling, exasperating soldier [who] ever wore a uniform"—this last according to his biographer William Manchester.[2]

As a combat officer, for instance, he adorned himself in a rakish, unorthodox style, removing the metal band from inside his hat crown so that the crown perked up and sat on his head in a jaunty manner. He wore highly polished boots, riding breeches, and long wool scarves knitted by his mother, which he threw about his neck in the manner of a British aristocrat. He also carried a riding crop (or "swagger stick") but, oddly, never a sidearm or weapon of any sort.

He was a natural leader and basked in the esteem his troops held him in for going out on dangerous patrols. But he also incurred the hostility of some influential staff officers in Pershing's headquarters, including a bright young colonel named George Marshall who was the commanding general's chief tactical planner, and who did not enjoy being second-guessed by staff officers at division level.

In any event, after the Battle of Sergy, MacArthur began reconnoitering beyond his forward outposts along the Ourcq River and heard strange noises coming from the German lines—the sounds of many truck engines and "vehicles on the move." There were explosions and other indications that the enemy was withdrawing. MacArthur reasoned that if he pressed the Germans now he would catch them in the midst of a retrograde movement—a tactical retreat—and they would have to run, leaving behind all of their great piled-up storage dumps and supplies with nowhere to make a stand until they reached the Vesle River nearly ten miles away, an enormous Allied gain.

There was no time to wait, MacArthur decided; he would take it on himself to organize a night attack without asking headquarters. He told the regimental commanders of the 42nd to move out in columns abreast with one battalion in line of battle, the next battalion in support, and a third battalion in reserve. He phoned for the artillery to open a barrage. It was 3:30 a.m. when they crossed into no-man's-land.

As usual, MacArthur was forward with a coterie of runners, riflemen, and aides on what would become an unforgettable journey.

"The dead were so thick in spots we tumbled over them," MacArthur wrote afterward. "There must have been at least 2,000 of those sprawled bodies. I identified the insignia of six of the best German divisions. The stench was suffocating. Not a tree was standing. The moans and cries of wounded men sounded everywhere. Sniper bullets sung like the buzzing of an angry hive of bees. An occasional shell-burst always drew an angry oath from my guide. I counted almost a hundred guns of various size and several times that number of abandoned machine guns."

As he moved deeper into the grim wastes of no-man's-land the sights became even more macabre. "Suddenly a flare lit up the area for a fraction of a minute and we hit the dirt, hard. Just ahead of us stood three Germans—a lieutenant pointing with an outstretched arm, a sergeant crouched over a machine gun, a corporal feeding a bandolier of cartridges to the weapon."

MacArthur held his breath waiting for the machine gun to open on them, but instead there was only a stony silence, punctuated by the distant cries of the wounded. They waited, frozen on the ground, until MacArthur's guide lay down the grenade he was about to throw, pulled out a flashlight, and scanned it over the Germans.

"They had not moved," MacArthur said. "They were never to move. They were dead—all dead—the lieutenant with shrapnel through the heart, the sergeant with his belly blown into his back, the corporal with his spine where his head should have been." MacArthur said they left them there, "gallant men dead in the service of their country."

The soldiers of the 42nd pursued the retreating Germans until just after dawn. MacArthur crossed over no-man's-land to visit his flanking regiment, the old "Fighting 69th" from New York City with its famous chaplain Father Francis P. Duffy and commander Colonel William "Wild Bill" Donovan, who would go on to head the U.S. Office of Strategic Services (OSS) in the next war. Duffy had just returned from the sad duty of burying Sergeant Joyce Kilmer, one of America's foremost young poets, who had been shot through the brain that morning reconnoitering a machine-gun nest. The burial took place, MacArthur noted, "under the stump of one of those trees he had immortalized."*

....

* *I think that I shall never see*
A poem lovely as a tree.

A tree whose hungry mouth is prest
Against the earth's sweet flowing breast;

MacArthur sent the regiments forward again but went himself to his division headquarters, where he found the corps commander Lieutenant General Hunter Liggett, as well as his commanding officer Major General Charles T. Menoher. MacArthur explained what he had done but soon felt so drowsy—he hadn't slept for four days or nights—that everything began to black out. He slumped into a chair and within a few moments was sound asleep.

"They told me afterward," MacArthur wrote years later, "that General Liggett just looked down at me and said, 'Well I'll be damned! Menoher, you'd better cite him.' My fourth Silver Star."

★ ★ ★ ★

DOUGLAS MACARTHUR WAS BORN January 26, 1880, at Fort Dodge, Arkansas, in what is now Little Rock, where his father, a captain in the regular army, was stationed. Like George Marshall and George Patton, MacArthur's family had immigrated to America from Great Britain, but instead of landing in Virginia the MacArthurs alit in Massachusetts, heart of Yankeedom. Neither did they arrive accompanied by some great chieftain, but a mere widow and her ten-year-old boy Arthur MacArthur I, in 1825, to escape the endless wars and poverty that afflicted all but the upper and royal classes during that period of European development.

It had not always been that way. In the long ago past of the dim Scottish Highlands the boy's ancestors had been among the wealthy and ferocious MacArtair clan—kilted, dirked, and with their own haunting

....

A tree that looks at God all day
And lifts her leafy arms to pray;

A tree that may in Summer wear
A nest of robins in her hair;

Upon whose bosom snow has lain
Who intimately lives with rain.

Poems are made by fools like me,
But only God can make a tree.

war cry: "Listen! O Listen!"—masters of all they surveyed along the shores of Loch Awe in the earldom of Garmoran. Until, that is, in 1427, during the reign of King James I, Lain MacArtair, chief of the clan, was summoned to Inverness where he was beheaded by the king for reasons that have vanished in the mists of time.[3] Afterward, the MacArtair clan—once said to be a thousand strong—lost its property and migrated to Glasgow where most of its members, being warriors and highland country people, became more or less civilized—but also mired in poverty and despair, and most remained so four hundred years hence.

Thus, in 1825 the newly arrived widow MacArthur took her son to the small settlement of Chicopee Falls, near the city of Springfield in the beautiful Connecticut River Valley. There she remarried, apparently handsomely, because her son was educated at Wesleyan and Amherst colleges, studied law in New York, and was admitted to the bar in 1840.[4]

In 1844 Arthur MacArthur I married Aurelia Belcher, daughter of a New England manufacturer (whose grandmother Sarah Barney Belcher [1771–1867] became the common ancestor not only of Douglas MacArthur but of Winston Churchill and Franklin Roosevelt as well). The following June Aurelia gave birth to a son, Arthur II. Then, for unknown reasons, Arthur I packed up his roots and moved the family way out to Milwaukee, Wisconsin, where he became a prominent Democrat and in 1855 was elected lieutenant governor of the state. He was forty years old.

Within two months of his inauguration MacArthur I found himself acting as governor of Wisconsin following a voting scandal that caused the newly elected holder of that higher office to resign in disgrace. The political issues of the day—namely the hated Kansas-Nebraska Act*—had nearly upset the peace of Wisconsin, a stronghold of the fledgling

* A piece of legislation sponsored a year earlier by the Democrats that allowed settlers in U.S. territories to decide whether slavery would be allowed within their borders. It led to much bloodletting between opposing sides and was a precursor of the American Civil War.

Republican Party. Nevertheless, this animosity did not seem to rub off on MacArthur, who in 1857 was elected as a circuit judge and served two terms. In 1870 he was appointed by President Ulysses S. Grant to become an associate justice of the Supreme Court of the District of Columbia, which governed the Federal District.[5]

Living in Washington, Judge MacArthur moved in the highest social and political circles, lecturing on history, law, and many other subjects in the capital's various clubs and lecture halls, and writing no fewer than ten books between 1875 and 1892 on history, education, law, and linguistics.[6]

General Douglas MacArthur remembered his grandfather well and spent time with him during these heady Washington days up until his death in 1896, when Douglas was sixteen. From his grandfather, Douglas got the sense that being a MacArthur meant commanding "the respect of important personages at all levels of government and society," and that he was "obligated to conduct himself with honor, gallantry and magnanimity." The "family heritage," according to MacArthur biographer Clayton James, "which [Judge MacArthur] largely created and passed on to Douglas, was one of nobility."[7]

He also taught his grandson how to play poker and when he was older Douglas liked to tell the story of the time he was holding four queens and bet "every chip I had," only to see his grandfather lay down four kings with the admonition: "My dear boy, nothing is sure in this life."[8]

★ ★ ★ ★

WHEN THE CIVIL WAR BROKE OUT IN 1861, Arthur II was fifteen and begging to join the Union Army. Instead his father sent him to military school for a year with a mind to get him into West Point (undoubtedly in the belief that the war would be over by the time he graduated). By that time the family was living in Washington and, armed with letters of recommendation from the Wisconsin governor and escorted by one of the state's U.S. senators, Arthur—then seventeen—got an audience with the president. Lincoln graciously but regretfully informed the boy that he had used all of his presidential vacancies for West Point until 1863, which prompted the headstrong boy to enlist immediately in the 24th Wisconsin Infantry, a volunteer regiment then being formed in Milwaukee. On August 24, 1862, he was commissioned a second lieutenant and became the regimental adjutant.[9]

Two months later during the Rebel general Braxton Bragg's incursion into Kentucky, the Confederates attacked the Federal Army of the Ohio near the town of Perryville. During the fierce and confused battle (which concluded more or less as a draw) young Arthur II was cited for conspicuous gallantry by his division commander, General Philip H. Sheridan, and breveted to the rank of captain.

Two months later, on the last day of 1862, Captain Arthur MacArthur II's army collided again with Bragg at the brutal Battle of Stones River, which produced 25,000 casualties over three days' fighting and a Union victory. The 24th Wisconsin bore the brunt of the fighting and suffered 40 percent casualties, including every mounted officer except MacArthur, who was again "mentioned in dispatches" for gallantry.

Nearly a year later, on November 25, 1863, Arthur MacArthur II was awarded the Medal of Honor for leading a charge that ultimately drove the Confederate States Army from the heights surrounding Chattanooga, Tennessee, and paved the way for William Tecumseh Sherman to march on Atlanta. Captain MacArthur, Douglas's father, seized the regimental standard of the 24th Wisconsin and, shouting "On Wisconsin!," personally planted it on the crest of Missionary Ridge when the Rebel army was repulsed.

MacArthur was promoted to major and given command of the regiment, which he held until the war's end. He participated in all of the vicious fighting leading to the Battle of Atlanta itself, where he was wounded in the chest and arm, but recovered in time to participate in the slaughter known as the Battle of Franklin, Tennessee. There, five Confederate generals were killed or mortally wounded in the last great Rebel charge of the war. MacArthur led a counterattack that broke the Confederate assault and restored the Union position, but he was shot in the knee, shoulder, and chest, putting him out of action for the rest of the war. Still, it earned him promotion to brevet colonel "for gallant and meritorious services." He was nineteen years old.

MacArthur began studying law under his father, but he found himself restless for the rough-and-tumble military life and decided to make a career of the army. The end of the war, however, produced a great riff, or discharging, of officers in the U.S. Army, and, despite glowing letters of commendation from politicians and other noteworthy people, the best that Washington would offer MacArthur was a second lieutenant's commission. A year later, however, he was promoted to captain, but a captain he would remain for the next twenty-three years.

★ ★ ★ ★

AT LAST IN 1874, after seven years on the Plains battling hostile Indians, the 13th Infantry was posted to New Orleans where the regiment hoped to enjoy the serene pleasantries of Southern civilization. Instead they found themselves involved in propping up a corrupt carpetbagger political machine at the direction of the Grant government in Washington. Distasteful as this task was, Yankee captain Arthur MacArthur II improbably met, fell in love with, and married a Southern belle from Virginia whom he encountered at a masked Mardi Gras ball in the winter of 1875.

She was Mary Pinkney "Pinky" Hardy, the vibrant, strong-willed twenty-two-year-old daughter of an aristocratic FFV* planter and cotton merchant from Norfolk whose family had been driven from their home Riveredge by the Union Army at the beginning of the war.† It was love at first sight.

Even though her three brothers boycotted the wedding—they were VMI graduates and former Confederate officers—Arthur and Pinky were

---

* First Families of Virginia. See chapter 2 for further explanation.

† The home was then occupied by the Union general Benjamin Butler who acquired the sobriquet "Beast" Butler while serving as military governor of New Orleans during the war, stemming from an order he issued suggesting that disloyal New Orleans women should be treated like prostitutes.

married that same spring amidst much pomp and gaiety at Riveredge, a three-story redbrick Federal-style mansion on the Elizabeth River. A child, Arthur III, came the following year and another, Malcolm, in 1878. For each birth Pinky came home to Riveredge.

At first the army seemed to have mercy on Captain MacArthur, assigning him to Washington where he and Pinky were for a time able to enjoy the company of his father, the judge, and the many friends he'd made in high places. But just as they were becoming comfortable, orders sent him back to Louisiana, then to Little Rock, Arkansas. There, in 1880, in a towered old arsenal building converted to married officers' quarters, Douglas MacArthur was born. He arrived "sooner than expected," so Pinky was unable to return to Virginia beforehand.[10]

At this point the army dealt Arthur a low hand, assigning him and Company K of the 13th Infantry to Fort Wingate, one of the most desolate and remote posts in the United States. It was in the northwest corner of the New Mexico Territory, one hundred miles from nowhere* between the vast Navajo reservation to the north and the hostile Apache territory to the south that Geronimo controlled.

In 1883 tragedy struck the MacArthur family when Malcolm, age five, died of measles and was buried at Riveredge. But army life in the Southwest went on as usual. The posts were rude and rugged, even for the men, while for the women such as Pinky MacArthur they were "Gethsemanes" of heat and dust and cold and dust, interspersed by storms, flash floods, rattlesnakes, scorpions, even Gila monsters—and always the eternal dust. Rainbows were rare.[11]

The following year, Company K was assigned to an even more god-forsaken outpost, tiny Fort Selden on the Mexican border, a 300-mile journey by wagon and foot. Douglas, then age four, wrote in later life that he specifically recalled marching next to the company first sergeant, Peter Ripley, at the head of the column during the monthlong trek toward the Rio Grande.

---

* "Nowhere" being Albuquerque, 100 miles to the east, a mere Indian trading post in those days.

The far-flung Fort Selden became the MacArthurs' home for the next three years while Company K chased after the elusive Geronimo and his band of Chiricahua Apache, which had gone off the reservation and onto the warpath. It was the army's duty to protect workmen on the Southern Pacific Railroad, the stage express, and various small settlements in the area. The garrison of the fort comprised Captain MacArthur and his executive officer, an assistant surgeon, and forty-six enlisted men who lived in one-story flat-roofed, dirt-floored adobe shelters.

Young Douglas adored it, and later he wrote that the first sound he remembered hearing was the post bugle. "It was here I learned to ride and shoot before I could read and write," he said afterward, "indeed almost before I could walk and talk." Yes indeed, Douglas MacArthur grew up in the last of the Old West, where once a band of bold and unhappy Apache warriors showered the fort with flaming arrows before riding off into the night.

One day he and his older brother, Arthur III, were out on their spotted Navajo ponies when away in the shimmering desert there appeared a strange-looking creature that proved to be, of all things, a camel. They stopped and gaped as the swaying camel trotted toward them, until it pulled up a few yards away, bared its teeth, and snorted. It was amazing and somewhat frightening to Douglas that real camels were so much bigger and more alarming than picture camels, but he stood his ground and yelled at the beast loud as he could until it turned and clattered off, swaying into the desert whence it came.* Later when the incident was reported to the senior MacArthur, Douglas having informed his father that he hadn't been afraid, the reply stuck with him the rest of his days: "Naturally, son. You're a MacArthur."[12]

....

* Evidently this was one of a large herd of camels brought from Egypt to the Southwest in 1855 by Jefferson Davis when he was the U.S. secretary of war. After a study, Davis had concluded that camels were much more useful in the desertlike terrain than pack mules and so they were used by army surveying crews until the Civil War when all the officers and soldiers returned east to fight and the camels were left to themselves. The last reported sighting was in 1927, in New Mexico, from a train.

About this time Pinky began the rudiments of an education that included, "above all else," MacArthur remembered, "a sense of obliga- tion. We were to do what was right no matter what the personal sacrifice might be. Our country was always to come first. Two things we must never do—never lie, never tattle."[13]

In 1886, because of MacArthur's noteworthy leadership, Company K was selected to be stationed at the new Infantry and Cavalry School at Fort Leavenworth, Kansas, to help train army officers. There, Douglas entered first grade in public school and was exposed for the first time to a regular academic discipline, at which he fared poorly according to his own account.

As the final decade of the nineteenth century approached, Arthur MacArthur II was in his twenty-third year as an army captain when he was finally blessed with a stroke of luck. General Alexander McCook— the old Indian fighter in whose command Arthur had served at the battles of Perryville and Stones River—was commandant of the Infantry and Cavalry School and gave Arthur a glowing recommendation for promo- tion to major in the Adjutant Generals Department in Washington, D.C. McCook's endorsement said of Arthur MacArthur, among other things, "He is beyond doubt the most distinguished captain in the Army of the United States." The appointment was soon forthcoming.

As Douglas put it afterward, when the family arrived in Washington it "was my first glimpse at that whirlpool of glitter and pomp," and he likewise got a taste, albeit from overhearing adult conversations, of the political, social, and financial intrigues infecting the American capital city. He also had time to spend with his grandfather, the first Arthur MacArthur, who was the epitome of Washington's "glitter and pomp," and for the next five years he attended a public school on Massachusetts Avenue where his grades remained "average."[14]

In 1893 Arthur was posted to Fort Sam Houston in San Antonio, Texas, a move that produced an epiphany of sorts for young Douglas, the reluctant scholar. He was enrolled for high school in the West Texas Military Academy that was run by an Episcopal bishop who was also rector of the post chapel. Suddenly Douglas found his horizons expanding with "a desire to know, a seeking for the reasons why, a search for the truth."

The dull Latin and Greek he'd learned in grade school now became pathways to the classics that George Patton so fervently craved. He studied Homer and Virgil and translated the *Iliad* and *Aeneid,* which described "the nerve-tingling battlefields of the great captains." He now saw the Bible in an entirely different light; the Old Testament became an epic story of wars and noble leaders, of plagues and floods and heroes and persecutors. His marks shot up and academic honors and medals came his way. He played sports—first team in football and baseball and the school's tennis champion. "My four years there were undoubtedly the happiest of my life," he would write seventy years later.

His father, now promoted to lieutenant colonel, was posted to the Department of the Dakotas in Minnesota, but the family made its headquarters in Milwaukee, which remained home. West Point, of course, became the natural, almost unspoken, goal for Douglas. When a competitive examination was announced for a vacancy in Milwaukee congressman Theobald Otjen's district, he began preparing, tutored by the principal of a local high school. In the spring of 1898 he passed the exam with flying colors; of thirteen applicants, he scored highest by far—with a 99.3 average to the next man's 77.9.

★ ★ ★ ★

MEANWHILE, BIG THINGS WERE AFOOT for Lieutenant Colonel Arthur MacArthur II—bigger than he ever imagined. In 1898 war was declared with Spain and MacArthur was made a brigadier general and given a brigade of forty-eight hundred men, which he expected to take to Cuba to fight. Instead, at the last minute, orders came to move the brigade to San Francisco and then board ship for the Philippines where the Spanish fleet had been sunk in the Battle of Manila Bay. The Spanish army was nevertheless persisting in holding on to what had been a Spanish possession for the past 350 years. Arthur had to send for a map for he didn't even know where the Philippines were.[15]

They arrived into a strange war in which the Spanish army was fighting an insurrection led by Emilio Aguinaldo, whose 60,000 to 80,000 Filipino rebels joined sides with the 11,000-man U.S. forces to eject the Spanish from the islands once and for all. When that was accomplished, however, Aguinaldo turned on the Americans, who had promised the Filipinos self-government, but only after a "period of adjustment" to ready them for democracy. Brigadier General Arthur MacArthur II pleaded with his superiors to make concessions to the rebels, but the American commander insisted that they must first lay down their arms.

In February1899 Aguinaldo attacked Manila, but Douglas's father, now a fifty-three-year-old major general, repelled them in a dozen savage battles that he personally commanded at the front. He narrowly escaped death several times. The fighting continued while more and more U.S. troops were thrown into the fray, until there were no fewer than 150,000 American soldiers in the Philippines fighting the guerrillas.

In May of 1900 MacArthur was put in command of the Philippines Territory with the title of military governor. Even as the fighting went on MacArthur began a civil action campaign to win the hearts and minds of the Filipino people: he built schools and hospitals, dug wells and improved roads and harbors; he rewrote the cruel Spanish laws and inserted the right of habeas corpus into the legal code. Strict penalties were enforced on American soldiers who abused the Filipinos, and even when Aguinaldo was at last captured, MacArthur took him into the Malacañang Palace, or governor's mansion, and befriended him to the extent that Aguinaldo told his people to lay down their arms.*

Despite this, the killing did not stop as pockets of guerrillas continued to attack Americans all over the two thousand inhabited Philippine

---

* Aguinaldo's capture is an amazing story. Brigadier General Frederick Funston and three other army officers, accompanied by U.S.-loyal Philippine scouts posing as *insurrectos,* marched into Aguinaldo's jungle hideaway pretending that the officers were captives being brought to the rebel general. When they arrived the scouts overpowered the rebel garrison and took Aguinaldo prisoner instead.

Islands. In exasperation, President William McKinley sent out a "U.S. Philippine Commission" to deal with the problem, which was causing him political headaches. Heading the commission was the colossal 325-pound William Howard Taft, an Ohio judge whose motto, "The Philippines for the Filipinos," did not square with Major General MacArthur's belief that the territory was not yet ready for self-government. Taft and MacArthur soon clashed and the relationship became so icy that Taft complained that the only time he stopped sweating in the Philippines was when he shook hands with his major general.[16]

To make matters worse, when McKinley was assassinated the following year, the new president, Theodore Roosevelt, appointed Taft as secretary of war. It did not bode well for Arthur MacArthur's future career.[17]

He spent the next ten years in a variety of menial duties beneath his rank and qualifications. There was only one assignment that paid off well for everyone, not least the military and the nation, and that was in 1905 following the Russo-Japanese War when General MacArthur was assigned to complete a nine-month "reconnaissance" of the Far East that included a grand tour of Japan, India, Singapore, Burma, Ceylon, French Indochina (Vietnam), Malaya, and Siam (Thailand) and ended up with several months in China. His reports on the political, social, and military situations in these nations became helpful to intelligence officers of the time and even later when America was on the verge of war in the Pacific and no one ever really knew it.

Upon the return of Arthur MacArthur—who remained a hero to the press and the nation—Congress bestowed upon him the four stars of a full general. But with Taft still running the War Department, MacArthur was passed over for chief of staff, which, as the army's senior general, should have been his. He was much offended by the slight, and when Taft won the presidential election of 1908 and moved into the White House MacArthur knew it was time to quit. He did so, formally, at the age of sixty-four, on June 9, 1909.

Three years later he was dead in the most prophetic fashion, as he had often expressed to friends that he sometimes dreamed of dying at the head of his old Civil War regiment, the 24th Wisconsin. On September 5,

1912, against the advice of his doctors and despite Pinky's admonitions, Arthur agreed to deliver the keynote address to the survivors of the 24th at their fiftieth anniversary banquet in Milwaukee.

He began by saying, "Comrades, I could not stay away on the great anniversary of our starting to war. Little did we think a half century ago that so many of us would be permitted to gather in this way." Then he "crumpled up upon the table in front of him." The regimental surgeon who had patched up the wounded so long ago rushed to him and after a brief examination said to the boys—now old men—whom Arthur had led up Missionary Ridge: "Comrades, the general is dying." Someone began saying the Lord's Prayer and they all kneeled and took it up. He was buried in Milwaukee, not Arlington, in a plain suit of clothes instead of his uniform, and as was his wish his funeral was "utterly devoid of military display," save an American flag on the casket. Lieutenant General Arthur MacArthur II was dead at the age of sixty-seven.[18]

★ ★ ★ ★

DOUGLAS MACARTHUR ARRIVED at West Point in June of 1899, accompanied by his mother, Pinky, who, because her husband was off fighting in the Philippines, had decided to take a suite at Craney's Hotel, just off campus, to be near her son.

Plebe year was rough in those times, perhaps more so than at any time in the history of the academy, because of the merciless hazing that the upperclassmen inflicted. Because of his father's fame and public stature, Douglas was singled out by sadistic "yearlings," or third classmen (sophomores), who ran the so-called summer camp for plebes before the academic year began. The summer camp was ostensibly designed to shape the plebes up for the coming year by teaching them the rules and customs of the academy and close order drill. In reality, it was more of an excuse to absorb the plebes in a brutal orgy of cruelty—as only nineteen- and twenty-year-old men who have just endured it themselves can conjure.

A man named Barry (later dismissed) had it in for MacArthur, and not long after he arrived in summer camp Douglas was called before Barry.

He and several other plebes were given the choice of "taking exercise" (hazing) or being called out by every member of the sophomore boxing team, one at a time. MacArthur was a fair boxer himself but the thought of his mother having to see him with all those cuts and bruises caused him to accept the "exercise."

It began innocently enough; he was told to stand at attention for one hour. Then the insults and the brutality began: "eagling," doing squats (deep knee bends) over jagged broken bottles with the arms flapping to the side like a bird's. He did fifty, then a hundred. He was then told to "hang by a stretcher"—hanging off of a tent pole; then more eagling; dipping (push-ups) fifty, then a hundred. In between these torments they mockingly made him recite his father's Civil War record, or his exploits in the Philippines, accompanied by an unrelenting torment of screaming in his face until he was covered with spittle, and then more eagling.

After twenty minutes and more than two hundred eagles he collapsed in a convulsive faint and was taken to his tent where his tentmate Frederick Cunningham caught him at the flap and laid him on the floor. MacArthur's legs suffered uncontrollable spasms and he asked Cunningham to put a blanket under them so the upperclassmen would not hear the noise. If he began to cry out, he asked Cunningham to stuff a blanket in his mouth.[*, 19]

Strangely, MacArthur's stoic performance during the hazing earned him the respect of his tormentors and, according to Cunningham, he was given a "bootlick," which was basically a free pass from further hazing at West Point. Afterward MacArthur privately vowed never to haze a fellow cadet, and if it was ever possible he intended to put an end to the practice.

During his days at the Point, MacArthur ran neck-and-neck for the top spots with Ulysses S. Grant III, grandson of the former general and president. Grant's mother, Mrs. Frederick Dent Grant, like Pinky,

---

* Cunningham soon quit in disgust and wrote an anonymous letter to the *New York Sun* revealing the brutality of West Point hazing, which prompted a congressional investigation at which MacArthur testified. He declined, however, to name any names except those who had already resigned or been dismissed from the academy.

resided in Craney's Hotel and the two cadets, Douglas and Grant III, would spend what time they had consulting with their mothers after dinner on Flirtation Walk, or in some cases sneak into the hotel itself for a treat from the dining room. His yearling year, MacArthur was second corporal to Grant's first, but that would be the only time. He arced across his West Point years like a shooting star, setting records some of which remain unmatched today.

He lettered in baseball, and in 1901 he scored the winning run in West Point's 4–3 first-ever victory over the Midshipmen of Annapolis. When first captain honors were announced it was Douglas MacArthur who was chosen, and he also held the top academic record his senior year. To his practice of rigid self-discipline, MacArthur added an almost uncanny intuitiveness that left even his instructors and tactical officers in awe. "He had style," a fellow classmate said many years afterward. "There was never another cadet quite like him."

At graduation, he led the ninety-three remaining cadets of the class of 1903 to their seats before the platform where Secretary of War Elihu Root left these words ringing in their ears: "Before you leave the army, according to all precedents in our history, you will be engaged in another war. It is bound to come. It will come. Prepare your country for that war."[20]

★ ★ ★ ★

THE YEAR 1903 WAS FILLED with weighty portent, marked by the Wright brothers' first heavier-than-air flight; the Nobel Prize in Physics awarded to Madame Marie Curie and her husband, Pierre, for their work with radium; the first wireless transmission; and the first appearance of the Crayola. It also saw Second Lieutenant Douglas MacArthur's acceptance into the U.S. Army's Corps of Engineers, the most elite branch of that service, and his transoceanic voyage to the U.S. Philippines Territory where guerrilla war still raged on some of the outlying islands.

His initial duty consisted of parochial construction work—the building of wharves and docks on the island of Leyte, for instance—but soon turned deadly in November 1903, when he led a party into the jungle looking for logs for pilings. MacArthur was aware that the jungle was dangerous, and that some previous patrols had been ambushed, but the fact was he had been directed to build the piers and needed the timber. His detail hadn't gone far when trouble sought them out.

Two *insurrectos* waylaid the patrol, one on each side of the narrow jungle trail, and the one to the right raised a rifle and fired into MacArthur's face. The slug tore through the crown of his campaign hat before slashing a small sapling tree behind him. MacArthur, an expert pistol shot from his childhood days on the frontier, whipped out his .38 revolver and "dropped them both dead in their tracks."[21]

His foreman, a regular army sergeant, rushed up and examined the dead men slumped on the ground, then noticed the still-smoking hole in MacArthur's campaign hat.

"Begging thu Loo'tenant's paddon," said the sergeant in his rich Irish brogue, "but all the rest of the Loo'tenant's life is pure velvut!"[22]

One day a captain who headed the Philippine constabulary invited MacArthur to the Army-Navy Club in Manila to meet two promising young Filipino law graduates. They were Manuel Quezon and Sergio Osmeña, both of whom would go on to be presidents of the Philippine Commonwealth.

In April 1904, less than a year after he'd entered the army as a commissioned officer, MacArthur was promoted to first lieutenant, and soon afterward he sailed for San Francisco. It might be recalled that it took George Patton seven years to get his silver first lieutenant's bars.

In San Francisco, MacArthur languished as an officer of engineers with duties that ranged from repairing yards and docks to supervising the cleanup of the environmental mess left in California's mountains and rivers following the Great Gold Rush of 1849 and its aftermath. In September 1905, to MacArthur's surprise and delight, he received orders to report to his father in Yokohama, Japan, to accompany him as aide-de-camp during his reconnaissance tour of the Orient. Douglas arrived in Japan at the end of October and together father and son sailed for Singapore where the British were erecting the greatest military fortress in the Far East—if not the world.

BEGINNINGS

From there they traveled to Burma, Calcutta, and Siam, where Douglas saved the evening for the king (who would become the model for the best-selling book *Anna and the King of Siam,* which begat the hit musical and movie *The King and I*) by changing a fuse in a lighting panel when the dinner party he was hosting went dark. The king was so grateful that he proposed to decorate Douglas for "conspicuous gallantry," an honor Lieutenant MacArthur politely declined.[23]

When the eight-month tour ended, Douglas had gained an immeasurably deep grasp of the Far East and its relationship with the United States—namely that from that time forth the Oriental world would be inextricably connected with the Americas and, more darkly, that at some point in time a conflict between the two would be inevitable. He also noted that while the British colonial system in India, Burma, Malaya, and elsewhere brought law, order, wages, religion, and other civilizing benefits, it also stifled the newfound aspirations of the colonized people, breeding resentment, apathy, and in some cases outright hatred. He concluded that, as in the U.S. occupation of the Philippines, colonial rule must be benevolent and temporary, as his father also believed.

In the following years Douglas MacArthur began climbing the ladder of military achievement with the air of a man who knew where he was going. Unlike some who struggled up it rung by greasy rung, MacArthur sauntered into Washington to attend the army's elite engineering school. Just before the new year of 1907 he was appointed aide to the dynamic and glamorous President Theodore Roosevelt who frequently sought MacArthur's views on the Far East while the dashing young lieutenant hobnobbed with senators, congressmen, cabinet members, and high-ranking military officers, each a potential stepping-stone for his brilliant career. MacArthur certainly seemed on his way to an early captaincy when, as it will, disaster struck—he fell in love.

He had gone on temporary assignment to his hometown of Milwaukee. The lady in question was Fanniebelle Van Dyke Stuart of New York, daughter of a millionaire, who had come to Milwaukee for a visit at the same time. MacArthur was immediately smitten, or "bewitched," as one of his biographers notes, and asked her to marry him. She declined.[24]

At West Point MacArthur had always been a sort of ladies' man and was said to have set some sort of record at one point by becoming "engaged" to eight different women at the same time. Doubtless there was a discrepancy of expression in the lingua franca of the day, and most probably what was meant was that MacArthur was *dating* eight different women at the same time; still, it was an astonishing accomplishment.

He began bombarding Fanniebelle with a kind of maudlin poetry that nevertheless registered a certain flair for the language of Romanticism.*

> *I live in a little house of dreams*
> *In the land that cannot be*
> *The country of the fair desire*
> *That I shall never see.*

He once wrote her an epic poem twenty-seven pages long in which he, himself, stars as a soldier doomed to be slain, but she continued to rebuff his advances, prompting him to pen mawkishly:

> *Fair Gotham Girl*
> *With Life awhirl*
> *Of dance and fancy free*
> *Tis Thee I love*
> *All things above.*
> *Why can't thou not love me?*[25]

Beyond the love lost, the worst thing the failed romance did was cause MacArthur to slip in his work. A superior officer during this period

---

* Poetry as a general art form has nearly passed from the scene, but in MacArthur's day—and Patton's and Marshall's—it was a common mode of expression among educated people, including big, burly soldiers. Alas, nearly all the large-circulation magazines that featured poetry have vanished, and more's the pity.

gave him a damning military efficiency report: "lacking in zeal," "absent from the office," "duties not performed satisfactorily" it read. Worse, the commandant of the engineer school placed in his file a letter stating that MacArthur "seemed to take but little interest in the work," and that he did only the "bare minimum needed to avoid failing the course."[26]

These are the sorts of evaluations that cause an officer to remain a lieutenant for years, if not forever, as MacArthur was well aware. He seems to have pulled himself together after this, however, and wrote an exceptional pamphlet entitled "Military Demolitions Illustrated," which was famously incorporated for use in all the service schools by the commandant of Fort Leavenworth, where he was soon to be assigned.

Once there, MacArthur organized an engineers' polo team to play against the cavalry, infantry, and other service branches, and he was also the manager/player on the Fort Leavenworth baseball team, which enjoyed immense success owing in part to MacArthur's peculiar style of gamesmanship. This involved the simple trick of inviting the opposing team to a sumptuous luncheon before the game, at which copious amounts of beer, wine, and spirits were provided. Afterward the thoroughly sober soldiers usually thrashed the inebriated visitors.

After a short stint at Leavenworth, MacArthur was ordered to the nation's capital where he was taken under the wing of General Leonard Wood, the new army chief of staff, a Harvard-educated surgeon who had made a name for himself without the benefit of a West Point ring. In 1913 MacArthur, now a captain, was appointed to the General Staff. Pinky, his now widowed mother, moved into an apartment building near the War Department to be with her devoted thirty-three-year-old son.

The following year, events conspired to propel MacArthur—still a very junior officer—into the highest echelons of military esteem. The eternal turmoil in Mexico spawned an insult to the American flag in Tampico. It seemed that the government of the Mexican president Victoriano Huerta mistakenly arrested nine U.S. sailors who had gone ashore to get fuel for their gunboat. The commander of the U.S. fleet insisted that the men be returned and that a twenty-one-gun salute be given to the U.S. flag by the Mexican garrison that had been holding the men. The Mexicans released the sailors but were unwilling to salute the American flag, prompting President Woodrow Wilson to order a fleet of battleships and detachment of U.S. Marines to seize the Mexican oil port of Vera Cruz and blockade its harbor.*

On May 1, Captain Douglas MacArthur set foot on the dock at Vera Cruz on orders from General Wood, who was himself preparing to lead an American expeditionary force to the city and make war on Mexico if open hostilities broke out. MacArthur's role was to "get the lay of the land" and report any useful information to General Wood when he arrived. It was just the kind of thing MacArthur was good at.

★ ★ ★ ★

AFTER SNOOPING AROUND FOR SEVERAL DAYS, MacArthur noticed that while there were plentiful boxcars and passenger cars in the rail yards, there were no engines to pull them. Nor were there any pack animals to speak of in Vera Cruz, which would put General Wood's army, if and when it arrived, in a bad way for transportation of its supplies.

MacArthur began searching for information on the missing railroad engines, when he encountered "a drunken Mexican" from whom he received "an inkling that a number of [train] engines were hidden somewhere on the line between Vera Cruz and Alvarado." Subsequently, "This man was sobered up and found to be a railroad fireman and engineer on the Vera Cruz and Alvarado Railroad. He consented, after certain financial inducements had been offered, to assist me in accurately locating the engines."[27]

---

* Insults to the American flag were far more serious then than now. In the days of so-called gunboat diplomacy following the Civil War the flag remained a revered symbol and exemplification of the national dignity, and one trifled with it at his peril. "Flag burning" was a concept that had yet to develop, and wars had been started for less.

This was dangerous business, as MacArthur well knew; a soldier who had recently blundered into Mexican lines had been lined against a wall and executed. But in his head MacArthur had visions of his father, the hero of Missionary Ridge, and while the Vera Cruz dustup wasn't much of a war, at the time it was the only war they had.

The distance between Vera Cruz and Alvarado was forty-two miles, and numerous Mexican army troops held each of the half dozen towns along the stretch. MacArthur's plan was to have the drunken Mexican meet him that night on the rail tracks outside the U.S. lines with a handcar, which they would use to take them up the rail line about fifteen miles to Jamapa, where the railroad bridge was down. From there they would find a way across the river and meet up with a second handcar manned by two of the Mexican's friends, and then pump along the tracks until they found the missing engines. In exchange for this, MacArthur said, the Mexicans would be paid $150 in gold,* once he was returned safely inside U.S. lines.

"The night was squally and overcast," MacArthur wrote in his official report of the matter. "At dusk I crossed our lines near the wireless station." He was in his uniform, carrying a small Bible, and armed with the new .45-caliber semiautomatic pistol that had been adopted by the army in 1911. As promised, the Mexican was there with the handcar; MacArthur frisked him, relieving the man of "a .38 caliber pistol and an small dirk knife," and they pumped off into the gloom. At Jamapa they camouflaged the handcar with bushes, stole a small native boat, and paddled across the river north of the town to escape detection. They discovered two ponies tethered near a shack and, proceeding now on horseback, continued along the tracks until they found the other two Mexicans and their handcar.

After hiding the ponies, MacArthur and his party kept stealthily following the tracks toward Alvarado; as each town approached he would get off the handcar and, with one of the Mexicans as guide (lashed to him to prevent escape), give the place a wide berth, catching up with the handcar on the other side of town.

---

* About $3,600 in today's money.

At last they reached Alvarado at 1 a.m., where they found five engines, three of which, after careful inspection, proved to be "fine big road pullers in excellent condition." Mission accomplished, MacArthur and his men began their escape back to Vera Cruz. At Salinas, however, they encountered "five armed men . . . evidently one of the marauding bands," who ran after them and opened up with rifle and pistol fire. Pumping furiously, MacArthur's handcar outdistanced all but two of the robbers whereupon, he said, "In order to preserve our own lives I was obliged to fire upon them. Both went down."

At Piedra, in a driving mist, they ran "flush in" to about fifteen more bandits, who were mounted. Immediately the bandits opened fire on MacArthur, whose clothes were riddled with several bullet holes. His main Mexican man was shot in the shoulder. In turn, MacArthur brought down "at least four of the enemy, and the rest fled." After bandaging up the wounded man, they "proceeded north with all possible speed," until, at the town of Laguna, they encountered three more armed and mounted men who again attacked them with gunfire.

Pumping the handcar desperately, they left two of the riders behind, but a lone gunman kept up and actually overtook the handcar, shooting through MacArthur's shirt. MacArthur fired on the Mexican rider and his horse, which toppled dead onto the track in front of the handcar.

At Paso de Toro they left the handcar, retrieved the ponies, and rode them back to the shack where they had taken them. Only MacArthur and the original Mexican were left, the two others having vanished during the gunfights. At the river they found the boat, but in crossing it hit a snag and sank. In the darkness MacArthur held his wounded companion's head above water until they reached the opposite shore where they uncovered the first handcar and miraculously made it back to Vera Cruz in one piece.*

....

* The so-called Vera Cruz Affair dragged on for another six months with American troops holding the city and its oil wells hostage until, in November 1914, an agreement was hammered out between the United States and the ABC Powers (Argentina, Brazil, and Chile—the three most powerful

MacArthur was put in for the Medal of Honor by General Wood himself, but as he later put it in his memoirs, "The War Department disagreed."

The rationale was that MacArthur had been acting on his own hook and not under orders from anybody, especially General Funston, who had been told specifically *not* to conduct the sort of escapade MacArthur had engineered. Nevertheless, the newspapers got wind of the story and made it into a splendid military exploit. For the first time MacArthur found himself a famous national hero. He was promoted to major upon his return to Washington and remained on the General Staff until April 6, 1917, when the U.S. Congress declared war on Germany.

....

nations in South America) and President Wilson withdrew the American forces. Two years later, however, with the Mexican Revolution in full swing, U.S. troops were again obliged to invade Mexico.

★ ★ ★ ★

Chapter Four

"SOME DAMNED FOOLISHNESS IN THE BALKANS"

For a hundred years historians, politicians, and military scholars have debated the causes of World War I. But one thing generally agreed upon is that the long and tortuous path began in 1871, when Germany organized itself into a nation.

Previously, Greater Germany had been a menagerie of twenty-five principalities and quasi-kingdoms governed loosely by the state of Prussia, which was ruled by the emperor, or kaiser, Frederick William III. In the 1860s, on the advice of the distinguished German statesman Prince Otto von Bismarck, the kaiser began to absorb this collection of domains into the Empire of Germany, thus making it the largest and most powerful country in Europe.

She then immediately began attacking and subduing her neighbors— Denmark (1864), Austria (1866), and France (1871). It was the conquest of France that caused the discontent. In the Franco-Prussian War, after laying siege to Paris and reducing its inhabitants to a diet of cat meat, the Germans demanded two French provinces along the Franco-German border: Alsace, rich in coal and iron ore, and Lorraine, an agricultural breadbasket. This humiliation vexed the entire French nation, whatever their class or political affiliation, and spawned a resentful and bitter animosity lasting for generations. It figures prominently among the bitter chemistry that ignited World War I.

With the exception of France, at the time a republic, Europe was ruled by monarchies. To the east lay czarist Russia, which controlled parts of Poland and the Baltic states. To the south of Germany was the Hapsburg empire of Austria-Hungary, including what is now Czech Republic, Slovakia, Slovenia, Croatia, Bosnia and Herzegovina, and parts of Italy and Ukraine. Southernmost still were the tempestuous and angry states of Serbia, Romania, Bulgaria, Albania, and Montenegro.

As Germany unified itself, Great Britain was the foremost industrial power in the world. But soon Germany began to challenge her, aided in no small part by the iron and coal of the conquered French provinces. The industrious Germans quickly eradicated illiteracy and made great strides in modern technologies: the production of steel, chemicals, electronics, transportation, finance, and, ominously, the most up-to-date military armaments. By the end of the nineteenth century Germany's economy was booming and, in terms of overall effectiveness, she had the mightiest army in the world.

The early twentieth century, however, was a time of peace, the last of the prosperous Gilded Age that saw development of electric lights, motion pictures, automobiles, vast railway systems, and luxurious transatlantic shipping. It also saw enormous improvements in weapons and weapons systems, such as the machine gun. Until nearly the close of the nineteenth century, artillery—with the exception of mortars—was fired "line of sight," meaning that gunners actually had to see the target. But the invention of high-tensile steel allowed the guns to get longer ranges and far more powerful to preregister fire over nearly every part of a battlefield. The machine gun of course revolutionized modern warfare almost overnight. One fully automatic weapon of the era, served by a three-man crew, could put out the firepower of an entire platoon of riflemen. The effect of these weapons on the battlefield would prove devastating when war broke out, and no one ever truly figured out how to defend against them except by dying in unacceptable numbers.

Winston Churchill summed up these great advances in technology as the nineteenth century came to a close: "Every morning when the world woke up, some new machinery had started running. Every night when the world had supper, it was running still. It ran on while all men slept." Yet despite this abundance of technology, an undercurrent of discontent roiled the European continent.

Amid the turmoil came both a dramatic rise of nationalism as well as a growing hatred between ethnic and religious groups: Catholic versus Protestant, Muslim versus Christian—and everybody against the Jews. Colonial possessions provoked an outburst of pride, greed, vanity, and mistrust among both the rulers and the ruled. Add into the mixture the rising creed of socialism and it is easy to see how the kettle was overheating. It was especially true in Russia where the iron-fisted czar Nicholas presided over a nation teeming with socialists who kept alive their utopian dream of a classless society where everyone got their fair share—a world without suffering, poverty, or political oppression.

The same was true in Germany, where dissatisfaction among the laboring classes had in fact produced the largest Socialist Party in the world, which was constantly plotting to overthrow the government and the capitalist system. While Germans had the right to vote, the reins of power remained in the hands of the kaiser, no matter what the populous decreed.

Around this same time, European nations undertook a flurry of military alliances, the most threatening of which was when France united in a mutual defense pact with Russia—a treaty under which if one was attacked by an enemy the other would promptly come to its aid. This agreement particularly galled the Germans, being located between the two of them. It also prompted the chief of staff of the German army, Count Alfred von Schlieffen, to draw up his famous battle stratagem under which, if war broke out, the German army would immediately rush through neutral Belgium to conquer France, and then turn on the Russians before they could fully mobilize.

Among the more remarkable things about European diplomacy prior to World War I was the intimate family relationships between the rulers who would ultimately become the belligerents. These unusual associations all began with Great Britain's Queen Victoria (granddaughter of King George III who reigned during the American Revolution). In 1837, at the age of eighteen, she became queen of England. With her husband, Prince Albert, a German, she had nine children who married into practically every royal house of Europe. Her oldest son, Prince Albert Edward, married a princess of Denmark and became king of England when Victoria died in 1901. His son George V succeeded his father as king of England just before World War I broke out.

One of Victoria's daughters married a German prince, and her daughter—Victoria's granddaughter—married Czar Nicholas II of Russia. Not only that, but Victoria's firstborn daughter became the wife of the German kaiser Frederick III, and upon his death in 1888 their eldest son ascended the throne as Wilhelm II.

Thus, Germany's Kaiser Wilhelm II, Russia's Czar Nicholas II, and England's King George V were all cousins—the descendants of Queen Victoria.

The new German kaiser was something of a military nut, especially regarding the navy, which was relatively small at the time of his ascension. He appointed himself a field marshal, as well as an admiral, and decreed that henceforth the attire for men at court would be the military uniform. He was particularly impressed with the Gatling gun (a gift of his cousin King George of England), and by the time World War I broke out the German army had twelve thousand of the Gatling's successor, the machine gun, incorporated into their fighting battalions—the equivalent firepower of a 700,000-man army of riflemen.

In 1890 the kaiser fired Bismarck and along with him the old diplomat's earnest desire to keep the peace in Europe. Not only that, he began treating Russia like an unwelcome relative, refusing to renew financial loans and provide other emoluments. This was where France stepped in with loans from its great House of Rothschild, and the aforementioned mutual defense alliance soon followed.

In the meantime the kaiser embarked on a foreign policy that seemed deliberately designed to vex his perceived enemies, which now included Britain, and he did so out of one of the world's worst motives—jealousy. Wilhelm coveted Britain's exalted position among the nations of the world. He desired its great worldwide empire upon which "the sun never set."

Before long, the kaiser embarked Germany on a worldwide land grab—beginning in Africa with the Cameroons, Togoland, Tanganyika (East Africa), and German Southwest Africa and concluding by going after several strings of islands in the Pacific, including (unsuccessfully) the Philippines, which Douglas MacArthur's father always suspected Germany had its eyes upon.

These conquests—if one might call them that—proved as much a burden as a boon. Just about everything worth taking in Africa and the Far East had already been claimed by the older imperial nations; the British had India, Hong Kong, Singapore, and the choicest colonies in Africa; the French and Italians had most of North Africa; the Dutch had what is now Indonesia; and the Belgians had the Congo.

Then, in the early part of the twentieth century, Britain and France began signing a string of colonial trade agreements that alarmed the German foreign service as it indicated a smoothing of Anglo-French relations, which had been somewhat chilled since the Napoleonic Wars. Also, Britain formed an entente with Russia, which was already allied with France, setting off new suspicions in the Teutonic mind. Now that Russia, too, was in the picture, Germany trundled out her hoary complaint about *Einkreisung,* or "encirclement" by enemies, a claim she had first developed under Frederick the Great to explain the Seven Years' War.

The kaiser reacted by authorizing a series of huge military appropriations designed to bring the German navy on parity with Great Britain's fleet—including construction of several dreadnought-style battleships.

This, in turn, alarmed the British, because supremacy at sea was the cornerstone of not only her national defense but also her position of worldwide power and empire. As Winston Churchill remembered: "All sorts of sober-minded people in England began to be profoundly disquieted. What did Germany want this great navy for? Against whom, except us, could she measure it, match it, or use it?" Thus began the greatest and costliest shipbuilding contest in the history of the world, which would continue unabated until the outbreak of war.

In the ensuing years Germany embarked on a foreign policy designed to harass, disturb, intimidate, and bully her neighbors, and the German press and public became exceedingly hostile to the French and British. As Churchill put it, "All the alarm bells throughout Europe began to quiver."

During this time the British and French began to surmise that if the Germans attacked France they would do it by coming through Belgium rather than simply crossing the Franco-German border, because after their defeat in 1871 the French had constructed a number of huge fortifications at Verdun, Belfort, and other locations to forestall such a maneuver. One tip-off had come some years earlier, following a conversation that the kaiser had with King Leopold. On that occasion the kaiser had politely asked the Belgian king whether, in the event of war, the German army could use his country as a doormat into France. Just as politely, King Leopold had refused, but in due course he informed the British about the kaiser's remarkable request.

Meanwhile, the turbulent southern regions—the Balkans—began to boil over. In 1912 they rose up and managed to fling themselves free of the Ottoman Turks, who had cruelly ruled them for centuries. Then they turned on one another in a squabble for territory and hegemony. Back in Germany, an unfortunate transition had taken place in the military hierarchy. Following von Schlieffen's resignation as the army's chief of staff, the post fell to Helmuth Johann Ludwig von Moltke, the fifty-eight-year-old nephew and namesake of the famous field marshal Helmuth von Moltke who had led the Germans to victory over France in 1871. This present von Moltke had been an aide to the kaiser who dabbled in mysticism and played the cello. But at the same time that Bismarck, even in retirement, was warning that "the Great European war could come out of some damned foolishness in the Balkans," von Moltke was declaring, "I believe war to be unavoidable and the sooner the better."

Thus the sun, day by day and year by year, inched itself across the horizon of the new century silently marking the grim inevitability of a world at war.

★ ★ ★ ★

THE EXPLOSION CAME SOON ENOUGH WHEN, on June 28, 1914, a nineteen-year-old Serb nationalist named Gavrilo Princip shot and killed Archduke Franz Ferdinand, heir to the Austrian throne, and his wife as they paraded, against all good advice, through the streets of Sarajevo, Bosnia. The furious Austrians (the country Churchill called Germany's "idiot ally") believed that Bosnia's neighbor Serbia had been behind the crime and delivered a series of "demands" on that seething nation that amounted to a humiliating ultimatum.

To everyone's great surprise, the Serbs acceded to all the demands except the last one, which would have in effect put Serbia under Austrian control. It would not have mattered, however, even if Serbia *had* acceded to the demand; the Austrians'—but, more important, the Germans'—minds were made up: Austria would declare war on Serbia. Even though Russia had sent a clear warning that if Austria attacked the Serbians she would mobilize her armies—as well as diplomatic warnings from France expressing dismay at such threats—on July 28, 1914, Austria declared war and two days later was bombarding Belgrade from gunboats in the Danube.

As promised, Czar Nicholas II, cousin of the kaiser (in telegrams they called each other "Nicky" and "Willie"), began a partial mobilization of the Russian army (mobilization was tantamount to war) to prevent an Austrian conquest of Serbia. Germany delivered an ultimatum threatening to mobilize if Russia did not cease, and when she did not Germany ordered a general mobilization of its forces and the Schlieffen Plan was immediately set into motion. France mobilized.

Coattails flying, diplomats from many countries rushed hither and thither but to no avail. On August 2, Germany invaded neutral Luxembourg and that evening sent an ultimatum to King Leopold saying that if neutral Belgium did not permit the German army to pass through its territory, Germany would declare war. Instead, the king of the Belgians ordered his army to mobilize.

Great Britain, which had hoped to keep out of the fray and whose statesmen were frantically trying to defuse the situation, delivered an ultimatum demanding that Germany respect Belgian neutrality. It based these demands on an 1813 treaty it had signed with the Belgians promising to guarantee its neutrality. That was the ostensible reason, but since time immemorial British diplomacy has been governed by a single question: "But what is best for Great Britain?"

In London and other English cities people took to the streets to get the latest newspaper headlines. German waiters by the tens of thousands and other German nationals packed up to board ships for home. Patriots waved the Union Jack and sang "Rule Britannia" and "God Save the King." Peace marchers sang "The Internationale." Soon fights broke out between them, while Britain waited in nervous excitement.

When the Germans did not respond and the ultimatum expired at eleven the next night, Britain declared war, prompting the British foreign secretary Sir Grey to make this melancholy observation: "The lamps are going out all over Europe. We shall not see them lit again in our lifetime."

★ ★ ★ ★

FOLLOWING THE OUTLINE of the Schlieffen Plan, Germany sent a token force to back up the Austrian army while Russia continued its mobilization on their eastern frontier. At the same time, the kaiser's main army of two million men smashed through Belgium and swooped into northern France with thirty-five army corps determined to envelop the French army and capture Paris. Instead, they ran into a buzz saw after the French unexpectedly amassed a new army just to the east of Paris and the fighting degenerated into a stalemate.

To protect themselves from the merciless effects of artillery fire, both sides dug trenches in the ground—rude ditchlike things at first, but over the years they became more like a gigantic underground city shored up by timber, complete with bunkers for sleeping and dining, on a line extending nearly 500 miles from Ostend, in northern Belgium, to the foothills of the Swiss Alps.

The British quickly sent their small, professional army of 250,000 men into the fight, but by the end of the first year it was nearly wiped out. That first year of the war became a kind of dreadful "learning exercise," in which both sides, to their horror, came to realize the sort of slaughter they had become involved with. The French, for instance, time and again marched into battle "conspicuous on the landscape," in the words of Churchill, "in blue breeches and red coats. Their artillery officers in black and gold were even more specifically defined targets. The cavalry gloried in ludicrous armor. The doctrine of the offensive raised to the height of a religious frenzy animated all ranks. A cruel surprise awaited them."

They were mown down or blown up by the tens of thousands—300,000 casualties in fact during the first several weeks of the war—operating under a battle plan that had been drawn up before the effects of modern armaments were fully understood.

Nineteen fifteen saw the introduction by the Germans of poison gas, a loathsome weapon soon employed by both sides. That same year a German submarine torpedoed the Cunard passenger liner *Lusitania* off the Irish coast, killing more than a thousand people, including Americans. An outraged President Wilson warned the Germans, who then retracted their scheme of unrestricted warfare at sea. But the incident was still fresh in American minds when the Germans reinstated the practice a year and a half later.

In February 1916 the Germans launched a million-man army at a French fortress known as Verdun—an attempt to "bleed the French Army white." Instead, it was the Germans who wound up being bled white, but not until nine months later. When it ended, the battle had cost both sides somewhere between 750,000 and a million men. In July of that same year the British set in motion a vast attack they were convinced would break through the German lines and end the war. It became known as the Battle of the Somme and produced 60,000 casualties on the first day alone—some 24,000 of them killed in action. When at last it ended later that autumn, the casualty lists were equal to Verdun, and less than two miles of ground had been gained.

As 1917 opened the Germans notified the Allies that they intended to resume the unrestricted sinking of ships in British waters. This was probably the greatest mistake of the war for Germany because it brought the United States into the conflict with a mobilized force of nearly five million men. By this time some thirty-two nations were involved. The Central Powers consisted of Germany, Austria-Hungary, the Ottoman Empire (Turkey), and Bulgaria. Everyone else was for the Allies including, before it all ended, such disparate players as Japan, China, Montenegro, Italy, Monaco, Guatemala, Brazil, and Chile.

★ ★ ★ ★

In June 1917 Captain George C. Marshall sailed the Atlantic with leading elements of the U.S. First Infantry Division, which was the first American combat unit to reach France. After a nervous seven-day trip zigzagging to avoid German submarines, they sighted Belle Isle at the mouth of the Loire. But these Americans arrived at an inauspicious time.

Morale among the Allied troops and the French population as well was at an all-time low. Nearly every French family had a relative who had been killed or wounded in the fighting. Less than two months earlier, the French had launched their own, much-vaunted attack under General Robert Nivelle advertised to "win the war," but it ended in disaster a week later. The French had estimated 10,000 casualties and a breakthrough of the German front. Instead they suffered 163,000 casualties and a continued stalemate. The British had endured a similar fate only a week earlier at the Battle of Arras, which cost them 158,000 casualties and no substantial gain of ground.

Though it was kept from the public, the French army was in actual mutiny, with many of the *poilus* refusing to join in further offensives and others refusing to fight at all. In northern Italy, the Italian army and the Austrians were stalemated. The Russian Front was deteriorating badly; Czar Nicholas had recently abdicated and the country appeared on the verge of revolution and civil war. The Germans, as we have seen, at the beginning of 1917 reinstituted unrestricted submarine warfare and in just six months so many ships had been sunk around the British Isles that the country was actually in danger of starvation.

The one bright light amid all of this gloom was the arrival of the American army. The citizens of Saint-Nazaire, where Marshall's ship finally put in, were lining the streets in force, expecting to see a crack American army outfit come marching down the gangway with the utmost military discipline. Instead, while a greatly "disturbed" Marshall looked on, the leading elements of the U.S. First Division disembarked as if "most of them were ignorant of the first rudiments of march-discipline and were busy looking in the shop windows and observing the French crowd."[1]

Many of these men had recently volunteered and had only a short time in various "camps" to gain military training and bearing. Immediately after Congress had declared war, General John J. Pershing was designated commander in chief of the American Expeditionary Forces. In turn, he had "hastily selected" four regular army infantry regiments from the Mexican punitive expedition against Pancho Villa, but in order to make up a full combat division of some forty thousand officers and men a number of untrained recruits and reservists had to be brought in. Presumably it was these who shambled off the troopship and so disappointed the French spectators on that warm June afternoon in 1917.

It was little better in the coming weeks and months as the Americans undertook to adjust themselves and train for the arduous tasks that lay before them in the dangerous, squalid trenches of France. There was as yet no motor transport, and horses for the officers had not yet arrived. Thus units, as well as their officers, were compelled to march nearly twenty miles to training fields and then back again in the evening to their encampment. There were shortages of practically everything. The American army, for instance, had never been equipped with helmets, and thus had to wear the wide-brimmed "tin pot," or "soup plate" helmet, supplied by the British. American pilots had no planes and were obliged to fly aircraft provided by the French. The same was true in many cases with small arms—rifles, grenades, machine guns, mortars—even tanks.

The Americans were trained by French officers, first on training grounds and later by linking them with French units in the trenches. Being completely unprepared for a European-style war, there was much to learn: about "trench raids," for instance, which both sides regularly conducted for reconnaissance, to capture prisoners, or just for the hell of it to keep their side in fighting shape and the other side on its toes. About "defense in depth"—lessons learned during the previous three years about protecting the rear areas as much as the front lines in case of a sudden enemy breakthrough. About telling the difference between incoming and outgoing artillery and what to do in a barrage (go to ground, get inside, pray). About avoiding otherwise harmless-looking terrain where deadly gas might be lurking in low-lying areas. And about a thousand and one other situations that American armies had never dreamed of: what the British army termed "wastage," for example, was approximately one thousand deaths a day—from random artillery, snipers, lingering gas, illness, accidents, and other mortal causes not associated with a regular battle. It was the same in the French army. It was the same in the German army. And it would be the same in the American army.

★ ★ ★ ★

GEORGE PATTON WAS FURIOUS—which is to say he was in his customary mood—after learning that General Pershing had persuaded the War Department to issue an order banning all soldiers' wives from France. After all, he'd already worked it out that Beatrice would come over and stay in the fine three-bedroom apartment he'd found off the rue Madeleine in Paris; she could shop while he went to war during the day. But it wouldn't work out like that now. Pershing explained to the unhappy, newly promoted Captain Patton that having wives would create all sorts of chaos and also morale problems for those who couldn't afford it. "You see," Patton told Beatrice, "the British had to send back 60,000 women who came over with the Canadians."[2] To salve his wounded feelings, Patton purchased a twelve-cylinder Packard automobile that cost him $4,386—a whopping $80,000 in today's money!

After saying goodbye to Beatrice, Patton sailed from New York on the RMS *Baltic* as commander of Pershing's advance headquarters staff on May 28, 1917. When the Mexican punitive expedition against Villa ended that winter, Patton had been assigned to command a troop in the Seventh Cavalry—George Custer's old outfit—but he had no sooner got his unit into top form when word came from Pershing that he was wanted on the general's staff. When he arrived in France, Patton became determined to learn the language, and while his comprehension was above the *"parlez vous?"* level, it wasn't by much. Quickly, he decided that as long as Beatrice wasn't coming to Paris he would install a French interpreter in his spacious three-bedroom apartment.

However, he had begun to chafe at his job, which was essentially a glorified *maître d'hôtel,* arranging automobiles and billets for superior officers—many among them scorned reservists—and looking after the needs, wants, and behavior of fifty-odd enlisted clerks, drivers, cooks, and other low-ranked personnel—meantime always being attentive to commanding general Pershing. Patton was smart enough to stick it out, though, as he told Beatrice in letters, because he'd rather be in France, near the fighting, "doing a jobber's work," than in Texas commanding a troop of cavalry. Here, something might happen, and he had a premonition that it would.

Patton had come to admire the French spirit but was appalled at their work habits; they took what amounted to a siesta for several hours in the afternoon during which "nothing could get done." In the mornings Patton fenced with a Monsieur Hyde, one of France's better swordsmen, who told him, "You have taught fencing." When Patton asked how he knew, the man replied, "Because you have all the faults of a teacher—you have the habit of letting yourself be touched." To Beatrice he reported, "If I go broke, or rather if you do, I can always teach fencing."[3]

In July, Patton was given an opportunity as temporary aide-de-camp to Pershing, who was planning a visit to the headquarters of the British commander General Sir Douglas Haig at Montreuil-sur-Mer, about 150 miles north. Patton was designated to prepare the best route for Pershing and thus in July began an arduous trip on muddy, troop-choked roads that took a full six hours. Of course for Patton it was worth it because at last he got to see for himself the horrendous scale of the fighting in northern France and Flanders. He saw the miles of mud, denuded forests, and no-man's-land near Ypres and Arras where you could smell the battlefield miles before you reached it; the sordid ever present odor of rotting humans, horses, mules, rats, and food mixed with the stench of excrement, lingering poison gas, and the repulsive aroma of quicklime—used to decompose the dead—and the acrid stink of high-explosive artillery shells. It was a place where men lived like troglodytes in slimy underground trenches and fought and died with such consistency that even on "quiet days" casualties ran into the thousands.

Patton looked on the bright side, however, telling a family friend about his "interesting trip," where he "saw the workings of over a million men from the inside. It is stupendous and fine. The more one sees of war the better it is. Of course there are a few deaths but all of us must 'pay the piper' sooner or later and the party is worth the price of admission."[4] Whether this was braggadocio or not it at least seems odd that Patton would take such a cavalier attitude of the terrible fighting that had left millions of men dead over the previous three years.

It was not long after this that Patton had another of his out-of-body experiences. He had been summoned to a secret meeting more than eighty miles distant and was riding in a staff car at night when he suddenly leaned forward and asked the driver if the camp they were going to wasn't just to the right. "No Sir, our camp where we are going is further ahead, but there is an old Roman camp over there to the right. I have seen it myself."

They rode on in silence until they arrived at the headquarters to which Patton had been summoned. After the meeting, as Patton was leaving, he asked an officer, "Your theater is over here straight ahead, isn't it?"

"We have no theater here," the officer replied, "but there is an old Roman theater only about three hundred yards away."

Later he wrote a poem about it; many of Patton's poems show a want of literary technique, but this one has a haunting quality about it.

> *So as through a glass and darkly*
> *The age long strife I see*
> *Where I fought in many guises*
> *Many names—but always me.*
>
> *And I see not in my blindness*
> *What the objects were I wrought*
> *But as God rules o'er our bickerings*
> *It was through his will I fought.*
>
> *So forever in the future,*
> *Shall I battle as of yore*
> *Dying to be born a fighter,*
> *But to die again once more.*[5]

It was but one of a number of experiences such as this that caused Patton to maintain a continuing belief that in some earlier incarnation he had been a part of powerful, ancient armies, even though he was not a mystic but a practicing Episcopalian.[6]

Meanwhile, Pershing had become lovelorn regarding Patton's sister Nita. Before leaving the United States, the two had spoken of her meeting Pershing in Paris, but considering the order forbidding wives to come to France Pershing now thought it would look bad and Patton, whom he had been consulting at length on the matter, agreed with him. "He has too much on his hands and it would make a bad impression at present," he wrote Beatrice. At the same time, Patton's own frustrations were giving him pause: "Don't think I am having a roaring time and not thinking of you for it is not so. Paris is a stupid place without [you] just as heaven would be under the same conditions."[7]

ONE U.S. INFANTRY OUTFIT, the First Division, the "Big Red One," of which George Marshall was operations officer, had been composed of regular army regiments and was already organizing to sail to France. A new one, styled the 42nd Infantry Division and composed of National Guard units, was in the process of assembling at Camp Mills, near Garden City, Long Island. Earlier Douglas MacArthur, acting on behalf of the secretary of war, had declared that this new untested unit deserved "the best colonel on the Army staff as its chief of staff." Secretary Newton Baker said he had already chosen the chief of staff for the 42nd Division and to MacArthur's amazement added, "And it is you."

MacArthur pointed out that the title of chief of a divisional staff called for a full colonel's rank, while he was only a major and thus ineligible, to which Baker further flabbergasted MacArthur by announcing, "You are now a colonel. I will sign your commission immediately." And when Baker asked MacArthur if he wanted his commission in the Corps of Engineers the answer was "No, the Infantry," thus positioning himself for faster opportunities of promotion to higher rank, which are always accorded to the infantry in time of war.

When Baker asked MacArthur how they could give "maximum effect" to President Wilson's decision to send the National Guard to war, MacArthur suggested that they call up units from as many states as possible, "so that a division would stretch over the whole country like a rainbow," and thus was born the famous "Rainbow Division" of World Wars I and II fame—all in all 27,114 U.S. citizen soldiers.

With good reason MacArthur was well pleased with "the excellent caliber of both officers and men." Most members of the regular army tended to look down on the National Guard and reservists as inferior troops, undertrained and underdisciplined, but as MacArthur noted in his memoirs with no idle boast that from the ranks of the 42nd Rainbow Division "came many of the great names that enrich the tablets of military fame." He noted the "splendid relationship" between the officers and enlisted men and the "comradeship" between the men themselves. The 42nd Division, he said, "soon took on a color, a dash, a unique flavor that is the essence of that elusive and deathless thing called soldiering."

In other words, they set out to prove they were just as good as regular army soldiers.

As chief of staff, MacArthur had wide latitude in selecting the senior officers of the division, often choosing men he had known at West Point. From France, Pershing telegraphed that, in observing British and French officers at the front, it was imperative that "only officers in full mental and physical vigor should be sent here." As for the enlisted men, he said, "Long experience with conditions in France confirms my opinion [that it is] highly important that infantry soldiers should be excellent shots."

On October 19, 1917, escorted by two destroyers and the cruiser *Seattle,* leading elements of the 42nd Division sailed from New York in half a dozen troop transports. MacArthur, aboard the USS *Covington*— formerly a German ocean liner seized at the beginning of the war—set the scene for what he called an "unnerving experience." Life belts were worn at all times. The ship was dark at night with no smoking in the open. All lifeboats were let down to deck level and all rafts unlashed and placed along the rail. The six-inch guns were constantly holding target practice with periscope-like targets that were towed. After ten days at sea they neared the coast of France and entered the high-danger zone for enemy U-boats. The ship began zigzagging in the freezing air and ice-cold sea and a report came in that enemy submarines were "moving in for the kill."[8]

Nothing came of it.* After several more days they spotted the lights of Belle Isle and the mouth of the Loire where they docked in "a misty, drizzling rain" at Saint-Nazaire and the infantry shipped out in the little "40 and 8" French boxcars. To his consternation, MacArthur found that all the careful attention he had paid to supplies was for naught. Most of the machine guns, uniforms, blankets, hats, rolling kitchens, munitions, food, and other vital items—including some fifty thousand pairs of marching shoes—had been confiscated by Pershing's headquarters "to make up for deficiencies in other divisions." Worse, almost, all but two

* On her return trip a few days later, however, the *Covington* was torpedoed and sunk by German U-boats.

of MacArthur's thirty-three meticulously hand-picked staff officers were "ordered away" by the General Staff.[9]

Worse still, he learned upon arrival that plans were in the making to dismember the Rainbow Division, breaking it up as replacements for a new corps that was just then forming. As it turned out, though, Pershing's chief of staff was an old friend of MacArthur's from the Manila days. He went to see this worthy and invited him to visit the 42nd and see for himself "whether such a splendid unit should be relegated to a replacement status." He did come, he saw, and he changed his mind, thus saving the 42nd for its future glory. The incident, however, also reared in MacArthur's suspicious mind a twinge of paranoia as he wrote long afterward that it "created resentment against me among certain members of Pershing's staff."[10]

★ ★ ★ ★

AT THE BEGINNING OF SEPTEMBER 1917, the Americans were still not yet in the fighting; the leading elements of the First Division were just as yet landing in France and would have to undergo extensive training before going to the front. Patton naturally found himself bored with garrison duty and chaffed to get into the action, but the closest he came was being named temporary town provost marshal, and even that was dull by comparison with war. "Yesterday," he wrote Beatrice, "I had to arrest a man for carrying a woman down the street in an inverted position. She was very angry when we arrested the man and [he] said he was only playing."[11]

To Beatrice, he gave an account of himself on September 17, 1917: "I ride from 8 to 9. I inspect barracks & kitchens from 9 to 10. Attend to various jobs in my capacity as adjutant from 10 to 12:30. Eat lunch from 12:30 to 1:30. Do a thousand and one things from 1:30 to seven. Read the 3 Musketeers [in French] from 8:30 to 10:30 and so to bed. I take a bath every morning."

Meantime, lists of promotions were coming over the wire every day. Many of Patton's classmates had been promoted to major, especially, he noticed, in the artillery. "There is a lot of talk about 'Tanks' here now," he wrote Beatrice, "and I am interested because I can see no future to my present job."*

★ ★ ★ ★

ONE OF GEORGE MARSHALL's initial staff assignments was to move the First Division from Saint-Nazaire to Gondrecourt, about fifty kilometers south of Saint-Mihiel. This was to be his first encounter with the notorious French battle trains, with their 40 *hommes*–8 *chevaux* boxcars that created great excitement among the Americans when it was pointed out that *hommes* were men and *chevaux* were horses, and the soldiers began looking to and fro for the herds of horses they were to ride with. In the coming months these trains would become as familiar to U.S. forces as they were to their allies, designed to move divisions around the battlefields, one regiment at a time—about fifty cars, half flat cars for equipment, the other half boxcars for men, with a couple of second-class passenger cars for officers at the end of the train and perhaps a first-class car for the commander. As operations officer for his division, Marshall organized all this while begging his superiors for a combat assignment. He was too valuable a staff officer, he was told, to be sent into the danger zones.

He came close in early October, however, when word came back in the dead of night that the first Americans had been killed. Marshall was sent to investigate the matter and just after sunup found himself at the scene of the action, staring down at the three dead men in a trench. One had been shot, another's throat had been slashed, and the third had his head bashed in by a rifle butt. The men belonged to the 16th Infantry Regiment, which had been among the first U.S. combat outfits to arrive in France with the First Division.

....

* Tanks—mechanized, armored, and armed fighting vehicles with caterpillar treads—had only recently been developed by the British and French as an answer to the three-year stalemate in the trenches.

In order to "accustom" the American units to the rigors of trench warfare, U.S. divisions had been paired off with French infantry divisions and placed in what was known to be a "quiet sector" of the front.

It did not remain a quiet sector for long. When the Germans got wind of Americans in the front lines they immediately organized a trench raid in the middle of the night. Standing atop the trench, Marshall could see where things had gone wrong. An enormous gap had been blown in the Americans' barbed wire, clearly marked with white tape that led from the German lines to the Allied positions. Twelve American soldiers had been taken prisoner and an equal number seriously wounded.

Following a brief but vicious artillery bombardment the Germans—about fifty of them—rushed across no-man's-land and exploded a Bangalore torpedo* in the wire, then leapt down into the American trench. The U.S. soldiers—most of them—had been sheltering from the barrage in bunkers built into the trenches, and here was where they were shot or captured.

A French general was on hand to question the lightly wounded, and Marshall was appalled that his questions seemed to imply that American cowardice was responsible for the incident. As the division's acting chief of staff, Marshall interceded and demanded to know why an order from the French command had forbidden the Americans from sending patrols beyond the wire. He further threatened to bring the matter to General Pershing himself, which caused the Frenchman to go stiff, but Marshall persisted. (In fact, the French and the German and Austrian units on the other side of this particular stretch of no-man's-land had adopted a kind of live-and-let-live attitude toward one another, and the French didn't want to spoil it with any American patrols stirring up trouble.)

The idea that Marshall was about to bring the matter to the attention of the American commander in chief became an anxious issue within the higher ranks of the French army, and several lower-ranked French officers begged Marshall to let the matter rest. He refused, however, on

* A long pipe loaded with explosives designed to clear a path through barbed wire.

grounds that Americans had been killed, wounded, and taken prisoner, which might have been prevented with vigorous patrolling, and that was all there was to it.[12]

The following day, perhaps by way of apology, the French high command staged a magnificent funeral to honor the fallen Americans, featuring a battalion of French infantry, a troop of cavalry, and miscellaneous troops "representing every unit in the French corps." Presiding over this was the French general with whom Marshall had quarreled, Major General Paul E. Bordeaux. He gave an eloquent benediction over the fallen soldiers that he concluded by saying: "The mortal remains of these young men [will] be left here, be left to us forever. We will inscribe on their tombs 'Here lie the first soldiers of the famous United States Republic to fall on the soil of France for justice and liberty.' The passer-by will stop and uncover his head. The travelers of France, of the Allied countries, of America, the men of heart, who will come to visit our battlefield of Lorraine, will go out of the way to come here, to bring to their graves the tribute of their respect, and of their gratefulness. Corporal Gresham, Private Enright, and Private Hay, In the name of France I thank you. God receive your souls. Farewell!"*, [13]

The French command continued to plead with Marshall to resist taking up the no-patrol issue with Pershing. American intervention was a godsend for the French, who felt in danger of losing the war. That an order issued by them might have caused the first deaths of American servicemen was nearly too embarrassing to contemplate.

Marshall understood, and even felt bad, but nevertheless he took up the matter with Pershing, who quickly had the antipatrolling order reversed. It was pure Marshall—no matter the pressure he knew the right thing to do and did it. However, it also showed Marshall's tendency to stand up to superior officers when he felt he was right, a practice that, in the army, is known to be dangerous.

....

* Thirty years later, as chairman of the American Battle Monuments Commission, Marshall had these words inscribed on a new memorial erected for the first Americans killed in France.

A few weeks earlier, Marshall had been on hand to witness a harsh chewing out by Pershing of the First Division's commanding officer, Major General William L. Sibert. The incident occurred during a training session at which Pershing charged that the division showed little evidence of training, comprehending tactics, or following directives. Making matters worse, in Marshall's estimation, was that Pershing "was severe with Gen. Sibert in front of all the officers." As Pershing "dismissed the chief-of-staff with an expression of contempt and turned to leave," Marshall stepped forward and put his hand on the general's arm, and told him, "There's something to be said here and I think I should say it because I've been here the longest."[14]

"What do you have to say?" Pershing demanded. Everyone from Sibert on down was horrified that Marshall had the nerve and ill manners to actually touch the commanding general. Marshall, his temper on the edge of control, responded with "a torrent of facts," not the least of which concerned a lack of supplies, help, and guidance from Pershing's own headquarters. Pershing listened and then walked away, saying, "You must appreciate the troubles we have." Marshall further horrified the staff by retorting, "Yes, General, but we have them every day and we have to solve them before night."[15]

Certain that Marshall would be fired before the day was out, the others—including most of all Sibert—offered their appreciation and gave their sympathies. Marshall responded by saying, "All I can see is that I might get field duty instead of staff duty, and that certainly would be a great success."[16]

In fact, there was no retribution; instead, whenever Pershing visited the First Division he immediately sought out Marshall and took him aside for private talks. "It was one of his great strengths that he could listen to things," Marshall wrote later.[17]

★ ★ ★ ★

PATTON HAD LONG SINCE GIVEN UP HOPE of getting Beatrice to France but had come up with a new scheme to bring her to England. The plan was that she would officially be a buyer for a fancy Boston furnishings establishment, which would give her a plausible justification to travel to London on an American visa. Meantime, he wrote her, "The English made a big attack yesterday that seems to have been successful but one can't tell for four or five days as the Germans don't hold well but make terrible counter attacks."* He added: "The Germans shoot a gas which makes people vomit and when they take off their masks to spit they shoot the deadly gas at them. It's a smart idea is it not?"[18]

But it was still the inaction and tedium of staff duty that had gotten under Patton's skin. He told Beatrice, "I am damned sick of my job . . . I would trade jobs with almost anyone for any thing." Shortly afterward he told his diary: "Col. Eltinge asked me if I wanted to be a Tank officer. I said yes." Though it was then in the formative stages, the American Expeditionary Forces was making arrangements with the French to supply and train American forces with as many as six hundred tanks, but as yet no formal unit had been organized.

On the advice of Eltinge, Patton wrote a letter to Pershing describing his desire to become a tank officer and explaining why he thought he was qualified. He put forth the novel theory that tanks—especially light tanks such as the French were producing—performed like cavalry "in normal wars," and that he was a cavalry officer who had commanded a machine-gun troop.

"I have run Gas Engines since 1917 and have used and repaired Gas Automobiles since 1905," Patton wrote. "I speak and read better French than 95% of American officers . . . I have been to school in France and always got along well with frenchmen. I believe that I am the only American that has ever made an attack in a motor vehicle," he asserted, referring to the killing of General Cárdenas during the punitive expedition in Mexico. "The request is not made because I dislike my present

----

* This was the horrendous Battle of Passchendaele in the Ypres salient in Belgium. The British captured the town, which was reduced to rubble, and the Germans indeed made "terrible counter attacks," which the British withstood, to the tune of 570,000 combined casualties.

duty or am desirous of evading it," he lied, "but because I believe that when we get 'Tanks' I would be able to do good service in them."

Meanwhile, he continued bemoaning his loneliness to Beatrice, writing her of a dance he attended that was given by American nurses in the local army hospital. "I have never seen such a lot of horrors in my life . . . and they dance like tons of brick. I don't think I shall go again. It is too much work with people out of one's class who are not dressed up."

"I certainly don't see any stars in prospect for me," he wrote his wife, "but one can always try. Some times I think I don't try as hard as I ought, but probably I do," he said. "I would give a lot to have you console me and tell me I amounted to a lot, even when I know I don't." He was thirty-two years old.

Then two things happened in quick succession. On October 20 Pershing telegraphed the War Department recommending that Patton be promoted to a major of infantry, and on November 10 orders were cut sending him to visit select French tank installations, "for the purpose of studying and familiarizing [himself] with tanks."

Patton wrote his father, "Here is the golden dream. 1st I will run the [U.S. tank] school. 2. Then they will organize a battalion. I will command it. 3. Then if I make good and the [tanks] do, and the war lasts, I will get the 1st regiment. 4. With the same 'if' they will make a brigade and I will get the star [of a brigadier general]."[19]

★ ★ ★ ★

NECESSITY BEING THE MOTHER OF INVENTION, the idea for the "tank" was conjured in late 1914 by a lieutenant colonel in the British army who one day observed a small caterpillar tractor in France. He thought if tractors could be armored, they would make formidable weapons on the battlefield where human flesh was utterly vulnerable. The enticing thing was that if a tank could be built large enough, it could cut the barbed wire, cross over the tops of the maze of enemy trenches, and get in the rear where it could do the most damage, with infantry following close behind. That had been the overarching tactical challenge for the past three years—how to break through the enemy's line on a large scale.

Churchill, then still in charge of the Admiralty, liked the idea of a "land ship" and supported it, which led to the development in England in 1916 of the first thirty-ton Mark I "heavy" tank, which had a top speed of three miles per hour. To deceive the Germans when they were shipped to France, the machines were carried on rail and ship's manifests as "water tanks," which they somewhat resembled, and the name stuck.

The British foolishly used them in the last days of the Battle of the Somme in 1916, employing forty-nine of the contraptions desperately seeking a breakthrough at Flers, even as the battle was winding down after more than two months of slaughter. There were not nearly enough tanks to make a difference, their tactics had not been developed, and many had to be abandoned and were captured by the Germans. The Germans had been surprised, but in the end not intimidated—and worse, they were now alerted to this formidable new weapon. Though no one understood it yet, the tank would change the entire concept of battle in the future.

Meanwhile, the French were developing the Renault light tank that was intended for reconnaissance and protection of the infantry by breaking up enemy machine-gun nests.* These were the tanks Patton would command. Known as TF-17s, they weighed six tons and had a top speed of ten miles per hour. Plans called for twenty light tank battalions (each containing seventy-seven tanks), but as of November 1917 there were not only no tanks but no one in the AEF knew how to operate one either.

Earlier, the British massed some three hundred tanks along a six-mile front at the Battle of Cambrai, which lumbered across no-man's-land and into and through the German trenches for more than four miles, the largest Allied advance of the war. Two German divisions were left

---

* Plans were made for the Americans to produce a forty-three-ton Mark VIII tank with an eleven-man crew and speed to six miles per hour but a scandalous incompetence among Washington bureaucrats resulted in tank production beginning only in the summer of 1918 when the war was almost over.

in ruins and some four thousand Germans taken prisoner as well as a hundred enemy guns. Unfortunately, the British celebrated while the Germans developed one of their "terrible counter attacks" that took back much of what had been gained and the British were unable to exploit their breakthrough.

Nevertheless, Cambrai proved that tanks were a highly valuable asset on the battlefield, a fact in no way lost on George Patton, who was attending the French tank school at Chamlieu. There he was learning about tanks from the ground up, studying and testing the machines from the standpoint of mechanics, gunnery, maneuver, and tactics. He became experienced in every aspect of a tank, as they crawled over hill and dale "in a most impersonal manner. They are noisy . . . [and] rear up like a horse and stand on their head with perfect immunity . . . The thing will do the damdest things imaginable," he told Beatrice.[20]

★ ★ ★ ★

AFTER FINISHING THE MONTH of November at the French tank school, Patton produced a fifty-eight-page paper entitled "Light Tanks" that in his own words "became the basis of the U.S. Tank Corps." The paper was "a masterpiece of originality and clear thinking," which detailed every aspect of armored warfare including organization, training, equipment, and tactics of the Tank Corps. Biographer Carlo D'Este calls it "an astonishing reflection of the visionary aspect of Patton's mind." Patton documented everything needed under every conceivable condition, even a list of tools and spare parts "down to and including extra wire and string."[21]

Despite his elation at having produced such a profound document, Patton's underlying inferiority complex began to dog him as he struggled to set up the new tank school for Americans. "Actually I'm in quite a funk," he told Beatrice, "for there is nothing but me to do it all. I am sure I will do it but just at this moment I don't see how . . . If I fail it will be only my fault. I won't even have you to pick on."

In mid-December Patton received official orders assigning him to organize and command the U.S. Light Tank School, using French

Renaults to begin with. He wrote, "This is my last day as a staff officer. Now I rise or fall on my own. I have always talked blood and murder and am looked on as an advocate of close up fighting. I could never look myself in the face if I was a staff officer and comparatively safe."[22]

Patton selected the town of Langres to set up his tank school. He was to report to Colonel Samuel D. Rockenbach, Pershing's chief of tanks (light and heavy). He visited with the British at Cambrai and the French at Flers to find out what lessons had been learned from their tank action. Patton concluded that the basic unit of his tank organization would be the platoon, which consisted of five tanks: one with a three-inch gun, two with six-pounder guns, and two with Hotchkiss machine guns—a total of five tanks and fifteen men. A company would consist of three platoons and a company headquarters—five officers, ninety-six men, twenty-five tanks, and twelve vehicles.

From what he had learned so far of the French and British in action, tanks were most successful when they were employed with infantrymen. It was when they outran the infantry that they got into trouble. In Patton's view, "The proper conception of a tank is as a heavily armored infantry soldier."

★ ★ ★ ★

MONTHS EARLIER, THE NEWS FROM the front had already proved unsettling. The fighting in Flanders had been so debilitating that the British army was a hundred thousand men short and there were not enough men left in the empire to clear the deficit; the French, also without replacements, were disbanding battalions by the score. The Bolsheviks, having seized power in Russia following the October Revolution, were now actively engaged in armistice talks with the Central Powers. Pershing projected that this would free a million German troops by spring to supplant those already on the Western Front, 260 divisions to the Allies 160 divisions—an unacceptable ratio. He soon would have five operational divisions and one training division in France but he still needed the additional eighteen divisions promised by Washington.

Time was not on Pershing's side, and the Germans were getting set to prove it.

German commander Erich Ludendorff, his forces engorged with the vast influx of German soldiers from the Eastern Front, had concluded that only a mighty all-or-nothing offensive would prevent Germany from losing the war. The unlimited U-boat campaign, in which so many high hopes of starving England out of the war had been placed, was foiled when the British discovered the value of putting heavily armed convoys of destroyers around their ships.

On the other hand, the British blockade of Germany was working splendidly. The German people were on a rationing system bordering on outright starvation. What was known as ersatz food was being offered, concocted by German chemical companies. Ersatz coffee, for instance, consisted of fine grains of acorns ground up with caffeine added. Bread was made with straw or sawdust; meat was almost unheard of. A year earlier the potato crop had failed and German civilians were forced to eat turnips—the "turnip winter," they called it. Demonstrations, strikes, and riots broke out. Already a million German soldiers had been killed and no end was in sight. With Americans arriving now at the rate of 240,000 a month, Ludendorff realized that the situation had become desperate.

After three and a half months of training, on February 13, 1918, the Rainbow Division moved to a "quiet sector" of the front, near Luneville in Lorraine, for a month's on-the-job training with a French corps. This sector, which was "strikingly similar" to the terrain of the Argonne Forest, was marked by steep ravines, sandstone ridges, and rocks and other debris washed down in the rivers Meurthe and Moselle from the Vosges Mountains twenty miles to the east. It was peopled by livestock farmers, basket weavers using river willows, and pottery makers using river clay, and had not been particularly active since the first year of the war. All that was about to change.[23]

By this point the division had acquired a new commanding officer, Major General Charles T. Menoher, an experienced artilleryman who had been Pershing's classmate at West Point. An able officer and thoroughly capable administrator, Menoher, noted MacArthur, preferred to supervise the division from his field headquarters where he "was in constant communication" with higher headquarters, "relying on me to handle the battle line." Father Duffy of the Fighting 69th characterized Menoher this way: "If he were out of uniform he would impress one as a successful businessman—one of the kind who can carry responsibility . . . and still find time to be human. He is entirely devoid of posing, of vanity, or of jealousy. His only desire is to see results."[24]

On February 26 MacArthur had his first encounter with the Germans. He had persuaded a French general to allow him to participate in a night trench raid to capture enemy prisoners. With blackened faces the patrol crawled across no-man's-land near Réchicourt beneath the overcast skies, unobserved until right outside the German trench a guard heard them and all hell broke loose. Flares went up; machine guns opened, a preregistered artillery barrage came crashing down—but the raid went on. The Frenchmen leaped savagely into the trench, killing a number of Germans while others fled.

Triumphantly they returned and delivered their quota of prisoners while MacArthur received slaps on the back, Cognac, absinthe, and the Croix de Guerre pinned on his tunic by none other than General Georges de Bazelaire himself, the French division commander. Moreover, American headquarters awarded him the Silver Star—the army's third highest decoration for valor—for "extraordinary heroism and gallantry in action," which, he later wrote, "seemed a bit too much," though he was nevertheless "glad to get it."

★ ★ ★ ★

DURING THE FIRST MONTH THAT the Rainbow Division was in the front lines, the soldiers had endured German raids and gas attacks, and on March 7 the Fighting 69th had its first men killed in battle when a German artillery barrage collapsed a dugout in the Rouge Bouquet sector, suffocating nineteen men. Corporal Joyce Kilmer composed one of his last poems to commemorate the tragedy, which Father Duffy read at a service held at the site of the dugout where the slain men remained entombed.

In a wood they call Rouge Bouquet
There is a new-made grave today
Built by never a spade nor pick
Yet covered with earth ten meters thick
There lie many fighting men
Dead in their youthful prime,
Never to laugh or love again
Or taste of the summer time;
For Death came flying through the air,
And stopped his flight at the dugout stair,
Touched his prey and left them there
Clay to clay.
He hid their bodies stealthily
In the soil of the land they sought to free
And fled away.

By then MacArthur had become almost legendary for his unorthodox choice of uniform—a gray turtleneck sweater and long, drooping scarf knitted by his mother, his jaunty officer's cap with the grommet removed and carrying, for some reason, a riding crop. He neither wore a helmet nor carried a pistol, but steadily walked the trenches giving pep talks to the men and their officers.

He was doing just that as he prepared for a retaliatory raid that involved a battalion of the 168th Infantry Regiment in the Salient du Feys. Zero hour was 5:05 a.m. MacArthur watched it approach from the top of the trench in the graying twilight as "pillars of flame shot skyward" over the enemy lines and the concentrated fire of sixty American artillery batteries unleashed their fury. Then, as the minute hand on the watch hit time and the artillery reached its most violent crescendo, MacArthur shouted into the ear of Captain Charles J. Casey, the battalion commander, "All ready, Casey."

The whistles blew and everyone scrambled over the top and into the inferno of no-man's-land. For a few moments, MacArthur felt that he was alone and his soldiers had failed to follow him. But before he could turn to check "they were around me, a roaring avalanche of glittering steel and cursing men."[25]

As they neared the German trenches they encountered "a hornet's nest of machine gun fire." MacArthur was everywhere, giving advice, orders, supervising the operations until the enemy position was carried. For this he was given the Distinguished Service Cross, the nation's second highest award for valor, citing his "conspicuous courage."[26]

Two days later MacArthur might have regretted spurning a gas mask when the Germans retaliated for the previous raid with a poison gas attack. He accepted treatment only from a first aid tent and refused to go to a hospital in the rear, requesting instead that his name not be included in the list of casualties. But the incident was serious enough to sideline him on his cot blindfolded for ten days. For this he received a purple heart and a heap of purple praise from Secretary of War Baker, who visited MacArthur's division and, after learning of his exploits, embarrassingly proclaimed him "the D'Artagnan of the AEF," and, somewhat prematurely, America's "greatest fighting front-line general."

★ ★ ★ ★

MEANWHILE, THE U.S. LIGHT TANK SCHOOL at Langres began to take shape. Young officers, many from the Coast Artillery, were either transferring or ordered to sign up for armored service, which no one at that point (except perhaps George Patton) even dreamed would one day become its own branch of the service. The school itself would assume the structure of a battalion, and Patton, with help from his able assistant Lieutenant Elgin Braine, sent in a requisition for supplies and equipment totaling some $20 million.* But still, they had no tanks, so Patton borrowed tools

---

* Nearly twenty times that in today's dollars.

from the quartermaster and secured an old Atlas truck for his tankers to take apart and put back together again to get a better notion of what made it run.

Patton ran a tight ship at the tank school. When officers failed to salute him, he stopped them and made them do it. He also reported a reserve lieutenant for profanity. "I expect some of them [reserve officers] would like to poison me. I will have to eat only eggs like Louis XI," he told Beatrice.[27]

Patton hadn't known it before, but an officer passing through told him that on December 15 he had been promoted to major (though as of February 17 the official promotion orders had not yet arrived). Patton didn't let that stop him; he took the captain's bars off his uniform and pinned a major's gold oak leaves on his shoulders and collar. "In spite of my increased rank I still love you," he wrote Beatrice, "I want you to be the same age when I get back as when I left."

By this time hundreds of enlisted men were arriving at what was now styled the U.S. Army Tank Center, and to Patton's delight he was getting all sorts of applications from officers wanting to join. But they still had no tanks, even though the French had long ago promised to send some. So Patton set the men to drills—in particular tanker signals consisting of the gunner kicking the driver in the back and head (gestures that told the driver when to turn, stop, go forward, or back up)—in addition to mapping, aiming, gas engines, reconnaissance, intelligence, and gunnery. As for himself, he composed a lecture on "obedience" and "discipline," which he was convinced were necessary qualities to win the war. Alluding to Philip of Macedon, Alexander the Great, the legions of Rome, and the ancient Greeks, Patton informed his startled subjects that without "instant, cheerful, and automatic obedience . . . you will die for nothing! With DISCIPLINE you are IRRESISTABLE."[28]

At last, on March 23, ten light Renault tanks arrived at Bourg by railroad flatcar. Patton backed them off himself because no one else knew how. They had arrived by design at night, camouflaged beneath tarpaulins, and would stay hidden in a wood away from the prying eyes of enemy observation planes. Having watched the procession of the tanks across the field in the moonlight, Patton wrote Beatrice almost as if he were again a proud father: "They are certainly saucy little fellows and very active. Just like insects from under a wooden log in the forest."

The tank school at that point had grown to several thousand men and several hundred officers. Barracks sprang up overnight, complete with latrines and company messes. The YMCA even opened a canteen, which pleased Patton because there were no amusements in town for the men. Patton was ambivalent about this last, for while it kept down venereal disease he felt that "men who are apt to be killed are entitled to what pleasures they can get even if it is not considered chic by some." The American singer and troop entertainer Elsie Janis gave a performance and afterward Patton took her and her mother out to eat. "She is not pretty but quite amusing though common in her pronunciation," he reported to Beatrice. "She wore an artificial leopard-skin coat."*, 29

On April 20 Patton went to Pershing's headquarters in Chaumont to have some teeth filled, and when he entered the officers' dining room for lunch a general, to Patton's astonishment, addressed him as "Colonel Patton." Behind him was the adjutant general who confirmed that orders had just come in from the States promoting Patton to lieutenant colonel. "How do you feel being a Mrs. Colonel?" he wrote to Beatrice. "We never thought to reach it so soon, did we?"

By this time—late April 1918—Patton was able to stage exercises or maneuvers on the field at Bourg simulating the tank in battle, supporting columns of infantry. These were very realistic and attended approvingly by high-ranking staff officers who followed the action on their mounts. Patton wrote about it later: "The enemy was unintentionally represented by members of the General Staff College who attended mounted . . . The horses objected to the tanks, and one officer was seen leaving the

....

* Eddie Rickenbacker, America's leading air ace in the war, had started a flock of rumors by escorting Elsie Janis to the elegant Farewell Dinner of his 94th Aero Squadron at the Waldorf. But the relationship went nowhere when she turned out to be a lesbian.

final objective on foot, after having been thrown five times. He held the record but the competition was close and general."[30]

On April 25 Patton held an amateur night in the YMCA tent where there was a stage and a piano, with boxing matches, skits, and speeches, capped by a song that the men had written about Patton saying, "We will follow the Colonel through hell and out the other side." "I don't see why they like me," he told Beatrice, "as I curse them freely on all occasions."

On April 28 Patton formed the First Light Tank Battalion with himself as commander and Captains Sereno Brett, Joseph Viner, and Earnest Herman as company commanders. He appeared everywhere, encouraging and bawling out his men. He wished to make them mirror images of himself, "ruthless, daring and dash." His words were powerful, theatrical, and memorable and the soldiers repeated them with embellishments that cultivated his legend.[31]

Patton laid down this law: "It must never be forgotten that boldness is the key to victory. The tank must be used boldly. It is new and always has the element of surprise. It is also very terrifying to look at, as the infantry soldier is helpless before it."[32]

★ ★ ★ ★

AT THE END OF MAY PATTON jumped at an invitation for a close-up look at the front by friends he had made in the French army. Simply going to the front was a highly dangerous adventure, and before leaving he wrote a letter to Beatrice that was to be sent in the event of his death here.

> Of course if I am reported killed I may still have been captured so don't be too worried. I have not the least premonition that I am going to be hurt and feel foolish writing you this letter but perhaps if the thing happened you would like it [better that I had written] . . .
>
> Beatrice, there is no advice that I could give you and nothing to suggest that you would not know better than I. Few men could be so fortunate to have such a wife.

All my property is yours though it is not much.* My sword
is yours, also my pistol, the silver one. I will give Sylvia [his
horse] to Gen. Pershing and Simalarity [his horse] to Viner.

I think that if you should fall in love you should marry
again. I would approve.

The only regret that I have in our marriage is that it was
not sooner and that I was mean to you at first.

If I go I trust that it will be in a manner such as to be
worthy of you and of my ideals.

Kiss Beatrice Jr. and Ruth Ellen for me and tell them that
I love them very much and that I know they will be good.

Beat I love you infinitely.[33]

Thus, brave Georgie Patton, who sometimes wondered if he wasn't
more like the cowardly lion in L. Frank Baum's story, went off to the
front to view what soldiers in an earlier war called "seeing the elephant."

About six miles from the lines Patton began to hear the roar of the
guns. It was a constant roar, he said, because there were so many guns
on both sides, a kind of dull throbbing that became so much louder the
closer they came that he reflexively began to flinch. He was riding in
an automobile with several Frenchmen and bragged later that while the
conversation was incessant he never spoke a word of English.

He spent the night at a French brigade headquarters and next
morning, May 30, he was escorted to the front by the commandant, a
Major La Favre. On the approach Patton was interested that everything
was camouflaged with enormous spreads of green sacking—acre after
acre of artillery batteries, sleeping areas, messes, buildings—against air
observation and strikes. At a point where it became too dangerous to
continue driving they got out and walked through a field potted with
shell holes. Then some shells began to explode about a hundred yards
away. Presently they came to a hill at the top of which was a farm "all

---

* Because of Beatrice's great wealth, Patton had conveyed his considerable
inheritance in Lake Vineyard to his aunt Nannie.

shot to pieces," and Major La Favre pointed out a line of trees several hundred yards away saying, "There are the Boche."*

La Favre said the Germans could see them, which was "quite evident," Patton wrote later, when two shells screeched over and exploded in a field behind them. Patton walked over and picked up a fragment, which was still hot, that he intended to send to Beatrice. They continued walking with Patton feeling "thrilled" but a little nervous the more they walked on the top of a French communications trench, which he frankly confessed he would rather have been in than on.

They passed by a freshly dug grave featuring a wooden cross that contained the body of a German soldier a French patrol had killed earlier that morning. Major La Favre paused to point out what an "excellent" field of fire the Germans had, which caused Patton to note that "we were the only available target and the range was deadly," adding that he disliked standing there turned as he was to Major La Favre in case it be recorded that George Patton died by being shot in the back.

La Favre then led his guest across what impressed Patton at the time as "the longest field in the world," in plain view of the German guns. As they neared the edge of some woods, the French major bent over, ostensibly to tuck trousers into his leggings, a pose that actually exposed his backside to the Germans in their trenches. Seeing this, and wanting to "express a contempt equal to his," Patton removed his helmet and lit a cigarette, smoking it while the two strolled across the ridge to the safety of the woods. Patton to the end of his days could not get over the fact that the Germans had not fired a shot at them.

"It was about the same thrill as riding in a steeplechase," he told Beatrice.

★ ★ ★ ★

ON MARCH 21, 1918, six thousand German cannons—the largest concentration yet seen in the war, or any war—opened up for several hours

---

* A derogatory term for Germans used by the French, meaning "stupid head" or "blockhead."

along a fifty-mile front that ran from Arras to the river Oise. This was followed at dawn by a massive German attack against the already jittery British that seemed to catch them completely, and strangely, off guard.

The Germans had developed new tactics they believed would win the war. Teams of "storm troopers" would rush forward after a tremendous but short artillery barrage, bypassing enemy strongpoints that could be mopped up later by more powerfully armed infantry. Light field guns would follow on the heels of the infantry attack; the entire idea was highly mobile warfare, the paramount objective being to infiltrate as far into the enemy rear as possible, sowing death and confusion. The result hoped for was to split the British and French armies and capture the channel ports, which would knock Great Britain out of the war and cause the French to sue for peace.

A million Germans emerged wraithlike out of the mists that shrouded no-man's-land, throwing hand grenades and mowing down what defenders remained after the bombardment. They overran the British frontline trenches first, followed by the reserve and support trenches, then the artillery positions, headquarters, and supply. Both sides were stunned at the German assault's success. Airplanes began taking off for fields nearer the coast; at one place, the British took time to evacuate the eight hundred inmates of a lunatic asylum.

The German onslaught seemed irresistible. The British suffered 150,000 casualties and had been pushed back twenty-five miles—more ground than they had given up at any time during the war. But though their line bent, it did not yet break, and, as George Marshall put it later, the German offensive "had assumed the proportions of a great catastrophe."[34]

In what became the greatest drama of the war, the Germans continued their attacks without letup. Both sides knew that ultimate victory or ultimate defeat hung in the balance. In the crisis, the French government gave Field Marshal Ferdinand Foch overall command of the Allied armies, including the American divisions. After the meeting at which the decision was made, the French premier Georges Clemenceau, who did not like Foch, told him, "Well, you've got what you wanted." Foch replied icily, "A fine present . . . you give me a lost battle and tell me to win it."[35]

★ ★ ★ ★

FOCH IMMEDIATELY ASKED FOR the American First Division to be thrown into the breach caused by the German onrush, and Pershing agreed. Marshall, who had been on temporary duty at Langres teaching a class for senior officers, hastily returned to his job as the First Division's operations officer. In November he had been promoted to major, and right after Christmas he wore the silver oak leaves of a lieutenant colonel. Now he had to scramble to find the right combinations of 40 hommes–8 chevaux to hurriedly transport the 40,000-man division from Lorraine to the fighting line in Picardy.

Upon arrival, the decision was made that the First Division would conduct an attack on the village of Cantigny, which the Germans were using as an artillery observation post. The assault was successful—at least at first. But the Germans began a series of violent counterattacks that left 200 Americans killed, 600 wounded, 300 gassed, and 16 missing. Marshall was often down in the front lines scouting around and was "officially commended for his bravery in carrying out his duties under fire."

At one point in the battle, a mud-spattered lieutenant stormed into headquarters wanting to know why his machine-gun company had been ordered back into the fight when it had just been relieved from the line. Marshall got him coffee, sat him down, and patiently explained that it was vital to hold Cantigny against the counterattacks and headquarters thought that his company was the best for the job. The lieutenant later remembered leaving "with a feeling of added pride in my outfit." When he relayed what Marshall had told him, "it restored officers and men to top combat efficiency."[36]

The Germans, however, continued their ferocious assaults, which for the Allies had reached crisis proportions. The Americans, including regiments of marines, were drawn into savage fighting at Belleau Wood and Château-Thierry. These sharp battles represented the first time American forces went on the attack. They successfully threw back the German army from the Marne, though not without more than twenty thousand casualties including particularly heavy losses in a battalion of the Fifth U.S. Marines. At the height of the action Gunnery Sergeant Dan Daley issued his famous remark, "Well come on, ya sons of bitches. Ya want to live forever?" The twin victories at Belleau Wood and Château-Thierry have been described as the turning point in the war, and certainly they erased any lingering doubts about the bravery and resourcefulness of the U.S. expeditionary force.

While the French and Americans were fighting the Second Battle of the Marne, a worried George Marshall began organizing two entirely new scratch fighting battalions out of the division's supply of men, stevedores, muleskinners, truck drivers, and various cooks and bottle washers. One of these was commanded by the division adjutant, the other by the judge advocate. When they reported for instructions, Marshall led them to a window, below which a lovely valley spread with a rail track running through it. "You are to die east of the railroad," he said, pointing. "That is all the orders you need."[37]

★ ★ ★ ★

ON JUNE 6 RUMOR HAD IT that Patton's tanks were to be used in a major upcoming operation, and he reorganized the Tank Center into two battalions to reflect the added men and equipment. Major Viner and Major Brett would each command a battalion and Patton would command what amounted now to a tank regiment.

But as the summer waned, there were no orders to bring the tanks to the fighting line and Patton was becoming antsy. He had honed his men and equipment to a fine edge and there they sat while the fighting raged. Out of exasperation and boredom, Patton decided to take the course at the Army Staff College that Pershing had set up at Chaumont.

Meanwhile, the battle being fought on the chalk plains of Champagne was long and bloody, and a "startling success" for the Germans. By the end of June an emergency was declared as the Germans appeared to be on the verge of taking the French capital. On July 4, 1918, the 42nd Division was pulled out of Baccarat and force-marched to the railheads of Champagne, scene of some of the bitterest fighting. They left behind more than two thousand of their comrades killed or wounded.

As chief of staff, MacArthur was of course in the midst of the loading when General Pershing showed up unannounced for one of his surprise "inspections." After watching the activity for a short while, Pershing suddenly strode up to MacArthur, who was busying himself on the loading ramp, and loudly said words to the effect that "This division is a disgrace! The men are poorly disciplined and they are not properly trained! The whole outfit is about the worst that I've seen." The ramp was crowded with dozens of officers and enlisted men who stopped whatever they were doing to listen to the commanding general's rant.

"MacArthur," Pershing shouted, "I am going to hold you personally responsible for getting order and discipline into this division! I won't stand for this! It's a disgrace!"[38]

Pershing's outburst left the Rainbow's chief of staff flabbergasted and flush-faced. Pershing strode away to his car and MacArthur left the loading ramp and walked into the nearby town of Charmes, where he sat on a park bench trying to fathom Pershing's reasons for singling out him and his division. What he didn't know was that "he had just been initiated into a growing fraternity of officers" who would become targets of Pershing's fury. In the AEF it had become something like a Red Badge of Courage to be publicly bawled out by the commanding general, who went around indiscriminately and at will making known his displeasure upon high-ranking subordinate officers.

MacArthur didn't see it that way. He began to harbor strong intimations that the "Pershing Faction" at AEF headquarters was persecuting him. This was an unfortunate side of MacArthur's personality and it would dog him for the remainder of his career. Something—some subtle distorted impulse in his psyche—led him to conjure conspiracies, designs, and intrigues against him by higher headquarters, which eventually included the Office of the Chief of Staff and the president of the United States. Even so, less than a week after his dressing down by the commanding general, MacArthur became the youngest brigadier general in the AEF.[39]

Now the Rainbow Division was under the operational supervision of the brilliant one-armed, one-legged French Fourth Army commander General Henri J. E. Gouraud. Popularly known as the "Lion of Morocco," Gouraud became so impressed with MacArthur during this period that an offhand but remarkably complimentary endorsement of the new brigadier found its way into MacArthur's permanent military records. Be that as it may, not everyone was as high on the "Boy General" MacArthur as Gouraud was. Once, after pinning a third Silver Star on him, the 42nd Division commander said, "Mac, there are people at GHQ [Pershing's headquarters] who consider you irresponsible. They feel you have no business leading attacks like some expendable line officer."

MacArthur replied that he didn't consider his line officers any more expendable than himself, adding that it makes for "a fighting spirit." Furthermore, it raised the question of whether MacArthur's seeming paranoia about General Headquarters actually had a reasonable basis in fact. Here he was, so to speak, down in the trenches, and around Pershing's headquarters they were calling him "the showoff."[40]

On July 14, Bastille Day, General Gouraud was seized by an implacable intuition that the Germans were going to launch a major attack in his sector. He invited all of the generals and senior colonels of the Rainbow Division to luncheon at his headquarters and told them so. It turned out that Gouraud was right. At midnight that night, the German bombardment began—5,500 guns on both sides firing at maximum rate so that "the whole sky seemed to be torn apart with sound," which could be heard in Paris, a hundred miles away. Four hours later the enemy attacked with three armies under Crown Prince Wilhelm—forty-seven divisions (500,000 men) in a two-pronged defensive on either side of the city of Reims through the forests and on the white-chalked plains of the Champagne sector.[41]

The storm burst into the 42nd Division's sector just after dawn as Germans began pouring into the Allied frontline trenches. What the enemy found there, however, startled them: almost nothing. As per the new Allied plan of "defense in depth," only a few troops were kept in the front line, and those mostly to signal back with flares and rockets that the enemy had arrived. The main Allied forces were entrenched in a well-fortified "intermediate line" about two miles in the rear. Every square yard of that distance was preregistered with Allied artillery.

All morning the Germans flung themselves into the trap and were thrown back. Again and again they re-formed and charged and were mown down with hideous losses. By midafternoon as they were repulsed for a final time it had become clear that the last great German offensive of the war was a failure and Paris was safe.[42]

On July 18 a desperate and hastily organized Allied counterattack was launched to destroy the German army. MacArthur's 84th Brigade was among the units spearheading the assault. Orders were that the enemy was retreating and must be pursued at all costs, in particular from the heights across the river Ourcq, which the Rainbow Division was told to surprise silently, with the bayonet only—no shots were to be fired. Here, however, the Germans had laid a death trap of their own. As the Americans waded across the river, the chalk bluffs to their front came alive with vicious stabs of machine-gun fire that turned the waters bloodred. MacArthur went immediately to the front and saw for himself where they had gone wrong. He vowed never again to launch a frontal attack unless he had personally reconnoitered the ground.

Now the Germans were playing a game of cat and mouse, ostensibly withdrawing, but apparently only for the sake of luring the Americans into a trap—or traps of their own. Allied intelligence had concluded that the enemy was retreating hastily with only small rearguard actions, but this was not so. The Germans had carefully set up strong, well-fortified positions among the myriad stone farm buildings of the fighting front, so that the only way to get at them was with suicidal attacks across open ground covered by precleared fields of fire.

The problem was that as intelligence kept reporting the Germans on the run Allied headquarters kept ordering close pursuit. It was frightening, demoralizing, and maddening—men crossing open fields only to be shot to rags by death-dealing automatic weapons hidden behind walls, rock, or clumps of trees.

Finally MacArthur told them to start fighting like the western Indians of his youth, creeping up along the ground in groups of twos and threes. During the next week, the Rainbow thus slouched forward in a series of horrid little encounters: La Croix Rouge, Ferme Beauvardes, Sergy, Meurcy Farm, Nesles, Forêt de Fer, Villers-sur-Fère, Hill 212—each place named on a military map that told nothing of the blood-drenched squalor that went on there. The Americans would crawl up Indian-style, throw grenades, and finish it off hand to hand with bayonets and rifle butts. Little or no quarter was given and little was asked.

Many times the enemy positions were wiped out to the last man, but the price was high. In those five days the Rainbow suffered an appalling 6,500 men killed or wounded. MacArthur's 84th Brigade was composed mostly of Alabama and Iowa National Guard infantry who were not held in high esteem by the regular army men. But they had learned to kill just as well as anybody else and MacArthur was immensely proud of them.

The battle had also taken its toll on MacArthur. Even though he earned a second Silver Star and the French Legion of Honor, something in his personality had changed. A group of officers was toasting the victory at a drinking party at Châlons, singing ever bawdier stanzas of "Mademoiselle from Armentières," but for MacArthur something was missing. "It may have been the vision of those writhing bodies hanging on the wire or the stench of dead flesh . . . Perhaps I was just getting old," he said. "Somehow, I had forgotten how to play."

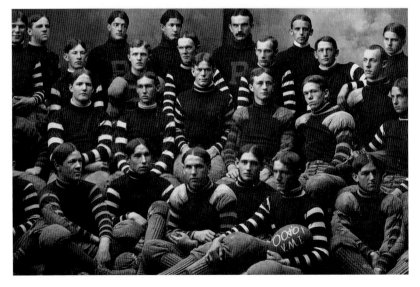

TOP: *George Marshall as first captain at VMI, 1901*
BOTTOM: *George Marshall (second row, second from right)*
with the VMI varsity football team, 1900

*The wedding party of Lily Coles (second from left) and George Marshall
(third from left), Lexington, Virginia, 1902*

*Colonel George Marshall (right) and his boss, General of the Armies
John J. Pershing, in France during World War I, 1917*

U.S. artillerymen fire a 14-inch railroad gun during the Battle of the Argonne Forest, France, 1918.

TOP LEFT: *George Patton, who was dyslexic, attended VMI for a year as a prep school before entering the U.S. Military Academy at West Point.*
TOP RIGHT: *Patton's marriage to Beatrice Ayer was one of Boston's main social events in 1910.*
BOTTOM: *Lieutenant Colonel Patton beside one of the vehicles he led as commander of the First U.S. Tank Brigade*

Among the finest horsemen in the army, Patton sails over a fence on his favorite jumper, Hukupu, to become champion of the 1933 West Point horse show.

American tanks head into the Battle of the Argonne Forest.

American soldiers in France, 1918, fire a 37mm gun at the Germans.

TOP: *Douglas MacArthur, age five, poses with his father, Arthur, who would become a high-ranking army general; older brother, Arthur; and mother, "Pinky," in San Antonio, 1885.*
BOTTOM LEFT: *MacArthur graduated West Point at the top of his class in 1903.*
BOTTOM RIGHT: *Colonel Douglas MacArthur wore his uniform in jaunty fashion while commanding the 42nd "Rainbow" Division in France, 1917.*

TOP: *MacArthur is decorated by
General of the Armies John J. Pershing in World War I.*
BOTTOM: *MacArthur, as field marshal of the Philippine army,
appears with Philippine president Manuel Quezon (left) in 1937.*

★ ★ ★ ★

CHAPTER FIVE

COURAGE WAS THE RULE

ollowing the Battles of Belleau Wood and Château-Thierry, the Germans reluctantly began winding down their great offensive but remained like a wounded and dangerous animal behind their fortifications on the Hindenburg Line. While German fortunes had changed for the worse, George Marshall's were changing for the better. Though he had repeatedly asked for field duty, each request was denied on grounds, as General Robert L. Bullard wrote, that "[Marshall] has no equal [in staff work] in the Army today." Instead, on August 21, 1918, he was promoted to full colonel and assigned to General Headquarters under Pershing himself.

That was just in time for what was about to become the first large American offensive of the war—the assault on the German salient at Saint-Mihiel. By this time Pershing had more than 1,600,000 American soldiers in France, with more pouring in at the rate of 10,000 a day. He had so far resisted pressure from Field Marshal Ferdinand Foch to put his divisions into battle piecemeal with the French, but held out until he was able to form a full U.S. army. Saint-Mihiel would be its battle test.

The salient had been a wedge-shaped bulge in the German lines that, since the commencement of the war in 1914, had jutted out to the French town of Saint-Mihiel and disrupted communications between Verdun,

Nancy, and Paris. In other words, it was a general pain in the neck for the Allies. Salients, such as the ones at Saint-Mihiel and at Ypres, in Belgium, are difficult to attack because at some point the majority of the attacking force will come under fire from the front and the side; the French had expended 60,000 men over the past four years in finding this out. Salients are equally hard to defend since they are vulnerable to enemy artillery fire from three sides. Nobody liked them, but the Germans refused to give theirs up—apparently on the notion that "ground gained was ground earned."

The Saint-Mihiel battle was to be conducted with fourteen U.S. divisions—more than 500,000 men—and had as its overall objective the capture of Metz, a critical German rail and transportation center. It would have to be done quickly, however, because larger plans were afoot for a more critical operation in the Meuse-Argonne region about forty miles to the north.

★ ★ ★ ★

As GEORGE MARSHALL DREW UP the battle plans for Saint-Mihiel— which included a ruse to deceive the Germans into reinforcing elsewhere—Patton was attending a lecture when a courier handed him an urgent note from General Rockenbach: Patton's tanks were to take part in a large-scale independent attack on the Germans to eradicate the Saint-Mihiel salient. He was to command a 144-tank brigade plus a French tank battalion of 72 machines, and the attack was to commence on September 12, which was less than three weeks away.

Suddenly everyone and everything became animated like a hive of hornets. Working under the attack orders drawn up by George Marshall and others on Pershing's operations staff, Patton planned an order of battle for his tanks. He of course decided he needed to reconnoiter the ground himself to make sure it was suitable for tanks. Dressed in French garb so as not to alert the enemy that Americans were spying on them, he went to the forward headquarters of a French division that fronted on no-man's-land on the floodplain of the Woevre plateau.

Patton's patrol, consisting of French officers and enlisted men, set out after dark and did the "burglar's crawl" across no-man's-land for about a mile and a half until they came to the German wire. Patton had worried that the ground would be too soft for tanks, but his patrol taught him otherwise. As Patton scooped up a handful of soil with some tiny flowers intending to send it to Beatrice, his troops cut the outer band of wire and kept on toward the German trenches when a whistle caught them. One of the Frenchmen whistled back. Patton was later told that the enemy whistle "meant that if the raid was pushed further the Germans would reluctantly be forced to fire." (In this particular stretch—which had been a "quiet sector" for more than two years—the two sides as previously noted had adopted a live-and-let-live custom. The French sergeant's return whistle acknowledged the first and indicated that the patrol would turn back, which it did—to Patton's disgust.) He had hoped for "an encounter."

Back at the tank brigade's new headquarters near the front lines everything was still buzzing along: telephone wire was laid, homing pigeons acquired from the signal corps, the tanks were fine-tuned, guns and personal firearms were cleaned, plans rehearsed and rerehearsed, and then, ten days before the attack was to begin, the whole operation order was changed and Patton's tank brigade would now support only the 42nd Division on different ground. The 42nd Division had never worked with tanks.

Once again Patton dutifully reconnoitered the area and found it suitable. Then rain came and threatened to foil all his carefully laid plans. Averaging (by his own estimate) three hours of sleep a night, Patton was highly aggravated when the artillery barrage for the attack awakened him at 1 a.m. on the morning of September 12, 1918.

★ ★ ★ ★

THE VERY DAY BEFORE the Allied attack began, the Germans, on their own accord, had decided the salient was "a defensive embarrassment" and began a withdrawal to the Hindenburg Line. As a result, when the

Americans (along with four French divisions) struck at daybreak on September 12, they initially gained ground all along a twenty-seven-mile front. At one point Patton encountered Brigadier General Douglas MacArthur, leading brigade of the 42nd Rainbow Division, walking upright on the battlefield through shot and shell and the whizz of German machine-gun bullets as their own "creeping barrage" rumbled inexorably toward them. Except for the general himself, MacArthur's infantrymen were all hunkered down in shell holes waiting for the barrage to pass, while Patton's tanks dashed hither and thither ahead seeking out enemy machine-gun nests. The two stood there making small talk, as Patton later wrote to Beatrice. "Each one [of us] wanted to leave but each hated to say so, so we let it [the barrage] come over us. It was very thin and not dangerous."

Soon after, Patton led his tanks toward Essey despite warnings from a Frenchman who said the enemy bombardment was too intense and suggested that they halt until it lifted. Regardless, Patton marched ahead of his tanks over a bridge not knowing if it was mined or wired with explosives and once more encountered MacArthur, who had come up into Essey with his infantry. Patton asked him if he could attack the next town, Pannes, about two miles ahead, and MacArthur assented, but before they could get there all but one of the tanks had run out of gas. Patton told the sergeant commanding the serviceable tank to enter the town but he hesitated given the sights of all the dead Germans and a smashed German battery with dozens of dead artillery horses still in their traces. Patton ordered him forward anyway, saying he was going to sit on the top of the tank as it went in to Pannes. The sergeant went forward.

As they got to the north end of town, Patton spotted some Germans who wanted to surrender and sent his runner and a Lieutenant Knowles to take them. Using their pistols only, the two returned with more than thirty German prisoners, whom they sent to the rear. When they passed out of Pannes toward the next town Patton, still sitting atop the tank, had what he described as a "horrible experience." Hearing an enemy machine gun firing, he was unable to locate it when he "glanced down the left side of the tank and about six inches below my hand paint was flying off on the side of the tank." This prompted Patton to instantly un-ass himself from the vehicle in order to make it "a less enticing target," according to his own action report, and dive into a shell hole where he remained until the machine gun was silenced.

The tank personnel, however, were unaware that their high-ranking passenger had jumped off, and the machine continued forward with the support of the infantry. In a hurry, Patton found the infantry commander and asked him to go forward to protect the tank but the answer was negative. Patton then asked the commander if he would send a runner, several hundred yards away, to tell the tank to fall back—the answer to which was, "Hell no, it ain't my tank."

Disgusted, Patton himself went forward running "like hell" and soon found himself facing the fire of four German machine guns. As bullets "sang about him," he managed to protect himself by dodging behind his tank where he beat on the hull with his walking stick. The tank stopped and the sergeant looked out, saluted, and asked, "What do you want now, Colonel?" Patton instructed him to turn back and walked ahead of him on the return trip, shielded by the tank, "quite safe" from enemy bullets.

By then the other tanks had refueled and returned to the battle area, capturing Pannes and a horde of German prisoners. Patton, meantime, was so hungry that he ate some crackers taken from the body of a dead German. Somehow in the confusion he had lost his haversack (it had been stolen by German prisoners), which contained among other things a bottle of brandy that he savored.

With Pannes occupied by Allied troops, Patton went to the left to see about his battalion under Brett. He found them at Nonsard, having taken that town with the loss of two officers and four men. But all twenty-five tanks were out of gas and Brett himself was crying in frustration and bleeding from a wound across his nose. Patton sent for fuel and comforted him, learning that Brett had personally shot two Germans out of a church steeple. "It was a most interesting walk over the battle-field," Patton told Beatrice. "Like the books but much less dramatic. The [enemy] dead were [all] about, mostly hit in the head. There were a lot of our men stripping off buttons and other things but they always covered the face of the dead in a nice way."[1]

Refueled after a delay of several hours, Patton's force moved on and halted for the night at Vigneulles, learning from the prisoners there that the seeming ease with which they were taking ground was because the Germans were actually in the process of evacuating the Saint-Mihiel salient. This disappointed Patton who had expected a big fight against Germany's best and most ferocious units. Still, he took solace in having learned a valuable lesson about tank battle tactics: a reliable fuel supply must be far more abundant and closer behind the fighting tanks.

★ ★ ★ ★

AT THIS POINT, the tank brigade's encampment was well beyond the stated objectives for the day, and the men took stock. Of 174 tanks that had gone into the fight that morning fourteen had broken down, three were destroyed, and twenty-two were ditched (stuck in trenches or shell holes). Nine American officers and men had been killed, fourteen wounded. Eighty American tanks and twenty-five French tanks would be ready to renew the assault in the morning. The *Chicago Daily News* and the *Los Angeles Express* carried stories with Patton's picture and the headline: "Californian Perched on Tank During Battle."[2]

General Rockenbach, however, was furious at Patton. A brigade commander was supposed to be at his headquarters or at least in close touch with it—to receive orders and transmit information—not running around on the battlefield. Patton was ordered—and he complied—to give a written statement in which he promised to remain at headquarters in future actions. Privately, however, he remained recalcitrant, if not defiant, writing to Beatrice, "At least I will not sit in a dug out and have my men out in the fighting." He had proved to his own satisfaction, he said, "that I have nerve." He further informed his wife that he had been the highest-ranked officer in the front line except for General MacArthur, "who never ducked a shell." ("I wanted to, but it's foolish because it does no good. If they are going to hit you, they will.") He enclosed for her a gift of some cap ornaments he took off a dead German, adding, "Personally I never fired a shot except to kill two poor horses with broken legs."[3]

★ ★ ★ ★

BY EVENING MacArthur had nearly reached the town of Mars-la-Tour, seven miles from their jumping-off point—an amazing accomplishment on a battlefield where for four years gains had been measured in yards.

While they were told to hold their positions, on the night of September 13–14 MacArthur and an aide sneaked through no-man's-land and made for a high hill. With binoculars they could see the strategic city of Metz glowing in the distance at the end of the valley. It was perhaps ten miles away but, through his glasses, MacArthur perceived that the town was undefended, a breathtaking prospect. "There it lay, our prize wide open for the taking. Take it, and we would be in excellent position to cut off South Germany" from the rest of the country and "lead to the invasion of Central Germany and . . . bring a close to the war," MacArthur concluded.

MacArthur rushed back to the division headquarters and reported what he'd seen. It was agreed that it was imperative to take Metz. It was the same at the corps headquarters and First Army headquarters as well. But Pershing had received orders from General Foch to halt the advance and move the troops south for the Meuse-Argonne Offensive. Even though Pershing and his planning wizard George Marshall sided with MacArthur, orders-was-orders for Pershing, and he reluctantly called a halt to the battle. MacArthur thought it was one of the great blunders of the war.

"It was an example of the inflexibility in pursuit of pre-conceived ideas," he wrote years afterward, "that is, unfortunately, too frequent in modern warfare. Had we seized this unexpected opportunity, we would have saved thousands of American lives lost in the dim recesses of the Argonne Forest." In any event, MacArthur, for his role in erasing the Saint-Mihiel salient, was awarded his fifth Silver Star, the Croix de Guerre, and the French Legion of Honor.[4]

★ ★ ★ ★

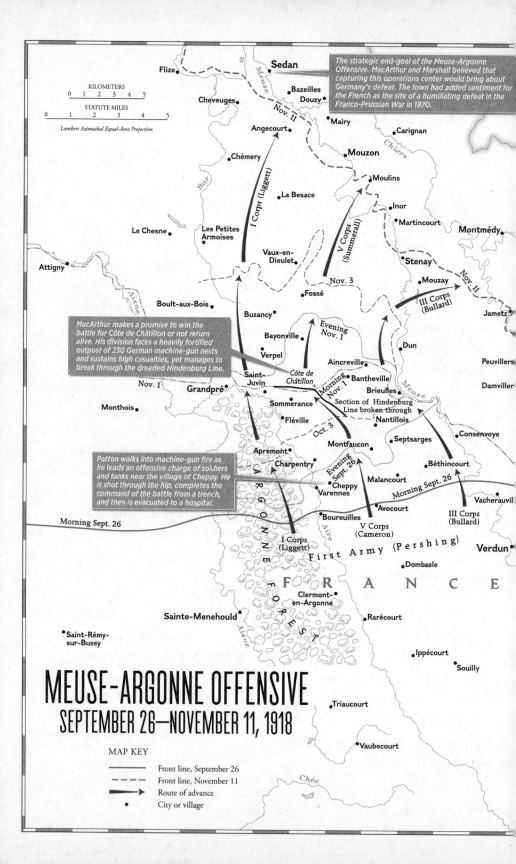

The strategic end-goal of the Meuse-Argonne Offensive. MacArthur and Marshall believed that capturing this operations center would bring about Germany's defeat. The town had added sentiment for the French as the site of a humiliating defeat in the Franco-Prussian War in 1870.

MacArthur makes a promise to win the battle for Côte de Châtillon or not return alive. His division faces a heavily fortified outpost of 230 German machine-gun nests and sustains high casualties, yet manages to break through the dreaded Hindenburg Line.

Patton walks into machine-gun fire as he leads an offensive charge of soldiers and tanks near the village of Cheppy. He is shot through the hip, completes the command of the battle from a trench, and then is evacuated to a hospital.

KILOMETERS
0 1 2 3 4 5

STATUTE MILES
0 1 2 3 4 5

Lambert Azimuthal Equal-Area Projection

Flize

Sedan

Cheveuges

Bazeilles
Douzy

Nov. 11

Mairy

Carignan

Angecourt

Mouzon

Chémery

Moulins

La Besace

Inor

Martincourt

Montmédy

I Corps (Liggett)

V Corps (Summerall)

Le Chesne

Les Petites
Armoises

Stenay

Attigny

Vaux-en-
Dieulet

Mouzay

Nov. 11

Nov. 3

Fossé

III Corps
(Bullard)

Jametz

Boult-aux-Bois

Buzancy

Evening
Nov. 1

Peuvillers

Bayonville

Dun

Damviller

Verpel

Aincreville

Saint-
Juvin

Côte de
Châtillon

Bantheville

Morning
Nov. 1

Brieulles

Nov. 1

Grandpré

Sommerance

Section of Hindenburg
Line broken through

Nantillois

Consenvoye

Monthois

Fléville

Oct. 3

Montfaucon

Septsarges

Apremont

Charpentry

Evening
Sept. 26

Béthincourt

Cheppy
Varennes

Malancourt

Morning Sept. 26

Vacherauvil

Boureuilles

Avocourt

III Corps
(Bullard)

Morning Sept. 26

I Corps
(Liggett)

V Corps
(Cameron)

Verdun

First Army (Pershing)

F R A N C E

Dombasle

Clermont-
en-Argonne

Sainte-Menehould

Rarécourt

Saint-Rémy-
sur-Bussy

Ippécourt

Souilly

MEUSE-ARGONNE OFFENSIVE
SEPTEMBER 26—NOVEMBER 11, 1918

Triaucourt

Vaubecourt

MAP KEY

Front line, September 26

Front line, November 11

Route of advance

City or village

Chée

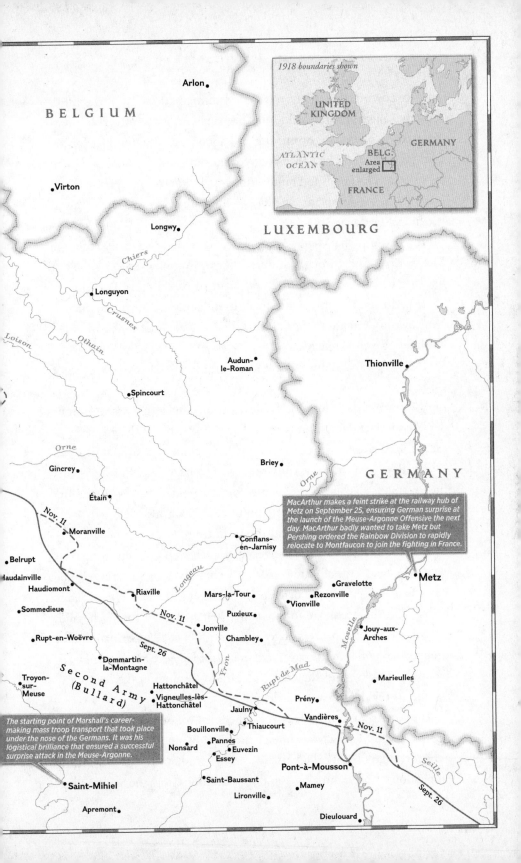

Arlon

BELGIUM

Virton

Longwy

LUXEMBOURG

Chiers

Longuyon

Crusnes

Loison

Othain

Audun-
le-Roman

Thionville

Spincourt

Orne

Gincrey

Briey

Orne

GERMANY

Étain

MacArthur makes a feint strike at the railway hub of
Metz on September 25, ensuring German surprise at
the launch of the Meuse-Argonne Offensive the next
day. MacArthur badly wanted to take Metz but
Pershing ordered the Rainbow Division to rapidly
relocate to Montfaucon to join the fighting in France.

Nov. 11

Moranville

Conflans-
en-Jarnisy

Belrupt

Haudainville

Gravelotte

Metz

Haudiomont

Riaville

Rezonville

Mars-la-Tour

Longeau

Vionville

Sommedieue

Nov. 11

Puxieux

Rupt-en-Woëvre

Jonville

Chambley

Jouy-aux-
Arches

Moselle

Sept. 26

Dommartin-
la-Montagne

Second Army
(Bullard)

Marieulles

Troyon-
sur-
Meuse

Hattonchâtel

Prény

Fron

Rupt de Mad

Vigneulles-lès-
Hattonchâtel

Jaulny

Vandières

Nov. 11

The starting point of Marshall's career-
making mass troop transport that took place
under the nose of the Germans. It was his
logistical brilliance that ensured a successful
surprise attack in the Meuse-Argonne.

Bouillonville

Thiaucourt

Pont-à-Mousson

Seille

Pannes

Nonsard

Euvezin

Essey

Saint-Mihiel

Saint-Baussant

Mamey

Sept. 26

Lironville

Apremont

Dieulouard

1918 boundaries shown

UNITED
KINGDOM

GERMANY

ATLANTIC
OCEAN

BELG.
Area
enlarged

FRANCE

THE FOLLOWING DAY, there was little fighting and even less the third, since the salient at Saint-Mihiel had been erased with some 7,200 Americans killed, wounded, or missing and about the same number for the Germans. The fight had been good for the tank corps' morale and good training for a far larger and more serious operation in the Argonne Forest known only to a few planning offices—including George Marshall's—at Pershing's headquarters.

The battle at the Meuse-Argonne was designed as a push along the Meuse River and through the neighboring Argonne Forest aimed at retaking Sedan (pronounced *sa-da*), a town of about 16,000 that in 1870 had been the site of the final, humiliating defeat of the French army by the Germans in the Franco-Prussian War. Thus it held an added sentiment for the French.

The U.S. First Army, created on August 10, 1918, consisted of three army corps—about 600,000 men—under General Pershing's command. It would be joined on the left by the much-depleted French Fourth Army of about 135,000 men. The ground was exceptionally difficult, consisting of hilly country rising above two river valleys that the attacking forces had to negotiate. For four years the Germans had been creating a multilayered defense—including fortified positions and concrete pillboxes (small, low shelters)—to a depth of thirteen miles behind the front lines.

As an illustration of the dangers of trench warfare even in the rear areas, George Marshall came close to becoming "wastage" himself one day when he went to the dentist. In the brief interval between Saint-Mihiel and the Meuse-Argonne battle, Marshall got a toothache and, while he was in the process of getting a tooth filled, "A German aviator dropped a bomb into the courtyard of the Intelligence Section of Headquarters, close by, and the explosion almost resulted in the loss of my tongue, as the dentist was a trifle gun-shy . . ."

The Meuse-Argonne attack was scheduled for September 26 at first light. George Marshall was one of the chief planners of the operation and, three days before the battle was to begin, he was tasked with the stupendous chore of moving 400,000 U.S. troops from the Saint-Mihiel battlefield to the Meuse-Argonne sector, sixty miles away, by night—and secretly so the Germans wouldn't find out about it.

It was an almost unheard-of proposition. He would have to pull fifteen divisions out of line at Saint-Mihiel, replace them with 200,000 French troops, and then move everything sixty miles: the various headquarters, field kitchens, ammunition, and supplies, 3,000 artillery pieces—light and heavy alike—90,000 animals, hospitals along terrible roads, and, because of lack of motor transport, a third of the men would have to march afoot.

He went into his office, closed the door, and thought for a while, realizing that if he made an error it could cost him his career. Then he called for a stenographer and standing before a large map began dictating. In an hour he was done and sent the plan on to General Hugh Drum, who would present it to Pershing.[5]

Next morning, Marshall was told to report immediately to General Drum, who somberly announced, "General Pershing wishes to speak to you." As they entered Pershing's office, Drum remarked casually to him, "That order for the Meuse-Argonne concentration you sent over last night is a dandy. The general thought it was a fine piece of work." Marshall was so flabbergasted that when he thought about it later he couldn't remember a single thing Pershing had said to him.[6]

★ ★ ★ ★

ARMED WITH A GREATER UNDERSTANDING of how his tanks and men would perform under battle conditions, Patton readied for the Meuse-Argonne attack. Patton again donned a French uniform, so as not to give away U.S. intentions, and went out on patrol to reconnoiter and discover if the ground he was to cover was suitable for his machines. He found the enemy trenches not as wide and the ground better than he had expected, although the German defenses were formidable. The Hindenburg Line had been constructed as a "defense in depth"; in this case, for twelve miles to the rear of its leading edges was a catacomb of bunkers, trenches, pillboxes with cannons, and mutually supporting concrete-protected machine-gun nests. The ground itself was pocked with innumerable shell holes, not a few of which were deep enough to envelope a tank.

Patton was given the responsibility of supporting (leading) two infantry divisions, the 28th and the 35th, in a northward drive up the valley of the river Aire that bordered the Argonne Forest. Patton situated Brett's battalion on the west side of the river with the 28th Infantry Division and Compton's battalion on the east with the 35th. The French battalion in support would bring up the rear.

His battle plan emphasized the offensive and presciently anticipated Germany's armored *Blitzkrieg* two decades into the future. To counter the enemy's defense in depth, Patton organized an offense in depth, in which the leading companies, after destroying the first line of enemy resistance, would hold the new line while the rear companies passed through and attacked the next enemy fortifications, and the French, in support, would pass through the whole in pursuit of the fleeing enemy. It was a dangerous, violent, hard-hitting stratagem.

Meanwhile, MacArthur was ordered to stage "a powerful double raid" in the Saint-Benoit sector to confuse the Germans into thinking the Americans were continuing their attack toward Metz. On September 25, one day before the Meuse-Argonne Offensive was to begin, MacArthur so effectively surprised the Germans that they were shelled out of their trenches and practically annihilated, while the American infantry were maneuvered "to make a lot of noise" but remained safely out of the line of fire. MacArthur, who had accompanied the raiders, earned his sixth Silver Star for his efforts. Afterward the Rainbow Division was ordered to the "vast and shifting" battlefield of the Meuse-Argonne.[7]

★ ★ ★ ★

THE BEST-LAID PLANS of Colonel George Marshall, however, did not go always as intended. Patton fumed on September 23, three days before the battle was to begin, "One fine example of efficiency has just happened. 10,000 gallons of gasoline arrived in tank cars with no pump.

Now we can't get it out except by dippers!!! It is a good thing I have a cheerful disposition."

That same day: "One whole battalion has failed to show up and I can't find it. The battalion commander [Compton] spent the day looking for a house instead of getting his tanks."

The following day he observed to his diary, "The Boche took [aerial] pictures of us so I guess we shall be shelled or something," and to Beatrice later that evening, "We had a very quiet day except that a shell took off a man's foot for which I am sorry."

Next day, September 25, the eve of battle, Patton reported to his diary that "one of our trucks full of [message] runners was hit by an artillery shell at 6:15 p.m.," and to Beatrice, "If I wrote all night I could not tell you how much I love you," and that he needed to eat and get to bed as "I shant be able to do [either] for the next few days."

The furious 1,400-gun artillery barrage began at 2:30 a.m. and promptly at 5:30 Patton's tanks, followed by tens of thousands of infantry, moved forward in the attack. "I am always nervous at these times," he told Beatrice, "just as at Polo or Foot ball before the game starts."[8]

★ ★ ★ ★

On October 1, MacArthur's Rainbow Division was carried in trucks driven by French army Vietnamese drivers to a dark and dismaying forest known as the Montfaucon Woods, where a desperate fight had recently concluded. The ground was torn with huge shell craters and the woods were "a mere graveyard of broken limbs and splintered stumps. Dead bodies, some of them in a bad state of decomposition, also littered the woods and slopes."[9] To make matters worse, it had turned bitterly cold.

America would send a million men into the Meuse-Argonne to attempt a breakthrough of the Hindenburg Line, known locally as the Krunhilde Stalling, a grim killing ground consisting of hundreds of machine-gun nests, concrete pillboxes, and barbed wire twenty-five feet deep, which the Germans thought to be impregnable.[10]

To the Americans' advantage, the Germans clearly were not expecting an attack through the Argonne, and in fact had fortified Metz a few days after MacArthur had pleaded to be allowed to take it, so that "an entire American field army would not be able to take the city." However, as soon as they perceived that the Allied attack in the Argonne was a major thrust and not a feint, the German High Command rushed twenty infantry divisions—200,000 more men—into the fray. Still, it was a high credit to George Marshall's planning that moved a full American field army across the entire enemy front without detection and it managed to get into battle formation in less than a week.

If successful, the attack would in MacArthur's view lead to the capture of Sedan and the defeat of Germany. This of course, like practically everything in the war, was easier said than done. The day after his arrival MacArthur watched from an old churchyard on a hill as the 79th Division unsuccessfully attempted a frontal attack on the German positions. It reinforced his conviction that frontal assaults in the age of the machine gun were a thing of the past. A particularly bloody impediment to the American advance was a group of hills known as the Côte de Châtillon, where first the 32nd Division, then the 91st, and finally the First Division—the Big Red One of regulars—had broken their backs, taking appalling casualties and recoiling in horror from the ferocious enemy fire. The Argonne was turning into a giant corpse factory. Now it became the Rainbow's time of trial.

MacArthur carefully studied the ground, the "desolate and forbidding terrain" of rolling hills and steep forested valleys where death lay everywhere behind the full horizon. He concluded that the Côte de Châtillon was the key to the entire enemy position in the Argonne; he proposed to capture it by concentrating his units in small batches directly at the center of the *côte*, rather than spreading them out on a line of battle in a full frontal assault.

The night before MacArthur's attack, the corps commander, Lieutenant General Charles Summerall, who had served under MacArthur's father, appeared out of the cold, dark, and rain in the doorway of MacArthur's headquarters in an old French farmhouse dripping wet and "looking tired and worn." MacArthur gave him a cup of steaming hot coffee, which he drank—then the general turned abruptly on MacArthur and said dramatically, "Give me Châtillon or a list of five thousand casualties."

"All right, General," the startled MacArthur replied. "We'll take it, or my name will head the list."[11]

Later that night, MacArthur was slightly wounded by shrapnel while conducting a final reconnaissance of the approaches to Châtillon. It was worth it, however, as he discovered something he'd expected all along: the Germans tended to give great strength to the center of their positions but often neglected the flanks. Châtillon was no exception. From the center, the deep belt of wire entanglements and entrenchments "dribbled out at the ends."

"There was where I planned to strike," said General MacArthur, "with my Alabama cotton growers on the left, and my Iowa pig farmers on the right."

The attack got off in a misty daybreak with MacArthur, white-faced and ill with some kind of bug, out of his sickbed to lead it. Within the hour, however, the advance had broken down and MacArthur, ironically, found himself in the same position as his father in Tennessee half a century earlier—at the base of a steep precipice preparing to lead his men in a grave and glorious uphill attack.

He sent the men forward in small units that "sneaked, crawled, side-slipped" from cover to cover; then, "when the chance came," they would form squads or platoons and spring up to envelope the enemy machine-gun nests and put them out of action. It was desperate, savage business, but as the sun sank over the Côte de Châtillon that day amid a field of dead bodies that a man could walk across without touching ground, the 168th Iowa clung by its fingernails to one of the position's main hills.[12]

★ ★ ★ ★

AT ABOUT THE SAME TIME MacArthur launched his attack, Patton's tanks and soldiers began making their way across the greasy shell-pocked mush of no-man's-land. Earlier, as four tank companies—some eighty tanks—tried to cross a bridge, a German counterbarrage killed the MPs who were directing traffic and caused the tanks to be delayed. From his command post, Patton peered impatiently into the gloom where his men were fighting and dying.

Finally he could stand it no longer and at about 6:30 took a captain, a lieutenant, and twelve runners carrying baskets of homing pigeons, telephones, and wire and stalked out of the CP northward toward the sound of the guns. After about two miles near a small town called Cheppy, Patton stopped his entourage in a railroad cut and took stock. The battle was still raging ahead of them; they could hear it clearly now, and Patton sent a pigeon back giving his location and situation as he understood it.

Half a dozen tanks appeared, which had encountered trouble navigating German trenches, and after a chat with Patton they moved on toward the fight. Suddenly enemy machine-gun bullets began kicking up dirt and Patton ordered his people back into the safety of the rail cut, then sent his orderly Joseph Angelo to scout for Germans or other trouble. Next, groups of American infantrymen began to appear, walking, running, disorganized toward the rear. They told Patton they had become separated from their units in the fog. Patton ordered them to join his group and soon the machine-gun fire became intense.

By now Patton had nearly a hundred stray soldiers in the cut. Evidently in the fog the tanks and infantry had unwittingly bypassed German machine-gun nests, which were now coming alive as the mist thinned. Patton noticed a small hill about one hundred yards to the rear and ordered everyone to make a dash for the reverse slope where they would be sheltered from the fire. No sooner had they done so than a breeze swept away the last of the fog and machine guns seemed to open on them from every direction.

Patton then saw several of Compton's tanks another hundred yards away at the base of the slope and sent his captain to order them forward immediately. When he didn't return, Patton sent his lieutenant to repeat the message, and after a while, frustrated, he marched himself down to the scene of the inaction. This was the storied moment when Patton as warrior emerged.

He discovered that one of the French machines, a Schneider (heavier and somewhat larger than the Renaults the Americans were driving), had got itself stuck at the only suitable crossing place of an enormous trench formerly occupied by the Germans. A French crew had begun digging at the banks but every time shells or bullets came near they dove back inside the trench for safety. Patton remonstrated with the French tankers and they resumed work; he then went to the American tanks and got them digging also. It was here that, when bullets or blasts frightened the Frenchmen, Patton stood on the parapet of the trench roaring, "To hell with them—they can't hit *me!*"

When a suitable passage had been excavated, Patton and others chained together several tanks for better traction and then he stood in front, backing up and leading the big machines with hand signals across the chasm the diggers had created in the enormous German trench. With about twenty of his men hit with bullets or shrapnel, Patton followed the tanks up the slope to where the stray American soldiers were waiting and told them to spread out in combat formation and follow him.

Shouting "Let's go get 'em—who's with me!" Patton started forward waving his large walking stick like the drum major of a college marching band. The soldiers jumped to their feet and followed Patton's orders until they had gone about a hundred yards over the crest of the hill where they were met with withering machine-gun fire from numerous German nests.

Everyone, Patton included, hit the dirt, but once on the ground Patton had a revelation about his ancestors, in which his grandfather, great-grandfather, and great-uncles from long ago wars appeared to him in a vision, watching him from a cloud over the distant German lines. This had a strange calming effect and Patton immediately got to his feet shouting, "Let's go! Let's go!" He began his forward march again, but only six of the men followed him this time, his orderly Angelo among them. By the time they had reached the forward battle area only Angelo remained, the others having been shot down.

Then a machine-gun bullet ripped through Patton's thigh, near his hip, and tore halfway through his body leaving a fist-size hole in his buttock. Patton tried to march on but soon stumbled and fell.

Angelo helped him into a shallow shell hole where he examined and bandaged the wound with what gauze he had and some he took from the body of a dead soldier. They were alone, the two of them, utterly pinned down by enemy machine-gun fire near the village of Cheppy. The Germans had reoccupied the railroad cut about forty yards distant and, every time Patton or Angelo showed their heads, would unleash a furious burst that skimmed the dirt rim of the shell hole. In the intervals they could hear the Germans chattering with one another.

Presently some of Patton's tanks came up, causing an immediate cessation in the German fire. Patton sent Angelo to tell the tankers where the German positions were and in no time at all two of the 37mm gun tanks had blown the enemy gunners out of the rail cut. It took the tanks more than an hour, however, to destroy all the German machine-gun nests in the area—at least twenty-five of them by some estimates. Meanwhile, one of Patton's sergeants, who had stayed behind the crest of the hill with other unarmed staff members, came forward. Patton sent him back with word that Major Brett was to command the brigade and under no circumstance was anyone to attempt to rescue him until the fire had died down. Men ran to find a stretcher, and a pigeon was released to headquarters telling of Patton's wounding. One of Patton's tanks stayed by the shell hole that he lay in, guarding him, he said, "like a watch dog."[13]

When at last it was possible to put Patton safely on a stretcher and carry him to the rear he insisted on being taken to the division headquarters to give his report before going to the hospital.

One doctor told Patton he "couldn't see how the bullet went where it did without crippling me for life." The doctor said he could not have run a probe "without either getting the hip joint, the sciatic nerve or the big artery. 'Fate' again."[14] But the wound turned septic and the doctors had to leave it open and insert drains that were uncomfortable.

Patton was removed by train—("cattle car," he said, where they were "put in racks three high")—to a recuperation hospital away from the front, where he languished in bed receiving visitors, reading, and answering mail.

★ ★ ★ ★

Although the Americans had the men, only a few were trained—let alone battle tested—by the time the First U.S. Army plunged into the forests and valleys of the Meuse-Argonne.

The Germans seemed utterly surprised, a tribute perhaps to Marshall's ability to secretly move that 400,000-man army and all its accoutrements in three days across the very face of the German front. At first the Germans gave ground—nearly three-quarters of a mile—but their resistance soon stiffened. As Marshall explained it, the problem was that inexperienced company and field-grade commanders lost control of their units after reaching their objectives and failed to exploit the gains by continuing the attack with the enemy on the run. In addition, the fast-moving armies had outrun their supplies and artillery support and needed time to regather.

Thus some of the political class (which rarely missed an opportunity for exploitation) began to grouse that the American army was failing and in some cases had already failed. Though there was no foundation for the scurrilous rumormongering, it soon found its way into newspapers, giving rise on Pershing's staff to speculation that these were actually political attacks centered on who would wield the power should a surrender or an armistice conference be declared. To some, it even appeared the gossip was mired in jealousy or envy that an upstart army could arrive after nearly four years of catastrophic war and claim credit for being in on the end. Marshall appraised it later as an even more sinister plot "that grew by leaps and bounds and like a snowball continued to gather weight and size . . . apparently for the purpose of depreciating the American [war] effort in order to weaken Mr. Wilson's powerful position."

Marshall also vented his anger at America's unpreparedness in not raising and training a large army much earlier on. "Everywhere on the battlefield individuals were paying the price," he said. "They paid with their lives and their limbs for the bullheaded obstinacy with which our people had opposed any system of training in time of peace."[15]

Meanwhile, the Central Powers had already begun crumbling as the attack in the Meuse-Argonne pressed on. The Germans gave ground grudgingly as casualties mounted heavily on both sides. Bulgaria had already signed an armistice with the Allies, and Austria was now threatening to seek one. The Turks had been driven by the British "in wild flight" from the Middle East, and Ludendorff was recommending to the kaiser that Germany seek some kind of peace agreement through the Americans, whom he thought would give them a better deal than the British or French.

By the first of October the French Fourth Army was lagging behind the fast-moving Americans, leaving the Americans' left flank "in the air,"* a situation the battlewise Germans quickly exploited by cutting off what came to be famously known as the "Lost Battalion." For five days this forlorn unit of the U.S. 77th Division lay benighted and besieged by the Germans, who had them surrounded and trapped in the wilds of the Argonne Forest. Gallantly, the approximately 555 men under Major Charles Whittlesey, a New York Wall Street lawyer, held their own against superior German forces until they were at last rescued on October 7 by the 82nd Infantry Division; the battalion, however, had lost some 350 men in the fray.

During this time George Marshall roamed over the battle area, cajoling, urging, ordering commanders, in the name of the commanding general, to reorganize and move forward.

Marshall put himself on hand to see that they followed those instructions. He was particularly concerned that he and his staff workers should share the privations of the front so that they would understand what it

---

* Both flanks need constant protection and security lest an enemy get into the unprotected rear of the formation.

was like when "Life became a succession of dangers, discomforts and hungers, with a continuous pressure being exerted on the individual to do more than he felt himself or his organization capable of accomplishing."[16]

★ ★ ★ ★

MEANWHILE, THERE WERE STILL 230 German machine-gun nests on the Côte de Châtillon and it "seemed almost impossible to move without getting shot." Ever since the offensive began, men had fallen around MacArthur but he appeared so magically untouched that his soldiers began to say he was "bulletproof."[17]

The battle had a profound effect on MacArthur. One night he was reconnoitering the German flank for a thin spot in the wire after the brigade had been held up all day on the Côte de Châtillon and his patrol suddenly came under a terrific enemy shelling and machine-gun fire. The men fell into craters to wait out the barrage and, when at last the flares had burned out, MacArthur crept from shell hole to shell hole whispering for the men to follow him. Getting no response, he shook the soldiers, thinking they had fallen asleep from exhaustion. But they were "all stone dead."

The journalist Frazier Hunt of the *Chicago Tribune* was hanging around outside MacArthur's headquarters when the general briefly returned during a slight lull in the action. Noticing a bullet hole in the sleeve of MacArthur's sweater Hunt asked, "When did brigadier generals get to be expendable?"

MacArthur laughed, embarrassed. "There are times when even generals have to be expendable," he said. "Come inside and we'll rustle up some coffee."[18]

The next day, MacArthur's brigade fought and clawed its way up one hill and around the other until at last, as night was falling, the 167th Alabama stealthily worked its way through a gap in the German wire. Every moment it seemed would bring a burst of machine-gun fire, or blasts from hidden German 77s, or a deadly explosion of enemy mortar shells from hidden positions.

Then out of the mists would suddenly appear Americans with bayoneted rifles, grim faced and bloodshot. On October 16, after three days of slaughter, Captain Thomas H. Fallow observed three companies' soldiers from the 167th Alabama pinned down by German machine-gun fire. He had had enough. He rose up and "jumped out in front of the men," leading a mass charge on the machine-gun nests. This produced an unexpected reaction in the German gunners, who, seeing the Americans "swarming down the hill in droves," jumped up and ran away, leaving even their guns behind.[19]

It was charges such as this that dispatched the Boche until, as dusk fell, MacArthur's 84th Brigade had silenced the last German resistance and the Bois de Châtillon and the Tuileries Ferme were in American hands. The price was high, however—awful, really. Of the Iowa regiment's original twenty-five officers and 1,425 men, only 300 men and six officers were still standing, and the 167th Alabama took similar casualties. "That is the way the Côte-de-Châtillon fell," MacArthur said afterward, "and that is the way those gallant citizen-soldiers won the approach to final victory."[20]

MacArthur's breakthrough at the Krunhilde Stalling put the Americans in rear of the Hindenburg Line, an untenable position, and the entire German army began to evacuate to the Meuse River, leaving behind tons of supplies and equipment that were invaluable and irreplaceable.

★ ★ ★ ★

FOR HIS PART, the kaiser was waffling about abdicating his throne—which obviously would have been a condition of any armistice request—proclaiming that "a successor to Frederick the Great does not abdicate." He blamed Germany's present woes on Jews and Communists, a dubious elucidation that was quickly seized upon by a woebegone Austrian-born corporal named Adolf Hitler somewhere in the lower ranks of the German army.

On October 4, 1918, President Woodrow Wilson received a telegram through German diplomats remaining in New York asking him to intervene with the British and French to call an armistice. Ferdinand Foch, now convinced that victory was in his grasp, was aware of this and determined to crush the German army before such a thing could happen. Thus racing against an armistice he now feared, Foch ordered an enormous assault by both French and American armies set for November 1.

Within two hours of the initial push, it was reported that the Americans had punched through the German line and were fanning out across the countryside. This sent the Germans into a general retreat while a mutiny convulsed the German navy and socialist riots broke out in almost every large city in Germany. Clearly the end was near and Foch was determined at least to capture Sedan. Because of the laggard French Fourth Army, it now lay squarely in the path of the Americans and Marshall had issued orders to take the city. But Pershing generously overruled his operations officer so the French could have the satisfaction of reconquering this emotional and symbolic landmark.

Marshall was in the process of issuing further orders for the Meuse-Argonne attack when word came down that the Germans were negotiating with the Allies and an armistice was declared beginning on November 11, 1918.

In some so-called quiet parts of the Western Front there was wild celebrating with German and Allied troops meeting in no-man's-land to trade caps, badges, and other souvenirs, and some French troops were said to have festooned their uniforms with flowers. But in those parts of the line where the fighting had been heavy there were still bad feelings and the Germans lay resentfully behind their fortifications with some weeping and much ugly muttering. In the British sectors, the mood was somber as well, and little was heard save an occasional rendition of "God Save the King" by a regimental band. Many on both sides merely poked their heads up above the trench line and looked around, as larks and other birds wheeled overhead, astonished that they weren't shot at.

★ ★ ★ ★

THE AMERICANS, IT WAS SAID, cheered wildly, which seems a bit odd considering that they had sustained more than 122,000 casualties—26,227 of them killed since the Battle of the Argonne Forest began six weeks earlier.* Many of them were from Patton's division. Of the officers, Patton had two majors, seven captains, and thirty-six lieutenants in the fight. Of these, both majors and all but one captain were hit, as well as seventeen of the lieutenants—plus himself. Almost all the tanks were either destroyed or rendered inoperable. On October 1 alone, fifty-nine of eighty-nine tanks that went into the battle were lost. Finally the outfit was reduced to a company-size "provisional" unit assigned to the 42nd Rainbow Division, consisting of twenty tanks, ten officers, and 140 men—all that was left of Patton's First Tank Brigade. And by the end of that day only 80 men remained of the original 834 who had started out the week.

On October 17 Patton received word that he had been promoted to full colonel and had been put in for the Distinguished Service Cross, America's second highest medal for valor. He told Beatrice he'd rather have the medal than the promotion.

One of his friends, a major in the French army, visited Patton at the hospital and said this: "My dear Patton, I am so glad you are wounded. For when you left I said to my wife that is the end of Patton. He is one of those gallant fellows who always gets killed." Patton wrote his father, "You know I have always feared I was a coward at heart but I am beginning to doubt it."

The battle for the Meuse-Argonne roared on for forty-seven days, until the war ended, inflicting 122,063 American casualties, the highest casualty rate of any U.S. battle, before or since. Patton finally got rid of his bandage the day that peace was declared, which was coincidentally his thirty-third birthday. To celebrate, or commiserate, he wrote a poem entitled "Peace—November 11, 1918," the last stanza of which is fraught with insolence and as much awful meaning as a Greek tragedy.

....

* This was by far the nation's deadliest battle. By comparison, at the Battle of Gettysburg in the American Civil War the *combined* total of battle deaths of both Union and Confederate soldiers was 7,863.

Then pass in peace, blood-gutted Boche
And when we too shall fall,
We'll clasp in yours our gory hands
In High Valhalla's Hall.

★ ★ ★ ★

THE RAINBOW DIVISION WAS PULLED OUT of the fighting to rest, heal its wounds, and receive replacements. It remained on the deadly killing ground near the Krunhilde Stalling and the Côte de Châtillon and was there when the armistice was announced. There was no cheering, for the men were "glad beyond expression," according to the regimental historian. The regimental chaplain of the 167th Alabama held an impromptu service in a half-ruined church. One of the members of the band played a doxology on the old organ, while more than three hundred men poured out their thankfulness by singing "Praise God from Whom All Blessings Flow."

Afterward they were told to march to the Rhine River and occupy a sector of Germany on its border with France. It took three days of walking but on December 16, 1918, the brigade marched down the valley of the Rhine with the regimental bands playing "The Star-Spangled Banner"—except for the 167th Alabama, whose band played "Dixie" for the curious and bewildered German spectators who lined the roads. During this procession, almost magically, the regimental historian said, a giant rainbow appeared over the valley of the Rhine.[21]

The Rainbow Division was largely MacArthur's creation and he would soon be appointed its commanding officer when General Menoher was given a corps to command. Secretary of War Baker continued to be fulsome in his compliments of MacArthur, calling him "the greatest American field commander produced by the war." Menoher was probably closer to the truth when, in citing MacArthur for promotion, he wrote, "On a field where courage was the rule, his courage was the dominant factor."

The Rainbow Division continued to rankle Pershing and other martinets but the soldiers remained oblivious. By comparisons such as ground gained, prisoners taken, enemy killed, days in combat, and decorations awarded, the 42nd Rainbow Division was second only to the Second Division, half of which was composed of marines. "They couldn't salute worth a damn and cared less what they looked like. The only thing they did superbly was fight."[22]

MacArthur was put in for the Medal of Honor but Pershing's head-quarters disapproved the recommendation.* Instead he received a second Distinguished Service Cross and his seventh Silver Star, which "more than satisfied my martial vanity," MacArthur said.[23]

★ ★ ★ ★

FOR HIS PART, George Marshall had missed coming out of the war with a general's star by only a hair, but he would face a long wait—sixteen more years, to be exact—a stern test in the backwaters for a man who could have resigned and entered civilian life at any point very high on the hog. But George Marshall was a soldier, and he was determined to rise as high as possible in the service of his country.

---

* Pershing did not think that officers, and especially general officers, should get the Medal of Honor, and furthermore he believed it should be awarded only in specific cases of uncommon valor.

PART II

BETWEEN THE WARS

★ ★ ★ ★

Chapter Six

THE SAD, GREAT HEAP OF *FLEURS BLANCHES*

Colonel George Marshall did not return to America and his devoted wife, Lily, until August 1919, almost two years since they had last seen each other. After the armistice with Germany, the question arose—posed chiefly by two of the major Allies, England and France, as well as by General Pershing himself—of whether or not Germany should be subjected to a major military occupation, including its capital, Berlin, for the purpose of proving to the German people that its army had been beaten.

Marshall was dead set against the proposal and said so in a letter to Pershing. It would be a different matter, he said, if occupation was required to put down an insurrection by the German Bolsheviks, but otherwise he proposed that the Allies send food to the defeated and starving Germans. This would later mark him as a target for criticism when, in the 1930s, Hitler rose to power partly because of his assertion that Germany had not been defeated on the battlefield but instead sabotaged by a craven government.

Most of Marshall's duty after the armistice was spent dealing with the nearly two million American soldiers in France who needed to be fed, clothed, and kept occupied and healthy in the face of one of the most deadly flu epidemics in history. After the continuous stress of planning for battles during the war, it might have seemed like a routine chore, were it not for the size of the undertaking.*

In April, Marshall went to Metz to receive the Legion of Honor and the Croix de Guerre, along with other members of Pershing's staff. By this juncture Marshall had decided to keep the army as a career, despite being offered $30,000 a year (about $400,000 in today's money) to join J. P. Morgan & Co. by one of the firm's partners, Dwight Morrow, who had become a top civilian aide to Pershing. Instead of leaving for Wall Street, Marshall became Pershing's aide-de-camp, even though he knew it would keep him from troop duty.

From then on, Marshall and Pershing were caught up in the vast ceremonies of victory, beginning in France with a bittersweet grand parade through Paris on Bastille Day 1919. The four years of war had been so horrendous—some ten million soldiers from both sides lay dead, millions more were maimed for life, and at least seven million civilians had also perished; entire nations were prostrated physically, spiritually, and monetarily—that it took more than half a year for anyone to contemplate a celebration of anything connected with the conflict. It was inevitable, however, that the victorious countries ultimately would need to find a way to memorialize the struggle.[1]

On a warm July morning, millions of spectators thronged to watch the parade down the Champs-Élysées to the Place de la Concorde, thence past the Church of the Madeleine, which had unfurled huge red banners between its magnificent Corinthian columns, to the reviewing stand at the Place de la République. At the Arc de Triomphe lay a single white casket, representing the 1.4 million French soldiers (nearly 4 percent of

---

* The Spanish influenza epidemic of 1917–19 killed nearly as many U.S. servicemen as had died in the war itself—almost 50,000 of them on both sides of the Atlantic. Marshall, of course, was charged with trying to help control the problem.

the population) who had fallen in the war, decorated by wreaths placed upon it by President Poincaré and Premier Clemenceau. The parade itself was led by a somber procession of a thousand mutilated veterans—lame, armless, legless, and blinded victims of the fighting—the *invalides* who came in wheelchairs and carts and on crutches to receive their thanks from the grateful throng.

Following this were Marshals Foch and Joseph Joffre and their staffs, on horseback, who arrived amid passionate cheering. Next came General Pershing and more wild accolades, followed by his staff including Marshall on a prancing white horse. Following them was the American "Victory Regiment," composed of one thousand crack U.S. soldiers marching with superb military precision.

Next came the British, Italians, Canadians, Algerians, Japanese, Senegalese, Australians, Serbs, Czechs, Poles, Portuguese, and others of the twenty warring nations of the Allies, each with accompanying marching troops (all except the Russians, who were not invited)—followed at last by the French with all the shining brass and polished steel for which its army was rightly famous. Marshall was deeply stirred by "the great military spectacle" of which he was now also a part, and he would have vivid memories of it for the remainder of his life.

After several hours, the parade and its accompanying exultation passed by and a great hush settled over the banks of spectators lining the famous *places* and *boulevards* and *avenues*. It now became the turn of the French people to mourn their loved ones. In single file they came all afternoon, and into the night, walking silently though the triumphal arch—the war-worn, heartbroken, *mesdames* and *mademoiselles* misty-eyed beneath their black veils, and the *mères* and *pères,* the *enfants* and *frères* and *soeurs* of the dead, each clutching a single white flower, often grown in their own gardens or window boxes, to place on the white casket, until by the end of the day there had risen a great sad heap of these *fleurs blanches,* like a big snowbank or a dune, covering where the casket lay.

★ ★ ★ ★

General Pershing, with Colonel Marshall now his aide, then embarked to England for the massive victory celebration, where Winston Churchill, now secretary of state for war, greeted them at London's Victoria Station.

For the rest of the week the American contingent was feted to luncheons and dinners with more counts, dukes, duchesses, etc., than inhabit a Shakespeare play. Marshall met the king and queen and sat next to princes and princesses of all nations during the ongoing festivities. He attended garden parties, balls, formal dinners, cotillions, and drunkouts with various celebrants, whose ranks included Lady Curzon, the prince of Wales, Mrs. John Jacob Astor, and the governor of Jerusalem.

Mrs. Astor's sister, the American socialite Nora Langhorne, was among those who caught Marshall's attention. "She was in a great gale and was very amusing," according to a notation in his diary. "She had on a black velvet cap, like students in the Latin Quarter wear, and was trying to pass herself off as one of that class."[2]

A formal dance that was given the night before the great victory parade seemed more in the nature of a melee. Marshall, for example, "had the pleasure of stepping on the foot of the King of Portugal, who was sitting on the sidelines" and who "looked quite furious," but no apologies were forthcoming as Marshall whirled right past. Meanwhile, according to Marshall's diary, General Pershing stepped on the foot of Princess Victoria "and left a black spot on her slipper," which she told a lady-in-waiting she intended to keep "as a souvenir."[3] These affairs, Marshall noted, often lasted until two or three o'clock in the morning, convivially fueled by whiskey and champagne. At one point in the proceedings, Marshall found an open window and lay down on the floor "to take a nap" but was awakened by other revelers and sent back into the fray.

★ ★ ★ ★

At the victory parade itself there was more consternation when it turned out that General Andre Brewster, the AEF's inspector general, was unable to manage the horse provided him by the British army. Marshall earlier had picked out a "nice, quiet-looking" horse for himself, but being an accomplished rider he offered to swap with the general and soon found himself aboard an animal that was "both fractious and vicious."

The crowd along the route of march was dense and enthusiastic, which, said Marshall, "did not add to the peace of mind of my animal [and] for eight miles I had the ride of my life." The horse, it seemed, "tried to kick everything in reach," and actually may have struck a small girl in the face. It refused to go straight, instead "going sideways," and every time Marshall would try to straighten it out it would buck and rear. This delighted the crowd, and they cheered even more wildly, which made the beast frantic.

When they reached Admiralty Arch, packed with spectators, Marshall was petrified that his horse "would have killed a few if I had allowed him to go sideways." Instead, when Marshall tried to straighten him out, the horse not only reared but reared so high that he toppled over backward. Marshall managed to jump off and roll out of the way and, as the horse was struggling to rise, he scrambled back aboard, having fractured a bone in his hand.

"As it was," Marshall said, "I entered the Arch on a horse, and came out of it on a horse—and did not even lose my place in the lineup. But," he added, "I lost my temper for the rest of the ride."[4]

After Marshall passed the Royal Pavilion where the king and queen were reviewing the parade he at last was able to rid himself of the disagreeable creature ("with a curse!" he said) and join others of Pershing's staff in stands where they watched the rest of the procession.

A national holiday had been declared and the festivities in England continued unabated as mobs of citizens thronged the streets dancing, singing, and drinking tankerloads of beer and ale. Though the people scarcely understood it at the time, this would mark the beginning of a social upheaval in Britain, which, like France, had lost nearly .4 percent of its population in the war.

But of the millions who had survived the fighting or had otherwise contributed to the war effort, many would not be content to return to the stern, prewar class-driven society from which they had been hurled into the trenches. This was just as true for the millions of British servants, plowmen, miners, hod carriers, and other menial workers who gleefully broke out in a novel popular song:

> *What shall we be . . .*
> *When we aren't what we are?*[5]

On August 19 Pershing and Marshall returned to France and embarked on a poignant tour of the battlefields of the war, in particular those upon which American blood had been shed.

After visiting Verdun, Pershing's party traveled to the Saint-Mihiel and Meuse-Argonne battlefields. Pershing wanted to see the massive new cemetery at Romagne where twenty-two thousand Americans were buried, and he lingered for some time in the vast graveyard. He walked up and down the seemingly endless rows of white crosses, somber and preoccupied as a man who has sent that many men to their deaths must be, even if he was convinced the cause was just. The commanding general of the American Expeditionary Forces must also have been contemplating his relationship with George Patton's sister, Nita. We have nothing in the historical record on Pershing's feelings during this period, but we can speculate that following the great outpouring after the victory he found himself much in demand by practically every eligible woman in Europe and America. That must have been on his mind.

Their train took Marshall and Pershing next to the Champagne, Château-Thierry, and Marne battlefields, and the following day by car they visited Soissons and the spot where the Germans had positioned their monster 240mm "Paris guns"—enormous Krupp factory railroad cannons with 110-foot barrels, which they used to bombard the city from eighty miles away. Marshall and Pershing went then to Lens in the British sector, a scene of utter destruction and desolation. Marshall later wrote, "To see a city, a great manufacturing center as large as San Francisco, completely leveled to the ground, gives one a better conception of the horrors of war than anything else."[6]

A train carried them north to the killing fields of Belgian Flanders and the battles around Ypres, another pulverized city, where markers for nearly 300,000 British soldiers testified to the hideous intensity of the war in that sector during the four years it lasted.*

After returning to Paris for a week, Pershing and Marshall set out for a whirlwind tour of the Italian battlefields, which turned out to be as much a goodwill tour as anything else. By train they visited Turin, Genoa, Venice, and Rome, greeted everywhere by formal ceremonies, luncheons, dinners, complete with brass bands, or orchestras if the occasion rose to it, declarations of national fealty, cheek kissing, and so forth. At Rome they met the king and someone took Pershing around to explain the ruins to him, while Marshall, as it was mid-August, begged off in favor of a bath.

★ ★ ★ ★

ON SEPTEMBER 1, 1919, Marshall and Pershing boarded the SS *Leviathan* (formerly the German liner *Vaterland,* seized by the United States at the beginning of the war) and arrived in New York City five days later to yet another tumultuous reception. Pershing and his staff, Marshall of course included, led the way to a gigantic ticker-tape victory parade up Broadway and eventually through the triumphal arch at Washington Square. After the obligatory rounds of banquets, receptions, and eternal speeches, the general's party attended similar congratulatory demonstrations at Philadelphia and Washington, D.C., before it all settled down again to the regular army routine. Marshall, like most colonels, lost his rank after the war and was demoted to captain, a rank of unhappy prospects when the army was reduced from more than four million men to a permanent 297,800, set by an act of Congress. Young officers had to wait for older officers to retire before getting promoted themselves.

---

* This includes 95,000 men whose remains were never found; they had simply been blasted to nothingness by the almost constant shelling. Their names are carved on the walls of the Menin Gate and the Tyne Cot British cemetery. British deaths in Flanders alone exceeded the entire number of Americans killed in World War II.

Marshall and Lily rented an apartment in the Adams Morgan section of the District of Columbia, across the street from Rock Creek Park with its many riding trails. Her frailty prevented childbirth, but the couple struck up a friendship with a precocious eight-year-old neighbor, Rose Page, who visited their apartment and often ate meals there. The Marshalls became her godparents when she was confirmed and the friendship lasted a lifetime.

Meanwhile, Pershing, who still commanded the AEF, which was, in effect, the U.S. Army, got into a kind of permanent row with the army's chief of staff. General Peyton C. March assumed that Pershing was his inferior; after commanding four million men Pershing thought no such thing, and the two men quarreled so bitterly that Marshall was often forced to play referee.

One bone of contention was the question of what size and shape the postwar army would assume, and it became a feverish political football in the years immediately following the war. Liberals, labor unions, and even big business favored a small peacetime army, for both economic and humanitarian reasons. They contended that the size of the German army before the war had led to that nation's militarism, while others argued that the immense costs of the war would prohibit the United States from maintaining a large permanent army. Pershing was of this mind as well, and he had approved a plan under which a smaller army would still be strong enough to handle lesser conflicts such as the Philippine insurrection, but also more than competent to train and organize a huge army of citizen soldiers if the occasion ever were to arise. At present, that possibility seemed so remote that people had begun routinely calling the late world conflict "the war to end all wars."

Pershing's stubbornness, his sternness, and his intransigence might have intimidated a lesser officer but Marshall was in fact just as stubborn, and often just as stern. In later years he recalled an incident in which Pershing, after he had replaced General March as army chief of staff, proposed a change in a military procedure that March had initiated. When he sent the proposal to Marshall for comment, Marshall's endorsement said that Pershing was "entirely wrong," and soon enough he was summoned to the general's office.

"I don't take to this at all. I don't agree with you," Pershing scowled.

"Well now, General, I have done a poor job on this," Marshall said. "Let me have the paper again."

So he rewrote his endorsement to tell Pershing in a whole different way that he was still wrong, and again Marshall received a summons to the general's office where Pershing slapped his hand on his desk and cried, "No by God! We will do it this way!"

"Now General," Marshall told his boss, "just because you hate the guts of General March, you're setting yourself up—and General Harbord, who hates him too—to do something you know damn well is wrong."

At this, Pershing returned the paper, grumbling indignantly, "Well, have it your way." And that, Marshall said, "was the end of the affair."[7]

Marshall was in the forefront of the practical world of army chiefs of staff, and he became indispensable to Pershing as he met frequently with President Warren G. Harding and his cabinet members, congressmen and senators of all parties, and foreign dignitaries. He wrote Pershing's speeches and sometimes even gave them for him. During the general's frequent absences and trips abroad, Marshall functioned almost entirely in his stead, acquiring in the process practically every nuance of the chief of staff.

★ ★ ★ ★

THE CLOSE OF THE WAR ALSO BROUGHT a bittersweet end to the romance between General Pershing and George Patton's sister Nita. In the spring of 1919 she had arrived in London to visit her sister-in-law Kay Merrill when Pershing wrote, asking to postpone their engagement announcement because "the feeling was gone." Not only that, but he had failed to include her on the guest list for the great victory gala in Paris on July 3. Brokenhearted and humiliated, Nita replied by returning the engagement ring.

Although he had counseled his sister not to come to France during the war, Patton now made entreaties to her to go to Paris for a "dignified reunion," but it was no good. Pershing was, in the words of Beatrice, "wined and dined and flattered and praised by the great and the near great and some of the most beautiful women in Europe who were not above falling at his feet to gain something for their heart's interests." Nita, she continued, "with her blond Viking good looks . . . and good sense . . . removed herself with all flags flying."

Neither Nita nor Pershing would marry, and several years later after turning down another suitor Nita wrote her aunt Nannie, "I am fated to be free. Unless I could mate with a master, I'd better steer clear of the shoals." In the estimation of her niece she "spent the rest of her life taking care of everyone."[8]

Beatrice had an even darker observation about Pershing after he had become chief of staff and a regular at their dinner table; she told her daughter Bee that "the General Pershing you children know is not the Black Jack Pershing" their aunt Nita had fallen in love with. "Lots of men die in wars but some of them with very strong bodies go on living long after the person inside of them is dead," Beatrice said. "They are dead because they have used themselves all up in the war. That's one of the most terrible things about war."[9]

On September 16, 1919, following the great victory hullabaloo in New York City, Patton had joined behind Pershing and Marshall in the Pershing "Triumph" parade in Washington. "I am to command the tanks," he wrote his mother, seriously doubting whether any of the American-made machines would finish the parade "as the engine usually [conks] out after about five miles." Peace, however, was Purgatory for George Patton, if not Hell itself. He was thoroughly a warrior—or a racehorse, as his friend and brother-in-law Fred Ayer likened him, a stallion penned in a small corral always kicking at the rails to get out. He was not without his humor and charm during this period, but Patton could also be rude, bitter, and cruel as events went against him and he watched his beloved tank corps and, in time, the very army he loved crumble before his eyes.

Like George Marshall, Patton lost his wartime rank and reverted to captain, but within seventeen months he had climbed back up the ladder to major. His first assignment was at Fort Meade, Maryland, which had become home to the U.S. Army Tank Corps.

For the first several months, Patton spent the majority of his time in Washington, on the board of a committee, preparing a series of reports on the future role of the tank. Its role in war was well studied and of increasing importance; its role in peace was not so certain, especially considering how dramatically the country's mood had changed in the 1920s. Tanks were expensive to build and expensive to keep up, but the nation had turned the page from militaristic to isolationist, as George Marshall, too, had found. The U.S. Army was quietly being relegated to the backwaters of America's attention.

Beatrice brought the family to Fort Meade, even though it was only sixty miles from their home in a fashionable section of Washington. For the Patton children, the fact that "daddy was home" soon became "far below our expectations," according to Ruth Ellen, then six.

"Everything I did was wrong," she said.

Much later Ruth Ellen put it in perspective. "I realize now that he was in considerable pain at the time . . . having a hangover from the war, which is a very real thing." She spoke of the "shrinking command of a handful of men and the narrowing horizons of peacetime duty"— and then the "tender trap" of home and family. "It is a let-down," she wrote, adding, "I guess things didn't come up to Georgie's [her father's] expectations either."[10]

Patton bought a very expensive Pierce-Arrow automobile because, he said, "I can afford it, and the war's over." When his efficiency report arrived from France it rated him "one of the strongest officers in the Army," and he was awarded the Distinguished Service Medal. He told his father he believed it was only the second time an officer had been awarded both the Distinguished Service Cross and the DSM—the other being MacArthur—but he was wrong. He gave all the credit and honors for the award to the officers and men of his tank corps. "They won the medal and fortune pinned it on him."[11]

In fall 1920 Patton returned to the cavalry branch of service—not only because he believed that on the battlefield of the future the tank would ultimately supplant the horse for reconnaissance and mobile shock value, but also because of his love for horses. At a time when even his colonel-ranked peers had to exercise frugality, Patton acquired a gorgeous string of polo ponies and became, in time, one of the finest polo players in the army. It was a highly skilled sport that required great confidence, foresight, and reaction. It was also very dangerous; broken bones and gashes from polo mallets were regular occurrences and death was not uncommon. For Patton it was a poor substitute for war, but it filled a void in him that almost obsessively craved perilous activity.

In time Patton came around to relaxing with the family. He bought a dog for the children, a white bull terrier that they named Tank, and soon he began to enthrall the youngsters—Ruth Ellen and Bee—by regaling them with elaborate fables made out of whole cloth from the medieval history he knew so well. Fabulous raconteur that he was, Patton's tales were filled with gallant knights, beautiful ladies, and horrible fiends "with no detail left to the imagination," Ruth Ellen wrote much later. "As the stuff of history is often cruel and bawdy and bloody and unfair, that's the way [he] told it," she said.[12]

★ ★ ★ ★

IT WAS AROUND THIS TIME that Patton met Dwight D. Eisenhower, also a lieutenant colonel, five years his junior, who had graduated from West Point in 1915—"the class the stars fell on." While Patton had been in France fighting Germans, Eisenhower had established and run the army's largest tank training center near Gettysburg, Pennsylvania. Frustrated that he never went to France, Eisenhower complained, "I suppose we'll spend the rest of our lives explaining why we didn't get into this war."[13]

The two men could hardly have been less alike in temperament—or more alike in ambition. They were also neighbors and played poker twice a week, not to mention rode, hunted and fished, and made Prohibition-era homebrew and bathtub gin together. Once they even staked out a dangerous road at night, armed to the teeth, looking to foil a highway robber who never took the bait.

Mostly they shared a common interest in the future of the tank, and the two became nothing less than zealots in absorbing every aspect of tank warfare, from the vehicle itself, to its armaments, to its usage on the field of battle. A new-styled tank created by a New Jersey inventor named J. Walter Christie intrigued them. It could travel up to sixty miles per hour, climb a two-and-a-half-foot wall, and jump a seven-foot ditch. Patton soon began working with Christie and his armored inventions—including a forerunner of the amphibious tank—in what would be a decade-long collaboration. Some said he personally financed Christie too.

But during those austere years, as the cavalry was being phased out of the army, few mechanized vehicles were brought in to replace horses. This was so frustrating to young, talented officers like Patton and Eisenhower that the two retorted by publishing articles in the *Infantry Journal* suggesting, among other things, that the tank would someday lead the infantry into battle.

The motto of the U.S. Infantry is "Follow Me," so this kind of heresy naturally elicited a strong response, including reprimands to both men from high-ranking infantry officers in the Washington military bureaucracy.

Even worse, during the congressional sessions to reorganize the army after the war, despite pleas by Secretary of War Newton Baker, Chief of Staff Peyton March, and the enormously influential Major General Charles P. Summerall to make the Tank Corps an independent branch of the army, opposing testimony by Pershing "sounded the death knell" of it. Instead, the Tank Corps was placed under the supervision of the chief of infantry and eventually would lose both its identity and its raison d'être—a bitter pill for Patton and his courageous pioneers whose blood stained the battlefields of Europe.

Given that the tank was now under the infantry, Patton would have to decide whether to change branches of service. With the Tank Corps' future seemingly at a dead end, Patton became once more the beau ideal of the gentleman cavalry officer. More than ever, he enjoyed the romance of that elite and social organization—foxhunting, playing polo, skeet shooting, tennis, engaging in events in swordsmanship, horse racing, and steeplechasing.

That same year, from the gloomy, greasy, dusty tank laagers of Fort Meade, Maryland, he was transferred to the spit-and-polish greenswards of Fort Myer, Virginia, where he arrived with a veritable stable full of animals to assume command of a squadron (battalion) of the Third U.S. Cavalry Regiment.

The Pattons moved into a spacious brick Victorian house at number 5 Officers Row, while George settled into running the business of the Third Squadron, which at Fort Myer was a mostly ceremonial unit that escorted funerals of dignitaries at the adjacent Arlington National Cemetery or rode in parades. This gave Patton plenty of time for his recreational sports at the various foxhunting clubs in northern Virginia and he and Beatrice became regulars on the high society social circuits in the Roaring Twenties in and about the capital city.

That is not to suggest that Patton had become a dilettante or a dabbler. He took his duties as a trainer of military men very seriously; in fact, his corps program was to train his officers to be trainers, and he personally delivered a lecture to his charges nearly every other day.[14]

Patton was a superior teacher and he drilled into his men his own special tenets of cavalry warfare. "Success in War," he wrote, "depends upon the Golden Rule of War: Speed-Simplicity-Boldness." "Offensive combat," he insisted, "consists of FIRE and MOVEMENT. The purpose of FIRE is to permit MOVEMENT." A leader, he said, if things go badly, "must ride up and rally his men personally." If his men still break and run, then the leader "SHOULD NOT SURVIVE IT. THERE IS NOTHING MORE PATHETIC AND FUTILE THAN A GENERAL WHO LIVES LONG ENOUGH TO EXPLAIN A DEFEAT."[15]

He also created at Fort Myer a monumentally successful money-raising ploy for the Soldiers Rest and Recreation Fund, a charity designed to help the enlisted men whose pay was so low that most could not even afford to marry, let alone partake of other off-post delights. Patton organized and inaugurated a succession of spectacular exhibitions in Fort Myer's large indoor riding arena. With nearly eighteen hundred spectators looking on, what came to be known as the Society Circus was held every Friday afternoon from January to April. It featured jumping, trick riding stunts, and acrobatics by the cavalrymen, as well as large routines involving music and dozens of riders performing precision drills. Soon these spaces were filled by the area debutantes and their families—the young ladies always interested in some handsome eligible bachelor officer. In succeeding years the event was held on Sunday afternoons, and wealthy families as well as cabinet members, congressmen, and senators bought boxes in which they threw fashionable luncheon parties while the regiment's expert horsemen entertained in the riding ring. The coffers of the Soldiers Rest and Recreation Fund swelled while Patton himself immensely enjoyed riding, jumping, and "doing his stuff" in front of the crowd.

Whenever Patton was not working or playing polo he darted off to horse shows up and down the East Coast, bringing back basketsful of ribbons and enough silver cups to line an entire wall at number 5 Officers Row. While training with the army polo team on Long Island, in the summer of 1922, Patton managed to make friends with the likes of the Belmonts, Harrimans, and other society swells, remarking in a letter to Beatrice that "These are the nicest rich people I have ever seen."

But beneath this veneer of social status and sportsmanship Patton seethed. Without a war to fight, he was bitter and unhappy, even lapsing into depressions that today might be diagnosed as bipolar disorder. When in a foul mood, he would do and say outlandish things, mostly to gauge the reaction of the unsuspecting. George Marshall said of him, "He would say outrageous things and then look at you to see how it registered; curse and then go write a hymn."[*, 16]

Yet Patton persevered. In 1923 during a day-sailing trip in rough seas off Salem, Massachusetts, Patton and Bea came upon a small capsized boat and managed to fish out of the water three boys who would have undoubtedly drowned had the Pattons not come to the rescue.

* Marshall's second wife, Katherine, would later confront Patton after some particularly boorish remark at Fort Myer. "George, you mustn't talk like that," she told him. "You say these outrageous things and then you look at me to see if I'm going to smile. Now you could do that as a captain or a major, but you aspire to be a general, and generals cannot talk in such a wild way."

Newspapers gave the story great play, and Patton was once again lauded as a hero.

Later that year, he attended the Advanced Officers Course of the U.S. Army's Cavalry School at Fort Riley, Kansas, finishing in the top percentile of his class. While there, he became a master at the machine gun, in addition to his swordsmanship. Patton's high standing entitled him to attend the rigorous Army General Service school (ultimately the Command and General Staff College), where, according to Patton's daughter, "more homes are broken up, there are more suicides and more cases of battered children from the tour at Leavenworth than anyone will ever officially know."[17] The competition to get high rankings—thus raising chances for promotion—was so great as to push men beyond their limits.

It was therefore doubly troubling for Patton when he was one day, in December 1923, summoned before the board and told that he had been accused of using an unauthorized study aid—in effect, cheating—that consisted of a mysterious bluish light that he allegedly employed while reading texts. The embarrassed Patton had to explain that he had recently purchased a "purple light" that purportedly was able to cure baldness, and a classmate who was passing by Patton's quarters while he studied at a desk by the window had apparently noticed it. "He stopped using the light—he went on getting bald," his daughter said.[18]

★ ★ ★ ★

THERE WAS NO GRAND HERO'S WELCOME for Douglas MacArthur and his famed 42nd Rainbow Division when they arrived in New York on the ocean liner *Leviathan* (ex-*Vaterland*) on April 25, 1919. Neither the division—whose soldiers had voted against "any welcoming parades"—nor American citizens, who by then "had tired of parading doughboys," were upset that they didn't have to engage in another great extravaganza. The soldiers, however, were nevertheless disappointed when the great ship pulled to the dock and barely a soul was there to greet them save for a "small urchin who asked if we had been in France," said MacArthur. He himself was dressed in an enormous raccoon-skin coat that he acquired from God knows where, and a long scarf knitted by his mother, Pinky. "We marched off the dock to be scattered to the four winds—a sad, gloomy end of the Rainbow."[19]

MacArthur received orders to report to the chief of staff of the army in Washington, who immediately appointed him superintendent of the United States Military Academy, informing the startled thirty-nine-year-old brigadier that "West Point is forty years behind the times."

It was too true. During the course of the war, the army had lost so many officers (nearly ten thousand had become casualties in France) that cadets were being graduated as eighteen- and nineteen-year-old plebes—after only one year of training and school. Consequently, the place was a mess. There were no upperclassmen to train the youngsters and discipline was almost nonexistent. The urgent need to cram military subjects down the throats of this inexperienced cannon fodder had turned West Point into just another officers' training school and the academy was "reduced to a pitiable state as a result of the actions of the War Department." Faculty had been let go to join the fighting and the curriculum was in chaos.

Worse still, there was an undercurrent of decidedly antimilitary sentiment in postwar America that argued: "Why have a West Point at all if the country had just fought the war to end all wars—the war to save democracy for all time?" These people, MacArthur found—including some in Congress—would have abolished West Point in favor of Reserve Officers' Training Corps (ROTC) in colleges in the name of economy and an attitude of "never again."[20]

Nevertheless, in June 1919, MacArthur moved into the imposing brick and filigree superintendent's mansion at the Plain with his sixty-six-year-old mother. Initially, MacArthur had resisted the appointment, arguing that he was "a field soldier," but the fact that, as superintendent, he would remain a brigadier general instead of reverting to his prewar rank of major convinced him otherwise.

As when he disembarked the *Leviathan*, there was no welcoming ceremony or review of the corps upon his arrival. This, however, was on MacArthur's personal instructions. They had marched enough already, he said, and would march far more during the courses of their lives, to have to march on his behalf. "They'll see me soon and often enough," he told his chief of staff.[21]

MacArthur quickly sought to restore order and took his case to Congress. Learning that it planned to restore West Point to a three-year college, the new (and youngest in more than a hundred years) superintendent persuaded that body to expand the cadet corps to a full four years of classes within two years. He quickly developed "a burning desire," in the words of biographer Clayton James, "to reform West Point on the basis of his experiences in the war."

During the fighting in France, MacArthur had numerous occasions to witness the behavior of West Pointers who, for the most part, performed admirably with one glaring flaw—an inability to cope with the civilian draftees and volunteers who made up the bulk of the modern army. Their experiences at the military academy had left them hidebound. Accustomed to ordering and receiving immediate obedience from those cadets beneath them, these officers were flummoxed and disconcerted when confronted by often rebellious soldiers for whom submission to military orders was a foreign notion.[22]

After months of studying and analyzing new criteria for the military academy and its cadets, MacArthur determined that "Improvisation will be the watchword." The changed conditions in warfare demonstrated by the First World War required a "modification of the type of officer [that West Point produced], a type possessing all the cardinal military virtues as of yore, but possessing an intimate understanding of his fellows, a comprehensive grasp of world and national affairs, and a liberalization of conception which amounts to a change in his psychology of command." Accordingly, MacArthur decreed that the corps would abandon its regular, limited summer encampment altogether and billeted the upperclassmen with regular army brigades in order for them to get a chance to see what the real army was all about.[23]

MacArthur ran into trouble, however, when he tried to change West Point's academic curriculum. He wanted less math and more of the humanities—literature, history, philosophy, government, social sciences, geopolitics. But the academic department was filled with mossbacks who resisted change. On the academic committee, the superintendent had only one vote, and many of West Point's longtime professors resented his intervening on what they saw as their turf. "Looks like another effort to wreck the Academy," one of them said.

Nevertheless, MacArthur did manage to coax some changes in favor of the liberal arts. He also saw—for the first time—that each cadet was given $5 a month, as well as six-hour passes on weekends. Among other innovations, each cadet was required to read two newspapers a day and told to be prepared to discuss current events. MacArthur introduced an honor system, under which the cadets were individually and collectively responsible to see that no one cheated. And he saw to it that Civil War battle maps in the tactics instruction rooms were replaced with combat maps from the recent world war.[24]

MacArthur didn't stop there. He ordered that the most modern of the army's weapons be brought to West Point for the cadets to learn and train with, and he organized an intramural sports program and required that all cadets not already playing on some varsity team participate. Upon the gray stone walls of the gym he caused this quatrain to be carved:

> *Upon the fields of friendly strife*
> *Are sown the seeds*
> *That, upon other fields, on other days*
> *Will bear the fruits of victory.*

When Army's baseball team routed Navy in 1921, the corps staged—against all regulations—a midnight parade that marched past MacArthur's quarters and made an enormous bonfire on the edge of the drill field where they kept up a raucous cheering into the night. Upon encountering the commandant next morning MacArthur asked, "How many of them did you skin?" When the answer was "Not a damned one," MacArthur broke into a grin and said, "Good! I could hardly resist the impulse to get out there and join them!"[25]

MacArthur's chief of staff during this period, Major William Ganoe, remained in awe of his boss, and wrote about it later, noting "his unwavering aplomb, his astonishing self-mastery. I had seen men who were so placid or stolid they were emotionless. But MacArthur was anything but that. His every tone, look, or movement was the extreme of intense vivacity. As he talked, so he walked jauntily, without swagger. His gait and expression were carefree without being careless. Obedience," Ganoe wrote, "is something a leader can command, but *loyalty* is something, an indefinable something, that he is obliged to win. MacArthur knew instinctively how to win it." A possible reason for all this carefree jauntiness might have been something of which Major Ganoe wasn't aware at the time. MacArthur had fallen in love.

She was not just any woman, but a thirtyish, formerly married with two children Baltimore socialite named Louise Cromwell Brooks who was said to bear some resemblance to the silent-movie actress Clara Bow. Until she met MacArthur, she had been squired around Washington by none other than the army's highest-ranking officer, John J. Pershing. To say that she and MacArthur had a whirlwind romance would be a vast understatement. They met at a fashionable party in Tuxedo Park, which lies between West Point and New York City, and before the evening was done they were engaged. If MacArthur hadn't asked her to marry him the first time they met, Louise told the newspapers, "I believe I would have done it myself." If one did not know MacArthur well, it would be easy to speculate that he had been drinking that night, but because his reputation for moderation was well established it must have been something else.

When the engagement was announced in the January 15, 1922, *New York Times*, "both Pershing's and Pinky's plans lay in ruins," according to MacArthur's biographer William Manchester. MacArthur's mother was mortified at her son's choice of a frivolous flapper, divorced with two children, and told a friend from her bed, fainting couch, or wherever, "Of course the attraction is purely physical." Pershing, who evidently assumed a proprietary interest in the woman, was said to be furious at having been bird-dogged and snaked by one of his own officers, nearly twenty years his junior.

Thus—although Pershing publicly denied having a hand in it— MacArthur soon found himself summarily relieved of duty at West Point, a year shy of what was customary, and sent with his bride, at government expense, on a honeymoon cruise to the Philippine Islands—for four years! There is a photograph of them arriving in Manila—he in a sharply tailored suit and she wearing a long featureless dress and one of those little hats of the period that look like a flower pot turned upside down, pulled low over her brow.

★ ★ ★ ★

IN 1920 MARSHALL WAS PROMOTED to major in the regular army, and in 1923 to lieutenant colonel. In 1924, General Pershing retired and Marshall put in for reassignment with the 15th Infantry Regiment, which had been stationed in Tientsin, China, since the Boxer Rebellion of 1900. On June 12, 1924, he, Lily, and Lily's mother from Lexington steamed out of New York on the U.S. Army transport *St. Mihiel.* After a lazy cruise of nearly three months, during which they visited his friends from AEF days who were posted all across the Pacific, they arrived in China on September 7. At last, Marshall had a troop command.

As a lieutenant colonel, Marshall was actually designated as the thousand-man regiment's executive officer, but in fact he became its commanding officer for nearly three months until a more senior full colonel arrived to take charge. Not only that, but when the new officer was relieved for neglect of duty, Marshall again assumed regimental command.

The regiment occupied quarters in a compound on Kaiser Wilhelm-strasse, which before the war had belonged to Germany, and was now renamed Woodrow Wilson Street. In the same area were troops from England, France, Italy, and Japan—all, like the Americans, there to keep order over the fractious Chinese ever since the bloody days of the Boxer Rebellion. While the Chinese attempted to establish a republic under Dr. Sun Yat-sen, Bolsheviks and other Communists were even then making inroads, and warlords of all descriptions continued to rule, fight, and commit depredations in the vast hinterland.

The basic mission of the regiment was to keep open communications with the American consulate in Peking and the sea, 135 miles away. It was also to serve as a sort of fire brigade, protecting American interests at a variety of points along the northern Chinese coastal region.[26] The 15th was a proud regiment, comprising old army hands, many of whom had been solid enlisted men during the war—but there was nothing of which it was prouder than its reputation for having the highest rate of venereal disease in the entire United States Army. "Today is pay-day," Marshall began a letter to his old boss General Pershing, "and we are up against the problem of cheap liquor and cheaper women."[27]

One of the first things Marshall did was begin taking Chinese-language instruction. It was not required but he thought it would be useful. One day he tried numerous times in his newfound Chinese to instruct his Chinese driver to bring around his car, but the man simply looked at him dumbfounded. "Oh hell," Marshall said in exasperation. "Just send my car," at which the man promptly left and returned with the automobile. A regimental chaplain overheard the incident and the story "got all over the army" within a month or two.

The Marshalls and other officers lived in "sumptuous" quarters, where a ten-room house that Lily described as "awfully nice," with ample servants' quarters, rented for $15 a month.[28] Marshall also acquired a Mongolian pony, which was considerably smaller than a horse, but he wanted to blend in more with the native population. He made a point of riding a dozen miles in the morning and twice that on weekends, and he also began playing squash and tennis with members of the U.S. legation. And, as a matter of great satisfaction for him, Marshall completed the two-and-a-half-year regimental Chinese-language course in only eleven months and found himself able to carry on casual conversations in Chinese so as to understand "even the wranglings and squabbles of the rickshaw men."[29]

Lily spent her time shopping, and in addition to "exquisite clothes," she acquired numerous furnishings of the finest sort—Chinese rugs, linens, lacquers, screens, silver tableware, and other larger fittings for the home she hoped to make for them in America at the end of her husband's tour in China.[30]

The Chinese seemed continuously in a state of uprising, with various "armies" operating ever closer to the compound that Marshall and the other foreign entities occupied. This led to incidents and tense armed confrontations between the American and European forces and the Chinese militarists. Marshall himself was involved in several that might have ended badly had it not been for his cool penchant for persuasion and psychological bluff. Toward the end of his tour of duty in China, Marshall wrote to Pershing, "There has been so much wrongdoing on both sides, so much of shady transaction between a single power and a single party; there is so much of bitter hatred in the hearts of these people and so much of important business interests involved, that a normal solution can never be found." Marshall anticipated that some kind of "evolution" of the people and culture might provide an answer, but predicted a "trying period that is approaching." That was in 1926. China's long agony was about to begin.

★ ★ ★ ★

THE MARSHALLS RETURNED to the United States in May 1927, but Lily soon fell ill from a flare-up of her old heart condition, so serious that an operation was called for. She was, at the time, too weak to stand the surgery so Marshall kept her at the home she had longed for all those years—one of the stately three-story brick white-columned officers' quarters on "Colonels' Row" at Fort Lesley J. McNair in Washington, while he lectured at the Army War College. There, amid her fine collection of Oriental furnishings, Lily attempted to regain strength, but her condition worsened, and in August she entered Walter Reed Hospital. Surgery was performed the following day but she remained in serious, sedated condition. After five days she seemed to improve, however, and Marshall was able to visit every afternoon for the next two weeks. "[It] helps me so," she wrote her aunt Lottie. "It puts heart and strength in me."[31]

On the morning of September 15, the doctor came in to tell her she could go home. She began writing a letter to her mother with the news when she slumped over, dead. The last word she wrote was "George."[32]

Marshall was in class lecturing when a guard called him to the phone. The guard stood by as Marshall took the call. "He spoke for a moment over the phone, then put his head on his arms on the desk in deep grief," the guard said. "I asked if I could do anything for him and he replied, 'No, Mr. Throckmorton, I just had word my wife, who was to join me here today, has just died.'"[33]

Pershing wrote him immediately when he got the news. "No one knows better than I what such a bereavement means and my heart goes out to you very fully at this crisis in your life." Marshall replied that Pershing's handling of his own tragedy, the fire that took his wife and children, gave him inspiration and hope, but he added, heartbroken, "Twenty-six years of intimate companionship, since I was a mere boy, leaves me lost in my best effort to adjust myself to future prospects in life . . . However, I will find a way."

★ ★ ★ ★

INDEED GEORGE MARSHALL FOUND A WAY. Even with the emptiness and sorrow left by Lily's death, he remained an extremely bright, energetic personality with an indomitable spirit that required military challenge. He felt hemmed in by his work at the War College and even the army understood that under the circumstances Marshall needed to find himself elsewhere. He was presented with a choice of several assignments, one of which impressed him—assistant commandant of the Infantry School at Fort Benning, Georgia.

Fort Benning, in the western middle part of the state near the Alabama line, comprised nearly a hundred thousand acres including some of the area's old Southern estates that the government had purchased. Marshall moved into one of these homes, a circa-1850s building that was "as old as the hills," by Marshall's telling, surrounded by flowers, a grape arbor, and stately magnolias. It was "the nicest [house] I've ever had," he said.[34]

As assistant commandant and head of the school's academic department, Marshall aimed to inculcate young infantry officers in the arts of combat and leadership, basing his lessons on his own experiences of the past few years, particularly his time in France. As his chief biographer Forrest Pogue observes, Marshall "was one of those rare teachers who make a difference, who open minds in such a way that they never quite close again or forget the excitement of a new idea." He kept what he called "my little black book," into which he recorded, "for future reference," the names of young officers whose talents impressed him. Once someone asked if his little black book was to take down the names of officers who were the opposite of talented. "There wouldn't be room," Marshall replied.[35] Pogue ticks off scores of names of Marshall's students in his five years at the Infantry School who would become the best generals in high command during World War II, including Omar Bradley, Matthew Ridgway, J. Lawton Collins, and Walter Bedell Smith. Marshall's classes were those from which the stars fell.[36]

He set up difficult field problems to challenge the young warriors' abilities to react in rapidly changing circumstances. When a blue force that had been in mock battle all day, for example, encountered a red force in retreat during the late afternoon, the blues would naturally assume that the problem was nearly over. Then suddenly, from an entirely different direction, another red force sent by Commandant Marshall would vigorously attack. Marshall drummed it into their heads: plan how to deal with whatever happens—think three or four steps ahead.

"We have to expunge this bunk," Marshall said when handed a copy of laborious field orders that required young officers to march their men from paragraph C to paragraph H. "To mobilize for war," Marshall insisted, "we must develop a technique and methods so simple and so brief that the citizen officer of good common sense can readily grasp the idea." What he was talking about was mechanized war, with tanks, armored cars, and planes. Everything would be much faster and the army must learn to fight faster, fire, and maneuver in the open. There would be no trenches in future wars, he believed.[37]

He set up a tank force at the school because of his view that tanks would play a far greater role in future combat than they had in the First World War. He set up air demonstrations from nearby Army Air Corps fields. He chose his instructors carefully, from the very best the army had to offer. Marshall refined training in the various infantry weapons and published a handbook, *Infantry in Battle*.

Marshall encouraged reserve and National Guard officers to attend the school and, on one occasion, two black reserve officers appeared at Fort Benning. This being the 1930s, a petition was circulated demanding their withdrawal. Marshall not only ignored it, he denied it. One of the black officers wrote him long afterward, "Your quiet and courageous firmness in this case has served to hold my belief in the eventual solution of problems which have beset my people in their ofttimes pathetic attempts to be Americans."[38]

Life was good for Marshall in many ways. He enjoyed his work at the Infantry School, and took long horseback rides on the Benning reservation or joined in foxhunts. There was good duck and quail hunting near Columbus and tennis at the officers' club and country club in town. He also organized theatricals and exotic horseback scavenger hunts, and during one of the latter it was heard-tell he rode up to the finish line wearing a Japanese kimono, a Filipino hat, and carrying a birdcage.[39]

Yet there was the inevitable absence in his life after Lily's death and he was miserably lonesome. He told a visiting Rose Page, now a young woman of nineteen, "I hate to let you go. I dread returning to an empty house." Then, in the spring of 1928, Marshall accepted an invitation for dinner at the home of a friend in Columbus. There, he met an out-of-town guest, Mrs. Katherine Tupper Brown of Baltimore, a recent widow, who had come with her sixteen-year-old daughter, Molly.

Marshall, on his doctor's advice, had quit smoking and given up liquor. Standing next to the handsome, sandy-haired army colonel Mrs. Brown remarked, "You are a rather unusual army officer, aren't you? I have never known one to refuse a cocktail before."

"Well, how many army officers have you known?" Marshall asked.

"Not many," was the answer.[40]

Throughout the evening the two found conversation easy and became increasingly comfortable around each other. "I will never forget," she wrote, "George had a way of looking straight through you. He had such keen blue eyes and he was straight and very military." At the end of the evening Marshall offered to take her to the house of friends where she was staying, assuring her he knew where it was. However, for what seemed like hours he drove her around, talking, until at one point she remarked that he didn't seem to know his way around Columbus very well. Marshall replied that he knew his way around well enough to keep off the street where he was supposed to deliver her. Next day he invited her to a reception on the post and sent a car and driver for her. Before she returned to Baltimore they agreed to write.[41]

Katherine Brown was a tall, striking woman from a distinguished line of Baptist ministers in Virginia, with an "unusual" story to tell, according to biographer Pogue. After graduating from staid Hollins College she scandalized the family by going to New York to become an actress. After completing two years at the American Academy of Dramatic Arts, in 1904 she went to London where she tried to get on stage in Shakespeare productions, only to be told she had to learn "English." Undaunted, Katherine found work in a traveling stage company, staying in cheap boardinghouses and chaperoned by her sister, an art student. Her first speaking role was offstage as the ghost in *Hamlet.*

When not on stage she worked on her diction and by her second season she not only was playing Shakespearean roles but had parts in *The Rivals, She Stoops to Conquer,* and *School for Scandal.* She was able to summer with her parents and sister in Lucerne and then signed a seven-year contract with the distinguished Shakespeare touring company of Sir Frank Robert Benson.

But as she began the new season, Katherine started experiencing severe abdominal and shoulder pain that was eventually diagnosed by British doctors as "tuberculosis of the kidney." When she returned brokenhearted to Baltimore a specialist gave a more favorable diagnosis—exhaustion. Recuperating in the Adirondacks, she reacquainted herself with a childhood friend, Clifton S. Brown, an important Baltimore lawyer, who asked her to give up the stage and marry him. She declined and found work with the National Theater in Chicago. But no sooner had she returned to the theater than the pain began again; at one point she found herself paralyzed and had to be carried off the stage after the curtain dropped. When she returned to the Adirondacks for more recuperation, who should be waiting there but Clifton S. Brown, once more asking for her hand. This time, after much agonizing, she acceded.

It was not an easy transition. For years Katherine could not bring herself even to go inside a theater, but in time she reconciled herself to the life of a Baltimore socialite and, eventually, a mother. Then all that came crashing down when a deranged client shot and killed her husband outside his office and a few months later the bottom dropped out of the stock market, leaving Katherine Brown a forty-seven-year-old widow with three children to care for. She had just returned from a trip to Hawaii with Molly, who was taking the death of her father very hard, and was returning to Baltimore when she "stopped fatefully" on the way in Columbus, Georgia, to visit college friends.

A relationship between Marshall and Katherine developed nearly immediately. They wrote and visited frequently and on October 5, 1930, they were married at the Emmanuel Episcopal Church in Baltimore with General of the Army John J. Pershing as best man.

The newlyweds entrained directly for Fort Benning as the Infantry School was already in session, and by all accounts the new Mrs. Marshall adjusted splendidly in the transition to army wife. Her two young boys adored the tall, witty man they called "the colonel," and daughter Molly became his companion for morning horseback rides. George Marshall had not only acquired a loving wife, but a family as well.

★ ★ ★ ★

On Christmas Eve 1924, at Avalon, the Ayer family estate, Beatrice gave birth to George Smith Patton IV, at last giving Patton the son he'd always wanted. The following year, Patton graduated with honors from Leavenworth, while Beatrice, meantime, wrote Aunt Nannie that, "George is having a grand time here and busy every minute. He seems like his old self again—he is so changed since the war I feared it was permanent! But this summer he is just like a kid again—every stern line has gone out of his face."[42]

Soon orders came posting Patton to Hawaii, where he arrived at Schofield Barracks in April 1925. Beatrice and the children followed soon afterward and, like at the towns prior, she and her husband soon became enmeshed in the Honolulu social scene, including friendship with the wealthy sportsman Walter F. Dillingham—who became "Uncle Walter" to the children. Patton organized a first-rate polo team at Schofield and Sunday afternoons were given to chic luncheons and polo matches.

In August 1926 Patton's regiment was called to attention to witness his decoration with the Treasury Life Saving Medal for rescuing the three boys whose boat had capsized. Unbeknownst to her husband, Beatrice had collected statements from the boys and sent them to the Treasury Department. Even though she had done as much as he had in saving the boys, Beatrice was ever thinking of her husband and his career advancement.

★ ★ ★ ★

PATTON DEVELOPED A GREAT and lingering suspicion during this period that the Japanese not only sought war with the United States—noting their stunning victory against the czar's fleet in the Russo-Japanese War— but also intended a sneak attack on Pearl Harbor. Patton noticed that Japanese migrant farmers had established shacks near important inlets and installations. Whenever Japanese ships arrived for visits, reported Patton's daughter, the officers would visit the little farm shacks ostensibly because they would have relatives there. It was a poor reflection on U.S. military at the time that such information wasn't forthcoming from intelligence personnel.

Patton was incredulous because he knew that under the Japanese caste system naval officers were highly unlikely to have peasants for relatives. "All these things he reported to Military Intelligence from where it disappeared into the vast maw of Washington unnoted."[43]

In June 1927 Patton's father died from tuberculosis and cirrhosis of the liver "from drinking more than was good for him." Patton could not find a liner to get him home to California from Hawaii in time for the funeral and arrived three days afterward in a state of "almost unreasonable grief." Upstairs Aunt Nannie had been screaming hysterically for a week for her "beloved George to come and take her with him," and that "it was she he had always loved and not Ruth." According to Patton's biographer Carlo D'Este, "The death of his father was the most traumatic event of Patton's life. He had lost the best friend he ever had."[44]

The next year Patton was reassigned to the Office of the Chief of Cavalry in Washington. There the family rented Woodley Mansion, a grand old estate near the Washington Cathedral dating to 1797 that had been home to a series of important or fashionable people, including President Grover Cleveland. At that time the Pattons also bought their first and only house—Green Meadows in the Myopia Hunt country near Avalon in Massachusetts, where George kept his ever growing stable of thoroughbreds.

At Woodley, Patton renewed his friendship with Henry Stimson, the former secretary of war, and joined him on long rides through Rock Creek Park. Three years later, Stimson was named secretary of state in the Hoover administration and bought Woodley, which the Pattons had been renting. George therefore moved his family into a nearby mansion that required nine servants and was thought to be haunted.

Like clockwork, the Pattons resumed their places on the social ladder. In addition to the normal foxhunting, steeplechasing, and polo playing, there were nightly dinners held at the Patton home. We learn from biographer D'Este that they were extraordinarily formal affairs, the women wearing long gowns and the men in dinner jackets. The fancy attire did nothing, however, to conceal the uncouthness that had become a staple of Patton's complex personality.

This was aptly demonstrated when one evening the telephone rang and "a gentleman with a cultured Harvard accent" inquired after Major Patton. "Thinking it was an old family friend," Patton replied, "Why Francis, you damned old nigger lover! What in hell are you doing in Washington, and who the hell let you out of jail?"—to which the caller replied, "This is the secretary of state. I called to see if Major Patton would like to come over to Woodley for a game of squash rackets and a drink."[45]

Regarding his career in the Office of the Chief of Cavalry during this period, Patton was dancing on the edge of a very sharp knife. On the one hand he realized that the tank and other new armored vehicles would one day replace the horse. But as a high-ranking member of the Chief of Cavalry staff, he could hardly come out and advocate the demise of his branch of service. He continued to dance, giving speeches and writing articles in such publications as *Cavalry Journal,* suggesting that there was still a valuable place for the horse on the battlefield. Still, he tempered the argument with an acknowledgment that the tank would also be a force to reckon with in future wars.

In 1931 Patton became a student at the Army War College in Washington, which aimed at preparing officers for high field command. As at Leavenworth, he performed exceptionally well, but remained a major, with bleak prospects for promotion—so much so that when active duty generals or colonels died there would be secret rejoicing among the lower-ranked officers.

That same year his aunt Nannie passed away at the age of seventy-three, and Patton journeyed back to Lake Vineyard for her funeral. It was during this visit that he finally became emotionally affected by the death of his mother, Ruth, who had passed three years earlier. He composed to her a moving letter that he left in a whatnot box on her desk.

> Dear Mama, here with your things before me you are very
> near. I never showed you in life the love I really felt or the
> admiration for your courage . . . Children are cruel things.
> Forgive me. I had always prayed to show my love by doing
> something famous for you . . . Perhaps I may but time grows
> short. I am 46. In a few moments we will bury the ashes of
> Aunt Nannie. All the three who I loved and who loved me
> so much are gone now. When we meet again I hope you will
> be lenient for my frailties. In most things I have been worthy.
> Perhaps this is foolish but I think you understand. I loved
> and love you very much.[46]

★ ★ ★ ★

IN SUMMER 1932, the height of the Great Depression, heated demonstrations known as the Bonus March put Patton and other army officers in a hard spot. For several months, destitute veterans of World War I had been pouring into Washington to demand early payment of a "bonus" that had been voted to them by Congress after the armistice. At issue were so-called service certificates, which were due to be redeemed in 1945. The certificates had been issued to the veterans using a complex formula of time and place served and had a maximum value of $625 (about $8,000 in today's money).

Earlier, Patton's former orderly Pfc. Joseph Angelo, who had saved Patton's life in the Argonne Forest, testified in full uniform before a committee of Congress, telling them, "I could go right over to this cavalry camp across the river and get all of the money I want or need from Colonel Patton. But that ain't right . . . He owes me nothing. All I ask is a chance to work or a chance to get my money on my certificate."[47]

As the encampment of veterans grew into thousands who styled themselves as the Bonus Army, a number of agitators or "troublemakers" turned to violence. Before long, bricks, rocks, and other debris were being thrown.

President Herbert Hoover's administration refused to recognize or assist the veterans, and Congress adjourned without addressing their demands, other than to enact a law allowing them to borrow against their certificates and only to the extent that it paid for their travel home. By mid-July, ten thousand or so veterans remained in the encampment on the mudflats of Southeast Washington's Anacostia River directly in sight of the Capitol. It was dubbed Hooverville, and the veterans were threatening to stay there until 1945 if necessary. The confrontations increased in both number and intensity while the protestors repeatedly blocked streets and crowded the lawns of the Capitol and other government buildings.

On July 28, in the heat of the season, the secretary of war declared what amounted to martial law. By this point, D.C.'s police were outnumbered and the police chief had been struck. A policeman responded by firing into the crowd, which resulted in the killing of two marchers and injury to three policemen. The chore of driving demonstrators out of downtown D.C. now fell to the Third Cavalry Regiment, of which

Patton was the executive officer. MacArthur too would be called on to contain the escalating chaos.

The regiment formed for riot duty with their steel helmets, rifles, and gas masks. Quickly, they moved across Memorial Bridge to the Ellipse, south of the White House, to await the arrival of an infantry battalion under MacArthur's command. Around 4 p.m. the army began sweeping the demonstrators off of Pennsylvania Avenue south, toward Hooverville. They did not go easy: more stones and bricks were thrown before the infantry used tear gas.

During the melee, a fire was set to one of the shacks in Hooverville and soon the entire encampment was ablaze. The next morning, with the cavalry on picket lines near the smoking ruins on the Anacostia River, a somewhat dubious story has it that Patton refused to speak with his former orderly Pfc. Angelo, who had asked to see him. What we do know from Patton's family is that they were all taken to see Joseph Angelo when he "somehow or other ended up in Walter Reed Hospital," Patton's daughter Ruth Ellen said. "He was a sad little man, all eyes, and we wondered how he could have dragged Georgie into the shell hole and saved him."[48]

The press were generally sympathetic to the veterans and appalled at U.S. Army troops violently ejecting U.S. citizens from the capital city. This, Patton later wrote, "insured the election [in November 1932] of a Democrat [Franklin D. Roosevelt]."[49]

★ ★ ★ ★

IF MACARTHUR WAS UNHAPPY with his new assignment he did not show it. In fact, he seemed glad to be back in the Philippines after eighteen years, installed in luxurious quarters in the lovely eighteenth-century House on the Wall that towered above the old fortified city of Manila. There he renewed his friendship with Manuel Quezon, who was a rising politico in the Philippines, and with other Filipinos of note, scorning "the color line," which often brought him at odds with the upper-caste white population.

One of his first jobs as commandant of the Military District of Manila was to arrange a military survey of the mountainous Bataan Peninsula and Corregidor—the Rock, as it was known. These two large terrain features figured prominently in the army's War Plan Orange, which, in the event of a sudden attack by the Empire of Japan, were to become the last-ditch defensive positions of American and Filipino forces until a relief expedition could arrive from the United States.

MacArthur had serious doubts about the plan, not least because the islands contained only one thin American infantry regiment "commanded by a dottering officer who had last fought in the Sioux war," and the Japanese were thought to be able to land 300,000 invasion troops within a month. Washington, however, refused to reinforce the garrison for fear of antagonizing Tokyo. Still, in the ensuing weeks, MacArthur "covered every foot of rugged terrain, over its trails, up and down its steep mountainous slopes, and through its bamboo thickets."[50]

Meanwhile, the new Mrs. MacArthur was less taken with her circumstances, considering that the social scene in Manila was somewhat different from what she was accustomed to in Washington, Baltimore, Philadelphia, and New York, respectively. She wrote home explaining that life in the Philippines was "extremely dull," and that she was trying to get her husband to quit the army and become a stockbroker—which at that, or any point, would have been patently ridiculous.

Out of boredom and a need for exercise, she joined a bicycle club and hung out with the American elite, but the marriage was strained. Meantime, MacArthur adored Louise's two young children, Walter Jr. and Little Louise, and doted on them while Louise used her influence with powerful people in Washington to have her husband promoted, which she saw as the easiest ticket out of the Far East.

Pinky MacArthur, languishing in the Wardman Park Hotel in Washington, likewise put up a lobbying campaign for her son with the War Department, including an almost pathetic letter to Pershing "presuming on my long and loyal friendship for you—to open my heart in this appeal for my boy . . ." Whatever the effect of these efforts, on January 17, 1925, MacArthur was able to pin on the extra star of a major general—the youngest two-star general in the army—and he, Louise, and the children sailed for home.[51]

Louise owned a 150-acre estate in the Green Spring Valley, which was generally considered to be hunting country. There, north of Baltimore, sat an elegant manor house that she renamed Rainbow Hill in honor of the 42nd Division. From this lofty perch the MacArthurs began taking in the eternal dinner parties and ceaseless rounds of hunts, debutante balls, and other social etcetera that attaches to the presence of a handsome two-star general with a wife connected to high society. MacArthur assumed duties as commander of III Army Corps, headquartered in Baltimore, a dull sinecure in which he made speeches, visited training camps, and organized ROTC programs.

Among his baggage that he maintained through all his years in the army was his father's vast library of literature and military history. At night, perched by the fire at Rainbow Hill, MacArthur read voraciously. Over time he had developed a particular antipathy toward ideologies such as Bolshevism, communism, and passivism, which he equated with the other two, thinking them highly dangerous to the American way of life and frequently speaking out against these subjects during his lectures to Rotary clubs and Kiwanis meetings. It was also during this time that MacArthur was assigned to a "most distasteful" duty—the court-martial of Billy Mitchell.

Mitchell, a brigadier general who like Patton would forecast with chilling accuracy the Japanese surprise attack on Pearl Harbor, had been the top U.S. air combat commander in World War I and a good friend of MacArthur since their days growing up in Milwaukee. He had been slated to take over the army's air arm but, in a series of ill-advised speeches and remarks, Mitchell so excoriated the administration of President Hoover for failing to properly fund military aviation that he found himself hauled before a court of twelve major generals accused of "conduct prejudicial to the military" and several like charges.

The press were generally favorable toward Mitchell—who was flamboyant and always good for a quote—and hostile to court officials, none of whom were fliers and who were seen as hidebound throwbacks, MacArthur included. After a fair trial, Mitchell was duly convicted and sentenced to five years' suspension without pay—later reduced by half. No one knows for sure how MacArthur voted; members of the court were sworn to secrecy and only a two-thirds majority was necessary for conviction. MacArthur would go only as far as to say that he had "tried to help" Mitchell as much as possible, and that he agreed in general with Mitchell's complaints about lack of administration support for military aviation. A reporter who rifled through a wastebasket in the jury room after the verdict claimed that he found a ballot for "not guilty" with MacArthur's handwriting on it. In any case, Mitchell remained on friendly terms with MacArthur for the rest of his life.*

MacArthur's duties to this point continued to border on the mundane; the army, as well as his marriage, seemed to be foundering. Needless to say, he was becoming restless, when up popped an opportunity that promised to be a restorative tonic. The president of the American Olympic Committee had suddenly died and MacArthur was offered the job for the 1928 games in Amsterdam. He had always been a strong supporter of athletics and the job seemed tailor-made.

The outlook for the U.S. team, in MacArthur's estimation, was "not bright" but he wasn't about to accept that as fact. "I rode them hard all along the line," he said later, noting that "athletes are among the most temperamental of all persons." He told them that they "represented the greatest nation in the world and we had not come 3,000 miles just to lose gracefully." As it turned out, the U.S. team dominated the Olympics, scoring more than twice the points of Germany and Finland, the nearest runners-up, and set seventeen records. The team returned to America as heroes coast to coast—a fine feather for MacArthur's cap.

When MacArthur returned to the placidity of Rainbow Hill Louise was not there; in his absence she had moved to East Fiftieth Street in

---

* Mitchell died in 1936 before his theories could be vindicated. But when war again came the army named a bomber after him—the B-25 Mitchell that was used in Jimmy Doolittle's famous raid on Japan in 1942—and in 1946 Congress authorized a special gold medal in his honor, and everything from mountains to roads, streets, and highways were named after him, including the eating hall at the United States Air Force Academy. In 1955 a first-rate movie, *The Court-Martial of Billy Mitchell,* was released starring Gary Cooper, and in 1999 Mitchell's portrait was put on a U.S. postage stamp.

New York City from where—the gossip columns reported—she was observed clinging to the arms of men not her husband. "Wild stories were circulating about her behavior in speakeasies and on Westchester weekends," writes biographer Manchester. All of this was duly noted by MacArthur, who—whether or not at his own behest—was ordered to assume command of all forces in the Philippines. "No assignment could have pleased me more," he remarked.[52]

Once back in his old quarters "On the Wall," MacArthur received a communication from Louise's attorneys saying she was going to Reno, and he agreed to a divorce (in the days before no-fault divorces) on "any grounds that will not compromise my honor." The grounds ultimately agreed upon were that MacArthur had "failed to provide support" for his wife, an accusation that was patently ludicrous since her family was worth more than $100 million. The decree was granted on July 18, 1929. MacArthur's lone comment on the subject was this: "I entered into matrimony but it was not successful, and ended in divorce years later for mutual incompatibility."[53]

What lay more heavily on his mind was his third tour of duty in the Philippines and the Japanese threat to the archipelago. Japanese migrants had been arriving in the northern islands in alarming numbers and, like Patton in Hawaii, MacArthur saw them as a potential menace. He was opposed in this, however, by his old friend Manuel Quezon, who saw the new arrivals as a business opportunity. A recent treaty that the United States and Japan had signed forbade building any new forts in the islands. MacArthur protested that the number of troops on hand were wholly inadequate for a proper defense of the Philippines, but in fact the administration had all but written off the islands, a position MacArthur refused to concede. "From 1928 onward," writes Manchester, "the chief obstacle to Japanese conquest of the Philippines was his implacable will."

Then, in 1930, a new chapter opened in MacArthur's life. He was made chief of staff, the highest-ranking man in the army.

ON NOVEMBER 21, 1930, MacArthur was sworn in and moved, with his mother, to the palatial Officers Quarters Number 1 at Fort Myer, Virginia. Somehow, having four stars seemed to stimulate MacArthur's eccentricities. Always casual about his military attire, he now took to wearing a Japanese kimono in his office and paced around fanning himself with an Oriental fan. He acquired a bejeweled holder for smoking his cigarettes and began speaking of himself in the third person. On journeys to Europe to watch maneuvers, he demanded his own railroad car for travel. Then he did what may have been for the time the ultimate eccentricity—he took a mistress.

She was a Eurasian girl in her twenties named Isabel Cooper, daughter of a Scottish businessman and an Asian woman. MacArthur began seeing her several months before leaving Manila. A Washington hostess who met her said, "I thought I had never seen anything as exquisite. She was wearing a lovely, obviously expensive chiffon tea gown and she looked as though she was carved from the most delicate opaline."* MacArthur kept her in an apartment in Northwest Washington, where he showered her with the finest gowns and lingerie, as well as a poodle. Before meeting MacArthur, she had been a chorus girl in Shanghai, "with all that that implied," and she called MacArthur "Daddy."[54]

Mistress or not, as chief of staff MacArthur had the stupendous task of trying to keep the army together in the wake of Congress's consistent budget cuts during the first full year of the Great Depression. The entire American army at home and abroad consisted of only 124,301 enlisted men (including 6,000 native "Philippine scouts")—compared with nearly five million at the end of World War I—and 12,255 officers, with a bill pending in Congress to reduce the officer corps to 10,000. MacArthur thus began a fight that only a man of his eloquence could wage. He told the House majority leader: "An army can live on short rations, it can be insufficiently clothed and housed, it can even be poorly armed and equipped, but in action it is doomed to destruction without the trained

---

* A decorative style of opaque or milky glass made in France during the reign of Napoleon III.

and adequate leadership of officers. An efficient and sufficient Corps of Officers means the difference between victory and defeat."

For months he spent endless days testifying before various committees. The world was again becoming a dangerous place but following the previous war the notion of pacifism took hold among a growing number of Americans, particularly among college students and citizens in the Middle West, and this was reflected in the thinking of many in Congress. While both Japan and Russia were actively operating a policy of international expansion in the Far East, Hitler and Mussolini were beginning to make names for themselves in Europe. The great international tragedy had begun to fester and brew.

Meanwhile, American pacifists were hard at work trying to undermine the nation's military power. In May 1931, 62 percent of nearly twenty thousand Protestant clergymen representing vast congregations throughout the land stated in a poll in the popular church magazine *The World Tomorrow* that they believed their churches "should now go on record as refusing to sanction or support any future war." Passivism was not merely a state of mind; in the 1920s and '30s it had become a powerful movement to be reckoned with. MacArthur responded in a letter to the editor, reminding him that "History teaches us that religion and patriotism have always gone hand in hand, while atheism has always been accompanied by radicalism, communism, bolshevism and other enemies of free government . . ." In return, he received a good deal of hate mail.

In 1931 and 1932 MacArthur visited Europe, notably France, where he told a group of French generals he had served with during World War I that "sooner or later Germany was going to try again." As a defense against this, the French constructed the infamous Maginot Line, a succession of fortifications running from the Alps to Belgium, which the Frenchmen told him was designed to hold and pin down the German army while a mobile force of the French army swung north into Belgium to flank and destroy the German right wing.

While he was in France, MacArthur's concubine Isabel was becoming restive. She wheedled a chauffeured limousine out of MacArthur in which she tooled around to Washington and Baltimore nightspots, according to Manchester, "seduc[ing], among others, George S. Abell, a descendant of the *Baltimore Sun*'s founder." Furthermore, she coaxed "a large amount of cash" out of MacArthur, which she blew on a toot in Havana. At length, the chief of staff received word of these activities and his "ardor cooled." For example, when she asked him to help find a job for her brother in Washington, MacArthur sent her a copy of the Help Wanted ads from the local paper. Furthermore, he mailed her a train ticket to the West Coast and passage on a liner to the Philippines, but instead she moved into a boardinghouse near his office at the State–War Department building on Pennsylvania Avenue. It was there that the syndicated columnist Drew Pearson found her and began asking questions.[55]

★ ★ ★ ★

IF MACARTHUR FOUND HIS DUTY in the trial of Billy Mitchell "distasteful," he certainly had a right to call his next assignment "disagreeable." President Hoover and Secretary of War Patrick Hurley instructed him to evict the veterans of the aforementioned Bonus March. MacArthur had been dealing with the march's leader, offering army tents and other camp equipment for the veterans. He had also sent a number of rolling kitchens to their encampment.* MacArthur was sure that most of the marchers were Communists, although later research has shown that the figure was probably closer to 10 or 15 percent.

When tensions heightened to the violence Patton and the Third Cavalry Regiment were also facing on July 28, MacArthur ordered a regiment of troops and a cavalry battalion—totaling about eight hundred men—to assemble on the Ellipse. Because they were located

---

* The kitchens were withdrawn after a House leader made a speech complaining that if the army agreed to feed the veterans indefinitely, it would cause the other eight and a half million out-of-work citizens to descend on Washington looking for their handouts.

in surrounding areas in Virginia and Maryland, the various units took until about 4 p.m. to converge. At 4:30 they set out to clear about three thousand of the Bonus Marchers from the area around Third and Fourth Streets in the shadow of the Capitol building. Against the advice of MacArthur's assistant Major Dwight Eisenhower, who was fairly close to him and had advised his boss that it was unnecessary and "highly inappropriate" for him to take the field with the evicting force, MacArthur appeared on the scene wearing what some reports described as "parade dress"—jodhpurs, high, polished cavalry boots, and a tunic bemedaled with ribbons.

The soldiers, with bayonets drawn, wearing gas masks, and tossing gas grenades, quickly cleared the streets and pushed the veterans back across the 11th Street Bridge, leading to their encampment in the Anacostia Flats, where they stood their ground in a flood of profanity and barrage of rocks and bricks, some of which damaged MacArthur's car. Secretary of War Hurley twice sent word to MacArthur *not* to cross the bridge and carry the eviction to the main camp on the flats, but the chief of staff was impassive. "In neither instance," Eisenhower said, "did General MacArthur hear these instructions. He said he was too busy," and the messengers were sent away. He then sent word through the police chief to the veterans that he would "proceed very slowly," and that "I would stop the command for supper so that full opportunity would be given for everyone to leave without being hurt."[56]

Meantime, as darkness closed in, an army intelligence report arrived saying that "all men that have firearms were told to use them against the first troops to cross the bridge." This apparently led MacArthur to believe that the marchers were regrouping for a "last stand" or even a counterattack. In any event, shortly afterward, the army crossed over the bridge and soon the entire veterans' encampment was on fire. All of the infantry commanders denied setting the blaze and some believed that the marchers acted "in spite," setting fire to the tents the government had loaned them.

Whatever the case, with unrelieved bitterness the marchers disbursed and the Bonus March was ended. MacArthur received much criticism in the press, and particularly by liberal publications, for his role in the affair.* He remained unrepentant and told the newspapers that the march might ultimately have led to "insurgency and insurrection," and pointed out that it was the most bloodless riot he had been in.[57]

★ ★ ★ ★

THAT DID NOT KEEP SYNDICATED COLUMNISTS such as Drew Pearson from maligning MacArthur for ousting the marchers in an "unwarranted, unnecessary, arbitrary, harsh, and brutal" manner. MacArthur filed a $1,750,000 libel suit against Pearson and his partner in the "Washington Merry-Go-Round" column, Robert S. Allen, which featured some most interesting twists before it was done.

In those days, before the Supreme Court made libel suits almost a thing of the past, Pearson and Allen had ample reason to worry. Then a Mississippi congressman informed them that until recently a suite on his floor in a Northwest Washington, D.C., hotel had been occupied by a beautiful Eurasian girl who in the evenings frequently received the U.S. Army's chief of staff, Douglas MacArthur. Newshound Pearson was able to locate Isabel and purchased MacArthur's love letters from her. Then, at a pretrial hearing, Pearson's attorneys startled the proceeding by saying that he intended to put one Isabel Cooper on the witness stand. MacArthur, thoroughly alarmed, sent Major Eisenhower to find Isabel—but Pearson had stashed her in Baltimore. Finally, MacArthur dropped the suit.

The columnists reported that no money was paid nor were apologies given. What was not reported was that Eisenhower or some other officer close to MacArthur had delivered $15,000 to Pearson's lawyers, which

---

* Later, prominent Communists and former Communists testified before Congress that on orders from Moscow they were instructed to foment trouble between the marchers and police, in hopes that the army would be called in. Then, it was further hoped that the army would fire on and kill some marchers, thus touching off a Communist-style revolution in America.

was given to Isabel for her part in the scheme. Afterward she moved to the Midwest where she purchased a hairdressing shop and later to Hollywood where she became a "freelance actress"; according to her death certificate, she died following an overdose of barbiturates in 1960.[58] When he heard about the affair, Admiral William Leahy remarked that MacArthur "could have won the suit. He was a bachelor at the time. He could have just said . . . so what? . . . you know why he didn't do it? It was that old woman he lived with at Fort Myer. He didn't want his *mother* to learn about that Eurasian girl!"

★ ★ ★ ★

IN MARCH 1933 Franklin Roosevelt took office, and though MacArthur liked him personally the two men thoroughly disagreed on military policy. Roosevelt wanted to spend less on the military and more on his social programs, while MacArthur opposed him. During one spectacularly intense discussion that included the secretary of the army, Roosevelt became sarcastic when MacArthur argued that the safety of the nation was at stake. "When we lose the next war," the chief of staff responded, "and an American boy is lying in the mud with an enemy bayonet through his belly, and an enemy foot on his dying throat, and spits out his dying curse, I want the name not to be MacArthur, but Roosevelt!"

At this, the commander in chief became livid and roared, "You must not talk that way to the president!"

MacArthur immediately realized he had been insubordinate and apologized, and then said he would resign his position. But as he reached the door, Roosevelt's voice came with that cool detachment that so reflected his extraordinary self-control, "Don't be foolish, Douglas; you and the budget must get together on this."

As he left the building, MacArthur vomited on the White House steps, but he noted later, "From that time on he [Roosevelt] was on our side."[59]

In 1934—as MacArthur's time as chief of staff was coming to a close—Manuel Quezon, his old friend from the Philippines, came to

America looking for help in case of a Japanese incursion. He went to see MacArthur, who told him that any place was defensible if enough men, munitions, and money were available. He told the Filipino, "It would take ten years and much help from the United States." Quezon then asked if MacArthur himself would undertake the job of supervising the raising and training of a Philippine army. MacArthur agreed.

CHAPTER SEVEN

★ ★ ★ ★

"I AM ALL HE HAS"

W hen the Marshalls left the Infantry School in 1932, seventeen million Americans, nearly 20 percent of the workforce, were unemployed. The stock market crash of 1929 had precipitated the Great Depression, which was to last the remainder of the decade. People were begging in the streets of large cities and millions, unable to find work, were on the move in tent cities across the country. The army too felt the pinch; appropriations were frozen, as well as salaries, and personnel, including the officer corps, were cut back.

Into this unfortunate state of affairs plunged the newly married George C. Marshall as commanding officer of a battalion of the U.S. Eighth Infantry Regiment stationed at Tybee Island, Georgia, seventeen miles south of Savannah. It was only a four-hundred-man outfit, but Marshall was glad for the opportunity to once again have a fighting infantry command. The post was a small one so he also served as post commander, with duties that extended to the civilian community in Savannah, a lovely but sleepy town that seemed a throwback in time.

No sooner had Marshall arrived than he was notified that his unit would be responsible for training a recent creation of the new president, Franklin D. Roosevelt, and his Democratic Congress called the Civilian Conservation Corps (CCC). The New Deal measure would employ hundreds of thousands of young men in flood and soil erosion control by planting trees and grasses, building dams, bridges, and campgrounds, and other methods to be mapped out by the U.S. Forest Service, Conservation Service, and Army Corps of Engineers. These youths had to be organized into military-style units, the better to control them and enable them to carry out their jobs. Marshall's quota of young men to train was seventeen hundred, but soon orders from Washington directed him to oversee nineteen of the CCC camps being built from Georgia to Florida. Marshall was charged with seeing that the young men had proper barracks, food, hygienic facilities, and direction. He loved the idea and threw himself wholeheartedly into the work, visiting and inspecting the camps regularly. If there were men who could not read or write properly he arranged for their education, and he encouraged them to learn to fish and swim and play team sports.

In 1933, Marshall was promoted to full colonel and sent to command the Eighth Infantry Regiment at Fort Moultrie, South Carolina, near Charleston. As the Depression deepened it took a harsh toll on the enlisted personnel, especially if they had families. Marshall arranged for the mess to fix lunch boxes with hot meals that the men could take home to their families for ten cents a day. He and Katherine also ate these midday dinners "until the custom was well-established," she said. "It saved the wives endless toil and was a godsend to the married enlisted personnel."[1] He also continued his work with the CCC camps, which he called "the greatest social experiment outside of Russia."*

No sooner, it seemed, had the Marshalls settled in at Fort Moultrie than the new bird colonel received a severe blow from the War Department. He was to leave immediately for Chicago, and there become chief instructor for the 33rd Division—a National Guard outfit. Marshall saw it as a demotion and a dead end and asked Pershing to write Douglas MacArthur, who was then chief of staff of the army. MacArthur affirmed the orders. What Marshall didn't know was that MacArthur had in

---

* At its height, the CCC would employ 2.5 million youths.

fact handpicked Marshall for the duty, which he knew was somewhat onerous. As Marshall might have—and should have—expected, politics was involved.

It seems that the 33rd Division's commander, Major General Roy D. Keehn, a prominent Democrat and lawyer for William Randolph Hearst, was smarting from accusations in "Colonel" Robert R. McCormick's *Chicago Tribune* that the division was in such a poor state of affairs it would be incapable of dealing with anticipated labor strikes and civil disorders in Illinois. McCormick was, of course, a prominent Republican and his paper made a point of attacking the Roosevelt administration. At Keehn's request MacArthur had specifically selected George Marshall to shape up the 33rd and end McCormick's attacks.

Unaware of all this, Marshall became despondent. Katherine wrote: "George had a gray, drawn look which I had never seen before, and have seldom seen since." He told visiting Rose Page, who had asked when Marshall would become a general and then chief of staff, "Rosie, it looks now as if I never will. If I don't make brigadier general soon, I'll be so far behind in seniority I won't even be in the running."[2]

Chicago was a dull, dingy Depression-era city with half its working population unemployed. Marshall as usual worked hard—and successfully—to bring the 33rd Division up to par, while Katherine shopped at antiques auctions, of which there were many given the state of economic affairs. Worried that time was running out on him because of age, Marshall implored his old friend Pershing to write a letter to the War Department urging his promotion. Instead, Pershing did him one better—he went personally to the president of the United States.

On May 24, 1935, Secretary of War George Dern received a note from the White House.

> General Pershing asks very strongly that Colonel George C. Marshall (Infantry) shall be promoted to brigadier.
>
> Can we put him on the list of next promotions? He is fifty-four years old.
>
> F.D.R.

On October 1, 1936, Marshall at last got his star and was assigned to command the Fifth Infantry Brigade at Vancouver Barracks, Washington. It was the deep boondocks but Marshall didn't care. He had a fighting command once more.

★ ★ ★ ★

AFTER FOURTEEN YEARS AS A MAJOR, George Patton was at last promoted to lieutenant colonel in 1934. That same year, his daughter Bee was married to Lieutenant John Knight Waters, a graduate of the U.S. Military Academy and future four-star general. Patton had taken her to West Point five years earlier, for his twentieth reunion, and asked the authorities to provide a suitable escort and the authorities had produced Waters, whom they considered "the most outstanding cadet at the Academy."

The wedding, which took place in the same church where Patton and Beatrice were married twenty-four years earlier, was a great social event. Bee wore the same wedding dress her mother had worn in 1910 (and the one her grandmother had first worn in 1884). Patton too looked dazzling, sporting his dress blues bedecked with medals. Photographs in the society sections of the newspapers show him smiling contentedly, although daughter Ruth Ellen had a different take. She would never forget her father's face, she said, as he walked Bee down the aisle. "He looked just like a child who is having his favorite toy taken away. All his determination to remain forever young was being undermined by having a daughter getting married. He was forty-nine years old and he had still not won a war or kept his part of the bargain with Grandfer Ayer about winning glory. He looked stricken to the heart."

For his part, Patton wrote to Beatrice, "No mother of a bride ever looked better or cried less."[3]

The following spring Patton was again ordered to Hawaii and, to celebrate the occasion, he bought a fifty-foot schooner. Named *Arcturus,* the boat was shipped to Patton by rail, from the East Coast to San Diego. He intended to sail solo across the Pacific to the Hawaiian Islands—despite the fact that he knew little or nothing about ocean navigating, telling Beatrice that he'd "rather be dead than be nobody."

Of course, in 1935, there weren't GPS or any other sort of electronic navigation system; getting from one place to another in the vast and trackless wastes of the Pacific was done by celestial navigation using charts, sextant, and chronometer. Patton therefore enrolled in a course in celestial navigation taught at the Naval Academy in Annapolis, Maryland, which he drove to from Washington three times a week.

Beatrice immediately announced, according to Ruth Ellen, that "she would not let George drown without her," and so she enlisted as the ship's cook despite the fact that she had never cooked in her life. By the time they cast off, the crew had grown to six, including friends, cousins, and a Norwegian seaman who had come with the boat. As they pulled away from the dock on a May morning, Patton looked forlornly at the varnished boxes containing the sextant and chronometer and remarked to Beatrice, "We can learn, can't we?"[4]

They arrived, somehow, fifteen days and 2,238 miles later, to be greeted at the dock in Honolulu by a brass band and a bevy of hula dancers courtesy of their many friends on the island. Quickly, Patton was made the G-2, or chief intelligence officer, for the Hawaiian Department, but his superior General Hugh Drum, a rather square man who secretly envied Patton's financial and social superiority, refused to back him up in the "things he discovered about the Japanese underground" and other nefarious activities that would ultimately lead to Pearl Harbor.

An all-expenses-paid two and a half years in Hawaii with your family might be a wondrous pipe dream for most, but in Patton's case he was "miserable," according to biographer D'Este and Patton's daughter Ruth Ellen. He loved Hawaiian life but he was frustrated by lack of promotion and the fact that he was now in his fifties without yet having discovered the end of the rainbow. He was drinking too much, Ruth Ellen noted—not more than usual, but too much "after a bad fall in polo [that] affected his drinking capacity for the rest of his life." Not only that, he was angry about growing old, and he began seeking the company of younger people including "the eternal harpies who are always standing in the wings of successful marriages hoping the wife will falter and the man will be there for them to feast on."[5]

Among these latter, unfortunately for everyone concerned, was twenty-one-year-old Jean Gordon, daughter of Beatrice's half sister Louise, who came visiting from Boston on her way to a tour of Japan and the Far East. An educated, good-looking young woman, she "made a play" for Patton.[6]

Beatrice seemed unaware of the affair until her husband and niece returned from several unchaperoned days on another Hawaiian island. While Patton was there on official business, the affection between the two upon their homecoming was too apparent to ignore.

A "powerful tension" then descended upon the Patton family, lasting until Jean's departure several days hence, when Beatrice turned to Ruth Ellen as Jean's ship was pulling away from the pier—and as Patton was "making a damned fool of himself" waving furiously at Jean—and delivered herself of one of the sagest, bravest, most selfless and eloquent lectures in the history of marriage. "You know," she told her daughter, "it's lucky for us that I don't have a mother because if I did I'd pack up and go to her now; and your father needs me. He doesn't know it, but he needs me. In fact, right now he needs me more than I need him."[7]

The infidelity had coincided with the publication of a novel—*Blood of the Shark*—that Beatrice had been putting the finishing touches on since their last posting in Hawaii in 1928. Such as it was, Patton's behavior had also cruelly "stolen her moment," as Beatrice explained to Ruth Ellen: "I want you to remember this; that even the best and truest men can be be-dazzled and make fools of themselves. So, if your husband ever does this to you, you can remember that I didn't leave your father. I stuck with him because I am all that he really has, and I love him, and he loves me."[8]

★ ★ ★ ★

ABOARD THE FAR EAST LINER *President Harding* with Douglas MacArthur was Jean Faircloth, thirty-seven, a zesty, attractive, five-foot-two, green-eyed heiress from Murfreesboro, Tennessee, whose grandfather, a Confederate captain, had fought against Arthur MacArthur at the Battle of Missionary Ridge. She had planned to visit friends in Shanghai before concluding a world tour, but revised her itinerary to take a suite in the Manila Hotel, which was also Douglas MacArthur's abode. The two had met at a cocktail party thrown by the ship's captain and were inseparable thereafter.

MacArthur had brought his eighty-six-year-old mother, Pinky, on board the ship but she was ill and remained in her cabin. Once in Manila he installed her in the hotel's penthouse suite next to his, but her condition worsened and within a month she was dead of cerebral thrombosis. It was an enormous blow to MacArthur, who had been extraordinarily close to her through the years—even to the extent that, when he was chief of staff, he would ride from his Washington office every day to Fort Myer to have lunch with her. He would carry her remains with him on his next trip to the States and bury her in the National Cemetery in Arlington, Virginia.

MacArthur grieved for months, but Jean Faircloth was a decided help. The two of them would go to the movies five or six nights a week, arriving for the 8:30 showing at one of Manila's many English-language theaters. Otherwise, MacArthur spent much of his time in the Philippines reading while sitting in his mahogany-paneled library in his six-room suite at the Manila. The library, like the rest of the suite, was palatial, with large maroon-colored leather chairs and an exquisite fifteen-foot Japanese bamboo table. In the spacious dining room, which featured a large Philippine mahogany table, MacArthur had his mother's early American silver on prominent display.

There were two long tiled balconies that overlooked Manila Bay, one with a breathtaking view of "The Rock," Corregidor, rising from the ocean, with the Bataan Peninsula as a backdrop. MacArthur would pace here for long periods, thinking. As biographer William Manchester tells it, pacing was MacArthur's form of exercise. He was going on sixty years old and was reasonably fit except for a slightly protruding belly. According to Manchester, he paced for miles each day in his office and in his suite.

James Gavin, then a young officer and soon-to-be four-star general, remembered the day MacArthur came "visiting us at Fort McKinley on Luzon to watch some test firings of a new 81mm mortar. We were observing mortar fire from the high ground when he strode up in a rather imperious way. There was an aura about him that seemed to keep us junior officers at a distance. He was impressive and, in his own way, inspired great confidence and tremendous respect. We knew him by reputation to be a man of great physical courage, and by professional behavior to be a man of vision, intelligence, and great moral courage."[9]

One of MacArthur's first actions in building up Philippine defenses was the acquisition of fifty sixty-five-foot torpedo boats known as PT boats, based on a British-made model. Unfortunately, the British had to cancel most of the order when war with Germany was declared. (Thus, only nine PT boats were available when the Japanese finally attacked on Pearl Harbor on December 7, 1941.)

MacArthur's most important element of defense for the islands was a ten-year program to train 40,000 men a year as soldiers so that by the end of a decade he would have, at his disposal, a Philippine army of 400,000 divided into forty 10,000-man divisions scattered around the archipelago. Their training would be by a cadre of regular Philippine soldiers led by officers graduated from the country's military academy that was modeled on West Point. "We are going to make it so very expensive for any nation to attack these islands that no nation will try it," MacArthur told *Collier's* magazine. He said it would cost the Japanese half a million men, three years, and a billion dollars to take the Philippines—a price they would not be willing to pay.[10]

They soon learned, however, that the principal enemy was lack of money. The United States, still suffering the Depression, would not appropriate nearly enough to fund such a force, and "the Philippine government simply could not afford to build real security from attack," according to Dwight Eisenhower, who had come along to be MacArthur's chief of staff ("My best clerk," MacArthur called him).

As it turned out, the vaunted Philippine army that MacArthur was building wasn't measuring up either. Armed with ancient World War I

Enfield rifles and clad in sneakers and pith helmets, their training progressed in fits and starts and many of the locals evaded conscription because, among other things, the Filipino soldiers were paid only $7 a month compared with $30 for a U.S. private. Worse, Quezon, who was now president of the Philippine Commonwealth, had turned against his old friend and was threatening to abolish MacArthur's ten-year plan, believing it might become a provocation to Japan.

Even with the setbacks, in the summer of 1937 the Philippine government made MacArthur a field marshal, the highest rank in its army. For the occasion, he had designed a uniform consisting of a white tunic, black pants, and a cap with the gold-braided "scrambled eggs" of a high-ranking field officer on the bill. Some historians have suggested that the uniform was ostentatious, or "Ruritanian," but in fairness it closely resembled the U.S. Army's regulation dress whites.

★ ★ ★ ★

THAT SAME YEAR MACARTHUR MARRIED Jean Faircloth in a simple ceremony at New York's city hall, following a disappointing visit to Washington, where the War Department turned down nearly all of his requests for military supplies, which were becoming increasingly urgent considering what was happening in Europe.

There, Hitler had seized absolute power and Germany was threatening her neighbors; Japan had invaded China. It was apparent to most knowledgeable observers that there would be no ten years' time to prepare for an invasion. The Philippines stood squarely in the way of the Japanese path to the wealth of the East Indies, which contained the oil, tin, rubber, quinine, and other raw materials desperately needed by Imperial Nippon. Observers in the northernmost of the Philippine archipelago daily could see the aerial maneuvers of Japanese warplanes based on an island the Japanese occupied barely forty miles away. Time was running out for General MacArthur and his Philippine army.

★ ★ ★ ★

UPON HIS ARRIVAL AT VANCOUVER BARRACKS, Marshall wrote to General Keehn in Chicago, telling him of the historic nature of his new post. His quarters, for instance, had been occupied at one time or another by a "succession of Civil War celebrities or Indian fighters," including Generals Nelson Miles, Edward R. Canby, George Crook, John Gibbon, and John Pope. The parade ground, in the shadow of Mount Hood, was surrounded by giant fir trees and bordered the Columbia River, which "emerges from its famous gorge a few miles above the post." There was excellent salmon fishing and pheasant hunting in the vicinity, as well as skiing on Mount Hood.[11]

In addition to his duties with the Fifth Brigade, Marshall also had thirty-five CCC camps scattered throughout Oregon and southern Washington. At one point, in June of 1937, he gained the national spotlight when a Russian plane intending to fly nonstop from Moscow to San Francisco was forced to put down in Vancouver. There was a great press clamor to interview the crew but Marshall declared that no interviews would be conducted until the Soviet pilots got some sleep. After lending the Russians his own sets of pajamas, Marshall then offered a fancy breakfast table for the fliers and invited the reporters in; as well, he brought the Russian ambassador, who had been awaiting the flight in San Francisco, up to Vancouver and gave him a presentation sword to honor the occasion, which elicited a "warm thanks" from the ambassador.

All of this was duly noted by the State Department, the American public, and the General Staff of the Army back in the capital. Marshall's earliest biographer, William Frye, notes that there was "strong evidence," but "no clear proof," that it was at about this point in Marshall's career that decisions had been made to bring him to Washington, D.C., as the successor to the chief of staff. If that were so, Marshall certainly had no idea of it, but he continued to distinguish himself as commander of the Fifth Brigade and overseer of the CCC camps.

★ ★ ★ ★

BY 1937 THE DEMOCRACIES RECOILED as Adolf Hitler firmly ensconced himself and his Nazi party as brutal regulators of German society. It was one of several dictatorships that ultimately sought to divide and control large parts of the world.

Following World War I, the victorious Allies had set up an organization they hoped would prevent future conflicts. Called the League of Nations, it was envisioned as a body that would not only mediate international disputes but settle them, if necessary, by force of arms. Almost immediately things began to go wrong. Principally isolationist sentiment in the United States caused the U.S. Senate to reject the idea of a "world government," and thus the most powerful nation on earth at the time would not lend its considerable teeth to a multinational plan for stopping wars before they got out of hand.

Throughout the 1920s and '30s American military might was dismantled in favor of domestic programs, the more so following the onset of the Great Depression. During this period American leftists, socialists, pacifists, and isolationists loudly denounced munitions makers and financiers such as J. P. Morgan for being responsible for all the misery caused by the recent war, and most American citizens assumed the attitude that "Europe's problems were Europe's problems."[12] This outlook was so pervasive that a measure known as the Kellogg-Briand peace pact was passed by the U.S. Congress, Britain, France, and other nations—including Germany, which actually *outlawed* war, and contained about as much authority as outlawing thunderstorms.

All of this played greatly into Hitler's and the other dictators' hands: decadent, idealistic, foolish democracies, thinking they could vote out war. Hitler made his first move in 1936, marching into the Rhineland, which had been set up as a buffer zone between Germany and France, in direct violation of the Treaty of Versailles. Neither the French nor the British did anything but protest to the League of Nations, which also did nothing. Hitler made numerous sham speeches intended for international consumption in which he stated, "We have no territorial intentions in Europe . . . Germany will never break the peace," and similar words to that effect.

Next the Nazis marched into Austria, claiming it had always been a Germanic province. The Western Allies merely watched. It was a continuing pattern of Hitler's: claiming he desired no territory but then seizing it. Soon it became Czechoslovakia's turn, on the pretext that there were German citizens living among the Czechs in an area known as the Sudetenland who wished to return to the fatherland. By then France and Britain were thoroughly alarmed. A permanent peace was sought by sending the British prime minister, Neville Chamberlain, to meet Hitler in Munich and draw up some binding accord. It was a fiasco. When the tall, umbrella-carrying, bowler-hatted Chamberlain returned to London he waved a Hitler-signed document and proclaimed, "This means peace in our time."

It meant no such thing. Among the leaders of Great Britain only Winston Churchill fully understood the machinations of Hitler. "The government had to choose between shame and war," he thundered. "They have chosen shame, and now they will get war." Barely six months later, in March 1939, German storm troopers annexed the rest of Czechoslovakia, including its large armaments factories at Skoda and elsewhere.

In August 1939 Hitler negotiated one of the most breathtaking diplomatic coups in history—a ten-year "nonaggression" treaty with the Soviet Union, thus making an ally out of his most powerful archenemy. This shocking news completely flummoxed Western Communists and their fellow travelers, who for years had been warned of the dangers of fascism. Now the Communist *Daily Worker* began preaching that Hitler and the Nazis were their friends.

Meanwhile, across the Pacific, the Empire of Japan had for a long time been flexing its muscles. In 1853 the American commodore Matthew C. Perry had steamed his squadron of sleek, black-hulled warships into Tokyo Bay, opening relations with the island kingdom of Japan, which had been the most remote civilized nation on earth.

Some months later Perry returned with a full U.S. fleet bearing champagne, modern tools, women's clothing, a telegraph, guns, pictures of New York City, and an English-language dictionary and sailed "triumphantly home having brought a mighty empire into the family of nations without bloodshed."[13]

Perry's feat set off a chain of events, which, fifty years into the future, changed the world, as Japan incorporated Western science, culture, and military technology into its burgeoning economic system. The Japanese began purchasing large warships from the British, whose naval officers trained Japanese sailors, just as German officers were hired to train its army. In 1894 Japan set out to become an imperial power by invading Korea as well as Manchuria and the great Chinese island of Formosa.

This alarmed the Russians, who ran the Japanese out of Manchuria and took it for themselves. But the Japanese were not done. In a chilling parallel to the Pearl Harbor raid in 1941, Japan in 1904 launched a sneak torpedo attack at Port Arthur that annihilated Russia's Oriental Fleet, including two of the czar's largest battleships, only afterward bothering to declare war. Land fighting continued, with the Japanese getting the better of it, inflicting a hundred thousand casualties on the Russians at the Battle of Mukden.

The shocked Russians sent their much larger Baltic Fleet halfway around the world only to fall victim to the worst naval defeat in modern history. Twenty Russian warships, including four new battleships, were surprised and sunk by the Japanese at the Battle of Tsushima Strait, and seven other Russian battleships shamefully struck their colors and were captured. Between four thousand and six thousand of the czar's sailors perished in the action and the world awakened to the fact that Japan was a major international power.

The Russo-Japanese War also unleashed the first wave of anti-American sentiment in the nationalistic Japanese empire. Since its victory in the Spanish-American War in 1898 the United States had come to acquire vast properties in the far eastern Pacific, including Wake, Guam, and Midway islands, as well as the enormous archipelago of the Philippines. All of these properties lay in what the Japanese regarded as their "sphere of influence," and American diplomats, including Douglas MacArthur's father, Arthur MacArthur, were even then privately warning that the emperor's military was casting a hungry eye upon these remote possessions.

Theodore Roosevelt, whose slogan was "speak softly and carry a big stick," decided to roll out the big stick for the Japanese in the form of a "goodwill" cruise by all sixteen battleships of the U.S. Navy, painted white to signify friendship. In fact, it was a supreme example of gunboat diplomacy. On October 18, 1908, this armada arrived in Yokohama, where it was greeted by cheering throngs of Japanese who showered the American sailors with gifts.

This was in direct contrast to recent charges of anti-Japanese racism in the United States. Japanese had begun immigrating to America—in particular to the West Coast—in large enough numbers to alarm many who termed the flood the "Yellow Peril," a phrase popularized by newspapers of the period. The San Francisco Board of Education in 1906 had ordered Japanese children to be segregated from the whites, and West Coast workers began rioting and attacking Japanese immigrants who, they claimed, were working for "coolie wages," thus putting them out of jobs. The California legislature passed a resolution that referred to the immigrants as "immoral, intemperate [and] quarrelsome."

All of this created a great stir in the Japanese Diet (parliament), where there was talk of declaring war on the United States, a suggestion echoed by reactionary newspapers in Tokyo. Meanwhile, the Japanese increased their orders of warships from Europe, including dreadnought-class battleships.

The arrival of the Great White Fleet, as if by magic, seemed to sweep away these animosities, but at least one of the American sailors, a young naval ensign and recent graduate of Annapolis named William F. Halsey, wasn't buying it. Destined for fame as a U.S. Pacific Fleet commander in World War II, "Bull" Halsey recalled, "I felt that the Japanese meant none of their welcome; that they actually disliked us. Nor was I convinced when they presented us with medals confirming the 'good will' between our two governments."[14]

Halsey's premonitions were sadly borne out as Japanese-American relations slowly soured over the next three decades. Beginning in the 1920s, a rise in murderous militarism swept Japan so that by the 1930s it was said to be ruled under a "government by assassination." Japan repudiated an international naval armament limitation treaty of 1924 and, in 1931, once again invaded Manchuria, bringing on war with China. There commenced riots and beatings of Caucasians in Japanese cities, often "within sight of the police," after the U.S. Congress passed an immigrant exclusion act that forbade Chinese as well as Japanese from settling on American soil. In 1932 Japan walked out of the League of Nations.

The Japanese war with China ground on with nightmare slowness and brutality. In 1937, the Japanese exacted what came to be known as the Rape of Nanking—a bloody six-week orgy of almost unimaginable savagery on the peaceful Chinese metropolis. International newspapers and newsreels recorded the deaths of some 300,000 helpless citizens, most of them women and children, who were murdered in the most unspeakable ways. The city was burned and people were thrown into the flames. They were roasted alive or buried alive in pits. Infants were torn limb from limb. More than 80,000 women and children, ranging from eight to eighty years old, were raped by Japanese soldiers. People were speared on bayonets or thrown headlong into wells. Beheadings were so common that they were held on a contest-level basis to see which Japanese army unit could perform the most.

This reign of cruelty was so abominable that people still writhe at the telling of it; the world, of course, was shocked and horrified but did nothing. Even as the films, photographs, and news stories came back to the Western world, the Japanese claimed they were exaggerated. Later investigations proved that, if anything, the barbarity was underreported. The Japanese army was then two million strong, about fifteen times larger than the army of the United States. It was apparent that the Japanese intended a conquest of the entire Far East but no one knew when or how it would begin.

As this ghastly situation unfolded, George C. Marshall was abruptly pitchforked onto the world stage.

★ ★ ★ ★

WHILE HIS HOME LIFE WAS TUMULTUOUS, Patton still managed to produce a paper for circulation among key officers that was eerily prescient regarding a Japanese attack on Pearl Harbor. Patton's suspicions about the Japanese began during his earlier tour in Hawaii and became amplified as the Imperial Japanese Army began to invade and conquer her Asian neighbors and establish hegemony over far-flung Pacific islands upon which they built air and naval bases. Entitled "Surprise," Patton's paper theorized that the Japanese, "during a profound period of peace," would sneak aircraft carriers and an invasion force to within two hundred miles of Oahu and launch aerial attacks on U.S. military installations before landing troops. Japanese submarines, he predicted, would be lurking around the entrance to Pearl Harbor to sink any ship that attempted to escape. Also prescient was Patton's plan for the incarceration of all Japanese in the Hawaiian Islands—including those who had become American citizens—at the opening of hostilities. Only four and a half years later, President Roosevelt's controversial executive order relocated millions of Japanese from the West Coast of the United States.[15]

While the army seriously considered Patton's warnings, its present state of affairs did not allow for much reaction, and in June 1937 Patton sailed the *Arcturus* from Honolulu back to California for reassignment on the board of the Cavalry School at Fort Riley. The crew this time consisted of Beatrice, young George, Francis "Doc" Graves, a cook named Suzuiki, and the Norwegian deckhand, who had originally come with the boat. With light westerly winds they made the voyage in just one day short of a month, nearly twice the time of coming over. Once on shore Patton sold the boat but vowed to get another when he reached the East Coast.

Before he had that chance, however, Patton was riding with Beatrice on the Myopia Hunt course when he did the thing he had so often warned about in the summer bluebottle fly season. He allowed the head of his horse to come even with the stirrups of Beatrice's horse, a position that put his leg right behind the other horse. When a horse is fly bitten it will often kick, and Beatrice's did, causing compound fractures of Patton's right tibia and fibula, which cracked with the sound of a pistol shot.

While the injury put him out of business for nearly six months, Patton was promoted to colonel in July of 1938 and sent to Fort Clark near San Antonio to command the Fifth U.S. Cavalry Regiment. He was to take his place in the ongoing war games staged by the Third U.S. Army, which were designed to test concepts of troop mobility. By then Patton had become a full exponent of mechanizing the cavalry—not only armored cars and mechanized machine-gun carriages but tanks as well.

Fort Clark was in wild country, much the same as when Patton had been on the Mexican border with Pershing against Pancho Villa. It had a great restorative effect on Patton, who not only was back in a combat command position but could hunt and fish and ride wherever he damn well pleased. His letters from this time are full of satisfaction, hope, and praise and he made solid friendships among the high-ranking officers on the post.

After only four months, however, Patton was ordered back to Washington to take command of the Third U.S. Cavalry Regiment at Fort Myer. Waiting for him was all the spit and polish of its ceremonial duties, as well as the "Society Circus," which had been going strong ever since Patton had organized it many years earlier. The reason for the transfer, according to Patton biographer Martin Blumenson, was that a man of Patton's wealth and social connections was needed as the present commander of the unit. Brigadier General Jonathan Wainwright had driven himself into debt trying to keep up with the constant social swirl on an army officer's salary.

This time, in addition to conducting funerals of prominent people at Arlington, Patton's command escorted many political dignitaries, including the president of Nicaragua and the king and queen of England, who arrived for a visit to Washington in 1939. In between throwing fashionable parties for Washington's high and mighty, in June of that year Patton and Beatrice bought an eighty-foot, two-masted schooner, the *When and If,* which they sailed down from Massachusetts into the Chesapeake Bay and up the Potomac to the Capital Yacht Club in Washington, D.C.

Of course, the vast majority of enlisted soldiers could not live like that, and by mid-month most had run out of money to spend. Curiously, about that same time, Patton's dog would "mysteriously disappear at the same time each month," and he would post a reward notice in the stables offering $2 (about $30 in today's money) for the return of the dog. Invariably the dog would turn up and some "lucky" trooper would collect his reward.[16]

By then, Patton's friend George Marshall had become the army's chief of staff and was "batching it" with Patton in Patton's quarters at Fort Myer. It was a temporary stay while the chief of staff's sumptuous house was being renovated. Beatrice and the children were in the country at Green Meadows and Katherine Marshall was visiting friends. This gave Patton a chance to curry favor with Marshall for other high-ranking officers not so conveniently located.

And while he was at it, he did the same for himself; when, for instance, Marshall was made a four-star general as chief of staff, Patton presented him a pair of sterling silver stars (eight stars in all) that he had commissioned from a New York jeweler. The army in those days was small and the scheming for promotion among officers resembled, at times, intrigues from the bewildering days of the Borgias. On July 29, 1939, Patton confided to Beatrice that Marshall "is just like an old shoe. Last night he was dining out and instead of having a chauffeur he drove himself! He is going out in the boat with me today [a Saturday]. He does not seem to have many friends."[17]

★ ★ ★ ★

ON FEBRUARY 21, 1938, Jean MacArthur presented her husband with a seven pound, eight ounce boy who was christened Arthur MacArthur IV. He was tended to by Jean and a Cantonese nurse named Ah Cheu, and quickly the boy became the light of the general's life. The baby soon learned to walk, and before long MacArthur had created a morning ritual of martial bearing. When young Arthur would toddle into the couple's bedroom about 7 a.m., MacArthur would spring out of bed and come to attention. Then they would parade around the bedroom with the field marshal of the Philippines making the sound of drums until he burst into song, usually those from the turn of the twentieth century, which he taught to Arthur IV so the two of them could sing duets.

The birth of the child had a profound effect on Douglas MacArthur, who was going on sixty but looked and now acted twenty years younger. Practically everyone who knew him commented on this.

Unfortunately, by then, MacArthur had created a number of powerful enemies in Washington, including the new chief of staff Malin Craig, who resented MacArthur's prominence in the press and ordered him to return to duty in the United States. Soon after, the field marshal of the Philippines resigned from the U.S. Army, while numerous members of Congress simply wanted the army to withdraw from the Western Pacific and make the Hawaiian Islands the extent of U.S. influence in that ocean. But MacArthur always had President Roosevelt, who repeatedly called him "our greatest general" (though he told him privately, to his face, that he would be "our worst politician"). And Roosevelt trumped everyone.

MacArthur and Quezon continued to be "estranged," with the president of the Philippines now publicly suggesting that the islands were indefensible. MacArthur was irate not only with Quezon but with the politicians in Washington, who continued to refuse to send any arms and had put the islands on a low defensive priority.

Another loss came when war broke out in Europe on September 1, 1939, and Eisenhower, now a lieutenant colonel, asked to be released and sent back to the States, where he hoped to receive a combat command. MacArthur graciously let him go, and as his replacement he selected Lieutenant Colonel Richard K. "Dick" Sutherland, a gloomy, unctuous Yale graduate, whose father was a retired U.S. senator. Sutherland had some strange political views that didn't sit well with MacArthur, and one night, at dinner, MacArthur set him straight. Sutherland told the general and several other officers that democracy should be abolished in wartime, that Congress wasted too much time arguing. Elections, he asserted, ought to be eliminated in favor of a presidential dictatorship.

"No Dick, you are wrong," MacArthur told him. "Democracy as we have it in the United States is the best form of government that man has ever evolved." When people have freedom of speech and thought, MacArthur continued, they will keep their minds flexible and progressive. But, he said, in a dictator state freedom disappears and people's minds become rigid and regimented—"especially in time of war." Then, the general concluded, "something always goes wrong in the dictator's plan and the free-thinking people will defeat him."

"The trouble with you, Dick, I'm afraid," MacArthur summed up, "is that you forget that we fight for the ideals and principles of democracy." Thus ended the lesson for MacArthur's chief of staff, and nothing more was said of it because Sutherland was just the kind of officer MacArthur wanted for his second in command—crafty, obedient, and ruthless.[18]

PART III

BRAVE AS LIONS, BOLD AS BULLS

Chapter Eight

★ ★ ★ ★

THIS MEANS WAR

During the summer of 1939 the world watched with mounting outrage and distress as Adolf Hitler threatened to bring it to war once more. By then, his Nazi army had absorbed the Rhineland, Austria, and Czechoslovakia and was threatening to invade Poland, at which point both Britain and France had vowed to take military action.

The United States was slow in mobilizing its forces; the army was woefully undermanned—perhaps equal only to that of a third-world nation—and the air corps planes and navy ships were mostly outdated. What limited force the country had also lacked anything near the German arsenal of heavy tanks, armored cars, self-propelled artillery, and other mechanized combat vehicles.

When Hitler at last attacked Poland, U.S. military minds were shocked at the stunning success of the German *Blitzkrieg*,* which caused the collapse of the Polish army; World War II had thus begun.

By that time the decision had already been made that Marshall was to be the new U.S. Army chief of staff, and formal ceremonies were

----

* "Lightning war."

scheduled. But those proceedings were hastily canceled in favor of an immediate induction on that fateful September morning, and Marshall was rushed to the War Department on Pennsylvania Avenue next to the White House. At 9 a.m. he raised his right hand before the adjutant general and was sworn in as a permanent major general in the army. Then, following a pause for congratulations and handshaking, he took a second and far more important oath, as a temporary four-star general and chief of staff of the U.S. Army. Then Marshall sped away to the White House for an emergency conference with President Roosevelt and the nation's top leaders.

★ ★ ★ ★

AT A TIME WHEN THE ARMY was trying to expand in response to the deteriorating international situation great military maneuvers were held in various parts of the United States, including Virginia, where Patton was detailed to command a large mobile infantry-cavalry component. He took his role very seriously and was judged "superior" by the exercise umpires, yet he still felt himself stuck in place as a colonel and was exasperated that no stars seemed in sight.

In army maneuvers later that spring, a hastily cobbled together armored division decisively defeated a division of cavalry. It spelled the end of the horse in modern warfare, even though there were clearly not enough armored vehicles to go around, and the isolationist-minded Congress was loath to vote money to build them.

But then Hitler ended an idle period in what had come to be known as the "phony war," by attacking and conclusively defeating France, overrunning it in a mere six weeks with yet another powerful blitzkrieg. At last, Hitler had America's undivided attention. The politicians poured so much money and means into manufacturing that the United States would soon have enough tanks for several large armies.

Patton's career, however, remained inert, no matter how many private letters he wrote, how many luncheons and dinners he and Beatrice threw, or how well he now managed to control his manners in public.

Outwardly Patton was the model of a well-bred army field officer—gracious, all creased, and spit-and-polished. Inwardly, he seethed.

★ ★ ★ ★

IN SEPTEMBER 1940, the Japanese signed a mutual defense agreement with Nazi Germany and Mussolini's Fascist Italy. Known as the Tripartite Pact, the three Axis Powers, as they came to be known, promised to come to the defense of one another should they be attacked by any nation not then a belligerent—namely, the United States. When France fell to the Germans, Japan immediately pounced on her East Asian colonies Vietnam, Laos, and Cambodia, thus putting itself on the flank of the Philippines in the South China Sea. Not only that, the Japanese octopus began to spread its arms even farther south, occupying strings of islands on which they were building air bases. It was becoming evident that they had their eyes next on Indonesia, New Guinea, and the Malay Peninsula.

Alarm spread through the Philippines and a state of emergency was declared. MacArthur insisted to Washington that he had an army of 125,000 men ready to fight, but he needed weapons—guns, tanks, planes, and supplies. But from the War Department there was silence, so MacArthur played his last card: he telegraphed George Marshall that he was resigning and moving with his family to Texas! That produced immediate results. On a Sunday morning in July, MacArthur learned through the newspapers that, by order of the president, he had been placed in command of all U.S. armies in the Far East. Not only was MacArthur to be restored to four-star rank, Roosevelt announced he was freezing all Japanese assets in the United States and cutting off any further American shipments of oil, iron, or rubber to Japan.

The Japanese reacted by calling a million reservists into the army and issuing a statement saying that Roosevelt's actions made U.S. relations "so horribly strained that we can not endure them much longer." At last, MacArthur was going to get what he'd been screaming for all those years—men, munitions, planes. Through all of his military career, Douglas MacArthur had preached that "the history of war can be summed up in two words:

'Too Late.' Too late in comprehending the purpose of the enemy, too late in preparedness, too late uniting forces, too late standing with one's friends."

★ ★ ★ ★

IN THE AUTUMN OF 1941, a high drama began to unfold between Washington and its far-flung outposts in the Pacific. American intelligence had penetrated the Japanese diplomatic code. Beginning in late November of 1941 tensions between Japan and the United States had risen to such heights that U.S. Army Chief of Staff George Marshall was convinced war could break out with terrible suddenness. He put the commanders in Hawaii, the Philippines, Wake, Guam, and Midway islands, and other remote stations and garrisons on what was called a "war warning"—an alert that hostilities could begin at any time.

Earlier that month MAGIC—the code breaker's name for the top-secret project of intercepting Japanese messages—had intercepted a message from Tokyo to a secret agent in Hawaii telling him to send the precise locations of each American warship in Pearl Harbor. This caused the U.S. chief of naval operations, Admiral Harold "Betty" Stark, to reiterate to his commanders in Hawaii the necessity of sharp vigilance. Even as he did this, the Japanese aircraft carriers were already skulking their way toward the Hawaiian Islands.

Then, on the evening of December 6, the first thirteen parts of a fourteen-part message from Tokyo arrived at the Japanese embassy in Washington, D.C., with the final part to come the next day, December 7. Most of the thirteen parts of the message merely ticked off everything the Japanese didn't like about the United States, including its continued presence in the Far East and the recent decision by the Roosevelt administration to discontinue selling oil, rubber, metal, and other needed material to Japan. It further stated, ominously, that when the fourteenth part of the message had been received the ambassador was to see to it that all major code machines and codebooks at the embassy were destroyed.

When Colonel Rufus Bratton of army intelligence, who was on duty that night, read the message he became alarmed and asked his boss for permission to wake up the chief of staff. But Bratton was told there was "little military significance" in the message and not to disturb General Marshall. When the message reached the White House, President Roosevelt was talking with his aide Harry Hopkins. Roosevelt read the thing and handed it to Hopkins, and when Hopkins finished reading it the president remarked, "This means war."[1]

Hopkins suggested that the United States might want to attack the Japanese first. "No we can't do that," Roosevelt replied. "We are a democracy and a peaceful people." Nor did the president initiate a call to General Marshall or Admiral Stark, possibly assuming that they had already been alerted.

The next morning, December 7, Marshall went out for his regular long Sunday morning horseback ride at Fort Myer, still unaware of the message. An aide finally found him around 11:30 a.m., and by the time the chief of staff got to his office and read the message it was around noon. Colonel Bratton was standing before him, fidgeting, holding the vital fourteenth part of the message, which had come in the early morning hours. At last, Marshall read it: the Japanese were breaking off negotiations, which was not exactly a declaration of war in itself, but the part about burning encoding machines and codebooks certainly sounded like war. The Japanese ambassador was instructed to read the message to the U.S. secretary of war Henry Stimson at exactly 1 p.m.

Bratton deduced that something was going to happen in the Pacific at that time, but he didn't know where or what. It would be dark in the Philippines, he knew, and about daybreak at Pearl Harbor, but he never thought the Japanese would attack there. After the original "war warning," Bratton would later explain, "everybody in Washington thought the fleet would be at sea." It occurred to no one, apparently, to check.

When the chief of staff had read the entire message he conferred with Admiral Stark, then scribbled out a communication to all military commanders in the Pacific including Panama and Alaska:

> Japanese are presenting at 1 p.m. eastern standard time
> today what amounts to an ultimatum, also they are under

orders to destroy their code machine immediately. Just what significance the hour set may have we do not know, but be on the alert accordingly. Inform naval authorities of this communication—Marshall

In Washington, people were returning home from church or going out for Sunday dinner. Fans were filling up Griffith Stadium (the D.C. football stadium, now demolished) for the Redskins–Philadelphia Eagles game. As the rest of America went about daily life, Colonel Bratton was designated to get the new war warning to Pacific commanders by the highest possible priority. It would prove a daunting task.

He rushed the message to the army communications center where it would have to be typed out, encoded, sent, and delivered. By then, there was still nearly an hour left to alert the Pacific to the coming danger, but fate intervened. A giant solar storm had brewed up overnight and the army's radio communications with Honolulu were interrupted. No one seriously thought about using the telephone, as historian Gordon Prang has pointed out. Even with a scrambler it was considered insecure, and anyone listening to Marshall's message would have been able to figure out that the United States was reading Japan's secret diplomatic messages.

The communications officer on duty told Bratton that the next best way to get the warning out would be through civilian services. So he had it encoded and sent by Western Union from Washington to San Francisco, where it would be cabled by RCA to Honolulu, and then delivered to the message center at Pearl Harbor. From there, it would be given to the army commanding general, who would then pass it to the navy admiral commanding the base. By the time it arrived neither officer would have need of a warning.

The Japanese fury first burst in the skies above the Hawaiian island of Oahu. Carrier-based planes from the Imperial Fleet wrecked the U.S. Pacific Fleet and surrounding air bases. December 7, 1941, was a day, Franklin Roosevelt famously said, "that would live in infamy."

A FEW MONTHS PRIOR, George Marshall had planned to check himself into a hospital in Hot Springs, Arkansas. He was physically and mentally exhausted and felt he needed time off to recuperate. Since taking over as chief of staff in 1939, he had driven himself almost to the brink in organizing the U.S. Army for war, preaching preparedness at every turn. And, at every turn, congressional isolationists opposed him, accusing him of association with the Roosevelt regime through their newspapers. The war changed all of that; the isolationists either changed their minds or went underground, and whatever Marshall wanted was now only a matter of possibility—no mean task in itself.

The nature of the war had already changed dramatically before the Pearl Harbor attack. In June 1941, the Germans—instead of invading England as had been expected since the fall of France—suddenly turned on their erstwhile ally Russia. They launched a four-million-man attack along an 1,800-mile front in an attempt to surprise and subdue her old enemy. This provided a measure of relief to the United States, because if Britain had fallen the Atlantic would have become impossibly dangerous and there would be no staging ground for American and British armies to attack the Germans in France.

And as for the Japanese attack at Pearl Harbor, although it decimated the American fleet of battleships, it failed to accomplish two highly important tasks that would vastly improve America's fortunes in the months to come—it did not wreck the naval stores and shops that were vitally important to maintaining the fleet, and it did not sink the navy's only two aircraft carriers then in the Pacific—*Enterprise* and *Hornet*—which were at sea when the attack occurred. Nevertheless, the American people were roused to a fury probably never known before or since.

Then a relatively small event in the developing scheme of things occurred the week after Pearl Harbor in the far-off waters of Malaya. There, Japanese bombers and torpedo planes sank two British battle cruisers, HMS *Repulse* and the *Prince of Wales,* forever changing the way navies would view their primary fighting strategy. Two incredibly expensive capital ships, free to maneuver in the open ocean, had been sunk by a handful of cheap airplanes. Even the Japanese senior naval officers in

Tokyo found it difficult to believe. Overnight came the painful revelation that if battleships were to play any role in the war, they would require massive protection from carrier-based fighters, and that the carrier itself had now become the principal instrument of sea war. Winston Churchill "writhed and twisted in my bed as the full horror of the news sank in. In all the war I never received such a direct shock."[2]

★ ★ ★ ★

THE PHILIPPINES FOLLOWED PEARL HARBOR. A little past 3 a.m. on December 8 (December 7 in Hawaii) a frantic message flashed out from naval headquarters: "Enemy Air Raid Pearl Harbor. This Is Not A Drill." It was received not by General Douglas MacArthur but by Admiral Thomas Hart, commander of the small U.S. Asiatic Fleet based at Manila, who did not inform the commanding general on the assumption that the army had its own means of finding out.

It did. An alert army radioman with a shortwave tuner had been listening to music on a San Francisco commercial station when the announcer broke in with a wire service bulletin. He went screaming into the night with the news.

When it eventually got to MacArthur, he dressed and asked his wife to bring him the Bible, which he read for an hour before going to headquarters. Admiral Hart was there and after a conference he received MacArthur's blessing to steam his fleet south toward Australia to escape the fate of the ships at Pearl. While that conversation was in progress, Lieutenant General Lewis Brereton, commander of the Far East Air Force, rushed in to see MacArthur, wanting to send thirty-five B-17 heavy bombers to attack Japanese airfields on Formosa (now Taiwan) five hundred miles to the north. MacArthur refused on grounds that Roosevelt had sent a telegram insisting that the Japanese "strike the first blow"—a decision that has stirred controversy from that day until this one.

After arguing unsuccessfully that the Japanese had already done so at Pearl Harbor, Brereton ordered his bombers to take to the air and scout for an enemy invasion force—and of course to avoid being caught on the ground by a surprise attack. Again he asked MacArthur if he could attack Formosa; again he was denied, but instead was told to go there and take pictures of enemy airfields. After another hour, word came that MacArthur had authorized the attack on Formosa. Brereton ordered his planes to land at Clark Field, north of Manila, refuel, and load up with bombs.

These behemoths had barely touched down when the Japanese arrived overhead in force. Worse, the modern American P-40 fighters that had been scouting all morning for enemy planes had been ordered to land at Clark and refuel, and thus were sitting ducks on the runway when the bombs began to fall.* The pilots, who had been having lunch in the mess hall, rushed outside to see hundreds of Japanese bombers, "glistening in the sunlight," hurtling toward them. The men immediately scattered to the four winds.

In a maddening stroke of bad luck, fog had also delayed the Japanese planes on Formosa—otherwise they would have arrived right when the P-40s would have been there to greet them, and the B-17s could have flown to safety.

No less than three warnings of approaching Japanese planes had been sent and all failed to get through. In one case, the Teletype operator, like the pilots, was eating his lunch when word came; in another, an unnamed lieutenant promised to sound the alert but never did. Most of the U.S. antiaircraft ammunition was ten years old and failed to explode, or it exploded thousands of feet below the Japanese planes. For the Americans, it was a debacle. When it was over an hour later, most of the Far East Air Force was a shambles—not only the planes but the hangars and stores had also been wrecked and the aviation fuel exploded. Brereton called it "one of the blackest days in U.S. military history."[3]

The smoke had barely cleared when Brereton's phone rang. It was Hap Arnold in Washington, chief of the U.S. Army Air Corps. He was furious.

....

* There are conflicting stories about the sequences of these events—Brereton's, Sutherland's, and MacArthur's. To this author Brereton's seems the most convincing but the true story probably never will be known.

"How in hell could an experienced airman like you get caught with his planes on the ground?" he demanded. "That's what we sent you there for, to avoid just what happened!"

Brereton was trying to explain the situation when yet another flight of Japanese fighters appeared and began strafing his headquarters.

"What in hell is going on there!" Arnold shouted.

"We are having visitors," Brereton replied sourly.[4]

For the next two weeks the Japanese continued to bombard and strafe airfields all over Luzon and the other islands, leaving the inhabitants only to wonder when the invasion would begin. They wrecked the great U.S. naval base at Cavite, and even though most of Admiral Hart's larger ships were gone there were submarines, seaplanes, tenders, barges, oilers, tugs, and other useful craft either sent to the bottom or badly damaged. Thus MacArthur was left with no navy and no air force to contend with the rapacious Japanese, which was all the more galling because of his genuine love for the Philippines and the Philippine people, as well as his promises.

His biographer Manchester suggests that MacArthur—during this period after the initial air attacks—seemed to be in some kind of "daze" similar to that which afflicted Napoleon, George Washington, and even Stonewall Jackson at critical moments in their military careers. Perhaps that was so; MacArthur was then sixty-one years old, an age when most people are looking forward to retirement, when suddenly upon his shoulders was thrust tremendous responsibility.[5]

★ ★ ★ ★

ON DECEMBER 11, 1941, Hitler's Germany and Mussolini's Italy foolishly declared war on the United States, even though the Tripartite Pact did not require it. (It called for an Axis nation to declare war only in the event it was *attacked* by another power.) Thus the United States went from being a peaceful nation trying its best to stay that way to a belligerent at war with three powerful enemies who had been preparing for the occasion for nearly a decade.

It wasn't as though America was totally surprised by her sudden entry into the war; five months before Pearl Harbor at a secret meeting aboard the heavy cruiser USS *Augusta,* Roosevelt and Churchill—with Marshall present—made the first grand strategic decision of the war, namely that Germany was the most dangerous enemy and must be defeated first. The American army Marshall oversaw was more than three times larger than the one before he became chief of staff. It had an authorized strength of 375,000 men, plus half a million National Guardsmen who could be activated if necessary.

But it was still woefully inferior to its enemies. Over the next year it would expand to an army of millions, all of whom—civilians, as in World War I—would have to be trained and provided for.

The magnitude of the task was simply overwhelming. The Germans and Italians had overrun Europe and North Africa—only tiny England hung on by a thread—and the Japanese were busy conquering Asia and the Pacific. The Imperial Navy subdued the U.S. possessions Guam and Wake, their garrisons made prisoners in ghastly POW camps. And of course the Philippines were under heavy attack. There were fears on the West Coast that the Japanese might invade California or the Pacific Northwest, and one large Japanese submarine did in fact surface off the coast near Santa Barbara. For about twenty minutes, it began bombarding an oil field and refinery there, killing a number of cows.

The secret agreement between Roosevelt and Churchill notwithstanding, the president wanted an immediate retaliation on Japan and was astonished when Marshall and other chiefs told him that none was possible at the moment—the United States simply did not have the strength. They might get a few submarines close enough to Tokyo or other cities, Roosevelt was told, but the fire from the subs' lone three-inch (76mm) deck guns would produce slight damage, and the subs would probably be lost. A carrier attack seemed the only feasible scheme, but carrier planes didn't have the range to penetrate Japan's defensive perimeter of picket boats four hundred miles offshore, strike Japan, and return to their carriers. Even if they did, the size of their bombs was so small that, like the deck guns on the subs, they would likely only invite derision from the haughty Japanese. But Roosevelt was adamant that something be done—"the people demand it." Marshall delegated the task to his air chief Hap Arnold.

In July 1940, Henry Stimson had again become secretary of war, and he procured a number of high-ranking civilians from the private sector—such as General Motors president William S. Knudsen—to oversee the vast production increases in tanks, artillery, planes, munitions, and the thousand and one other items necessary for an army to have a fighting chance. In retrospect, this was a brilliant move, because these powerful capitalists were unfettered by a lifetime in the military bureaucracy where justifications, reports, and other inflexible rules and regulations often made it difficult to quickly accomplish complex and expensive tasks. Automotive manufacturers ceased making cars and began turning out tanks, jeeps, and army trucks. Appliance manufacturers stopped making refrigerators, fans, and stoves and started making parts for military use. The great American arms industry retooled for military weapons.

It became urgent to build a formidable combat air fleet, not only of fighters and bombers but also of troop transports, cargo carriers, observation planes, and so forth. Sixteen thousand planes were expected to roll off the assembly lines, with double that number the following year, double again the year after that, and so on. Before the war's end Henry Ford's giant plant at Willow Run, Michigan, was the largest airplane manufacturer in the world, turning out a bomber an hour.

★ ★ ★ ★

IN THAT SUMMER OF 1940, during the calm before the storm, Patton had gone on leave to attend the Beverly Farms wedding of Lieutenant James W. Totten and Ruth Ellen, who would become the third Patton to don the wedding dress of Beatrice's mother. But not without considerable ado. "Goddamnit, you can't marry him," Patton fumed, when told Totten was on the way to ask for Ruth Ellen's hand. "He's too short, he's a field artilleryman, and he's a Catholic!" Then he told her to go and mix up a pitcher of martinis without any vermouth. "I know you're serious," he told her, "because if you were just thinking about it you would have told your mother first."

A few weeks earlier, when visiting in California, Ruth Ellen had tried the idea of marrying Totten on her aunt Nita, who took "the dimmest possible view of me marrying a Catholic," said Ruth Ellen. She replied in tears, "Well, then I guess I will never marry; I'll just stay home and take care of Ma." At this, Nita drew herself up and "fairly shouted, 'What! And be like me? One sacrifice on the altar of family loyalty is enough. Go home and marry your young man, and God help us both. I'll come to your wedding!'"

Beatrice was also against the marriage, but not because of Totten's height (he was five-foot-five) or the field artillery angle; her objection was also on religious grounds. When Totten arrived that night Patton arose and stalked out, sitting through the same movie three times at the post theater. Beatrice held what amounted to night court as Totten sat speechless while being given a long summation "on the evils of Catholicism, and how he ought to be an Episcopalian." Ruth Ellen, meanwhile, sat mortified and "paralyzed by the whole scene."

After half an hour Beatrice wound up and asked, "Well Mr. Totten, what about it?"

Totten rose and went over to her and very politely asked, "Mrs. Patton, what do you think of turncoats?"

"I don't approve of them," Beatrice replied.

"Neither do I," said Totten, and took his leave.

Patton returned about an hour later to find both his wife and daughter distraught and in tears.

"Is it over?" he asked.

"Yes," Beatrice replied. "He wouldn't change."

Patton said he never thought he would.

Several days later, Totten told Ruth Ellen he intended to "brave the lion in his den" and ask Patton for her hand. This he did the same night, and his request was granted.[6]

AROUND THIS TIME, Patton was perusing the newspaper when he found an article about himself that reported he had been reassigned to the Second Armored Division at Fort Benning. It was official; he was back in the tanks and as delighted as ever. Patton immediately wrote the division's commanding general to say how excited he was at the prospect of his new assignment, closing with, "Best regards and looking forward to a short, and bloody war, I am Very sincerely."[7]

On July 26, 1940, Patton assumed his duties over one medium tank regiment, two light tank regiments, a field artillery regiment, and a battalion of combat engineers. There were 350 officers, 5,500 men, 383 tanks, 202 armored cars, and 24 105mm howitzers. More tanks were coming and additional soldiers were arriving at the rate of about a hundred per day. Though a brigade is traditionally commanded by a brigadier general, Patton remained a colonel. He was thoroughly pleased with his situation nevertheless.[8] He was certain now that the war would at some point draw in the United States, which would allow him to fulfill what he saw as his destiny—to become a great captain of the armed services.

Patton had championed the horse cavalry when he was a horse cavalryman, but now he sensed the strength of the fully engineered and developed tank: its great mobility that allowed for wide turning movements to get on the flanks and into the rear of a foe; its ability to produce shock and awe; and its efficiency in disrupting and degrading the enemy. Official army doctrine for the tank had always been "to assist the advance of infantry foot troops, either preceding or accompanying the infantry echelon," but the German blitzkrieg against France had just rendered that mission obsolete.

The tank was a new weapon for a new age in warfare, where the battlefield was fluid and the commander who arrived first with armored weapons would likely win the day. Patton saw himself as that man.

★ ★ ★ ★

Chapter Nine

THERE WILL BE
A BIG TANK BATTLE
IN THE MORNING

With the onset of war, Patton's promotion was meteoric. In the nine months between July 1940 and April 1941 Patton rose from the rank of colonel in charge of an armored brigade to the rank of major general commanding the Second Armored Division. Within another year he was in command of an armored corps, and then leading the Fifth U.S. Army during Torch, the Allied invasion of French North Africa.

Neither Dwight Eisenhower, who retained overall command of the operation, nor Patton, who would lead the landing force at Casablanca, much liked the plan or gave it a better than even chance for success. Writing in his diary from England on August 9, 1942, where Allied planners were setting up the invasion, Patton—after dining with Eisenhower—said, "We both feel that the operation is bad and mostly political. However, we are told to do it and intend to succeed or die in the attempt. If the worst we can see occurs [heavy resistance during the landing by the French army] it is an impossible show. But with a little luck it can be done at a high price, and it might be a cinch."[1]

Two months later, and a little over a month before the invasion fleet would sail from Norfolk, Virginia, Patton's opinion remained gloomy but somewhat more optimistic. He told Eisenhower he could "rest assured that when we start for the beach we shall stay there either dead or alive, and if alive we will not surrender. When I have made everyone else share this opinion, which I shall certainly do before we start, I will have complete confidence in the success of the operation."

Back in Washington and preparing for Torch, Patton dined with General Jimmy Doolittle, who five months earlier had returned a hero from his splendid air raid. The navy had finally figured out how to get sixteen army "Mitchell" B-25 bombers* aboard an aircraft carrier—in this case *Hornet*—and carry them within striking distance of Japan. The planes were launched in the North Pacific on April 18, 1942—eight hours early because an enemy picket boat had spotted the carrier force. It surprised the Japanese, who had been told no enemy could ever successfully attack the homeland.[2]

The real trouble for Doolittle came afterward, however, when his bombers reached China, where they were supposed to have safe landing fields. Because of the early takeoff, the planes arrived over Japanese-held China at night, in a rainstorm. With no airfields visible, they flew on until they ran out of gas and the crews bailed out in dark mountainous terrain. Two were killed and half a dozen were captured by Japanese—several of whom were executed—but the majority of the raiders survived and were conducted back to American lines by friendly Chinese.

....

* The B-25 "Mitchell" was named after the late General William "Billy" Mitchell who had lobbied so hard for improvements in American airpower that he was court-martialed for insubordination and suspended from the service. In 1925 he had predicted the Japanese attack on Pearl Harbor almost exactly as it occurred sixteen years later.

The raid was not only a great American morale builder in a time of frightful disasters, but it also caused the Japanese to use their communication system so heavily as to enable U.S. code breakers to decipher a majority of the Imperial Navy's top-secret messaging. This, in turn, allowed the U.S. Navy to ambush the Japanese fleet at the Battle of Midway, sinking four of their top-line aircraft carriers and halting Japanese expansion in the Pacific for good.[*,3]

Doolittle would now be commanding the 12th U.S. Army Air Force, which would support Patton's North Africa campaign. When Patton remarked that he was getting all the men and equipment he had asked for, Doolittle swilled a last glass of gallows humor: "Yes, George. They always give the condemned man what he wants to eat for his last meal."

Patton then called on General Pershing, his old friend and mentor, who was now eighty-two and at first barely recognized his former protégé. Pershing told Patton that he hoped he would carry with him to North Africa the same pistol with which he had killed the Mexicans and use it to kill Germans.

"I can always pick a fighting man and God knows there are few of them," Pershing declared. "I am happy they are sending you to the front at once. I like generals so bold that they are dangerous. I hope they give you a free hand."

When he left, Patton kissed the old man's hand and asked for his blessing and at the door turned and gave a salute, which Pershing returned, crisply as ever. Pershing had been the same age as Patton when he led the American army into France. Later Patton told his diary, "He looks very old but his mind seems quite clear. It is probably the last time I shall see him, but he may outlive me."

---

* From 1943 onward the Doolittle Raiders held annual reunions traditionally drinking a toast in special silver cups with their names engraved on them. When a raider died, his cup was placed in the raider's cabinet upside down. In 2014, the last two raiders drank their final toast, sharing a bottle of fine brandy bottled in 1896, the year of Doolittle's birth.

Much was expected of Torch, and of the army Patton would command. The tide of war had turned in the Pacific but this was not yet apparent to the Allies. U.S. Marines had landed on Guadalcanal and were in the final stages of wiping out the Japanese army there, though at a terrible cost. In June 1942 an American task force had ambushed and sunk the Japanese carrier fleet, permanently blunting Japanese expansion in the Far East. But no one could see the end of things yet, only the enormous amount of bloodshed that lay ahead.

In Europe the situation was worse. The Nazis, whose armies had penetrated deep into the Soviet Union, were solidifying their "impregnable Atlantic Wall" against the possibility of an Allied invasion. In the Egyptian desert, the British Eighth Army had battled to a bloody stalemate with German forces under Field Marshal Erwin Rommel at a railhead named El Alamein and were preparing for a second attack. If it was unsuccessful Rommel's army might well turn westward and fall on the American and British forces of Torch.

On October 23, before boarding the heavy cruiser USS *Augusta* that would serve as his command troop transport, Patton told his diary, "This is my last night in America. It may be for years and it may be forever. God grant that I do my full duty to my men and to myself." To Beatrice he wrote, "It will probably be some time before you get a letter from me but I will be thinking of you and loving you."[4]

Little did Patton know that on that same day the British Eighth Army attacked and defeated Rommel's German-Italo army in the Second Battle of El Alamein and were pushing them into Libya. If Torch was successful and the Anglo-Americans took Tunisia, Rommel would be caught in a trap between two Allied armies.

★ ★ ★ ★

PATTON'S COMMAND CONSISTED of 35,000 troops including the U.S. Second Armored Division and the Third and Ninth U.S. Infantry Divisions, aboard a hundred-ship convoy. Like so many Allied operations at the beginning of the war, Torch got off to a rocky start. This had much to do with the lack of time given to properly train the army troops in an amphibious landing. The army and navy tried a number of rehearsals, but because of the German U-boat menace along the Atlantic Coast they were confined to practicing in the Chesapeake Bay, which presented none of the large surf and strong weather associated with landings in Morocco.

A great fear of George Marshall and other planners had been that the Germans would learn of the invasion plans. The historian Thaddeus Holt points out in his book *The Deceivers* that by sailing time as many as five thousand American troops knew at least some of the plan, and the U.S. military worried it had been compromised by the Axis. If it is not a miracle that they never found out, it ought to be.

★ ★ ★ ★

AT SEA, TWO DAYS BEFORE the landings, Patton told his journal, "In forty hours I shall be in battle, with little information and on the spur of the moment will have to make momentous decisions. It seems that my whole life has been pointed to this moment. If I do my full duty the rest will take care of itself."[5]

The morning of the landings broke hazy and relatively calm and "almost too good to be true," according to Patton. "Thank God. I hope He stays on our side." Optimism that the French would not oppose the landings was quickly disabused, however. Just before 5 a.m. huge shore-bound searchlights went on and began playing across the sea looking for Torch ships. Heavy firing from French shore batteries and naval vessels followed immediately, splashing great gouts of water all around the ships. A French warship, likely a corvette patrol boat, came roaring out of the harbor and U.S. destroyers "opened fire and shot off the mast and killed her captain. I think she sank," Patton said.

On November 8, just before a soggy, gray dawn broke amid intense blasts from ship and shore, six thousand American soldiers—the first wave of the invasion—scrambled down cargo nets into waiting Higgins boats and navy launches. They were headed toward the lights of Casablanca that twinkled in the distance. The surf rolling onto the beach

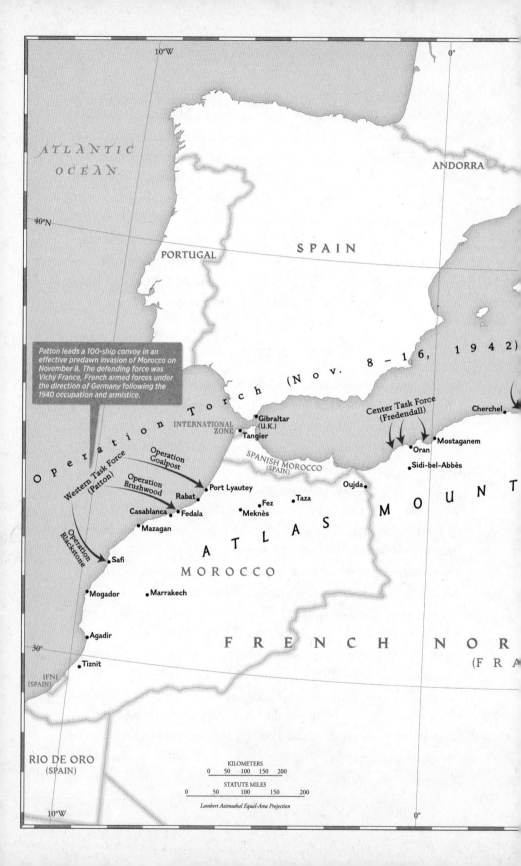

ATLANTIC
OCEAN

ANDORRA

40°N

PORTUGAL

SPAIN

Operation Torch (Nov. 8 – 16, 1942)

Patton leads a 100-ship convoy in an
effective predawn invasion of Morocco on
November 8. The defending force was
Vichy France, French armed forces under
the direction of Germany following the
1940 occupation and armistice.

Center Task Force
(Fredendall)

Cherchel

Gibraltar
(U.K.)

INTERNATIONAL
ZONE

Tangier

Mostaganem

SPANISH MOROCCO
(SPAIN)

Oran

Sidi-bel-Abbès

Operation
Goalpost

Western Task Force
(Patton)

Operation
Brushwood

Port Lyautey

Oujda

Rabat

Fez

Taza

M O U N T

Meknès

Casablanca

Fedala

Mazagan

A T L A S

Operation
Blackstone

Safi

MOROCCO

F R E N C H   N O R

Mogador

Marrakech

(F R A

Agadir

30°

Tiznit

IFNI
(SPAIN)

RIO DE ORO
(SPAIN)

KILOMETERS
0   50   100   150   200

STATUTE MILES
0   50   100   150   200

Lambert Azimuthal Equal-Area Projection

10°W

0°

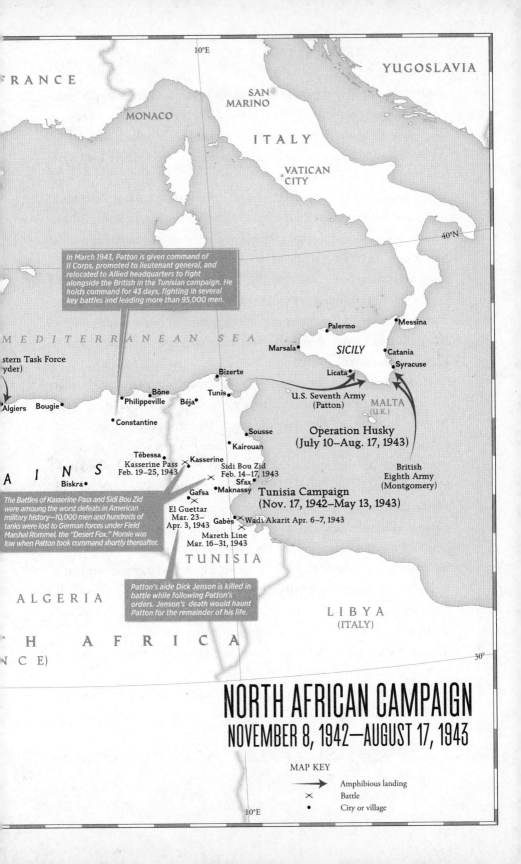

FRANCE

MONACO

SAN
MARINO

ITALY

VATICAN
CITY

YUGOSLAVIA

40°N

10°E

In March 1943, Patton is given command of
II Corps, promoted to lieutenant general, and
relocated to Allied headquarters to fight
alongside the British in the Tunisian campaign. He
holds command for 43 days, fighting in several
key battles and leading more than 95,000 men.

M E D I T E R R A N E A N   S E A

stern Task Force
yder)

Algiers   Bougie •

Constantine •

Bône •
Philippeville •

Béja •

Tébessa •
Kasserine Pass
Feb. 19–25, 1943

Biskra •

Bizerte •

Tunis •

Bijerte

✕ Kasserine

Sidi Bou Zid
✕ Feb. 14–17, 1943
Sfax •

Maknassy •

Sousse •

Kairouan •

Palermo •

Marsala •

SICILY

Messina •

Catania •

Licata •

Syracuse •

U.S. Seventh Army
(Patton)

MALTA
(U.K.)

Operation Husky
(July 10–Aug. 17, 1943)

British
Eighth Army
(Montgomery)

A I N S

The Battles of Kasserine Pass and Sidi Bou Zid
were amoung the worst defeats in American
military history—10,000 men and hundreds of
tanks were lost to German forces under Field
Marshal Rommel, the "Desert Fox." Morale was
low when Patton took command shortly thereafter.

Gafsa •
✕
El Guettar
Mar. 23–
Apr. 3, 1943

Gabès •

Tunisia Campaign
(Nov. 17, 1942–May 13, 1943)

✕ Wadi Akarit Apr. 6–7, 1943

Mareth Line
Mar. 16–31, 1943

T U N I S I A

ALGERIA

Patton's aide Dick Jenson is killed in
battle while following Patton's
orders. Jenson's death would haunt
Patton for the remainder of his life.

L I B Y A
(ITALY)

H   A F R I C A
N C E)

30°

NORTH AFRICAN CAMPAIGN
NOVEMBER 8, 1942—AUGUST 17, 1943

MAP KEY

→   Amphibious landing

✕   Battle

•   City or village

10°E

masked the sound of the boats' engines but soon enough the searchlights caught them. It could have been disastrous but gunfire from American destroyers shot the lights out almost immediately with "quad-fifty"-caliber machine guns and the boats continued to shore where they were met by intense small arms fire.

A naval battle continued for several hours, while landing craft took more American soldiers to the beach. Patton's boat, containing all his belongings including the ivory-handled pistols, swung on davits on the gun deck. "The first blast from the rear turret blew [it] to hell and we lost all our things except my pistols," Patton said.*, 6

The battle continued to rage chaotic on land and sea with the American forces slowly gaining the upper hand. A wind came, raising waves. By noon five French destroyers had been wrecked and just as many French submarines sunk.

Patton was several times soaked by seawater from enemy shells that hit near the *Augusta,* but in due time he secured another landing craft. At half past noon, he went over the side to rapturous cheering by a crew of sailors who were leaning over the rail. The fighting was still going on when Patton hit the beach, soaked again in the surf, "but I had no bullets," he complained. There he learned from the two colonels he had sent ashore that the French had declined to surrender, which was patently obvious. Disorder reigned along the landing beaches, which Patton personally began patrolling, kicking soldiers "in the arse" whenever he found them wanting. French aircraft regularly strafed the beaches, while in the harbor a transport carrying ammunition and "400,000 pounds of frozen beef" was torpedoed by a French sub and exploded, sending chunks of beef all over the beach to further the confusion.

Back in Washington, news of the landings broke over the radio at 9 a.m. A Paramount News crew showed up at Beatrice's door wanting to film her. With a microphone in her face Beatrice said, "This is America's

---

* The pistols were rescued by Patton's loyal aide-de-camp Richard Jenson, son of a childhood sweetheart of Patton's back in California. In time Patton "came to cherish [Jenson] as deeply as his own son."

hour of triumph. Safely our men have crossed the sea to fight our battle. The spirit of victory is in their hearts. They will not fail." When the cameraman moved from behind his camera, Beatrice could see he had tears in his eyes.

The Allied invasion was successful all along the North African coast but hundreds of Allied troops were killed before the French at last gave up on November 11, which coincidentally was not only World War I's Armistice Day, but also Patton's birthday. He had arranged with the U.S. Navy to bombard Casablanca with gunfire from the battleships, and at 5:30 a.m. he sent an officer to tell the French commander there that if he did not surrender, the city would be destroyed. An hour later the officer returned with news that the French had quit. To make sure, Patton ordered his Third Infantry Division into the city with orders not to shoot unless attacked. They were not, but Patton told his diary that "the hours from 7:30 to 11 were the longest of my life, so far."

At 2 p.m. the French admiral and French general who were commanding the Vichy forces in Morocco came to American headquarters to treat for terms. Patton opened the conference "by congratulating the French on their gallantry and closed it with champagne and toasts." He then gave the Frenchmen an American guard of honor back to their quarters. "No use kicking a man when he's down," Patton said.

The task now turned to getting American forces eastward, across the Atlas Mountains and into Tunisia, which had been defended by the French. But when Hitler got word of Torch he immediately began airlifting strong German army forces into the country. Mussolini began sending troops too. Following Rommel's defeat at El Alamein, he also had his Afrika Korps hightail it for Tunisia fifteen hundred miles to the west, where he hoped to make a stand or be rescued by Italian ships to fight another day. So swift was his flight that the British couldn't catch up with him.

★ ★ ★ ★

THE SITUATION IN MOROCCO settled after the French capitulation but remained tense. Patton had gone to great lengths not to humiliate the

French in front of the Moroccans, lest it inspire an Arab revolt. He was also concerned that the chaos of the invasion might arouse one or more of the Arab tribes to try and overthrow the sultan, Mohammed V, who ruled from Rabat. Then there was always the possibility that the Germans, Italians, or even Franco's Spanish, who ruled Spanish Morocco next door, might decide to invade. This last, regarding the Spanish, Patton privately told his diary he would welcome, "as it would give our soldiers some practice."

The French, for their part, claimed to be worried about the Moroccan Jews, who were rumored to be stirring up trouble. On orders from Vichy, the French government in Morocco had stripped the Jews of their rights to vote and work in most professions, similar to the way they were being treated in Germany. Furthermore, Germans operating within Vichy had propagandized the North African Arabs to believe that the Allies' arrival meant the establishment of a Jewish state as had been done in Palestine after World War I. When the Americans sought to restore rights to the Jews, the French demurred, saying it might cause the Arabs to revolt.

Patton's job now became largely political, which is to say ceremonial, an especially annoying development since his every nerve and sinew strained to get into the fight. "We have been here for a month today," he wrote to General Thomas Handy, a friend and aide to George Marshall, "which means that for 26 days we have not had any fighting. This is regrettable."

In keeping with his diplomatic duties, Patton and an aide drove from Casablanca, "a city which combines Hollywood and the Bible," to Rabat where the sultan was located. First he stopped by the residency of the French governor of Morocco, General Charles Noguès, whom Patton invariably described in letters and memos as "a crook." Guarding the residency, a magnificent marble structure, were a squadron of Spahis (Arab cavalrymen) and a company of Goums (short for Goumiers, native Moroccan infantry, which Patton understood was pronounced "goons").

Patton's party entered an inner court, filled "with white-robed men in biblical dress," and encountered the grand vizier, "in white, with enormous gold-filled teeth," who took them up three flights of stairs to see the sultan. The sultan, a handsome, frail young man, rose and shook hands, and speaking in Arabic (though Patton claimed the man spoke perfect French) he made a speech of welcome.

They then got down to business, which was to reassure one another that they must "make common head against the enemy." Before they left, the sultan admonished Patton about American soldiers not "showing proper respect for Mohammedan institutions," and Patton reassured him, saying he hoped if any such acts would occur that the sultan would report them to him personally. A few days later Patton flew across the Mediterranean—with an escort of four P-40 fighters—to see Eisenhower at his headquarters at Gibraltar.

"Ike lives in a cave in the middle of the rock—in great danger," Patton noted sarcastically in his diary. Patton was not, apparently, in a great mood that day. Eisenhower had just informed him that his deputy Major General Mark Clark—eight years Patton's junior at West Point—was to be commander of the new Fifth Army, which would combine all the American forces that had landed in North Africa. Patton had desperately wanted that job, and in his estimation Clark, whom he neither liked nor trusted, "seem[ed] more preoccupied with bettering his own future than in winning the war."

At lunch with Eisenhower, Patton met the British governor of the Rock, "an old fart in shorts with skinny red legs," who asked Patton if Clark was a Jew. "At least one quarter," Patton replied ignobly, "and probably a half." On the way back to Casablanca "the Spanish at Tangier shot at my left escort and possibly at me, but their aim was bad." He had trouble sleeping that night, he wrote Beatrice, but would "get ahead" of Clark yet.

★ ★ ★ ★

WINTER IN NORTH AFRICA is the rainy season and, as the Allies continued their push into Tunisia, the tanks and trucks could scarcely move along the greasy roads even when not confronted by German and Italian strong points. Worse, the tank models the Americans put up were the woefully outdated General Lee and General Stuart tanks that ran on gasoline with a 37mm gun that could not penetrate the armor on German tank hulls. German diesel Mark IV Tigers, however, were armed with an 88mm main cannon more than twice as powerful. The Americans called their tanks "flaming coffins," and one old soldier—seeing a column of high-profile Lee models clanking down the road—remarked that the tank looked like "a damned moving cathedral."

Even with these challenges, the Americans and British crawled forward on the main road that led from Algeria into northern Tunisia. They headed toward its capital, Tunis, which on a clear day could be seen gleaming tantalizingly white against the cobalt blue of the Mediterranean Sea. It would "remain a haunting memory through many tough days ahead," as the Germans were now streaming in great strength from their bases in Sicily and Italy, while Rommel's horde of 80,000, pressed hard by the British, was slouching Sphinx-like across the desert toward Tunisia.[7]

Patton had heard that the Americans in Tunisia were taking enormous losses against the Germans, and in early December he flew to Algiers. From there he went by staff vehicle to the Tunisian battlefields to see for himself what was going wrong. Tunisia was the land of the Carthaginians of antiquity who had made a great Mediterranean empire, fought the Punic Wars against Rome, and lost their civilization because of it. The Romans then began a prosperous centuries-long occupation until their hour came at the hands of the Vandals, plunging Western culture into a thousand years of darkness. Patton knew all about this, savoring it in his absorbent mind, for here upon this bountiful land, amid the olive groves, vineyards, and fields of golden wheat, were being fought some of the fiercest tank battles of the war.

Ernie Pyle, the diminutive and beloved Scripps-Howard correspondent, observed that "The battlefield was always an incongruous thing . . . some ridiculous impingement of normalcy"—in this case, the Arabs. "They were herding their camels as usual, some of them continued to plow their fields. Children walked along, driving their little sack-laden burros, as tanks and guns clanked past them. The sky was filled with planes and smoke burst from screaming shells."[8]

Patton visited his son-in-law John Waters, Bee's husband, now a colonel commanding a tank battalion that "had lost 39 tanks—two-thirds of its original strength." There, Patton found he was the only American general the men had seen their entire time at the front.

Leadership, poor tactics, and the inferiority of the American tanks and their ammunition were the culprits, Patton concluded. When he returned to Algiers he wrote up his notes and gave them to Eisenhower and Clark, neither of whom had visited the front. On a nighttime flight back to Casablanca, Patton had "the most dangerous experience I have had [so far] in this war." His plane was caught in an impossible rainstorm and they were considering jumping out. When the aircraft landed miraculously safe, Patton noted in his diary, "Again, God has saved me for something."

At last, on Christmas Eve, Eisenhower visited the fighting front after George Marshall himself ordered him to stop worrying about political considerations and concentrate on beating the Germans. He watched, appalled, during the fifteen-hour drive from Algiers in his big armored Cadillac staff car, witnessing firsthand the continual sights of men straining and struggling to free vehicles that were hopelessly mired in mud that "had the consistency of glue," in the words of the First Infantry Division commander. An army could never conduct offensive operations under those conditions, Ike concluded, and he called off the battle until spring. It was a terrific letdown, all the wasted lives, all the lost time, but there was nothing to do except wait until the ground dried out.

No sooner had Eisenhower returned to headquarters than he received an alarming message. As if Eisenhower didn't have enough on his plate, in less than three weeks President Roosevelt, Prime Minister Churchill, and all their top aides and staff were going to descend on Casablanca for a high-level conference to decide what to do next, assuming that they took North Africa from the Axis. The man Ike detailed to receive this great assembly of free world leaders was none other than George Patton.

Most of the pomp and circumstance was to be muted because of the secrecy imposed, but Patton personally scoured his army units for a band that could play "Hail to the Chief." He located a compound outside Casablanca where everyone could stay, and as Churchill, Roosevelt, and their people arrived at the airport, they were hustled into automobiles whose windows had been smeared with mud to conceal the identities of those inside. Patton was irked when a gaggle of Secret Service agents got into a jeep and rode behind Roosevelt brandishing pistols, as if his 50,000-man Western Army Corps was unable to provide enough security for the president. (Afterward Patton described the agents as "a bunch of cheap detectives always smelling of drink.")

★ ★ ★ ★

IN MID-FEBRUARY 1943, the Axis became worried at the advance of the Allies, slow as it was, across the Atlas Mountains and into Tunisia. Rommel, the infamous Desert Fox, had arrived in the area and linked up with the forces of General Hans-Jürgen von Arnim, but the Germans feared that the Americans and their Allies might drive deeper into Tunisia and split their armies. The decision was made to attack. On February 14, von Arnim's tanks surprised and overwhelmed the American forces under General Lloyd Fredendall's II or Eastern Corps at a place named Sidi Bou Zid. More than a hundred tanks and several thousand troops were lost, including those of Patton's son-in-law John Waters, who went missing when his battalion was cut off and destroyed by a force of eighty German tanks.

Patton was devastated, not only for himself but for his daughter "Little B." "I could not feel worse," he wrote Beatrice, "if [his son] George had been in John's place. I feel terribly sorry for B, but John may turn up yet."

Five days later, the Germans under Rommel attacked the Americans at the Kasserine Pass inflicting even worse losses and driving the Allies back more than fifty miles to the western passes of the Atlas Mountains. The Battles of Sidi Bou Zid and Kasserine Pass were among the worst defeats in American military history—some ten thousand men and hundreds of tanks lost. Worse, there were reports of incompetence, shirking, and even cowardice. The Americans, it seems, despite verified accounts of undaunted courage, were not performing—although they did manage to rally after the retreat and, with massed artillery barrages, successfully blocked Rommel from entering any of the passes along what was known as the Western Dorsale. With that, the Battle of Kasserine Pass, while still a defeat, was not an unmitigated Allied disaster; Rommel concluded that with Allied reinforcements he would be unable to break through and wreak havoc, so he ordered the Afrika Korps to return to its original positions along the so-called Mareth Line, a series of captured French-built forts in southern Tunisia.

Two weeks after the Kasserine Pass debacle, Patton "got a sudden call to go to the vicinity of the place where John [Waters] was last seen." When he reached Algiers, which had become Allied headquarters, Eisenhower told Patton that he was going to replace Fredendall as commander of II Corps. It was because "the fighting in Tunisia is a tank show and I know more about tanks," Patton wrote on March 6.

Fredendall, it seemed, had badly bungled the job. He was a likable and mostly able commander, but in Tunisia he never visited his front lines and positioned his infantry units from maps at headquarters, allowing them to be cut off in detail. Nor was he very cooperative with the British, a serious offense in Eisenhower's mind. Ike sent him a brief note to clear out and Patton now found himself in charge of both American corps in North Africa. The two corps constituted an army—except that they were separated by a thousand miles of some of the most hostile terrain on the African continent.

Six days later Patton heard from the radio that he was promoted to lieutenant general and, courtesy of his aide Captain Richard "Dick" Jenson, who had been carrying them for months, had a third silver star pinned on his shoulders. Patton told his diary that night: "When I was a little boy at home I used to wear a wooden sword and say to myself, George S. Patton, Lieutenant General."

Getting back to work, Patton's first move was to make Omar Bradley his deputy commander. It was an odd move, inasmuch as Bradley was nearly as different in personality from Patton as was possible. Bradley was a teetotaling, straitlaced midwesterner who found Patton's penchant for profanity appalling. But the cautious Bradley also acted as a kind of brake on Patton when he was in one of his loose-cannon frames of mind.

Patton's problems began almost immediately, some of them brought on himself—not the least of which was that he had become an inveterate Anglophobe when his II Corps was to be under the tactical command of the British general Harold Alexander. Patton immediately flew to Constantine to meet with Alexander, who "seems competent," he told Beatrice, yet impressed Patton by giving him a free hand with his corps, as opposed to being directly under British authority. Still, Patton resented being placed under the overall command of the British, and resented even more Eisenhower's acquiescence to it. "I think he [Eisenhower] has sold his soul to the devil with this 'cooperation,'" he remarked.

Patton's new command contained about 90,000 men in four divisions: Terry Allen's First Division, Orlando Ward's First Armored Division, Manton Eddy's Ninth Division, and Charles Ryder's Thirty-fourth. Upon his arrival in the combat zone, Patton immediately took note of the decidedly unmilitary bearing of the troops and issued orders that the soldiers would wear clean uniforms with ties, shined boots, polished brass, and helmets. GIs would always salute officers and discipline would be rigidly enforced. "It's absurd to believe that soldiers who cannot be made to wear the proper uniform can be induced to move forward in battle," explained his thinking on the subject. Worse than their dress, Patton found that the men's morale was low, and he believed the best way to raise it was to be seen and heard as much as possible.

As a result, when he was not in conferences planning the next move, Patton was out giving pep talks to the troops the language of which, in the opinion of his then deputy corps commander Omar Bradley, "would not be suitable family fare."[9]

One of the most pressing military issues Patton had to face was a lack of air cover. The British seemed unable to intercept German fighter-bombers that continually bombed and strafed his troops, adding to the morale problems. The Englishmen dismissed Patton's complaints and pleas, insisting that the British had complete air control. After a particularly nasty contretemps between Patton and a British air commander, a meeting to resolve the problems was arranged by the British air marshal Arthur W. Tedder and U.S. Lieutenant General Carl "Tooey" Spaatz at Patton's headquarters. They had barely finished formalities when four German Focke-Wulf fighter-bombers roared in, strafing the streets with their machine guns and dropping bombs that sprayed plaster from the ceiling and dislodged Patton's office door.

When the fracas was over and the German planes roared off, Spaatz asked Patton incredulously, "Now how in hell did you manage to stage that?" Tedder rose from the floor and said to Patton, "I knew you were a good stage manager, but this takes the cake." For his part, Patton dusted himself off and replied with a grin, "I'll be damned if I know, but if I could find the sonsofbitches who flew those planes I'd mail them each a medal."

Meanwhile, Allied air and sea power had "virtually isolated" the German and Italian armies in Tunisia from resupply and reinforcements. Rommel, sensing a disaster, flew to Berlin to try and organize a Dunkirk-style plan to evacuate his Afrika Korps. But Hitler, suicidal even then, utterly refused and insisted that they fight to the death. The toady-like Mussolini did the same for his Italian command.

Alexander's plan in North Africa was to defeat the Axis by initiating a "squeeze play" in which General Bernard Montgomery's Eighth Army would attack and smash Rommel's Germans at the Mareth Line, while another British army under Kenneth Anderson (including some 50,000 converted Vichy French) would hold the north and north-central sectors of Tunisia. For the Americans, whose battleworthiness Alexander held in contempt, was reserved a minor role of "demonstrating" (i.e., feinting, taking a few small objectives, mostly making noise) to convince the Germans they were about to be attacked. They were expressly prohibited from making a thrust into the coastal plain.

Disgusted, Patton resigned himself to the situation and drew a battle plan in which the First Infantry Division would march out of the Western

Dorsale and drive to Gafsa, while the First Armored Division would strike at Maknassy in the Eastern Dorsale. The Ninth Division would stay behind in reserve and the Thirty-fourth Division would hold back until the Axis retreated and strike them at Sbeitla.

On March 16, the night before the battle, Patton told his astonished staff: "Gentlemen, tomorrow we attack. If we are not successful, let no one come back alive," then went to his room to pray.[10] He wrote in his diary, "The hardest thing a General has to do is to wait for a battle after all the orders are issued." At 11 p.m. he heard firing from the direction of Gafsa and wrote, "Well, the battle is on. I'm taking off my shoes to go to bed."*

Patton joined the First Infantry troops in the front line when they jumped off before dawn. The Americans easily rolled over the initial objectives. Gafsa was taken without much fanfare. It wasn't much in the way of big battles, but it served to restore the Americans' confidence after Kasserine and added mightily to Patton's reputation back in the States. ("If any American officer ever had the will to win that officer is Lieutenant General George S. Patton," crowed a prime-time radio show.)

He wrote to Beatrice: "The weather is frightful cold and wet. The Roman ruins are wonderful and one gets quite used to passing huge cities without even knowing the names. It's hard to believe the Romans were here for 700 years. I have found out why all the pillars are broken: the Romans pinned them together with bronze pegs, and the Arabs pushed them over to get the metal. What a race! I feel sorry for the men in this cold."

On March 19, Patton joined the First Armored Division that was utterly bogged down in mud on its way to attacking the Maknassy Pass. It was important to Patton, because if the pass were breached the Americans would threaten to break out into the coastal plain with possibly disastrous results for the Afrika Korps. After a forty-two-mile jeep ride

----

* This was a night action preliminary to the main attack in the morning.

that took three hours Patton arrived at the command post of General Orlando Ward.

"He is in a sea of mud, really awful," Patton told his diary. "He fears that tanks can't move, due to mud, but I told him to do it with his infantry. I want to hit Rommel before he hits us, also to help Eighth Army, which attacks tomorrow night." What Patton didn't know, however, was that the Germans had already taken the bait and moved the Tenth Panzer Division into the gap at Maknassy.

The next day, Patton rode to his various divisions, urging them on. After retiring he was awakened at midnight by Bradley with news that his son-in-law John Waters was safe, captured. Patton's aide Dick Jenson wrote to Beatrice, "If the General gets any more good news I think we will have to sit on him to keep him down. I think the hex is over." On March 21, while pushing General Ward to attack the Maknassy Heights, Patton closely escaped death himself when a salvo of large German artillery shells exploded on a hillside where only moments earlier he had been standing.

Continuing the push two days later, Terry Allen's First Infantry Division ambushed a battle group of tanks and infantry of the Tenth Panzer Division. The battle raged from morning throughout the afternoon, during which American artillery and M10 tank destroyers demolished several dozen enemy tanks and slaughtered a large number of infantry before the Germans retreated in disorder. It was a significant victory not only because it set up a further American offensive to clear all of the Tunisian Eastern Dorsale of Axis units, but also because it was the first American victory against the German army.

On March 26, the attacking British Eighth Army drove the Germans from the forts of the Mareth Line. Four days later—disgusted with Ward's lack of progress—Patton moved a substantial portion of Ward's armor to the First Infantry Division for a lightning strike down the El Guettar road, which would threaten the left flank of the retreating Afrika Korps. Both Patton and Bradley attached their aides to this force not only because it was short of staff officers but also to give the aides some combat experience. "There will possibly be a big tank battle in the morning," Patton wrote Beatrice. "We are trying to cut Rommel off and he don't like it."

The American attack was almost immediately bogged down and Patton was furious. He called Ward and told him to assault the Axis positions at Maknassy and, if necessary, to take casualties "up to twenty-five percent," adding, "Goddamn it! I want that hill in front of you. Get off your ass; get a pistol in your hand, and lead that attack yourself."

"I feel quite brutal to order people to take such losses, especially when I personally am safe, but it must be done," Patton told his diary that night. "Wars can only be won by killing and the sooner we start the better."

The next day, April 1, Patton received one of the great shocks of his long, shock-filled career. "Dick Jenson was killed this morning," he wrote Beatrice. "It was my fault in a way," he said, and told her what had happened. Jenson was at the forward command post with Omar Bradley when twelve Junkers 88 fighter-bombers came. Everyone jumped into a slit trench, but a 500-pound bomb landed just on the edge near Jenson and killed him instantly. "It was concussion that got [Dick]. He was not mangled in any way," Patton wrote, brokenhearted.

"We brought him to the cemetery here at Gafsa and will bury him at 4:00 p.m.," Patton continued. "Gaffey* and I went out to see his body wrapped up in a shelter half. I knelt down and kissed him on his forehead. He was a great character and loyal, long-suffering friend. I shall miss him very much. I feel very sorry for Echo [Jenson's mother]. I cut a lock of his hair and sent it. I will send all his trinkets as soon as I can find them."

While Patton grieved over Jenson's loss, his offensive with the First Infantry Division had broken through the German and Italian defenses and was rolling on out of the mountain passes and into the Central Plain. Alexander at last gave Patton a chance to wedge his forces between the two German armies in Tunisia and cut them off.

---

* General Hugh J. Gaffey, a member of Patton's staff.

But before doing so Patton paid respects to his fallen aide. "Stiller, Sgt. Meeks, Sgt. Mims and I went to the cemetery at 1600. Dick was wrapped in a white mattress cover. We had a squad and a trumpeter, but did not fire the volleys, as it would make people think an air raid was on. The Corps chaplain read the Episcopal service and he was lowered in. There are no coffins here, as there is no wood. He was a fine man and a fine officer. He had no vices. I can't see the reason that such fine men get killed. I shall miss him a lot." Patton's biographer Carlo D'Este has written: "Like nothing else he had ever experienced, Dick Jenson's death haunted Patton for the remainder of his life, and served as a constant reminder of the awesome responsibility of being a commanding general. Correspondents calling on him in Gafsa after the funeral found him still in tears."[11]

As the fighting moved on, so did Patton. He set up new headquarters in Constantine (founded by Trajan in A.D. 200 or 100, he noted) and had lunch at the mess of U.S. Army Air Corps general Tooey Spaatz. Afterward, he reflected that "Men . . . are too damned polite. War is very simple, direct, and ruthless. It takes a simple, direct and ruthless man to wage war."

Before leaving Gafsa, Patton had once more visited Jenson's gravesite and took a picture of it to send to his mother. "I picked some nasturtiums in the yard and I went to the cemetery to tell Dick goodbye," he wrote. "There are more than 700 graves there now." Patton later received this in reply. "You gave him the happiest years of his life," wrote Mrs. Jenson. "After his father's death, you took his place, and his admiration and affection for you were unbounded. I quite agree with you that he should not be moved from Africa." She said she wanted Patton to keep Jenson's personal belongings "with undying gratitude for making it possible for him to do all the things he wanted to do."

★ ★ ★ ★

IN CONSTANTINE, PATTON WAS relieved of II Corps, which was no surprise, and Bradley took his place. His new job was to plan for and lead the American forces in Operation Husky, the amphibious invasion of Sicily to knock Italy out of the war. George Marshall telegraphed: "You did a fine job [with II Corps] and further strengthened confidence in your leadership."

The campaign for North Africa concluded successfully for the Allies shortly thereafter. Rommel had gone back to Germany before the end, but in mid-May some 250,000 Axis troops surrendered, and more than 40,000 had been killed. The Allies counted nearly 60,000 dead, but North Africa was free of Germans and Italians—a major turning point in the war. Meanwhile, Patton had become even more bitter over Eisenhower's insistence that U.S. forces cooperate with and even serve under the British.

"So far this war is being fought for the British Empire and for post-war considerations," he wrote in his dairy. "No one gives a damn about winning it for itself now." It was too true. The British, and to some extent the Free French, were planning the war politically to reclaim the North African empires that the Axis had conquered. To Patton's dismay and disgust, the wily British general Harold Alexander was placed in charge of ground forces in the Sicilian operation.

For his part, Patton had led the corps for forty-three days, fought several successful battles, commanded 95,800 men, lost twenty pounds, and gained a third star "and a hell of a lot of poise and confidence, and otherwise I am about the same."

★ ★ ★ ★

THE BUGABOOS THAT BEDEVILED Patton in North Africa plagued him in Operation Husky as well. Alexander, still mistrusting the American army in combat, had given Patton a secondary role in the Sicilian campaign. Patton's forces—initially consisting of the nearly 96,000 men of his two North African corps, but soon to become nearly triple that number and designated the Seventh U.S. Army—were to protect the left flank of Montgomery's Eighth British Army as it landed upon Sicily's southern shores. They would then march up the coast to capture Messina, the capital of the Italian province of that name and the jumping-off point for an invasion of greater Italy.

Patton had learned not to question Eisenhower on matters of British control; it became a sore point with the Allied commander. Instead Patton outwardly welcomed the chance to participate in any operation that contained a role in it for himself, and privately he waited to seize any opportunity to expand that role into one of overwhelming importance. "This is what you get when your Commander-in-Chief ceases to be an American and becomes an Ally. The U.S. is getting gypped," Patton groused to his diary.

After weeks of preparation for Operation Husky, the planning had become a royal mess concocted by the various entities involved. For one, the U.S. Navy was reluctant to use ships in what it saw as a risky situation in range of Axis fighters and bombers. To make matters worse, nobody could decide where to land the two armies. At last Montgomery cornered Ike's deputy Bedell Smith in a North African air force officers' latrine, where he steamed up the lavatory mirror with his breath and drew an outline of a convincing assault plan. Eisenhower endorsed it, breaking the impasse.

With motorcycle escorts, blaring sirens, and other hoopla of his exalted rank, Patton meanwhile darted from unit to unit of his command delivering a pep talk for the upcoming operation. On Memorial Day, he laid out for the troops what might be deemed the Patton philosophy of war: "We must remember that victories are not gained solely by selfless devotion. To conquer we must destroy our enemies. We must not only die gallantly, we must kill devastatingly. The faster and more effectively you kill the longer will you live to enjoy the priceless fame of conquerors."

Around that time, Patton got word that his son, George IV, like his father before him, had flunked mathematics in his first year at West Point. And, like his father before him, he wrote that he planned to take the reexamination and return to the academy next September to repeat his plebe year.

"I am naturally distressed by George's failure but apparently he came by his mathematic ability very naturally," Patton wrote his brother-in-law Frederick Ayer, "and I now feel convinced he will wind up at least a lieutenant-general, that is, if he continues to follow so accurately in my footsteps."

★ ★ ★ ★

HUSKY KICKED OFF IN THE EARLY morning hours of July 10, 1943, with a thunderous naval bombardment. Watching from the deck of the cruiser *Monrovia*, Patton was convinced that the Italians "must be scared to death"—though he himself recorded an anxiety similar to that of "before a polo match."

After the initial shelling the First Infantry Division waded ashore and took the German-Italian airfields at Gela, led by Lieutenant Colonel William O. Darby and his force of Army Ranger Battalions. The next morning the Germans and Italians counterattacked, but after initially penetrating the division's perimeter they were smashed by naval gunfire during a fierce battle that included paratroopers from the 82nd Airborne Division.

Guns blazing, Patton could no longer stand being on the ship. Accompanied by several aides, he waded ashore at 9:30 a.m. to inspect the battlefield. They arrived at Darby's command post in Gela to witness an Italian armored counterattack; from a rooftop they watched enemy tanks roll across a plain straight toward him. When Patton saw a navy forward observer standing in the street below with a radio, he hailed him, "Hey, you with the radio!"

Pointing to the tanks Patton shouted, "If you can connect with your Goddamn Navy, tell them for God's sake to drop some shellfire on the road!" Soon large-caliber shells from the cruiser USS *Boise* were blasting the Italian tanks into junk metal. Before leaving the Rangers, Patton ordered them to "kill every one of the Goddamn bastards!"[12]

According to biographer D'Este, that day marked the beginning of the deterioration in relations between Patton and Omar Bradley, which, until then, had been good. Patton, it seems, had countermanded an order Bradley gave to the First Infantry Division, and though he later apologized he apparently told Eisenhower that Bradley was "not aggressive

enough." When asked about it by Ike, Bradley responded that the remark was "an unforgivable slur."[13]

During the early days of fighting, the Italians and Germans committed such an inordinate number of atrocities and tricks that "there are more enemy dead than usual," Patton wrote Beatrice. On July 16, Patton told her, "The enemy has been booby-trapping his dead, which has made our men very mad. Yesterday I drove over some of our battlefields and smelled dead men for ten miles. The [Germans and Italians] have now pulled the white flag trick four times. We take few prisoners."

★ ★ ★ ★

FOLLOWING THE SUCCESSFUL LANDINGS, Alexander essentially allowed the American and British armies to develop their own operations with the general understanding that the Americans would be the "shield in the left hand" protecting the Eighth Army, whose right hand contained "the sword"—pointed at Messina, the main strategic objective in Sicily. Alexander bungled an opportunity, however, when he issued orders that forbade Bradley from moving quickly up Highway 124, a main artery, to encircle and obliterate the German defenses at Enna. This error caused excessive delays to Montgomery's plans for taking Messina and gave Patton his chance. After writing Beatrice that "Monty is trying to steal the show," Alexander's dithering allowed Patton to march swiftly across the northwest face of Sicily to capture the city of Palermo, the country's major port on the Tyrrhenian Sea. This he did on July 21 to a wild reception by thousands of cheering, flag-waving, disillusioned Sicilians shouting, "Down with Mussolini!"

Declaring that future students "at the Command and General Staff School will study the campaign as a classic example of the use of tanks," Patton described for reporters how his army had marched 200 miles over crooked roads, killing or wounding 6,000 Italians and capturing another 44,000. If anyone in the United States had failed to know who General George Patton was before, they certainly knew it then; he was the leading subject of newsreels across the land, his face plastered on every newspaper in the country.

★ ★ ★ ★

WITH MONTGOMERY STILL SLOGGING it out in the eastern hills of Sicily, Patton cast his gaze on Messina, which the British initially intended to gloriously and victoriously capture. A wrinkle, however, had developed in the form of savage German resistance to the British Eighth Army. Realizing that he was bogged down, Montgomery visited Patton in a conference to discuss strategy. He utterly astonished the American commander by proposing that Patton's Seventh Army take Messina if the Eighth Army could not break free.

Despite this, Patton suspected that Montgomery was being disingenuous and meant somehow to trick him into *not* getting to Messina first. Patton quickly regrouped his army, turned the II Corps 90 degrees to the right, and began a march toward Messina on the north Sicilian coastal highway. Along the way, he sent a note to Major General Troy Middleton, one of his division commanders, saying, "This is a horse-race in which the prestige of the U.S. Army is at stake. We must take Messina before the British. Please use your best efforts to facilitate the success of our race."[14]

The "race" had slowed to a walk, and then a halt, as the Germans ferociously resisted the American advance, giving way only at the expense of immense bloodshed. To counter this, Bradley ordered his division commanders to maneuver the enemy out of their positions rather than assault them frontally, until Patton stopped Bradley on the road with the following exhortation: "I want you to get to Messina just as fast as you can. I don't want you to waste time on these maneuvers, even if you've got to spend men to do it. I want to beat Monty into Messina." Bradley was "shocked" and "sickened," and he ignored the order, refusing "to waste lives merely for the sake of winning a meaningless race."[15]

Still, Patton was all over the battlefield, ordering, cajoling, suggesting. At one point he encountered a column of troops stuck in a holdup on a bridge while a local farmer tried to budge two stubborn mules pulling his wagon. Patton roared up in his jeep, pulled one of his ivory-handled pistols, and shot both animals behind the ear, then ordered his men to throw the carcasses off the bridge. It might seem to be an example of Patton's cruelty, but he was more concerned for hundreds of his men to run the risk of being strafed by the Luftwaffe than he was with the mules.

To slow the Allies, the Germans blew up bridges behind them and sowed thousands of land mines. Bradley and Patton dreamed up what they called their "end run" tactic, a night amphibious landing to leapfrog behind the German lines utilizing U.S. Navy landing craft that had originally carried the men to the beaches. By August 16, with the British still stuck miles from Messina, the end-run amphibious landings had combined with an almost superhuman effort by Lucian Truscott's

Third Division and others and together the American troops entered Messina. Hitler, at last having learned a lesson from the mass surrender of his troops in North Africa, had allowed the German forces in Sicily to evacuate.* They would fight again another day.

At 10:30 a.m. the next morning, Patton and Truscott—accompanied by aides and escorts—triumphantly entered the city. Patton was resplendent in his brown gabardines and shining helmet liner. The sirens on his jeep blared, its "three-star pennants gleaming in the sunlight," as the convoy entered the piazza in the town's center. About an hour later the first units of the British column "clanked into the city."[16]

For his part, Omar Bradley was fuming that Patton had ordered this circus-like atmosphere to stoke his own ego while Bradley's men were stuck in the hills "to watch helplessly as the last of the Germans fled the city." He later said, "I was so angry . . . that I was half tempted to enter the city and greet him on a street corner when he arrived." The rift between the two former friends was complete.[17]

The monthlong campaign of what Patton called "one of the fiercest sustained battles in history" had been a smashing success; at a cost of 24,850 Allied casualties (5,837 of these killed in action) some 20,000 Germans were dead and approximately 150,000 Italians were lost. More important, the defeat caused the already shaky Italian people to rise up and overthrow the Fascist regime. Mussolini fled to Germany and the Italians surrendered—which might have ended matters, but the Germans had no intention of giving the Allies a foothold in Italy from which they could bomb and even penetrate Germany easily from the south. Many months of terrible fighting lay ahead along the boot of Italy, but Patton would not be connected with it. Another shoe was about to drop that would stain the fabric of his illustrious career.

★ ★ ★ ★

* In the course of a week the Germans evacuated 40,000 of their own soldiers, 70,000 Italians, 10,000 vehicles, and 200 guns plus tanks, ammunition, fuel, and other supplies.

PATTON HAD PERFORMED brilliantly in the Sicilian conquest. Everyone said so, from President Roosevelt to George Marshall to Ike, each of whom wrote letters of high praise.

Patton, however, remained in Sicily, headquartered in a palace, worried about his army, his future, and his weight. He began walking two miles a day for exercise while having sumptuous lunches, teas, or dinners with local gentry that he often recorded for Beatrice's edification: "The other day I had tea with a very fat Bourbon Princess who has a black beard which she shaves. She talks bad French at the top of her powerful lungs, yet when she was young she must have been quite lovely."

In the meantime, Patton was losing his army right out from under him. With the war raging as the Allies slowly climbed up the Italian boot toward Rome, Eisenhower was ordering away Patton's divisions piecemeal to join Mark Clark's Fifth Army on the Italian mainland. Patton was appalled at the American tactics, which pitted nine U.S. divisions against eight of the Germans. He did not see how the Allies, without a clear superiority in manpower, could advance "at any speed at all" with the Americans on the attack and unable to rest their men, while the Germans—in the mountainous terrain favoring defense—could rest theirs constantly.

★ ★ ★ ★

BETWEEN HIS OFFICIAL DUTIES, which included receiving American dignitaries, Patton passed the days speculating in his letters and diary on what the army next had in store for him. Then, on August 20, a brigadier general from the Armed Forces Surgeon General's Office showed up with a personal and secret letter to Patton from Ike. It began: "I am attaching a report which is shocking in its allegations against your personal conduct."

Ever since his days at West Point, Patton had been a bellicose figure. He had always and genuinely loved his troops, but at the same time he despised inefficiency, laziness, and especially cowardice, which he considered the ultimate sign of weakness in a soldier. Patton was convinced that cowardice was the fault of the commanding officer, who either himself was a coward or permitted such behavior through dereliction of duty.

During the Sicily campaign he had encountered the perfect setup to raise his legendary temper to the boiling point—and beyond—when, during a temporary stalemate in the action, he entered a field hospital tent to hand out medals and encountered a man suffering from "battle fatigue" or "shell shock." Patton did not believe in shell shock, despite the fact that its symptoms were well known in military medicine. He lost his temper, accosted the soldier, slapping him across the face, and ordered him out of the ward, shouting, "I don't want any yellow-bellied bastards like him hiding their lousy cowardice around here, stinking up this place of honor." As if that were not bad enough, a week later Patton discovered another shell-shocked soldier in a hospital ward and waved his ivory-handled pistol in his face, saying, "You ought to be lined up against a wall and shot," even threatening to do it himself. He also slapped this soldier across the face.[18]

Doctors at the hospitals had filed formal complaints against Patton that Eisenhower was duty-bound to deal with. Instead, Ike ordered the complaints locked away in his top-secret files and wrote a stern letter to Patton ordering him to make a full report of the incidents, and to apologize personally to the doctors, nurses, and soldiers involved as well as to his entire army. Adding to Patton's humiliation was information in the report that the first soldier Patton slapped had chronic dysentery, malaria, and a temperature of 102 degrees; the second soldier's best friend had been bloodily wounded next to him, was on sleep medication, and even though the twenty-one-year-old boy begged the unit medical officer not to, against his wishes he had been ordered evacuated to the hospital where Patton found him. Ike's letter closed with this admonishment: "I assure you that conduct such as described in the accompanying report will not be tolerated in this theater no matter who the offender will be."

Patton was mortified and chagrined, but not beyond words. That night he told his diary: "Evidently I acted precipitately and on insufficient knowledge. My motive was correct because one cannot permit skulking to exist. It is just like any communicable disease. I admit freely that my method was wrong [and] I shall make what amends I can . . . I feel very low."

It is a court-martial offense in the U.S. Army for an officer to strike an enlisted man—let alone for a three-star general to strike a buck private—but reporters who learned of the incident decided by mutual agreement not to reveal it. The furious Eisenhower was poised to relieve Patton of command but was dissuaded by Marshall, who told some fellow officers at the War Department, "Georgie's in trouble again. He's always in trouble. But I'm not getting rid of Patton. He was solely responsible for Sicily."

★ ★ ★ ★

PATTON SPENT A GREAT DEAL OF TIME in the coming days justifying his actions even as he was personally delivering the ordered apologies to those involved and to his army, division by division. When he reached the last of the divisions, Truscott's Third Division, the men who had captured Palermo and Messina, "Patton's audience sensed that he was about to make a statement of apology. Before he could do so, they began a spontaneous chant, 'No, General, no, no, no, General no, no,' with increasing persistence." Patton tried again to start his apology but each time he was cut off, "No, General, no, no, no," and stood there on the stage, erect as the Washington Monument, the tears rolling down his cheeks as the chant reached its crescendo, "No, General. No, no, no!" and followed him, ringing in his ears as he turned smartly and exited the stage to his waiting car, "No, General. No, no, no!"[19]

He called in the second soldier that he had slapped and explained that he had "cussed him out in the hope of restoring his manhood." After telling the soldier that he was sorry, Patton told him that "if he cared, I would like to shake hands with him." They shook. Two days later Patton met with the first soldier and made more or less the same explanation. They also shook hands.

To Beatrice he wrote, "I have been a passenger floating on the river of destiny. At the moment I can't see around the next bend, but I guess it will be all right. Once in a while my exuberant personality gets me in a little lame with Devine Destiny, which seems to have the trait of believing the worst of everyone on insufficient evidence." He wrote to Eisenhower, "I am at a loss to find words to express my chagrin and grief in having given you, a man to whom I owe everything, and for whom I would gladly lay down my life, cause for displeasure with me."

Eisenhower meanwhile wrote to George Marshall, without mentioning the slapping incidents, that "Patton is preeminently a combat commander . . . He is a one-sided individual and particularly in his handling of individual subordinates is apt at times to display exceedingly poor judgment and unjustified temper. But his outstanding qualities must not be discounted." He added that they could not afford to lose those qualities, unless he ruins himself.

★ ★ ★ ★

FOR FOUR LONG MONTHS PATTON languished in an anguished limbo while the war went on around him. "I have joined the army of the unemployed," he wrote Beatrice. "I seem destined to either fight like hell or do nothing . . . I would serve under the Devil to get into a fight . . . apparently I am a man of deeds, not words. Except when I talk too much." He called in his staff and said, "Gentlemen . . . if you can find a better job, get it. I will help you all I can. You may be backing the wrong horse, or hitched your wagon to the wrong star." No one left him, which moved Patton very much.

Patton had been feeling very low when, unannounced, Jimmy Doolittle paid him a visit. The 12th Air Force commander and famous raider of Japan had become close with Patton when he was in North Africa, and he'd heard that his friend Georgie might need some bucking up.

When he arrived over the airfield Doolittle identified himself to the control tower and asked for permission to land and pay his respects to the general.

When he landed, Doolittle found Patton waiting for him in his jeep with the three stars of a lieutenant general adorning the hood, wearing his famous ivory-handled revolvers and polished helmet liner. Patton, his face beaming like a harvest moon, rushed to Doolittle when he climbed down, threw his arms around him, and burst into tears, exclaiming, "Jimmy, I didn't think anyone would ever call on a mean old son of a bitch like me!"[20]

Not long afterward, Patton became the subject of a major story in the *Reader's Digest* entitled "Old Man Battle," and he wrote a poem called "God of Battles" that was published in the *Woman's Home Companion*. On November 11, he had been overseas for a year and four days when his staff celebrated his birthday. He was fifty-eight years old. To his son, George, now repeating his plebe year at West Point, he wrote, "It is getting pretty cold here and we have no fires in the palace, so we dress and undress fast. I wish I could find out what we are going to do and when, but nobody knows a damned thing." Then the other shoe dropped.

The columnist Drew Pearson got wind of the slapping incident and, after confirming it with several sources, published a sensational story about the affair that blew like wildfire through the national media. Eisenhower was of course chagrined because the press intimated he was trying to sweep it under the rug. Congressmen and senators were inundated with angry letters calling for Patton's dismissal.

While a surprisingly large number of the letters were also supportive of Patton, he remained in what he considered the doghouse. "Regret trouble I am causing you," he cabled Eisenhower. To his diary on November 25 he said, "Thanksgiving Day. I had nothing to be thankful for so I did not give thanks."

★ ★ ★ ★

On December 7, Pearl Harbor Day, President Roosevelt, Eisenhower, Assistant Secretary of War John J. McCloy, and Roosevelt's top aide Harry Hopkins appeared at Patton's headquarters in Sicily after their big Allied conferences in Cairo and Tehran. It was a cordial meeting during which Ike told Patton he was certain he would be ordered to England to get an army. McCloy told him the same. Harry Hopkins took Patton aside and said, "Don't let anything that s.o.b. Pearson said bother you." These were gratifying reassurances but still nothing was definite.

Then, on January 18, Patton was informed by his orderly Sergeant William Meeks, who had heard it in a radio broadcast, that Eisenhower had announced Omar Bradley would lead the cross-Channel invasion. It came as a severe blow, even though Patton must have known that he was never seriously considered for the job. "I had thought that I might get this command," he told his diary. "It is another disappointment, but so far in my life all the disappointments I had have worked out to my advantage."

Four days later, a cable arrived ordering Patton to England, where he would serve under Omar Bradley. "Well, I have been under worse people and will surely win," he wrote Beatrice.

CHAPTER TEN

★ ★ ★ ★

"I SHALL RETURN"

For about three weeks, MacArthur's Philippine army battled the invading Japanese, but they were outmanned at every turn. Major General Jonathan "Skinny" Wainwright, a hard-drinking former West Point first captain and cavalryman with 28,000 ill-trained, ill-equipped Filipino troops and 3,000 U.S. regulars, was no match for the Japanese general Masaharu Homma's landing force of 43,000 well-trained and well-equipped soldiers. But Wainwright's defense was ferocious, including the last large-scale cavalry attack in modern warfare. "We lost more than a few of our first class fighting men," Wainwright lamented, "and a number of fine horses—including my Little Boy, who took a bullet through the head."[1]

To spare historic Manila from destruction by bombing or attack, MacArthur declared it an "open city." On Christmas Eve, 1941, when it became apparent that the Japanese could not be thrown back into the ocean and that they were preparing a giant pincers movement to trap MacArthur's army, he invoked the dictates of War Plan Orange. The army thus withdrew into the mountainous jungle of the Bataan Peninsula, from which it was to fight until the U.S. Navy arrived with reinforcements and supplies.

It took MacArthur's army two weeks to fully invest Bataan, where War Plan Orange drew five defensive lines. He knew the terrain well, since he had surveyed it as a young first lieutenant. At each line the American and Filipino troops gave a magnificent account of themselves. Provisions—enough food, ammunition, equipment, and spare parts—for an army to defend Bataan for up to six months had been stored in Manila, and much was being hastily trucked into Bataan.

Unaware of Roosevelt's and Churchill's "Europe First" policy, MacArthur was so sure that relief for him was on the way—with U.S. carriers ferrying over planes—that he ordered his engineers to build thirteen air strips in remote areas to house them. He wired General Marshall: IF THE WESTERN PACIFIC IS TO BE SAVED IT WILL HAVE TO BE SAVED HERE AND NOW. But by then General Marshall had come to accept that the Western Pacific could not be saved—at least not now—though he was loath to impart this bad news to MacArthur. MacArthur cabled his superior that he needed several dozen P-40 fighter planes, adding, almost pathetically, CAN I EXPECT ANYTHING ALONG THAT LINE? The simple fact was that, after Pearl Harbor, Japan still had its full complement of sixteen battleships and eleven aircraft carriers while the U.S. Pacific Fleet had no battleships and only three carriers. There would be no victorious "March Across the Pacific" by the American navy at this time.

From the onset, the fighting on Bataan was desperate and costly. One Filipino battalion attacked the Japanese line for an entire day, pushing the enemy back and blowing a bridge, but returning with only 156 out of the 655 men who had started out. Battles such as this went on day after day; military historians have lauded the Bataan retrograde as one of the finest withdrawal movements in the history of warfare. "Stand and fight, slip back and dynamite," MacArthur wrote afterward. "It was savage and bloody but it won time."[2]

By New Year's Eve the Americans had retreated deep into the peninsula. They at last blew the huge swinging bridge over the impassable Pampanga River, stranding themselves. By then, of Wainwright's original army corps of 28,000, only 18,000 remained. The soldiers were in rags and slowly starving. A total of 80,000 troops were on Bataan, and by early January provisions were down to one month's supply. MacArthur put the soldiers on half-rations. An old-timer sergeant in an antiaircraft battery remarked, "They'll eventually get us, but they'll pay dearly for their efforts."

The Japanese, nevertheless, were dissatisfied. General Homma had used more than half of the fifty-day deadline Tokyo had given him to secure conquest of the Philippines. His frustration was palpable. On January 9, his main attack had failed to dislodge the defenders and he ordered a banzai charge.* From a standing sugarcane field a thousand Japanese came dashing straight into American barbed wire and point-blank 75mm guns at midnight. The attacks went on without success until dawn, when the Americans counted several hundred bodies in front of them. However, most of the Americans agreed that people who would do that were an enemy to be reckoned with.

MacArthur's tenacious defense of Bataan earned him hero status in the United States, upset the Japanese timetable for military conquest of the southwestern Pacific, and became "a universal symbol of resistance" against the Japanese. It also proved to be an inspiration for the Allies in Australia and elsewhere who were being hard pressed by Japanese aggression. From George Marshall's office in Washington came disingenuous cables saying that "every effort is being made to send air and troop replacements and reinforcements." Marshall, of course, knew this was impossible.[3]

On January 10, MacArthur received a note from General Homma that began, "You are well aware that you are doomed." It went on with some admiring language about the defense MacArthur had put up so far ("Your prestige and honor have been upheld"), but continued with the usual threats of annihilation and offer of peace "to avoid needless bloodshed," if only the Americans would surrender.

The Japanese had deviously driven into the Allied lines almost the entire population of the nearby province of Zambales, knowing that MacArthur would feed them. Thus, on January 11, he was forced to cut his soldiers' rations again, halving the half-rations to one-quarter rations

---

* *Banzai* stood for, more or less, "May the Emperor live a thousand years."

of a thousand calories a day; within the month men who had weighed 170 or 200 pounds were down to 150 and scarcely a python, pangolin, or monkey remained uneaten in the steaming jungle. At night they were treated to scathing radio diatribes by the Japanese propagandist "Tokyo Rose," who aggravated starving American and Filipino troops by quoting from the *New York Times* about huge stores of food and supplies the United States was sending to Russia.

From his headquarters in the Malinta Tunnel on the island of Corregidor, MacArthur had a panoramic view of the siege the Japanese had laid against his army. At any time, day or night, he could see and hear the fiery explosions and columns of smoke from artillery shells and bombs, or watch as scores of the badly wounded were brought into the tunnel's hospital lateral after being ferried from Bataan. The entrance to the lateral was drenched in blood, and ambulances would often wait in line to pick up blanket-covered corpses for burial between bombing attacks.

The bomb-impervious tunnel had been completed in the 1920s, carved through the stone and dirt that composed Malinta Hill. It was more than a quarter of a mile long and had fifty laterals, or branches, some of which were four football fields long. Life in the tunnel was miserable; at times it contained as many as 10,000 men and a few army nurses.* Bomb blasts often sent choking clouds of dust and acrid smoke into the excavation and the electricity frequently went out, leaving everyone in the dark. About the only bright spot was when MacArthur's four-year-old son Arthur, dressed in a sailor's suit, would respond to the siren by rushing up and down the tunnel shouting, "Air raid! Air raid!" At least that gave some people a chuckle.[4]

★ ★ ★ ★

THE JAPANESE CAME ON IN GREAT RUSHES and were killed by the thousands. Unfortunately for MacArthur, however, the Japanese sent troop

* The nurses were evacuated by submarine before the surrender, a feat that later became the inspiration for the 1959 Cary Grant movie *Operation Petticoat*.

transports with replacements to the tune of 100,000 men, "while I could only bury my dead," he said bitterly. Laudatory messages poured into MacArthur's headquarters from President Roosevelt, Secretary of War Stimson, the king of England, General Pershing, and other notables with encouraging remarks and comments—but that did not take the place of food, men, and supplies, which were fast running out.

The troops were filthy, many barefoot, wearing tattered clothes over their bony skin. They would grin when they saw MacArthur among them, he said—"that ghastly skeleton-like grin of the dying"—and then roar in unison, "We're the battling bastards of Bataan, no papa, no mama, no Uncle Sam."

"They asked no quarter and they gave none," he continued. "They died hard, those savage men—not gently like a stricken dove folding its wings in peaceful passing, but like a wounded wolf at bay . . . and around their necks as we buried them would be a thread of dirty string with its dangling crucifix. They were filthy, and they were lousy, and they stank. And I loved them."[5]

By the end of February it had become apparent that Bataan was on the verge of collapse and Corregidor was unsafe. The question arose of what to do with MacArthur. The spectacle of him as a prisoner being paraded in chains through the streets of Tokyo was bad enough, and Tokyo Rose had announced gleefully that, if captured, MacArthur "would be publicly hanged on the Imperial Plaza in Tokyo." Or what if he should die with his men as he had promised? The army would lose one of its most brilliant and prestigious commanders.

Chief of Staff Marshall told Roosevelt the only way MacArthur would leave the Philippines would be if he received a presidential order to do so. Roosevelt so ordered it. MacArthur objected, but in the end he agreed to go to Australia and take command of all U.S. forces in or bound for the Far East.

On March 12 MacArthur, his wife Jean, his son Arthur, the Cantonese nanny Ah Cheu, and seven staff members boarded one of four PT boats and roared off toward Mindanao, six hundred miles south. There, at a Del Monte pineapple plantation, he was to meet a B-17 bomber sent from

Australia to complete his deliverance. As he stepped on board MacArthur heard someone ask, "What's his chance, Sarge, of getting through?" and came the gruff reply, "Dunno, he's lucky. Maybe one-in-five." It was an excruciating journey, according to MacArthur, as extremely rough seas tossed the boats around like corks and made everyone seasick. He later compared the experience to "spending two days inside a cement mixer."[6]

By 9 a.m., March 16, MacArthur and party arrived in Darwin, Australia, just in time for a major Japanese air raid on the city. Luckily, MacArthur's party had left the airfield ten minutes before Japanese dive-bombers roared in and obliterated it. He remarked later to his chief of staff Dick Sutherland, "It was close, but that's the way it is in war. You win or lose, live or die—and the difference is just an eyelash."

It was here that MacArthur made his famous proclamation to reporters about the Philippines: "I came through, and I shall return." It was vintage MacArthur. The phrase was printed and broadcast around the world. It was stamped on the covers of matchbooks provided by the army to GIs in the Pacific theater. The proclamation was headlined in newspapers and featured in radio broadcasts. It was glazed into pottery, engraved on cigarette lighters, and scrawled above public toilets, and it slipped easily into the American lexicon. MacArthur had become a legend in his own time.

★ ★ ★ ★

MACARTHUR WAS AWARDED the Medal of Honor for his role in the Philippines, but there were undertones that he had received it only to offset any criticism to his reputation for leaving during the fight. It was made worse when news reached him three weeks after his arrival in Australia that the American army in the Philippines had surrendered to the Japanese.

By the first of April it was clear that the food issue was critical. A quarter-ration can keep a man alive, but his ability to be active is greatly diminished. When the Japanese began a large offensive all hope was lost. One unit reported taking 2 percent casualties *per hour* from enemy artillery alone.

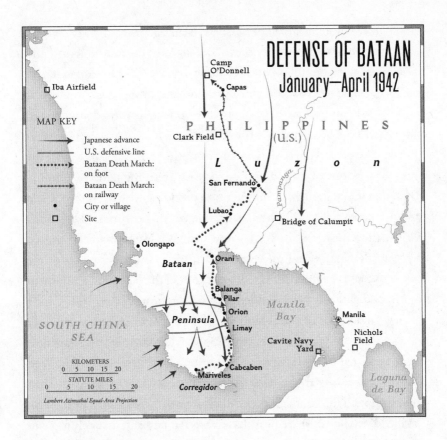

On April 9 an artillery major at the American headquarters in the Malinta Tunnel reported seeing General Wainwright on the phone with General Edward P. King, one of the senior commanders on Bataan. "'You can't surrender!' he shouted, 'You can't!' As Wainwright listened intently, his gaunt frame seemed to sag, and tears rolled down his cheeks. 'Why don't you attack with I Corps?' he asked. We clearly heard a voice say, 'I Corps no longer exists.' General Wainwright slumped into his chair."[7]

What ensued over the next week remains a prime example of studied cruelty in the history of the world. Starving and ill, the 78,000 troops on Bataan, unarmed and helpless, started northward on the infamous sixty-five-mile Bataan Death March. About 10,000 soldiers perished from starvation or thirst or were murdered by sadistic Japanese guards. Anyone who thought reports of Japanese atrocities in China were exaggerated was soon set straight. Private First Class Blair Robinett's first encounter with a Japanese soldier went poorly. "He stepped out, came across, and took my canteen out of its cover. He took a drink, filled his canteen, and poured the rest of my water on the ground and dropped my canteen at my feet. When I bent over to pick up my canteen he turned around and hit me over the head with his rifle butt."[8]

Screaming at the prisoners in Japanese, the guards began to sort the men into groups of a thousand or so, with sixteen guards to a group. There was much shouting, clubbing, and prodding with bayonets. When one American fell behind he was bayoneted in the throat. "He gasped for air, then was dead," a witness testified. When the marchers passed a sugarcane field several men went toward it to break off pieces of the cane. "When they reached the edge of the field the Jap guards shot them down, and clubbed the wounded survivors to death."[9]

Several survivor accounts recall a grisly incident in which an obviously ill American soldier was staggering along when a column of Japanese tanks appeared from the opposite direction. A Japanese guard "grabbed this sick guy by the arm and guided him to the middle of the road. Then he just flipped him out across the road. A tank pulled across him. Well, it killed him quick. There must have been ten tanks in that column and every one of them ran over him. When the last tank left there was no way you could ever tell there'd been a man there. The man had disappeared, but his uniform had been pressed until it had become a part of the ground."[10]

After robbing the prisoners of such things as watches, money, and wallets, the Japanese guards began pulling out gold teeth and chopping off fingers to get wedding rings. Two soldiers were carrying their captain, who had become prostrate with dysentery, when a guard rushed up and ran his bayonet through the captain's stomach. Anyone who lagged behind was murdered. For men in the rear of the march it was particularly traumatic since they had to pass by all the thousands of mutilated bodies who had died ahead of them.

At last they reached their destination, Camp O'Donnell, a half-completed American airfield. It was as close to hell on earth as any of the survivors could imagine. The camp commander, Captain Yoshio Tsuney-oshi, greeted them with a ranting, jumping-up-and-down harangue in which he compared the prisoners to dogs and concluded by telling them, "You think that you are the lucky ones? Your comrades who died on Bataan are the lucky ones!"[11] In the ensuing days the death toll rose for the 68,000 miserable prisoners—150, 200, 250, 300 lifeless skeletons a day, until it leveled off at 500 dead per day.

★ ★ ★ ★

FOR HIS FIRST ACT AS SUPREME COMMANDER of the South West Pacific theater, MacArthur met with the Australian prime minister John Curtin and reassured him that "We two, you and I, will see this thing through. We can do it, and we will do it. You take care of the rear, and I'll take care of the front."

The situation MacArthur found himself in was nothing short of desperate. The bulk of Australia's ground troops were fighting the war in the Middle East under British command when suddenly the Japanese came knocking at the door. To counter an invasion that was expected "momentarily," the Australians had devised a defensive plan that sacrificed more than three-quarters of their country to the enemy in order to defend a line from Brisbane to Adelaide that protected the most populous cities.

MacArthur rejected the proposal on grounds that it was a "passive defense" that would "result only in eventual defeat." Even if it was successful, MacArthur predicted it would "trap us indefinitely on an island continent ringed by conquered territories and a hostile ocean," with no hope of taking the offensive. He opted instead to move the fight fifteen hundred miles northward to the mountains of Papua New Guinea, where the Japanese invasion force was struggling up the Kokoda Trail, rung by grueling greasy rung, on the steep far side of the towering Owen Stanley Range.

MacArthur's legendary good luck was reinforced by the arrival of Major General George C. Kenney who, at the request of MacArthur's chief of staff Richard Sutherland, had come to replace General George

Brett as commander of the Allied air force. Sutherland was thought of as high-handed, even rude—especially by airmen. But because he spoke for MacArthur, or at least thought he did, most gave Sutherland a wide berth. Kenney was a diminutive, feisty pilot who set Sutherland straight the first time he met him. Waiting for a meeting with MacArthur, Kenney found himself in Sutherland's office on the receiving end of a lecture on how to run his air force.

Kenney listened for a while, then went over to a table and picked up a blank sheet of paper. He took out a pencil and put a dot in the center of the paper and handed it to MacArthur's chief of staff. "That dot I just put there represents what *you* know about the use of airpower. All the rest of this sheet of paper represents what *I* know about the use of airpower," he told the startled staff officer. After that, Kenney had little trouble out of Sutherland, and within an amazingly short period Kenney put on a dazzling display of the proper use of airpower that saved the faltering New Guinea campaign.

Still, the lingering problem for MacArthur was how to pull together an Allied force with enough strength to attack the Japanese before they reached Port Moresby on the southern shore of the island, which was only three hundred miles across the Torres Strait from the tip of Australia. The Japanese had already tried an amphibious landing at Port Moresby but were thwarted by a U.S.-Japanese naval engagement that came to be known as the Battle of the Coral Sea. Each side lost a carrier but it caused the Japanese to recall their transports with the troops to seize Port Moresby.

By then, MacArthur had only one American infantry division, a National Guard outfit that was undersized, undertrained, and under-supplied. The air force consisted of obsolete, mostly grounded planes with few spare parts, and his navy was without any capital ships what-soever. To make matters worse, New Guinea was possibly the most undesirable place to fight a war.

The Owen Stanley Mountains were a 15,000-foot-high barrier that ran the length of the island and featured some of the most inhospitable land on earth. Below were swamps consisting of "a stinking jumble of twisted, slime-covered roots and muddy soup," trails that were "a sea of mud," and man-high stands of treacherous razor-edged kunai grass. Among the diseases awaiting the defenders were malaria, dengue, the nearly always fatal blackwater fever, amoebic dysentery, hookworm, ringworm, scrub typhus, and billions of insects to bite, sting, or suck. New Guinea was in a state of nature nearly antithetical to human coexistence, and modern man had not made appreciable inroads. In addition to disease, encounters were to be had with leeches, scorpions, an astounding variety of ants, crocodiles, poisonous snakes such as the death adder and taipan, huge constrictors like the python, and the cassowary, a five- to six-foot-tall man-killing flightless bird with powerful legs and a daggerlike claw on its toes.

When they arrived, the Japanese were completely surprised to find that MacArthur had occupied Port Moresby and began bombing it twice a day. At stake for both sides was air control of the Coral Sea, and for Japan the freedom to bomb and invade Australia at will.

New Guinea natives believed that the Kokoda Trail that ran up and across the Owen Stanleys was haunted. It rained incessantly—300 inches a year—in blinding deluges that left men knee-deep, and sometimes waist-deep, in filthy mud. The trail was so steep that, in some places, men slept roped to jungle plants or trees. One man was found, so the story goes, after being attacked while asleep by a large constricting python. His body was said to be completely flattened, like a deflated balloon, as if every bone in it had been crushed.

Thanks to the successes of U.S. marines on Guadalcanal in the nearby Solomon Islands, in early September some five thousand Japanese troops were pulled out of New Guinea and sent to deal with the upstart Americans, and the Japanese push to take Port Moresby was postponed. But this still left around ten thousand Japanese infantry on the north shore of the island, dug into a position between two villages, Buna and Gona. The Allied troops first had to cross the Owen Stanleys—the Australians by the Kokoda Trail and the Americans by the lesser-known Kapa Kapa Trail, which was so remote no white man had been known to climb it since 1917.

The U.S. divisions (by then MacArthur had two) were "un-battle-hardened," meaning they were undertrained and out of shape. The strain of days of climbing in the leech-infested jungle left many prostrate along the trail. Officers went to the rear but, in many cases, could not get the stragglers to move. At one point along the route, "reek[ing] with the stench of death," lay the corpse of an enemy soldier on a crude stretcher, abandoned by his comrades in retreat. "The flesh is gone from his bones and a white bony claw sticks out of a ragged uniform sleeve, stretching across the track."[12]

On the far side of the mountains the Americans were flabbergasted when they stumbled on the Japanese positions at Buna and Gona. The surrounding terrain was waist-deep sago palm muck and jungle. The only practical approaches were heavily fortified by preregistered Japanese mortars, machine-gun nests, and direct artillery fire from protected coconut-log bunkers. Snipers were everywhere—in trees, behind trees, and in root jungles beneath trees. It was one of the most obnoxious positions from the attacker's point of view in the entire war.

MacArthur soon became aware of reports that the behavior in some of his units was marginal at best. There were accounts of soldiers refusing to obey officers' orders and stories of outright cowardice. MacArthur summoned his new corps commander, Major General Robert L. Eichelberger, and told him to go to Buna and relieve the commander of the 32nd Infantry Division, and also to relieve anyone else who wouldn't fight and replace him with someone who would—even if it meant putting sergeants in charge of battalions and corporals in charge of companies. Then he gave one of the most extraordinary orders to be issued in modern times (George Patton excepted). "Bob," MacArthur said, "I want you to take Buna or not come back alive." And, as if for emphasis, he pointed a long forefinger at Eichelberger's startled chief of staff, saying, "And that goes for your chief of staff, too."

★ ★ ★ ★

WHAT EICHELBERGER FOUND BEFORE BUNA was a miserable excuse for a U.S. military outfit. The 32nd Division was a National Guard unit composed of Wisconsin and Michigan natives, every man of them running a malarial fever. One of the inspecting officers wrote: "They wore long dirty beards. Their clothing was in rags. Their shoes were uncared for, or worn out . . . When Martin and I visited a regimental [headquarters] to observe what was supposed to be an attack, we found it four and a half miles behind the front line. The regimental commander and his staff went forward from this location rarely, if ever. The attack had been ordered and it could be entered on the headquarters diary, but it didn't exist."

Eichelberger visited the front, with MacArthur's "don't come back alive" orders ringing in his ears, only to discover there *was* no front. Everything was so jumbled no one seemed to know who was who or what was what. Eichelberger ordered the fighting—such as it was—halted for two days so things could be sorted out. Then he started firing people.

When the two days were up Eichelberger ordered an immediate attack, as it was obvious that in any stalemate the Japanese would win, "for they were living among the coconut palms along the coast on sandy soil while our men lived in swamps." Eichelberger took a personal hand in the assault, in which he claimed to MacArthur that the men were "fighting hard." But as one of his regimental commanders remarked, "We have hit them [the Japanese], and bounced off."[13]

The American soldiers were repelled by more than bullets. At one point, odors emanating from the Japanese positions, blown directly at them by a prevailing onshore ocean breeze, began causing severe nausea. When at last on December 14, 1942, Allied forces carried the Buna stronghold, what they found was beyond revolting. "Rotting bodies, sometimes weeks old, formed part of the fortifications. The living fired over the bodies of the dead, slept side by side with them." Inside one trench they found the body of a Japanese soldier who could not stand the strain. "His rifle was pointed at his head, his big toe was on the trigger, the top of his head was blown off." Almost worse, there were obvious signs of cannibalism. Parts of carved-up Allied bodies—which the Japanese apparently preferred to eat before eating their own—were scattered around the position.[14]

It soon became apparent to Eichelberger that no amount of artillery or bombing was going to dislodge the Japanese from their bunkers; the only way to beat them was to go in and kill them hand to hand with bayonets, rifles, and grenades. The Americans and Australians built a large roadblock to keep the Japanese put. Then soldiers began the bloody process of reducing the position bunker by bloody bunker.

Almost to a man, the Japanese fought to the last, taking a terrible toll on the Allied soldiers. The fighting went on for more than a month while MacArthur in his briefings disingenuously described it as "a mopping up action." It wasn't until January 22, 1943, that the major Japanese outposts in Papua New Guinea had been cleaned out.

Also, almost as an afterthought, it became the first American army victory in the Pacific.

★ ★ ★ ★

THE SOUTH PACIFIC IS LITTERED with small islands and island chains, upon which the Japanese army had nimbly crawled during the past decade, erecting small airstrips and turning these islets and atolls into stationary, unsinkable aircraft carriers from which to interdict an enemy's shipping.

MacArthur's next moves were governed by the dictum issued from the notable Hall of Fame outfielder from the turn of the century Wee Willie Keeler—"Hit 'em where they ain't." His decision to bypass many of these Japanese strongpoints and "leapfrog" northward toward the Philippines was controversial because it meant leaving powerful Japanese forces in the Allies' rear. But MacArthur was confident that, following the great navy success at the Battle of Midway the previous June, the Americans could keep the sea-lanes clear and, by selectively attacking only strategic Japanese installations, cause many enemy bases to wither on the vine and starve for lack of supply.

MacArthur's strategy was hampered as well by the navy's refusal to provide carrier airpower to help reduce the Japanese bases (apparently out of fear of losing its flattops to land-based enemy warplanes). This infuriated MacArthur, who intoned, "In the present state of development of the art of war, no movement can safely be made of forces on land or sea without adequate air protection."

Thus his advance across the Pacific would require Allied forces to storm an island's beaches to seize the enemy's air base, then use it to launch attacks on the next strategic island up the chain. The distance between the seizures was limited mainly by the radius of Allied fighters, which were necessary to protect the longer-ranged bombers that would be "softening up" Japanese defensive positions on the islands.

With a plan of action, MacArthur's next move was to reduce Japanese forces on the north coast of New Guinea proper, which would become the gateway for offensive strategy. "Island hopping" was a term MacArthur disliked because he said it implied storming the mass of Japanese-held islands "with extravagant losses and slow progress." Instead, he proposed selective strikes on less heavily defended outposts, leaving in his wake a chain of greatly weakened enemy bases.

The Japanese themselves soon recognized the danger, issuing a top-secret report that read, "New Guinea, especially, was the strategic point on the defensive line and if it should fall into the hands of the enemy . . . it would be a case of giving to the enemy the best possible route to penetrate into the Philippines." The report went on to note the differences in terrain between northern and southern New Guinea and concluded that the strategic value of the island was "of immense importance."[15]

Accordingly the Japanese, having lost Guadalcanal, decided on a last-ditch reinforcement of their positions on New Guinea. To that end, at the beginning of March 1943, nearly seven thousand soldiers from the sprawling Japanese base on the island of New Britain were loaded aboard eight troop transports, escorted by eight destroyers, with a dozen squadrons of Zero fighters providing air cover. They steamed out into the Bismarck Sea toward the town of Lae on New Guinea's northwest coast.

The Japanese had been assured that bad weather would mask their convoy, but when General Kenney received intelligence that the convoy was on its way, he managed to scramble together more than two hundred heavy bombers to intercept them. The Japanese meteorologist turned

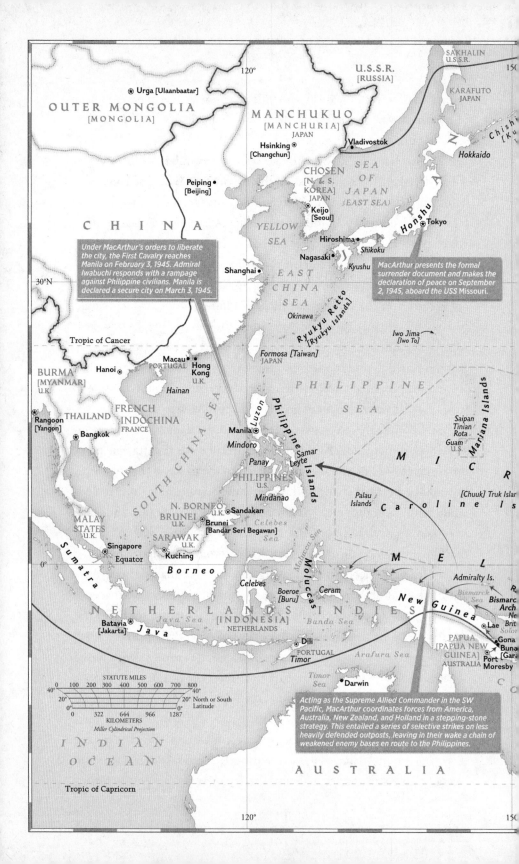

SAKHALIN
U.S.S.R.

⊕ Urga [Ulaanbaatar]

KARAFUTO
JAPAN

OUTER MONGOLIA
[MONGOLIA]

U.S.S.R.
[RUSSIA]

120°

150°

MANCHUKUO
[MANCHURIA]
JAPAN

Hsinking ⊙
[Changchun]

● Vladivostok

Chishi
[Ku

Hokkaido

C H I N A

Peiping ●
[Beijing]

CHOSEN
[N. & S.
KOREA]
JAPAN

SEA
OF
JAPAN
(EAST SEA)

Honshu

Tokyo ●

Keijo ⊙
[Seoul]

YELLOW
SEA

Hiroshima ●

Shikoku

Nagasaki ●

Kyushu

Under MacArthur's orders to liberate the city, the First Cavalry reaches Manila on February 3, 1945. Admiral Iwabuchi responds with a rampage against Philippine civilians. Manila is declared a secure city on March 3, 1945.

Shanghai ●

EAST

CHINA

SEA

MacArthur presents the formal surrender document and makes the declaration of peace on September 2, 1945, aboard the USS Missouri.

30°N

Ryukyu Retto
[Ryukyu Islands]

Okinawa

Iwo Jima
[Iwo To]

Tropic of Cancer

Formosa [Taiwan]
JAPAN

Macau ●
PORTUGAL

Hong
Kong
U.K.

P H I L I P P I N E

Hanoi ⊙

BURMA
[MYANMAR]
U.K.

Hainan

SEA

Saipan
Tinian
Rota
Guam
U.S.

Mariana Islands

FRENCH
INDOCHINA
FRANCE

Luzon

THAILAND

Rangoon ●
[Yangon]

⊕ Bangkok

Manila ●

M

I

C

R

Mindoro

Panay

Samar
Leyte

Philippine Islands

[Chuuk] Truk Islar

Palau
Islands

Caroline Is

PHILIPPINES
U.S.

Mindanao

MALAY
STATES
U.K.

N. BORNEO
U.K.

Sandakan

Celebes
Sea

Molucca Sea

M

E

L

Singapore ●

BRUNEI
U.K.

Brunei
[Bandar Seri Begawan]

Admiralty Is.

SARAWAK
U.K.

Equator

Kuching ●

Borneo

New Guinea

Bismarck
Sea

Bismarc
Arch
Ne
Brit

Sumatra

Celebes

Moluccas

0°

Boeroe
[Buru]

Ceram

Solor

N E T H E R L A N D S   I N D I E S

Lae ●

Batavia ⊕
[Jakarta]

Java Sea

Java

[INDONESIA]
NETHERLANDS

Banda Sea

PAPUA
[PAPUA NEW
GUINEA]
AUSTRALIA

Gona
Buna
[Gara

Dili ●

Port
Moresby

PORTUGAL
Timor

Arafura Sea

STATUTE MILES

0   100 200 300 400 500 600 700 800
40°   40°
20°   20° North or South
0°   0°   Latitude
0   322   644   966   1287
KILOMETERS
Miller Cylindrical Projection

Timor
Sea

● Darwin

Acting as the Supreme Allied Commander in the SW Pacific, MacArthur coordinates forces from America, Australia, New Zealand, and Holland in a stepping-stone strategy. This entailed a series of selective strikes on less heavily defended outposts, leaving in their wake a chain of weakened enemy bases en route to the Philippines.

I N D I A N

O C E A N

A U S T R A L I A

Tropic of Capricorn

120°

150

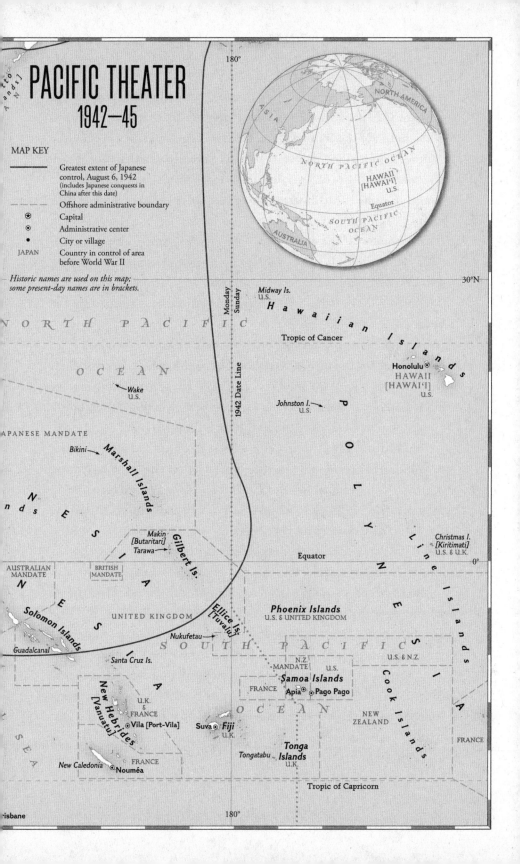

out to get the weather wrong by a day, and as the clouds began to clear, waves of U.S. planes appeared from the south. In what became known as the Battle of the Bismarck Sea, Japanese antiaircraft gunners on the destroyers ran to their weapons, only to be startled when the big bombers came in at mast-top level, like torpedo bombers. They released their bombs into the sea in an astonishing display of skip bombing, which Kenney's air force had perfected.

The bombs hit the water and "dapped" like stones skipping across a flat calm pond. All eight of the troop transports were sunk, as were four enemy destroyers, and sixty enemy Zeros were shot out of the sky. Only 1,200 of the 6,900 Japanese soldiers were rescued by the remaining destroyers.

This ended further Japanese attempts to reinforce New Guinea or go on the offensive, but there still remained large numbers of enemy soldiers who had shown at Buna and Gona that dislodging them would involve more than one bloodbath. Or, as General Kenney put it, "There'll be a lot of Bunas and Gonas before this thing is finished."

On April 18, MacArthur's air force scored one of the greatest coups in World War II. It shot down the commander in chief of the Japanese Imperial Navy, Admiral Isoroku Yamamoto. He had served for a time in the Japanese embassy in Washington, D.C., and had occasion to tour the United States. Prior to Pearl Harbor, Yamamoto was against war—he had noted the Americans' enormous industrial might—but when war was ordered, he sided with his country and planned the attack on Hawaii.

The U.S. code-breaking operation MAGIC, which in May had tipped off the navy that the Japanese would be attacking Midway, had also now intercepted a message saying that Yamamoto would be inspecting Japanese bases in the Solomons and flying from Rabaul to Bougainville ". . . to personally reconnoiter the bloody ground campaign there." American code breakers sent word to MacArthur's headquarters, giving Yamamoto's route, his air cover, and the rendezvous point off the west coast of Bougainville.[16]

Eighteen U.S. Army Air Force P-38 Lightnings were detailed to intercept the admiral at his rendezvous point. They would "wave hop" to the target maintaining radio silence. But when they arrived at the rendezvous point shortly before 3 p.m. nothing was doing except a storm brewing in the southeast. U.S. Army major John W. Mitchell was about to give the order to return to base when dead ahead there appeared Yamamoto's flight—two large transports beneath an umbrella of Japanese fighters.

American fighters rose to engage the Zeros, while others attacked the transports. One transport containing the admiral's staff was shot down in flames almost immediately, while the other undertook violent evasive action. Twisting and zigzagging at treetop level, Yamamoto's plane was desperately trying to escape the fire of Captain Thomas G. Lanphier, who was on his tail with all guns blazing. A wisp of black smoke on the big transport quickly became a red flame as Lanphier's bullets tore into the skin of the Japanese aircraft. Suddenly it rolled over and crashed through the thick triple-canopy jungle, killing all aboard including Admiral Yamamoto, architect of the Pearl Harbor attack.

Washington was elated at the news, but immediately the affair was branded top secret for fear it would alert the Japanese that American cryptologists were reading their code.

★ ★ ★ ★

AT THIS STAGE IN LATE 1943, additional troops finally began arriving in Australia from the United States, as well as a new organization to control them—the U.S. Sixth Army, commanded by Lieutenant General Walter Krueger, who had been MacArthur's war plans chief when MacArthur was chief of staff. Later, MacArthur would say of Krueger, "I do not believe that the annals of American history have shown his superiority as an army commander." His praise went on: "Swift and sure in attack, tenacious and determined in defense, modest and restrained in victory—I do not know what he would have been in defeat because he was never defeated."

With more than 100,000 men now under his command—including three splendid Australian infantry divisions that Winston Churchill turned loose from the Middle East—MacArthur proceeded with plans to eradicate the large Japanese presence at Lae and the rest of northern New Guinea. General Kenney put it this way: "It was no use talking about playing across the street until we got the Japs off our front lawn."

The first step was an amphibious landing of the recently returned Ninth Australian Infantry Division—the tough, battle-hardened "Rats of Tobruk"—about ten miles east of Lae, which was garrisoned by about 10,000 Japanese troops. The next day 1,700 American paratroopers of the 503rd Parachute Infantry Regiment would jump on a Japanese air base at the town of Nadzab and hold it so that the Seventh Australian Infantry Division could cut off any escape route of the Japanese in Lae.

On September 4, the Australians went ashore unopposed except by enemy bombers from Rabaul that killed about one hundred army and naval personnel. For the Nadzab operation, General Kenney had assembled ninety-seven troop transport planes at Port Moresby when a horrible accident occurred. As the 503rd Parachute Infantry was load-ing its people into the planes, a B-24 Liberator bomber crashed on the runway, plowing through five trucks and killing sixty paratroopers and injuring a hundred others.

Still, the attack went off like clockwork and the Japanese base at Nadzab was seized. MacArthur went along to be with "my kids," even though one of the engines quit in the plane he was riding. He told the pilot—who had suggested turning back—"I know the B-17 flies almost as well on three engines as four."[17]

★ ★ ★ ★

IN A FEW MORE DAYS JAPANESE strongholds at Salamaua and Fin-schhafen had fallen to Allied forces, which meant much of New Guinea's Huon Peninsula was now in MacArthur's hands. "Remember, gentlemen," MacArthur told the press. "We can only advance as far as the bomber line."[18]

In late December, George Marshall, returning from the Tehran Conference featuring Roosevelt, Churchill, and Joseph Stalin, passed through MacArthur's theater and had a candid discussion with him. MacArthur was appalled to learn that the navy—in the form of its chief of operations Admiral Ernest King—was actually jealous of him. According to Marshall, MacArthur said, "King claimed the Pacific as the rightful domain of the Navy and seemed to regard the operations there almost as his own private war." According to MacArthur, Marshall went on to say that Admiral King resented the part MacArthur had played in the Pacific war and was highly critical of MacArthur—and "encouraged Navy propaganda to that end."

Marshall told MacArthur that the navy believed that the only way it could erase the stain of Pearl Harbor "was to have the Navy command a great victory over Japan." MacArthur responded that "the Navy had no greater booster and supporter than [himself]," and expressed his dismay "that inter-service rivalries or personal ambitions should be allowed to interfere with the winning of the war." To this, Marshall seemed to agree but, MacArthur noted sourly, "Having been chief of staff myself I realized how impossible it was to have professional and objective matters decided on the basis of merit and common sense."

MacArthur then cast his eye—previously on the huge Japanese concentration at Rabaul—toward the neighboring island of New Britain. The enemy was using it as a staging base for troops and supplies for their operations both on New Guinea and in the Solomon Islands. MacArthur thought if Rabaul could be eliminated it would remove a large thorn in his side, as well as for the marines and soldiers who were then fighting on Guadalcanal. Admiral King, again worried that he might lose ships, persuaded George Marshall that an attack on Rabaul was too risky, which once more left MacArthur fuming. Instead, after Guadalcanal was secured, the navy continued "island hopping" in bloody, ghastly frontal attacks with its Marine Corps at such places as Tarawa and Kwajalein—islands that MacArthur would have bypassed.

MacArthur then drew plans to attack the Japanese in the tiny Admiralty Islands, an island group several hundred miles to the north of New Guinea that intelligence had told him was lightly defended. Rabaul might have had a magnificent harbor for the navy to gather its ships,

but on the island of Manus in the Admiralties there was also a fine natural harbor. From there, with naval warships and Kenney's warplanes,
MacArthur decided he could not only neutralize, isolate, and bypass
Rabaul, but also create a valuable stepping-stone for his next advancement toward the Philippines.

On February 29, 1944, nine U.S. fast destroyers and a cruiser
appeared in the harbor of Los Negros, an island neighboring Manus.
Aboard the destroyers were a 1,200-man reinforced squadron of the
Fifth U.S. Cavalry Regiment, which was the outfit that had once come
to the rescue of MacArthur's father during the Indian campaigns in New
Mexico. Aboard the cruiser was MacArthur himself, as a guest of Vice
Admiral Thomas C. Kinkaid. After a brief naval and air bombardment
under rainy, murky skies, the cavalrymen went ashore. MacArthur went
with them. With a few bullets singing in the air he waded from one of
the landing craft. Later a cavalryman told his buddy about it.

"You mean General Chase, don't you?" the buddy asked.

"No dammit! I mean General MacArthur," insisted the first trooper.
"He was right there with us. He ain't afraid of nothing."[19]

When MacArthur did step foot on land, there was little enemy opposition on the beach, which was as expected since aerial reconnaissance
had shown no Japanese on Los Negros. But that quickly changed.

It turned out that a sizable contingent of four thousand Japanese
inhabited Los Negros, reported by MAGIC and other sources but unbeknownst to MacArthur. Before long a battle erupted, one so ferocious
that the commanders ordered the rest of the 25,000-man division
brought up from its staging bases in New Guinea. MacArthur spent
most of the day at the scene of battle, personally handing out medals for
bravery. It took nearly two months, but by the first of May the Admiralty
Islands had fallen to the Allies and an important new air base began
building up in the southwestern Pacific.

Around this time, MacArthur learned that his name "was being ban-
died about" as a possible Republican candidate for president. He issued
a statement insisting that he had no desire to do anything but whip
the Japanese in the Pacific, but to no avail. Someone leaked a series of

correspondence between MacArthur and a congressman named Arthur Miller from Nebraska in which the two discussed the possibility of MacArthur's candidacy. It caused a furor in the newspapers, prompting MacArthur to issue a further clarification that ended with the statement, "I request that no action be taken that would in any way link my name with the nomination. I do not covet it nor would I accept it."

In the meantime, MacArthur unearthed among his midst a man even more famous than himself, which was a surprising discovery, all things considered. Reports had filtered up from below that among the P-38 fighter groups flew the man who had swept the world nearly two decades earlier with the first nonstop solo flight across the Atlantic from New York to Paris. Wondering how the celebrated aviator Charles Lindbergh could have found his way into his theater without him knowing the first thing about it, MacArthur sent a wire to the 475th Tactical Fighter Group summoning Lindbergh to his headquarters at Brisbane. He signed it, ominously, "MacArthur."

When he arrived, Lindbergh first had a meeting with the air force chief George Kenney, and then with Chief of Staff Sutherland, before at last speaking with Douglas MacArthur himself. Lindbergh, the famed "Lone Eagle," was wearing the uniform of a "technician," indicating that he was to be treated as an officer but with no insignia of rank. How he came to be there was just the kind of tale MacArthur enjoyed.

After the war in Europe broke out, the Americans were divided, bitterly in many cases, on whether the United States should enter the contest on the side of France and England. Lindbergh, as well as a host of other notables including politicians, college presidents, and Hollywood actors and other celebrities, was against such intervention. Being so famous, Lindbergh's eloquent speeches against provocative acts such as the Lend-Lease program—the administration's process of supplying Great Britain and Russia with war materials in exchange for real estate—soon earned him the enmity of President Roosevelt. After Pearl Harbor, when there was no question that America was at war, the president pettily refused to restore Lindbergh's colonelcy in the Army Air Corps, a rank Lindbergh had given up after the president publicly questioned his loyalty.

For six months, wherever he turned to find a job useful to the fight, Lindbergh was rebuffed by Roosevelt officials who, Lindbergh would discover, delivered veiled threats of loss of government contracts if he was hired. At last he found the one man even Roosevelt would not cross: Henry Ford.

Lindbergh—who at that point probably knew as much about aviation or more than any man alive—became a senior technician at Ford's Willow Run complex, the largest airplane manufacturer in the world, which meant in effect that he was mostly a test pilot. After a year and a half in that capacity, Lindbergh concluded he had done as much as one could in a factory setting; what was needed was to test the aircraft under conditions in which they were being utilized—that is, in combat.

Through intercessions by old friends in military aviation, the forty-two-year-old Lindbergh secured permission to go to the war in the Pacific and test-fly both single-engine Corsairs—workhorses of the U.S. Navy and Marine Corps—and twin-engine P-38s—the mainstay of army fliers in the Pacific. Before long, Lindbergh had completed more than a dozen combat missions in Corsairs, flying out of Guadalcanal, Bougainville, and other islands in the Solomon chain. Afterward he secured a similar assignment in New Guinea with the renowned 475th Fighter Group (Satan's Angels), which was conducting operations against Japanese holdouts in the far northwest of the island. Lindbergh had flown about twenty missions with the P-38s of the 475th and become a revered figure to young airmen half his age when MacArthur's summons arrived.

It seemed that the flap over Lindbergh's presence was not so much *because* he was there as it was over *how* he got there without MacArthur's headquarters knowing about it. When that was straightened out (lack of communication), MacArthur asked for Lindbergh's assessment of aerial operations. He was startled to learn that by manipulating the fuel mixture in the P-38's engines' carburetors, the celebrated airman had managed to increase the flying radius of his group's planes by nearly 600 miles—with no reduction in speed—adding 300 miles to their range. As the fighter group's commander Colonel Charles H.

MacDonald explained later, "It meant the bombers could hit targets three hundred miles farther out [than was previously possible] and still have their 'little friends' along. Lindbergh had, in effect, redesigned an airplane."[20]

Such news was a godsend to MacArthur, whose advance into the Pacific had been limited to the range that fighters could accompany his bombers. He asked if Lindbergh would return to the combat area and instruct all the fighter groups in his fuel-saving techniques.

"There is nothing [I] would rather do," Lindbergh replied.*

★ ★ ★ ★

THE ALLIED SEIZURE OF THE ADMIRALTY ISLANDS had caught the Japanese off guard, and within three months after the Lindbergh meeting MacArthur had yet another surprise for them—a strike at the huge Imperial Army supply base at Hollandia on the north coast of New Guinea. An Allied invasion fleet comprising two hundred ships and fifty thousand infantrymen sailed northwest on April 21 to deceive the Japanese into thinking the invasion was going to be in the Palau islands, which had been recently bombarded as part of the ruse.

The Allied landing was such a shock that most of the six thousand Japanese ran off into the jungle, leaving behind their still-warm breakfasts and personal belongings. (Their emaciated corpses were later found strung out over the hills and mountains as they tried to reach the nearest supply base over three hundred miles away.) Enormous quantities of supplies fell into Allied hands and Hollandia became the jumping-off place to bomb and launch future invasions at the tip of the Huon Peninsula, where the Japanese 18th Army was now trapped.

....

* In the course of his Pacific tour Lindbergh flew in excess of fifty missions, more than was required from the army fliers; he flew frequently through enemy flak, bombed and strafed enemy ships and installations, and, during a dogfight, shot down a Japanese fighter.

What's more, Hollandia quickly became the principal staging area and supply dump for MacArthur's planned move toward the Philippines. It also gave rise to the rumor that MacArthur had built himself a million-dollar mansion on Lake Sentani. In fact the building was "a neat-looking structure of rough timber" that became his headquarters. MacArthur's wife and son soon arrived to share two rooms in the building.[21]

MacArthur then turned his attention to securing the bulk of New Guinea from the remaining Japanese garrisons on the island's north coast. This would begin his great leap—or leapfrog—northwestward toward the Philippines, which were still sixteen hundred miles away with approximately 250,000 Japanese soldiers in between.

Some of these troops were stationed at airfields at Aitape, Wakde, and the islands of Biak, Noemfoor, and Sansapor in the Dutch East Indies several hundred miles to the northwest. Because of the danger the Japanese fighter-bombers posed to his shipping and air transport, and the fact that he needed the landing strips for his own planes, MacArthur felt compelled to seize them in what he envisioned as a series of lightning assaults beginning in mid-May 1944.

If MacArthur thought these small bases could be easily rolled over, he received a rude awakening when his 41st Division attacked the little island of Biak. The landings went smoothly but the enemy had dug into a series of ridges honeycombed with interlocking caves, and when army engineers began work on the runway the Japanese unleashed a murderous fire of heavy weapons upon them. What should have taken a week, according to MacArthur's command schedule, ground on in a bloody shot-for-shot slugging match that lasted into June and cost the Americans nearly 3,000 casualties—plus another 3,400 down from scrub typhus.

Intelligence had underestimated enemy troop strength on the island by more than half, and as it turned out the 12,000 U.S. infantrymen were about evenly matched man for man with their Japanese counterparts. As the fighting continued and the Japanese hung on with Buna-like tenacity, their leaders began, hopefully, to consider Biak as the battle that would stop the Allied advance and turn the war in Japan's favor.

However, various attempts by the Japanese to reinforce the island were turned back or sunk by Allied air and naval attacks. By the end, which came on July 22, some 10,000 Japanese—virtually the entire garrison—were dead, and 434 captured.

At the end of July MacArthur then launched another succession of assaults on Japanese-held ports and islands on the Vogelkop Peninsula, the "head" of New Guinea's peacock (or turkey) silhouette. Battles big and small, now largely forgotten, were fought in the steaming malarial jungles as the final phases of MacArthur's strategy to either destroy or isolate all Japanese garrisons on the island took shape. All the while, he was moving closer to the Philippines, which now lay but some six hundred miles from MacArthur's forces.

A month later, the final extirpation of the Japanese on New Guinea was accomplished. In the process, by employing methods utilized in the building of the Panama Canal, the army had also conquered malaria in the Allied areas of the island—in itself a Herculean feat—and, with fighter planes, PT boats, and submarines, had, in the bargain, destroyed the Japanese coastal supply fleet, sinking more than eight thousand enemy shipping vessels.[22]

★ ★ ★ ★

THE PREVIOUS MONTH, George Marshall had summoned MacArthur to Pearl Harbor for a conference. MacArthur suspected the principal conferee would be President Roosevelt, but he had no way of confirming it. He also divined that the purpose of the conference would involve matters "closely affecting" himself and his future plans, but he took with him to Hawaii no staff officer, plans, or maps. MacArthur was disgruntled at being called away from "[his] war," when his personal B-17, the *Bataan,* landed at the Hickam air base, Oahu, some twenty-six hours after it took off.

Roosevelt arrived aboard the navy cruiser *Baltimore* where he was greeted enthusiastically by fifty high-ranking army and navy officers— but no MacArthur. Instead of joining the other officers to greet the president, he had gone to Fort Shafter where quarters awaited him. Samuel I. Rosenman, one of Roosevelt's speechwriters, tells what happened next.

> After waiting for quite a while for General MacArthur, it was decided that the President and his party would disembark and go to the quarters on shore assigned to them. Just as we were about to go below a terrific automobile siren was heard, and there raced to the dock and screeched to a stop a motorcycle escort and the longest open car I have ever seen. [Belonging, we are told, to the madam of a well-known brothel in Honolulu.]
>
> In the front was a chauffeur in khaki and in the back one lone person—MacArthur. There were no aides or attendants. The car traveled around the open space and stopped at the gangplank. When the applause died down the general strode rapidly to the gangplank all alone. He dashed up the gangplank, stopping halfway up to acknowledge another ovation and soon was on deck greeting the President.
>
> He certainly could be dramatic—at dramatic moments.
>
> "Hello, Doug," said the commander in chief. "What are you doing with that leather jacket on—it's darn hot today." [The leather jacket that MacArthur wore was still nonregulation.]
>
> "Well, I've just landed from Australia," he replied. "It's pretty cold there," he told the president. [Australia, in fact, was in the dead of winter.]
>
> Greetings all around—and we proceeded to leave the ship.[23]

All the next day, Roosevelt toured military facilities in and around Pearl Harbor and that night after dinner he invited three admirals and two army generals into a private conference room where he told them they were there to "determine the next phase of action against Japan."

The admirals included Chester Nimitz, commander of U.S. naval forces in the Pacific; William "Bull" Halsey, commander of the Third U.S. Fleet; and William D. Leahy, a top adviser to Roosevelt. The generals were Robert C. Richardson, who commanded the army forces in Nimitz's area, and MacArthur.

Taking a long bamboo pointer, the president touched the Philippines on a large wall map, turned to MacArthur, and said, "Well, Doug, where do we go from here?"

Speaking strictly extemporaneously, according to Leahy, MacArthur launched into an impressive, well-organized defense of his plan to invade the Philippines, stressing the "moral obligation" to drive the Japanese from the islands, as well as to free American prisoners there. He said that if the Philippines were liberated, "It would enable us to clamp an air and naval blockade on all supplies from the South Pacific to Japan, which would paralyze Japan's industries and force her to surrender."

He also expressed the opinion that the American people would have an "adverse reaction" (presumably at the polls in November's presidential election) if the Philippines were bypassed. Nimitz, however, speaking for the navy, insisted that the next objective should not be Luzon and the Philippines but the Japanese island stronghold of Formosa, which was strategically located for an invasion of Japan.[24]

The conference lasted until past midnight, with Nimitz and MacArthur parrying with each other on the differing strategies and Roosevelt acting as referee—or "chairman" of the conference, as MacArthur put it. On the whole it was an entirely congenial meeting with Leahy remarking afterward that it was "both pleasant and very informative to have these two men who had been pictured as antagonists calmly presenting their differing views to the commander in chief. Roosevelt felt it was "an excellent lesson in geography," adding that geography was one of his favorite subjects.

The following morning the meeting resumed. MacArthur reiterated that by capturing Luzon the Allies could deny Japan all of the oil, tin, rubber, and rice that she was siphoning from the conquered territories, when Roosevelt interrupted: "But Douglas, to take Luzon would demand heavier losses than we can stand."

MacArthur replied with a dictum. "Mr. President," he said, "my losses won't be heavy, any more than they have been in the past. The days of the frontal attack should be over. Modern infantry weapons are too deadly, and frontal assault is only for mediocre commanders. Good commanders do not turn in heavy losses."[25]

No decision was made by the president when the conference ended and MacArthur boarded the *Bataan* for the long flight back to Australia. He was "shocked," he said, at the appearance of Roosevelt, whom he had not seen since 1937. "Physically he was just the shell of the man I had known. It was clearly evident that his days were numbered," MacArthur wrote.

Two weeks later the president sent MacArthur a personal note saying, "You have been doing a really magnificent job . . . Personally, I wished much in Honolulu that you and I could swap places, and personally, I have a hunch that you would make much more of a go of it as President than I would as a General retaking the Philippines," and adding, "Some day there will be a flag-raising in Manila and I want you to do it." MacArthur had won after all.

★ ★ ★ ★

THE NEXT LINE OF THE ALLIED ADVANCE up the Pacific was what MacArthur called the Halmahera-Palau Line, a watery axis suspended between the island chains of those two names. He had come north across the southwest Pacific with extremely low casualties compared with those of the navy, which was slamming the marines through the central Pacific. MacArthur was now poised to attack the Netherlands Indies (Indonesia) island of Morotai (about the size of Martinique in the Caribbean), which lay barely three hundred miles from the southernmost Philippines.

It was lightly defended, but a fierce battle raged for a few days between some 57,000 American, Australian, British, and Dutch troops and approximately 500 stubborn Japanese. Only a few weeks prior, a much larger enemy garrison had existed on Morotai. It had been moved to a neighboring island, which the Japanese wrongly believed that MacArthur intended to attack. U.S. intelligence had snatched the message out of the air from Japanese radio traffic, and MacArthur again set in motion his now standard tactic, "Hit 'em where they ain't."

Realizing their mistake, the Japanese rapidly began to reinforce Morotai but to no avail. Most of their troop and supply barges were sunk by the U.S. Navy. Though the fighting continued until the following January, organized resistance was finished by September 24 and army engineers began improving Japanese landing strips and building new fields. Allied casualties were 30 dead and 85 wounded—this in contrast to the Battle of Peleliu in the Palau islands, which began around the same time, in which the navy suffered 1,600 marines killed and 6,600 wounded.

From Morotai, General Kenney's air force B-17s began systematically destroying Japanese airfields and military installations on Leyte in the central Philippines. It was a tremendous gamble, as MacArthur himself pointed out: "The operation to take Leyte without a preliminary landing in Mindanao [the southernmost Philippine island] was a most ambitious and difficult undertaking . . . I knew it was to be the crucial battle of the war in the Pacific."

The initial invasion of the Philippines had originally been set no earlier than December, but reconnaissance planes from Admiral Halsey's fleet of carriers had overflown the area around Leyte in early September and discovered "serious weaknesses" in Japanese air reaction and defense. He recommended to MacArthur that landings be made immediately.

When General Kenney reminded MacArthur that, until Japanese air bases in the Philippines were captured, Leyte was more than five hundred miles from the nearest land-based fighter protection for his big bombers, MacArthur responded, "I tell you I'm going back there this fall if I have to paddle a canoe with you flying cover in your B-17." Halsey solved the problem by suggesting that his carrier fighters escort the B-24s and B-17s to the enemy stronghold. MacArthur and Halsey cabled their proposal to George Marshall and the Joint Chiefs, who were attending a major war conference at Quebec with both Roosevelt and Churchill in attendance; within ninety minutes they had their answer—"Go ahead."[26]

On October 16, 1944, the invasion fleet swung out of Hollandia with MacArthur aboard his flagship cruiser, the USS *Nashville*, amid "one of the greatest armadas in history . . . ships as far as the eye could see," consisting of battleships, aircraft carriers, cruisers, destroyers, and transport, supply, and landing craft of all description. On board were 200,000 American fighting men, a majority of whom were battle-hardened veterans. The Japanese had twice that many soldiers but they were scattered throughout the Philippine Islands.

Lest anyone doubt MacArthur's ability to inspire the spirit with dramatic prose, hear him describe the scene with a tinge of purple verbiage:

> We came to Leyte just before midnight of a dark and moonless night. The stygian waters below and the black sky above seemed to conspire in wrapping us in an invisible cloak as we lay to and waited for dawn before entering Leyte Gulf . . . Now and then a ghostly ship would slide quietly by us, looming out of the night and disappearing into the gloom almost before its outlines could be depicted. I knew that on every ship nervous men lined the rails or paced the decks, peering into the darkness and wondering what stood out there beyond the night waiting for the dawn to come. There is a universal sameness in the emotions of men, whether they be admiral or sailor, general or private, at such a time as this.[27]

MacArthur had dressed snappily that morning, in typical MacArthur fashion—pressed and creased khakis, the matchless "crushed" hat with the gold "scrambled eggs" embroidered on its band and bill, the trademark corncob pipe and sunglasses. "He was as excited," said an aide, "as a kid going to his first party."[28]

As day broke in hazy grays, the big guns roared out from the battleships, cruisers, and destroyers with a din "like rolling thunder"; flashes of red lit the beaches and plumes of smoke billowed above the palm trees. The *Nashville* had anchored two miles offshore and from its bridge

MacArthur could clearly see the invasion taking shape. Landing craft were circling the transports, swarms of airplanes swooped down on the beach areas dropping bombs and strafing, and rockets flashed off from gun decks, leaving their vapor trails in the air.

Through the fiery maelstrom, MacArthur caught a glimpse of Tacloban, the American army post that had been his first assignment after leaving West Point as a second lieutenant some forty years earlier, in 1903. Then the troop-filled Higgins boats began their run toward the beaches and the naval barrage moved inland. MacArthur went in, he wrote later, with the third assault wave, although one of his biographers, William Manchester, claims it was four hours from the opening of fire. Whatever the case, it took much of the day to get 200,000 soldiers off the ships and into the boats and onto the beach, where enemy sniper fire continued to zing through the air.

MacArthur's entourage included his old friend the journalist Carlos Romulo—now a general in the Philippine army who had served as an aide to MacArthur on Bataan and Corregidor—and Sergio Osmeña, the new president of the Philippines following the recent death of Manuel Quezon. It was planned to dock the landing craft at a wharf ashore but fifty yards from the beach the boat ran aground.

Impatient, MacArthur ordered the ramp lowered and stepped off into knee-deep water without even allowing its depth to be tested. He then slogged to the shore, which was still smoking and seething from the tremendous naval bombardment. Ahead Japanese machine guns frequently opened and snipers fired from trees or "octopus traps," the Japanese term for foxholes. From overhead, an unexpectedly large number of Japanese warplanes dived on the still-contested beachhead, followed in hot pursuit by U.S. Navy Corsairs from the carriers.

MacArthur seemed oblivious to all these dangers, marching from unit to unit, inquiring about their progress. Periodically, said General Kenney, who accompanied MacArthur's party, Japanese soldiers could be heard shouting their usual billingsgate: "Fuck Erenor Roosfelt!" and "FDR eat shit!" which was gleefully answered by U.S. GIs, "Tojo eat shit!" (referring to the Japanese dictator). At one point a voice with a Japanese accent hollered out amid the sniping and machine-gunning, "Fuck Roy Acuff," alluding to a popular country music singer of the day.*

As MacArthur stepped over a large log on the beach an infantryman crouched behind it gulped, "Hey, there's General MacArthur." His buddy, hunkered beside him, still staring ahead, responded, "Oh, yeah? And I suppose he's got Eleanor Roosevelt along with him."[29]

By late afternoon the American and Philippine flags flew atop two stripped coconut trees on Red Beach, the latter having been sewn together the night before by a sailmaker on the troop transport *John Land*. MacArthur paused for a moment to compose a letter to President Roosevelt, scribbled on a field message pad, which, being the first letter sent from the freed Philippines, MacArthur said he hoped might prove a welcome addition to Roosevelt's famous stamp collection.

He told the president that the invasion was "going smoothly" and that when completed it would cut off the Japanese defensive line, while tactically severing in two the Japanese army in the Philippine Islands. MacArthur then arguably stepped over the line by advising the president to grant the Philippines independence immediately, a diplomatic move that would "electrify the world and redound immeasurably to the credit and honor of the United States for a thousand years."

At one point, with gunfire rumbling in the distance, MacArthur stood before a microphone wired to a sound truck and in his best stentorian voice he delivered what would be remembered among his greatest orations. "People of the Philippines—I have returned," he said. "By the grace of God our forces stand again on Philippine soil . . . The hour of your redemption is here . . . Rally to me. Let the indomitable spirit of Bataan and Corregidor lead on . . . Strike at every favorable opportunity. For your homes and hearths, strike! For future

---

* A number of years ago the author found himself in the same makeup room with Roy Acuff at a public television station and asked about the story. He said, with some amusement, that he had heard it also, a number of times from different people, and assumed it was true.

generations of your sons and daughters, strike! For your sacred dead, strike! Let no heart be faint. Let every arm be steeled. The guidance of divine God points the way. Follow in His name to the Holy Grail of righteous victory!"

It had begun to rain and was getting late. MacArthur returned to the *Nashville* and slept the sleep of a satisfied mind. It was only a toehold they had on Leyte, but he felt confident that in the end his army would remain victorious. How he knew this was uncertain, but for a man with such a mind and such an ego, MacArthur was wise enough to realize that his deeds must match his words. Come morning he would visit with his troops again, unaware that something very nasty was brewing out on the dark and misty ocean.

★ ★ ★ ★

CHAPTER ELEVEN

OVERLORD

George Marshall's gravest concern of the war revolved around Overlord, the vast Allied amphibious invasion of Europe that almost everyone knew would be necessary for victory.* Not only was there constant friction with the British over the timing of the plan, but no one it seemed in the British government or its army could decide if they wanted to try it in the first place. The Americans had hoped to invade France in 1942, when the operation was code-named Sledgehammer, mainly to keep Russia in the war after Soviet dictator Joseph Stalin had warned his country might lose to the Nazis unless the Allies opened a "second front" to draw off German troops.

But the British, ever cautious, didn't feel the Allies could concentrate enough strength at that period and British officials—principally Winston Churchill—talked Marshall out of Sledgehammer until it was abandoned. Instead, at Churchill's behest the U.S. and British armies launched Torch, the amphibious invasion of North Africa to take Tunisia, drive the Axis from the Mediterranean, and secure the Suez Canal.

---

* Some high officers in both the U.S. and British air forces believed that Germany could be brought to its knees by heavy bombing of its cities and industrial sites.

The landings, as we know, were successful, with George Patton leading the American contingent, but operations then bogged down and, instead of reaching Tunisia in a matter of weeks, it was nearly a year before the Germans and Italians were forced to surrender.

While Torch played out, Marshall once more began pushing for the big Allied invasion across the English Channel—now code-named Roundup—but again he was thwarted by Churchill, who pressed instead for an Allied assault to clear Sicily of Axis forces. Roundup was shelved, and the invasion—now, and forever, code-named Overlord—was rescheduled for 1944. Marshall was determined there would be no more postponements.

Incidental to Overlord was the question of American strategic bombing, which also produced friction with British planners. Early in the war, the Royal Air Force began attacking Germany with its long-range bombers, but it was soon discovered that between enemy fighters and antiaircraft fire the British were losing planes at an alarming rate. They switched from daylight to nighttime bombing and insisted to the Americans that daylight bombing was doomed to failure. Marshall and his colleagues in the U.S. Army Air Forces disagreed. They claimed that the new U.S. B-17 "flying fortress" was so heavily armed—ten to twelve .50-caliber machine guns—and well armored that the heavy bomber could fight off most enemy planes.

The argument went on, with Churchill "paint[ing] such vivid pictures of the ghastly casualties in store" that the British were gaining the upper hand. Until the Casablanca Conference, that is, when Marshall summoned the U.S. Eighth Air Force commanding general Ira C. Eaker from England to come to Morocco. When Eaker's plane arrived, air force commander Hap Arnold was waiting for him with news that they had lost the argument and the Eighth Air Force was going to have to fly its missions at night. Eaker asked for one last try and a meeting was arranged with Churchill.

"What torpedoed Churchill was a phrase," according to William Frye, an early Marshall biographer. Churchill was a master phrasemaker, Frye explained, "and was vulnerable to them too." Eaker had come up with a doozie: "Bombing around the clock," with the Eighth Air Force by day and the RAF by night. Eaker asked the startled prime minister what could be better to put the Germans off balance. Churchill thought for a moment, and then roared, "You haven't convinced me you can do it! But you have convinced me you ought to have a chance!"[1]

While the resulting bombing campaign might not have shortened the war, it certainly proved highly destructive to Germany; 160,000 Allied airmen were killed and 33,700 Allied planes were lost, but as a consequence the principal German cities were destroyed and the main German manufacturing plants wrecked. Yet, even so, the Germans fought futilely on.

★ ★ ★ ★

AFTER SICILY FELL TO THE ALLIES came the question of whether to invade Italy. The dictator Mussolini had been deposed and he'd fled to Germany, and the Italians essentially surrendered to the Allies, but the Germans retained a strong military presence in Italy and Hitler was not disposed to give it up. Churchill and the British were all for invading Italy, partially on the notion of being able to bomb Germany from bases in the north once the Germans were evicted. Churchill even argued that the Allies might be able to send an army through Italy into southern Austria—his hoary strategy of attacking Germans through Europe's "soft underbelly."

The British, nevertheless, had a reason to proceed very carefully with any cross-Channel invasion of the French coast; in 1942 they sent a 7,000-man amphibious force, consisting mostly of Canadians, to assault the French village of Dieppe along Hitler's Atlantic Wall. The operation was a total disaster with half the men shot, drowned, or captured. Marshall, therefore, understood Britain's reluctance to undertake a cross-Channel invasion, but he still believed that attacking the Germans in France was the most effective strategy. It was a constant worry of his that the British might again try to postpone Overlord, even though a hundred thousand American soldiers had poured into England, with more to come.

There was also reason to believe, however, that Churchill's opposition to invading through France wasn't purely rational. His personal physician informed Marshall, "You are fighting the dead on the Somme" (the 1916 battle in World War I in which 50,000 British soldiers were killed). The physician said Churchill thought half a million Allied soldiers would be lost invading France and that the English Channel would be "littered with floating bodies." (Churchill had an obsession with the Channel, his doctor said.) Marshall came to believe that because of their horrendous experiences in the First World War the British simply did not want to fight in France—ever.

Still, as the proper time for Overlord approached, it was assumed that Marshall would personally command the operation—which would become the largest amphibious assault in the world. He had been in the army more than forty years and on only a handful of occasions had he commanded troops. There is no doubt that Marshall craved the assignment.

Secretary of War Henry Stimson had personally gone to Churchill in the summer of 1943 to secure his blessing for Marshall as commander. At first, Churchill was reluctant, not because he mistrusted Marshall's abilities—"he regarded Marshall as the greatest military figure of the war"—but because he believed that he could do more good in his present position. Stimson weighed his options carefully, and during the Allied conference in Quebec in August, with Churchill's blessing, he named Marshall commander of the greatest military operation of the war.

After the Marshall decision was made, highly placed individuals began discussing it "with long faces and shaking heads." Admirals King and Leahy, and air force chief Hap Arnold—privately and separately—urged Roosevelt to reconsider the nomination. They argued that Marshall was too much needed as head of the Joint Chiefs. When Roosevelt asked King for an alternative, he replied, "Eisenhower is a natural."

Others involved with the Joint Chiefs or with army affairs worked behind the scenes to scuttle Marshall's assignment. A letter to the president signed by none other than the aged General of the Armies John J. Pershing warned that Marshall's absence from Washington "would be a fundamental and very grave error in our military policy."[2]

Marshall apparently knew nothing of these intrigues and never told a soul—unless it was Mrs. Marshall—how he felt about the issue, which came to a head several months later when Roosevelt sent for him.

The president wanted to know if Marshall thought he could better help the war effort by going to England for Overlord or by staying in Washington with the Joint Chiefs. Marshall demurred, telling Roosevelt that "personal preferences were of no account in war," and that whatever the president's decision it would be "all right." That constituted one of the most selfless acts of the war and of Marshall's career as well.[3]

★ ★ ★ ★

As the war progressed, Marshall relentlessly contended with matters great and small. He was pleased with the way MacArthur was going about his business in the South Pacific but aggravated by his constant sniping at the navy, which Marshall feared would foster noncooperation between the services. MacArthur allowed reporters to hang around his headquarters and did not stoop to scruples in using them for his purposes. Stories would be printed charging that the navy had refused carrier escorts to one of MacArthur's invasions, or that the navy was more worried about losing ships than winning the war. MacArthur wouldn't necessarily say these things himself, but had allowed them to "leak" from one of his staff members.

Inevitably the stories would be printed in Honolulu newspapers, setting off Admiral Nimitz with a full head of steam; then Admiral King and others in Washington would receive angry cables and the whole thing would eventually wind up in Marshall's lap. The chief of staff in turn sent MacArthur everything from polite requests that he refrain from criticizing his fellow service to stern reprimands, but it did no good. The sniping continued throughout the war and what in hell could Marshall do? *Relieve MacArthur* for talking to the press? MacArthur was a great hero to the American people and, most important, he was winning battles. There were limits to what a chief of staff could do, and first and foremost Marshall was for winning the war.

To make matters worse, MacArthur did not limit his depreciatory complaints to the navy but also often referred in the press to "that bunch in Washington," usually Marshall and the War Department staff, but it could have included everything and everyone from Congress to the president himself. Supplies and ammunition were short, or defective, MacArthur complained, or the wrong kind was sent. MacArthur used the press as if it were a part of his command.

Despite the enormous pressure of his daily duties, Marshall was not above tackling the kinds of problems that could be handled at lower levels. Early in the war a rumor got back to Washington that U.S. fighter planes in MacArthur's theater were taking a beating from the lighter and faster Japanese Zeros because the Japanese fighters could get above the American planes to shoot them down. Marshall was always keen on correcting those kinds of issues and dispatched an air force general to New Guinea with instructions to "talk to the individual pilots, and the first thing you tell them is that if there is anything they want done to their planes, I will have it done."[4]

In fact, when he first learned of the problem, Marshall had ordered one type of plane in the United States stripped of everything to get its weight down, but it was found that the greatest item of weight that could be safely removed was the armor plate around the cockpit seat. When Marshall's emissary met with the pilots and gave them the option of removing the armor and weighing similar to the enemy Zero they turned it down. "Their clamor out there," Marshall said, "boiled down to one thing—they wanted girls. I sent word to the pilots that I was sympathetic, but I couldn't supply them with girls."[5]

There were other headaches. Malaria was a constant issue in the southwestern Pacific, particularly for air corps ground crews who had to work throughout the night on the planes to keep them in flying condition. Toiling under electric lights and without mosquito netting, they were either eaten alive by mosquitos or beginning to turn yellow from "terrible doses of Atabrine" (a malaria preventive, taken as a pill). The pilots were afraid that the mechanics "were so dopey they weren't certain they were putting in the cotter pins and things of that sort," Marshall said. When this came to his attention, it was evident to Marshall that these men would have to be relieved first and sent back to recuperate, but the snag was that the staff had not anticipated such problems and were training far too few mechanics and ground service crews as replacements.

The subject of replacements wasn't of course limited only to mechanics. Marshall always tried to keep his units up to full strength, he said, for morale as well as for fighting purposes. In one instance, fighter pilots flying out of England and other theaters of the war needed to have replacements in a way that kept the mess table always full. "If they fail to come in" (meaning they were shot down), "the [replacement] had to take their place because to sit down and find half the mess table empty was very depressing to the men."[6]

★ ★ ★ ★

PATTON HAD FOR MUCH OF HIS CAREER been a trial to his superiors and his behavior continually aggrieved Marshall—the more so because he knew Patton and liked him. He'd known him in World War I, roomed with him at Fort Myer, sailed with him on the Chesapeake, and written in his little black book that "Patton will take a unit through hell and high water."

"Give him an armored corps when one becomes available," he'd added. "But keep a tight rope around his neck." Marshall thought Patton was one of the finest, brightest tacticians in the army and had great admiration for his ability to whip a body of troops into shape. But slapping an enlisted soldier—and a hospital patient to boot—was outrageous. It appeared to Patton that Eisenhower and Marshall were deliberately letting him wither on the vine, with his Seventh Army being dismantled piece by piece—some units going to Mark Clark's Fifth Army in Italy, others to England to prepare for Overlord.

In fact, the Allies had concocted various ruses under the code name Operation Fortitude to mislead the Germans about where and when the Overlord invasion would occur, and Patton figured prominently in these schemes. Eisenhower, meanwhile, was content to keep Patton guessing as to what his role in the great invasion, if any, would be.

First, Patton was sent around the Mediterranean areas, including the island of Corsica, ostensibly for ceremonial purposes but the notion was to make the Germans believe his presence signified an Allied invasion somewhere in that region. When Patton was finally called to England in January 1944, Eisenhower told him he was going to command the U.S. Third Army, as yet on its way to England.

Meanwhile, due to his prestigious military reputation among the German High Command, Patton was given the additional assignment of commanding the First Army Group, a purely fictitious entity under Operation Fortitude, designed to fool the Nazis into thinking the Allies were preparing to invade France at the Pas-de-Calais—the shortest distance between England and France—in mid-July 1944. The actual invasion was to take place several hundred miles south, and a month earlier, on the Normandy coast.

The First Army Group consisted of several imaginary field armies, complete with bogus radio traffic and dummy landing craft at English ports close to Calais. Soon after its formation, Allied intelligence in the form of ULTRA—the British code-breaking project corresponding to the United States' MAGIC operation in the Pacific—revealed that the Germans were swallowing the bait and that Field Marshal Rommel was holding his 15th Panzer Army in the Pas-de-Calais in anticipation of an invasion by Patton.

Patton played along, making his presence known in the small town of Knutsford, England, where the Third Army was headquartered, and where he committed a political indiscretion that nearly did him in.

On April 25, scarcely six weeks before Overlord was to commence, at the behest of the British Ministry of Information Patton made an appearance at a club for women, whose purpose it was to welcome American soldiers. It was not his intention to speak but merely to be present to acknowledge the group for helping entertain his men.

When Patton arrived three press photographers were waiting for him outside wanting to take his picture. He agreed, remarking that he was there unofficially and stipulating that the pictures could not be published, to which the photographers agreed. After several introductions and addresses, a Miss Foster Jeffery, head of the British Women's

Volunteer Services, suddenly turned to Patton and asked him to "say a few words." Then a Mrs. Smith arose and introduced him, reminding the audience of about two hundred that he was there unofficially and his "presence was not to be disclosed."

Thus on the hook, Patton took to the stage and began telling the audience:

> Until today, my only experience in welcoming has been to welcome Germans and Italians to the "Infernal Regions." In this I have been quite successful . . .
>
> I feel that clubs such as this are of very real value, because I believe with Mr. Bernard Shaw, I think it was he, that the British and Americans are two people separated by a common language, and since it is the evident destiny of the British and Americans, and of course the Russians, to rule the world, the better we know each other, the better job we will do.
>
> A club such as this is an ideal place for making such acquaintances and for promoting mutual understanding. Also, as soon as our soldiers meet, and get to know the English ladies, and write home and tell our women how truly lovely you are, the sooner the American ladies will get jealous and bring this war to a quick termination, and I will have the chance to go to the Pacific and kill Japanese.[7]

Several lengthy speeches ensued, followed by the singing of "God Save the King" and "The Star-Spangled Banner," after which Patton departed. The next day all hell broke loose.

Around noon, Eisenhower's headquarters reached Patton asking what he had said about the Americans and British ruling the world. Patton replied that he had included the Russians, but apparently some British newspapers had omitted that part. It was certain to create a great commotion within the suspicious Soviet Union.

Worse, the British Press Association had released the story on the wire where it was immediately picked up by practically every newspaper in the United States and given front-page play. It didn't help much when the BPA later issued a correction including "the Russians" in Patton's address. The damage had been done.

Marshall had cabled Eisenhower that American newspapers were carrying "lurid" stories about Patton's speech, and that official Washington was in an uproar. It was the business about "ruling the world" that inspired the most reactionary outrage. A senator from South Dakota denounced Patton for "stepping out of bounds" in overriding diplomatic prerogatives. Letters to the editor poured in condemning Patton as a "Fascist" and for being "insulting to other nationalities." Newspaper editorials widely pronounced Patton's remarks "irresponsible." One described Patton as "Chief-foot-in-Mouth" and a congressman even compared him to Hitler.[8]

Coming on the heels of the slapping incident, Patton's latest gaffe became vastly overblown, and the Senate even held up his confirmation for promotion to the regular army rank of major general. A livid Eisenhower again sought Marshall's consent to fire Patton, and once more it was tactfully refused. The chief of staff told the Supreme Allied Commander in Europe that if he felt Overlord could succeed without Patton then he was free to relieve him. However, if he had any doubts about Overlord not succeeding in Patton's absence, he ought to keep him. Then Marshall pointed out "the unmistakable fact that Patton is the only available Army commander for his present assignment [Third Army] who has actual experience in fighting Rommel and in extensive landing operations followed by a land campaign of rapid exploitation."[9]

Eisenhower's reaction to this heavy hint was to call Patton onto the carpet and then let him stew for several weeks worrying whether Eisenhower or Marshall was going to fire him. Though he had already made the final decision on his fate, the notion of Patton dangling in perdition for all the trouble he had caused gave Ike no small amount of satisfaction. Knowing full well how Patton craved battle, and most especially this one, it was the cruelest cut of all and, evidenced in his personnel correspondence, Patton suffered grievously.

To his daughter Ruth Ellen Totten, Patton wrote, "Jesus only suffered one night but I have had months and months of it, and the cross is not yet in sight, though probably just around the corner. At least I have the *When and If* [his eighty-three-foot sailing schooner]." And to Beatrice he said, "My final thought on the matter is that I am destined to achieve some great thing—what, I don't know . . ."

It wasn't until the following week that Patton received a telegram from Eisenhower: "I have decided to keep you . . . Go ahead and train your army." Patton immediately wrote back, thanking Eisenhower, and to his diary said, "He [Ike] called up in person and was very nice. Sometimes I am very fond of him, and this is one of the times."

Two days later Patton wrote a paper on the use of armored divisions and told his diary, "I have completely gotten back in the swing of things, thank God."[10]

Eisenhower had warned Patton about saying anything publicly, which Patton initially interpreted as forbidding him to speak openly even to his infantry and armored divisions. When that was straightened out he made a series of speeches to these units as they arrived in Great Britain, telling them, among other things, "DO NOT TAKE COUNSEL OF YOUR FEARS." To his officers Patton said, "The only worry I have about this show is how I'm going to get the Army across [the English Channel] and assembled on the other side. For the fighting I have no worry." He'd instructed his commanders to visit the front daily, to observe, not to meddle, that issuing an order is only 10 percent of the problem—the rest is ensuring it is properly carried out—and to visit their wounded personally and frequently.

An army historian noted that Patton rarely cursed when speaking to his staff but was highly profligate with military billingsgate for the edification of his troops. He talked their turkey and they loved him for it. He would make speeches to division-size audiences—20,000 to 30,000 men, who would gather in a sea of brown uniforms before a stage decorated with bunting and an army band playing martial marches and popular tunes. "His speeches became galas in themselves," writes biographer Carlo D'Este, noting that Patton would arrive in a black Mercedes driven by a sergeant behind an MP escort with sirens blaring.

"He would emerge in his buff-and-dark-green uniform, helmet, and highly shined cavalry boots, and march through the crowd to the front of the platform," from which he intoned such sentiments as "A man must be alert at all times. If not, some German sonofabitch will sneak up behind him and beat him to death with a sockful of shit!" The men roared and clapped and slapped their thighs. One of his more famous speeches went:

> Everyone has a job to do. Every man serves the whole. The Ordnance is needed to supply the guns. The Quartermaster is needed to bring up the food and clothes for us, for where we are going there's not a hell of a lot to steal. Every last man in the mess hall, even the guy that heats the water to keep us from getting diarrhea, has a role to play. Even the Chaplain is important, for if we get killed and he is not there to bury us we would all go to hell. We don't want yellow cowards in the army. They should be killed off like flies. If not, they will go back home after the war, goddamn cowards, and breed more cowards. The brave men will breed more brave men. One of the bravest men I saw in the African campaign was the man I saw on a telegraph pole in the midst of furious fire . . . I stopped and asked him what in hell he was doing up there and he answered "Fixing the wire, Sir."
>
> "Isn't it a little unhealthy up there right now?" I asked.
>
> "Yes sir, but this goddamn wire has got to be fixed."
>
> That was a real soldier . . . I'm not even supposed to be in England. Let the first bastards to find out be the goddamn Germans. Some day I want them to raise up on their hind legs and howl "Jesus Christ, it's that goddamn Third Army and that goddamn sonofabitch Patton again!"

The troops ate it up and when he'd finished one had the impression, according to numerous accounts, that to the last man they would have followed him to hell and back.[11]

★ ★ ★ ★

A WEEK BEFORE THE ALLIES' ARMADA embarked for Normandy, Marshall returned to his home on General's Row at Fort Myer with an expression of deep sorrow on his face. He had come to tell Mrs. Marshall that her son, Second Lieutenant Allen Tupper Brown, had died that morning as his tank unit moved toward Rome.

Allen was Marshall's favorite stepson. He had volunteered for the army even though he was married with a young son, and he graduated from the Armored School at Fort Knox. He had survived the bitterest fighting in North Africa, Sicily, and in Italy around Monte Cassino. He was approaching the Alban Hills when a German sniper's bullet struck him in the head as he rose up with binoculars through the turret of his tank.[12]

"He came in, closing the door behind him," Mrs. Marshall wrote years afterward, "and told me Allen was dead. He had given his life . . . in a tank battle on the road to Rome."

In one of his last letters Allen had written his wife, "Today is a beautiful day. It is warm out and the feel of spring is in the air. It is hard to believe that men are killing and being killed all around us. The noise of the artillery is a reminder, however, and no matter how beautiful it is, it is bound to be a sad day for many people as it is every day of this war."[13]

Marshall was heartbroken, but with Overlord looming on the horizon he made every effort to block the family tragedy from his thoughts.

★ ★ ★ ★

OVERLORD GOT OFF TO A DUBIOUS START when Eisenhower, on June 4, postponed the invasion scheduled for the following day. Despite continued threatening weather on June 5, Marshall's office was notified that the invasion was on for June 6. It was a terribly agonizing condition for old-time sailors who knew the English Channel. They shook their heads and clamped their jaws at the prospect of landing in high winds and surf. But the weather forecaster had told Eisenhower there was reason to hope for a brief period of calmer weather between approaching fronts.

Marshall notified Secretary Stimson of the decision and went to bed. He has left no record of his reactions, although one might assume he would have been a bit wistful, knowing that the greatest command in history had eluded him. He got up the next day as he always did and went to the office where messages from Ike began informing him that the operation apparently was successful. To cap it off, the previous day, Mark Clark's army had marched into Rome.

Marshall, along with Arnold and King, chiefs of the air force and navy, respectively, decided to fly to England the day after Overlord to be on hand in case anything went wrong, and also one might fairly suspect to at least get a look at this greatest of all invasions—the one they had argued over, planned over, sweated over, and often anguished over—that would anticipate the liberation of Europe and the end of the war.

Once in England, on June 8, the American service chiefs briefed their counterparts on the British general staff as to their plans for the rest of the war, including Pacific operations. It was also then decided to dust off the long-shelved Operation Anvil (its new code name: Dragoon), a plan to invade southern France along its Mediterranean coast. Its aim was to both further confuse the Germans about Allied intentions and employ the more than 250,000 Free French soldiers currently languishing in North Africa.

The American chiefs joined the ebullient Prime Minister Winston Churchill in his private train for an expedition to the battlefront. That night as the train chugged toward Portsmouth, the chiefs enjoyed a sumptuous dinner in the prime minister's dining car where they celebrated Overlord with many toasts of champagne.

At Portsmouth they were met by a glowing Eisenhower and split up for the Channel crossing—the Englishmen boarding a Royal Navy destroyer that would carry them to the British zone (where Churchill insisted he was going to take a shot at the enemy) and the Americans boarding the USS *Thompson* to take them to the U.S. Army sector of Normandy. Once on French soil, the distinguished visitors were greeted by General Omar Bradley, who had been chosen to command the American ground forces of Overlord. It was George Marshall's first return to France since he'd left it twenty-five years earlier as an aide to General Pershing, when they said their goodbyes to Field Marshal Foch and his staff.

From the beaches, the party moved inland past a large sobering temporary cemetery where at least a portion of the several thousand Americans killed in action had been lain. One of Marshall's aides carried a bag full of medals with which to decorate men for acts of bravery. Having served in World War I he recognized the value of high-ranking general officers going among the fighting troops and personally presenting honors for acts beyond the call of duty.

It was hot and dusty and the roads were crammed with thousands of American soldiers, German prisoners, and vehicles—tanks, trucks, jeeps, ambulances filled with wounded and dead—in a continuous stream going to and from the battle area. This was the bewildering "flow of battle," which, as biographer Pogue points out, "could never be envisaged by use of even the most sophisticated visual aids in the Pentagon."

It was not long before General Bradley called a halt to the proceeding, stressing the catastrophe that just a single German sniper could cause, and took everyone to his headquarters in an old apple orchard where they lunched al fresco on army C-rations washed down by water in tin canteen cups.

Marshall cabled Roosevelt that "Conditions on the beachhead are generally favorable." The German army, he said, did not appear able to launch a counterattack of any consequence, at least for "some days to come." He commended the morale of the troops and their officers and was especially impressed with the confidence and aggressive attitude of the commanders. Overall, he told the president, he was highly impressed with the development of "a remarkable scale of efficiency."

★ ★ ★ ★

AFTER TWO WEEKS IN ENGLAND, Marshall visited the Italian front where Fifth Army commander General Mark Clark gave him a tour of the battle area, then a hundred miles north of Rome along roads littered with the twisted and burned remains of German vehicles, tanks, and guns. Approaching the town of Grosseto, close to the fighting front, the windshield on Marshall's jeep was lowered "to avoid reflecting the sun which would have attracted the attention of the Germans."

Near the end of his trip, Marshall took time to visit the gravesite of his stepson Allen. It lay near the flagpole on the main pathway through the seven-thousand-grave cemetery. Afterward he took a small plane and flew low over the terrain where Allen had been killed. With the help of Clark, he met with a lieutenant who had been in the tank immediately behind Allen's, and with the driver and gunner of Allen's tank. The lieutenant produced Allen's map, "a much rumpled paper with the various lines and objectives noted in crayon."

Using the map, the lieutenant described Allen's last battle in detail. Still not satisfied, the general again took a plane and, using the map, had the pilot circle slowly at 300 feet above the scene of the action, which lay about twenty miles southeast of Rome. That done, he returned to Rome and wrote Allen's widow of three weeks that he had both visited the gravesite and been able to pinpoint the place where her husband fell. It wasn't much, but it was something he alone could do in wartime; other widows hadn't even that small comfort and grieved never knowing where their loved ones had fallen.

★ ★ ★ ★

AFTER A MONTH OF TERRIFIC FIGHTING, the Allies broke out of their bridgehead in Normandy and, led by the U.S. Army, began to sweep across France with breathtaking success. In the Mediterranean, Operation Dragoon was successfully launched as well, spearheaded by the U.S. Seventh Army and an army of Free French, which fought its way up the valley of the Rhône, clearing southern France of Germans and linking up with the main Allied force near Paris.

Meanwhile, the Russians, who had been so badly tried by the German attack in 1942, had reversed their fate and were now counterattacking all along the Eastern Front. All of this as Allied bombers continued to reduce German cities, including the capital, Berlin, to rubble.

As the Allies were clearing the last Germans out of France, in the Pacific Douglas MacArthur had made good on his promise to return to the Philippines, having established a bridgehead on Leyte, in the middle of the archipelago. Marshall was profoundly satisfied with these developments, for all the hard work and burning of midnight oil seemed at last to be paying off after the years of consternation, disappointment, and fret.

Just as Marshall was feeling good about the progress of the war, however, a bugaboo arose to once again break him into a sweat. The Allies in Europe—particularly the American armies—had raced across France so quickly they had outrun their supplies.

Toward the end of September, Field Marshal Montgomery launched Operation Market Garden, in which a large part of his army—including 41,000 paratroopers—aimed for the town of Arnhem in Holland to secure a bridgehead across the Rhine into Germany.

But stronger-than-expected German defenses and overstretched supply lines caused the operation to be aborted with 17,000 Allied casualties. In turn, Eisenhower had been compelled to halt the powerful American offensive led by Omar Bradley in order to transfer supplies—principally tank fuel—to the British. This left everyone in a huff, especially George S. Patton, whose Third Army was spearheading the drive.

To see what could be done, in October, Marshall made another trip to the fighting front. On the seventh, he visited Patton after having his pilot fly low over the World War I battlefields in the Meuse-Argonne sector. Patton was straining at the leash with no fuel, no replacements, and a lack of other supplies; Marshall soothed him, saying these would arrive all in good time, and the meeting was amicable. When Marshall got to the British headquarters, however, Bernard Montgomery was in a snit.

He complained about Eisenhower's running of the war, saying Eisenhower had gotten his army "into a real mess." Marshall later stated to an interviewer that he "came pretty close to blowing off out of turn," and he condemned the field marshal's "overwhelming egotism."

Marshall couldn't accomplish the impossible and the war would have to wait until the reinforcements and supplies caught up with it. To a friend, General Frank McCoy, he highlighted his trip: "I went through five armies, army corps, sixteen divisions, and also saw the commanders and staffs of eight other Divisions." After returning to the United States he informed Beatrice Patton that her husband "looked in splendid health and in fine fettle and full of fight."[14]

★ ★ ★ ★

MacArthur, having just invaded Leyte, wrote Marshall asking for more supplies for the Pacific, adding, "These frontal attacks by the Navy [marines], as at Tarawa, are tragic and unnecessary massacres of American lives." Marshall agreed but it was a navy decision. As the two American prongs of the road to Tokyo began to intersect, new dangers arose. Combat planes from Japanese-held islands could reach out farther than the planes from U.S. carriers but, again, it was the navy's problem to solve.

In June, the navy nearly annihilated the fast carrier fleet of Admiral Jisaburo Ozawa, sinking three Japanese aircraft carriers and downing more than five hundred enemy planes. As a consequence, MacArthur wanted to take his invasion force north to attack the big island of Luzon, location of Manila, the Philippine capital, as well as 250,000 Japanese soldiers. He had come this far, so Marshall gave MacArthur the nod.

In Europe that December the Germans launched a surprise, all-out attack on Eisenhower's army in the Ardennes Forest on the Belgium-Luxembourg border that threatened to split the Allied armies in two. After a week of ferocious fighting, however, the Germans were forced to withdraw. Three months later, the Americans crossed the Rhine into Germany with astonishing success, capturing more than 350,000 enemy soldiers in the Ruhr. That broke the back of German resistance in the West and, led by the armies of Patton and General Courtney Hodges, the Americans pushed into central and southern Germany with unparalleled speed.

Meanwhile, the Soviet army was overrunning German forces in Poland and eastern Germany in its advance toward Berlin and Prague, leaving in its wake an orgy of rape, looting, and other unmilitary marauding violence.

The question of postwar politics now became intense. The British asked Eisenhower for permission to seize Berlin before the Soviets arrived there. Churchill, in particular, was highly suspicious of the motives of Soviet Premier Stalin, believing the Russians were anxious to acquire the formerly Nazi-occupied countries to enhance the spread of international communism. But Eisenhower refused, and Marshall agreed with him on grounds that such operations were political, unjustified, and that the focus of the Allied armies should be first to put the German war manufacturing enterprises out of business. In the meantime, the Soviets were establishing tightly held "zones of occupation" in the conquered countries, leaving no doubt that they intended to grab as much land as possible.

For Germany, it was only a matter of time. Most of the vast Nazi empire that had stretched from the English Channel to the outskirts of Moscow had been reconquered and the German economy was wrecked. Three and a half million German soldiers had been killed thus far. The principal German cities lay in rubble from the Allied bombing campaign, and a million and a half civilians were dead. Still, Hitler had vowed to fight to the death.

Even this was becoming nearly impossible after the Allies captured the Romanian oil fields that had fed the Nazi war machine. Allied intelligence noted an increased use of horses and cattle as dray animals by German soldiers at the fighting fronts.

That suited the U.S. Treasury secretary Henry Morgenthau Jr. just fine. For his part, Morgenthau was recommending to Roosevelt that Germany be turned into a permanent agrarian enterprise policed by the Allied powers, with no significant manufacturing of any sort—a land of grain farmers and goatherds—the better to ensure there would be no repeat of Nazi-style rule.

★ ★ ★ ★

BACK IN THE PACIFIC, MacArthur was charging into the Philippine Islands to establish bases from which U.S. planes could attack Japan directly. At the same time, navy task forces were driving westward across the ocean, closing in on Japan, expelling enemy military forces from the islands that would also be used by the Allies as permanent, unsinkable aircraft carriers.

Like the Germans, the Japanese were severely handicapped by a lack of oil after the Allies had cut off the petroleum supply from the East Indies. And like the Germans, all major Japanese cities were in ruins from Allied bombing. Trade was nonexistent and the Japanese economy was exhausted. Two million soldiers were dead as were several hundred thousand civilians. But again, like the Germans, the Japanese leaders refused to surrender and vowed to be wiped out to the last man—and woman—as a matter of national honor.

The Allies had come a long, hard way since the early 1940s. George Marshall, as U.S. Army chief of staff, had shepherded the tremendous effort with what would later be regarded as a calculated ease, although it was anything but.

Now he was on the crest of a great victory, with the Allied armies on the outskirts of the enemies' homeland. The two predator nations lay like wounded, exhausted beasts in their lairs—panting, furious, ferocious, and on their own terrain, their sacred soil. The trick now, Marshall knew, was a final conquest without the terrific bloodbath that both Axis nations had vowed in spades.

Chapter Twelve

★ ★ ★ ★

LET'S WIN IT ALL

D-day was, as the British were fond of saying, "a near run thing." Horrid weather caused a day's cancellation with 160,000 soldiers waiting in the holds aboard troopships. But the next day Eisenhower gave the word and the invasion armada of 5,000 ships completely surprised the Germans, which, considering the number of people involved, must go down as a miracle in itself. The British and American infantrymen of Omar Bradley's First Army and Bernard Montgomery's Second Army* stormed the Normandy beaches just after daybreak on June 6, 1944, and fought their way inland, in some cases—particularly in the American sectors at Utah Beach and Omaha Beach—up steep cliffs in the face of murderous machine-gun fire.

At day's end they had effected a tenuous lodgment all along the fifty-mile stretch at a cost of about 10,000 casualties—nearly half of them KIA. Also killed were approximately 10,000 French civilians caught in the preinvasion aerial and naval bombardment. Operation Fortitude had worked as

....

* Although the British and Americans made up most of the invasion force on D-day there were also troops representing Australia, Canada, and New Zealand as well as Norway, Poland, Greece, Czechoslovakia, Belgium, France, and other nations occupied by the Germans.

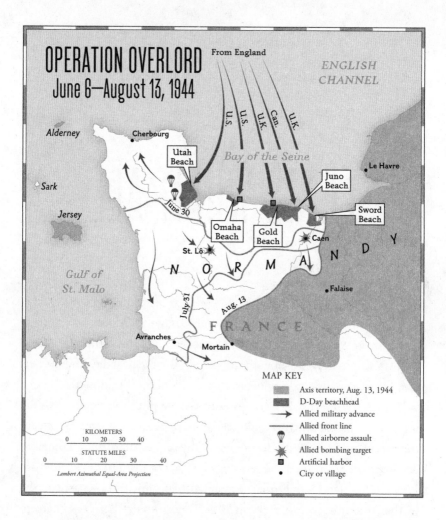

planned, with the Germans expecting Patton to land a vast army group at the Pas-de-Calais. If the enemy had utilized the forces he was keeping in Calais the result of Operation Overlord might have been very different.

The fighting in Normandy continued with pitiless intensity as the Allies pushed out from their beachhead into *bocage* country, where the land was divided into farm fields separated by dense hedgerows designed to resist soil erosion and sunken roads. These were particularly dreaded by the Allied troops because they invariably contained German machine-gun nests that had to be cleared out, often by hand-to-hand combat. Luckily for the Allies, a furious Adolf Hitler persisted in making all the big decisions about the battle himself from his aerie perch high in the mountains of Bavaria. After learning of the invasion he had relieved his senior army commander Gerd von Rundstedt and appointed Field Marshal Günther von Kluge to hurl the Allies into the sea, unaware that von Kluge had been involved in a recent plot to kill him with a bomb.

Meanwhile, Patton was feverishly training the Third Army for its role in Operation Cobra, the big Allied breakout from Normandy. Cobra was hatched between Bradley and Montgomery about a month after the Allied advance began to stall in the terrifying *bocage* country. Eisenhower feared the Germans might conclude they'd been tricked by Fortitude and unleash their 15th Army languishing in the Pas-de-Calais to assault the Allied pocket with overwhelming force.

On July 25 the British attacked the Germans near the town of Caen. When von Kluge rushed reinforcements to that front, Bradley attacked with his First Army toward the port of Cherbourg with the notion of liberating it for use by the Allies, who presently had only the artificial "Mulberry harbors" on the Normandy beaches to unload men, equipment, and provisions for what was rapidly building to a two-million-man army.

Patton had arrived in France on July 7, full of pep and ideas about how the Allies could break out of the Normandy-Cotentin Peninsula front and into Brittany, where he could employ his tanks in the mobile warfare for which they were designed. "I fear the war will be over before I get loose—but who can say?" he had told his diary. "Fate and the Hand of God still run most shows."

At the new U.S. airstrip on Omaha Beach he was mobbed by personnel from all services who had heard of his arrival, which was technically still supposed to be secret. Never one to shun an audience, Patton mounted his jeep and addressed the throng: "I'm proud to be here to fight beside you. Now let's cut the guts out of those Krauts and get on to Berlin. And when we get to Berlin," he added, "I am personally going to shoot that paper-hanging son of a bitch [Hitler] just like I would a snake."*, [1]

---

* Hitler at one time held a job as a wallpaperer.

Patton's advance party was in the Cotentin Peninsula where everything shook constantly from the firing of the large artillery guns emplaced along the line. The day he landed, Patton lunched with Omar Bradley, now his boss, Montgomery, and the commander of French forces General de Guingand. He was told that when the Third Army had arrived and become operational, it was to clear the Brest region of Germans, then push east toward Paris.

Until then there was nothing to do but wait and take care of recent troop arrivals. Patton had hurt his toe in England when a window blackout sash had fallen on it. Now it became infected and he had the nail pulled off after breakfast on July 10. "It hurt like hell and I can't wear a shoe," he wrote Beatrice. Three days later he told her, "[General] Teddy R[oosevelt Jr.] died in his sleep last night. He had made three landings with the leading wave—such is fate. I am going to his funeral tomorrow night. He was one of the bravest men I ever met."

★ ★ ★ ★

NEITHER THE BRITISH NOR THE AMERICANS seemed able to break out of their beachhead. In a full month since the landing, they had gained a mere eleven miles of ground, and Patton, who had been in France for a week, was chomping at the bit. He blamed Montgomery and Eisenhower for doing little or nothing to end the stalemate. Patton's plan would have been to put an armored division in the lead and, covered by heavy air bombardments, burst right through the German defenses. Ike, however, thought it was still too risky.

Then the Cobra plan was decided upon, but before it could be implemented Patton's Third Army public relations officer made the drastic mistake of briefing the press corps on Cobra, which at the time was a top-secret operation. It was a serious breach and Patton was mortified; he relieved the officer and told the war correspondents they must not print the story. "A terrible crime has been committed," was the way he put it to them.

The reporters kept mum, but rain held up Cobra because the bombers could not be precise in bad weather. In fact they couldn't be precise even in good weather, a fact stressed by General Jimmy Doolittle, who now commanded the U.S. Eighth Air Force. But Eisenhower insisted that the bombers attack the German front lines, which they did, often with tragic results.

By July 24 the skies had cleared and Bradley gave the order to attack. The 2,400 American bombers that preceded the breakout on the first day killed twenty-five U.S. soldiers and wounded more than one hundred. One of Patton's close friends, Colonel Harry "Paddy" Flint, was shot dead leading his regiment in the attack. Earlier, Patton had remarked of him in a letter to Beatrice, "He expects to be killed and probably will be."

The next day Lieutenant General Lesley McNair was also killed, along with 111 of his men, in another aerial misdrop by the bombers. McNair became the highest-ranked military man to be killed in the war and had come to France as a stand-in for Patton in the fake American army group of Fortitude. Appalled, Doolittle again argued to Ike that his big four-engine B-17s were unsuitable for close air support, but again he was overruled because Ike wanted the firepower.

★ ★ ★ ★

FIRST ARMY HAD BROKEN THROUGH the German lines by the second day of Cobra. Bradley told Patton to take over VIII Corps while waiting for the Third Army to become operational in four days. Patton immediately ordered two armored divisions through the break in the enemy lines and then, unable to stay away from a potential fight, went forward to see for himself.

On the outskirts of Coutances, Patton encountered General Robert W. Grow, commander of his Sixth Armored Division, sitting beside the road with several other officers, reading a map. The unit was being held up "by some German fire" at a small stream. Patton asked Grow if he had been down to look. The answer was negative. Patton replied that if Grow didn't "do something, he would be out of a job" and went himself to look at the stream, which was less than a foot deep. He saw no Germans. The Sixth Armored Division thus got itself moving toward Brittany, where it could fight in open territory.[2]

Patton was becoming frustrated by Omar Bradley's cautiousness. Bradley wanted the attack to be meticulous, steady, irresistible; Patton wanted speed and audacity. "I think we can clear the peninsula very fast," he told his diary. "The thing to do is to rush them off their feet before they get set."

By July 30, less than a week into Cobra, the town of Avranches, gateway to Brittany, was taken by Cobra forces. Patton ordered his VIII Corps to cross the Selune River and make for the Seine and Paris. The U.S. Fourth Armored Division captured a series of dams that it was feared the Germans might blow up and flood much of the countryside.

Patton continued his habit of writing poetry at night and penned this last of five stanzas of a piece called "Absolute War" that exuded his penchant for aggressiveness.

So let us do real fighting, boring in and gouging, biting.
Let's take a chance now that we have the ball.
Let's forget those fine firm bases in the dreary, shell raked spaces,
Let's shoot the works and win! Yes win it all!

Patton's army was now moving so quickly that it kept running off maps—so quickly that the Germans could not organize a counterattack. As usual Patton was at or near the front lines. "It always scares me and lures me like steeplechasing," he told Beatrice.

On August 6 Patton took time out to write a letter to a Mrs. T. Taylor of Pasadena accepting her request to become godfather to her son. "I am sure he could never find a more God-fearing, God-damning Godfather than myself," he wrote her.

Finally, in the early hours of August 7, the Germans launched their long-expected counterattack. Patton had gotten wind of it the day before through a secret source (probably ULTRA) and told his diary that he thought it was a German rumor to cover a withdrawal. To be on the safe side, however, he stopped two infantry divisions and one armored division "just in case something might happen."

The Germans attacked with three panzer divisions before Allied air attacks and a ferocious defensive effort by the 30th Infantry Division halted the enemy thrust, and Patton continued his end-run sweep around the German left flank. Eventually, by moving so swiftly, Patton's army wound up conducting a huge envelopment of not only the Germans' attacking force but most of the Germans in Normandy. This created what came to be called the Battle of the Falaise Pocket. Elements of ten enemy panzer divisions plus infantry and supporting troops—most of the German Army Group B, as many as 150,000 in all—were trapped in the pocket that was sealed by Patton, Bradley's First Army, and Montgomery's British and Canadian armies.

On August 16, 1944, the aforementioned Field Marshal Günther von Kluge declined, from his headquarters in the Falaise Pocket, to waste his command in yet another useless counterattack that Hitler had ordered. By late afternoon, von Kluge thought Hitler had come around to accepting his plea to withdraw the army, but Hitler instead changed his mind after it had occurred to him that von Kluge might instead surrender to the Allies. The next day, Hitler relieved von Kluge and ordered him to Berlin, whereupon von Kluge committed suicide by taking cyanide, fearful that the Gestapo had uncovered his involvement in the July plot against Hitler.*

The Führer then sent Field Marshal Walter Model to replace von Kluge, but his report to Berlin was immediate and dismal—withdraw or lose the army. Hitler agreed and the Germans began a long retreat.

As many as 100,000 Germans managed to escape the Falaise Pocket due to its not being quickly and completely sealed off by the Allies. Patton blamed Bradley for ordering him to abandon territory he held that was in the British sector and instead concentrate near Argentan, and of course he blamed Montgomery for complaining about it. Bradley, however, later wrote that he was worried about Patton overextending himself and becoming vulnerable to counterattack. "I preferred a strong

* Later an SS officer named Stroop, who claimed he was on von Kluge's trail regarding the bomb plot, asserted that he had shot and killed von Kluge after the field marshal refused to take the cyanide capsule he offered him.

shoulder at Argentan to the possibility of a broken neck at Falaise," was how he put it.[3]

When, on August 19, Bradley learned that Patton was pushing to the Seine he was "fit to be tied," according to Major Alexander Stiller, a member of Patton's staff. Stiller recorded a scene in which Bradley stormed into Patton's headquarters to announce it had been decided at an Allied joint conference that Patton should not go to the Seine, but instead leave an escape route for the Germans in the Falaise Pocket.

"General P told General B that since he was already to the Seine River, in fact had pissed in the river that morning, what would he want him to do—pull back?"

Bradley had information that the Germans in the Falaise Pocket were very strong and "didn't think General P would be able to contain them." He ordered Patton to leave the Germans an escape route in the east.

Patton then asked Bradley if he ever knew him to give up a piece of ground he had taken. Bradley said, "No—but this was different."

Patton responded that he "could and would hold it, if General B would agree."

After some more back and forth, Bradley finally relented and said that Patton could close the escape route if he would hold it.

More than 50,000 Germans were trapped in the pocket and eventually were either killed and wounded or captured along with an enormous amount of heavy equipment and weaponry. It is estimated that 10,000 to 15,000 Germans died. Eisenhower, walking over the battleground two days later, described it as "one of the greatest killing fields" of the war. "It was literally possible," Ike said, "to walk for hundreds of yards at a time, stepping on nothing but dead flesh."[4]

The Battle of the Falaise Pocket broke the back of German resistance in Normandy and opened the way for the liberation of Paris. Patton's lightning-like thrusts thrilled readers of U.S. newspapers and listeners of American news broadcasts; the *Washington Star* opined that his generalship in the campaign "vindicate[ed] a man who may be short on diplomacy but whose qualities as a fighting officer are beyond dispute."[5]

Of his part in the Falaise operation Patton told Beatrice, "I could have had it a week ago but modesty via destiny made me stop."

★ ★ ★ ★

Now the army was taking so much ground that Patton was forced to fly in an army Piper Cub to visit his foremost units. "I don't like it," he said. "I feel like a clay pigeon." On August 17 he took time to write to George Marshall in Washington, summarizing his exploits thus far as well as reassuring him that he had made no statements or newspaper interviews and would continue that policy in the future. He closed by thanking the chief of staff for his "many acts of forbearance."

On August 19, Patton spent the day with the French general Koechlin-Schwartz, an old friend from World War I days, who remarked on Patton's tactics of allowing his armored forces to roam around without infantry support. "Had I taught twenty-five years ago what you are doing," the Frenchman said, "I should have been put in a madhouse, but when I was told that an armored division was headed for Brest, I knew it was you."

The next day a regimental combat team of Patton's 79th Division crossed the Seine—the first crossing by an Allied force. The liberation of Paris had begun. Third Army had been operational in France for three weeks and had inflicted 108,000 casualties on the Germans—killed, wounded, and missing. They themselves suffered 15,029.

At every town and village they passed, Patton's army was cheered. The locals tossed flowers and apples and offered wine. "It will be pretty grim after the war," he wrote Beatrice, "driving one's self, and not being cheered. I am convinced that the best end for an officer is the last bullet of the war."

The next day he reported to his dairy, "We have, at this time, the greatest chance to win the war ever presented . . . if they will let me move on." Patton wanted to jump ahead with three armored divisions and six infantry divisions into eastern France before the Germans could reorganize themselves. He believed they could be in Germany in ten days.

With Paris saved, Patton continued to pressure Bradley for pushing quickly into Germany. But Montgomery was having difficulty overcoming stubborn German resistance to the north and kept complaining to Eisenhower that the British needed more time. Patton's Third Army was advancing so quickly it was running out of its supply line, which remained in large part back on the beaches of Normandy.

When he returned to his mobile headquarters the day after Paris fell, Patton informed his diary, "I found that a flock of Red Cross doughnut girls had descended on us." It was no ordinary flock, however, for among its number was none other than the beautiful and talented Jean Gordon, the niece Patton had had an affair with in Hawaii before the war. He had been alerted to her presence in France by a letter from Beatrice, which has not survived, so Mrs. Patton's express warning to her husband will never be known. However, Patton had replied, "The first I knew about Jean's being here was in your letter. We are in the middle of a battle," he added, "so I don't see people. So don't worry."[6]

By then, Patton's army was ranging all over central-western France, fighting battles and gobbling up terrain sometimes at seventy miles a day. They held a front of nearly three hundred miles, from Brest at the far tip of the Brittany peninsula to Verdun on the Meuse east of Paris—and all the old, bitter battlefields of World War I in between. As a measure of the hard combat encountered that week, the Third Army's total casualties since beginning operations in France rose to 24,860, including nearly 3,000 men killed, while inflicting approximately 152,000 German casualties during the same time period, including 19,000 killed.

A radio announcer in the United States gave this description of Patton: "A fiction writer couldn't create him. History itself hasn't matched him. He's colorful, fabulous. He's dynamite. On a battlefield, he's a warring, glaring comet."[7]

Patton continued to agitate for cracking Hitler's Siegfried Line (the German defensive position roughly along the Franco-German border) and pressing quickly into Germany. On August 30 Patton went to Eisenhower's headquarters to present his case. "I had to beg like a beggar," he complained, "for permission to keep on the line of the Meuse." But Ike turned down his request to push on out in front of the British and First Army. Patton told his diary that night that Eisenhower's staff was letting Montgomery "overpersuade" Ike, "a terrible mistake."

★ ★ ★ ★

DURING THIS PERIOD, the Third Army became notorious for "scrounging," or scavenging, particularly for gasoline, of which it was severely short. Officers and men of Patton's army were alleged to sew on the patches and other identifying insignia of other units in order to purloin caches of fuel from their dumps, or even hijack tanker trucks making deliveries. In one instance, according to Patton, "a colored truck company [stole] some for me by careful accident" and, fortuitously, his army captured more than a million gallons at a German fuel dump. "It is poor gas but runs a hot engine," he said, meaning that higher-octane American gas would have to be used to start the tank. "If they would give me enough gas," he continued, "I could go anywhere I want."

Patton's chief of staff wrote in his journal that the feeling around headquarters was that the lack of gasoline was a plot by Eisenhower and his staff to stop Patton's Third Army from continuing to advance. Worse, some thought that it was in order to placate the British, who wanted in on the glory but remained stuck against stiff German resistance in the Pas-de-Calais and Antwerp and were still trying to ferret out the launching sites for the V-1 and V-2 rockets that were terrorizing and destroying London.[8]

Still, the shortages prevailed, prompting Patton to tell Eisenhower that if he just had enough gas he could "rupture that goddamn Siegfried Line. I will stake my reputation on it." When Ike laughingly deprecated the value of Patton's reputation, Patton reminded him, "That reputation is pretty good now." Nevertheless, he got no gas and Eisenhower told him to go on the defensive at the Moselle until Montgomery and the British could catch up.

A furious Patton did as ordered, but soon he picked a fight with the Germans in the fortified city of Metz on the Moselle, which had been such a disagreeable bone in the Allies' throat during World War I and, according to Patton, had last fallen to an outside power when Attila the Hun sacked it in A.D. 451.* As Patton's army approached Metz it was nearly undefended, but with the capture of Nancy the Germans decided to make a stand. Metz was a tough nut to crack, ringed by no fewer than thirty-three separate forts and protected by moats, stone walls, and difficult terrain features.

Patton was first told that Metz could be taken by a battalion, but that proved to be an error. A second battalion was thrown in, then a third, and so forth until elements of an entire corps were engaged at a steep price. Third Army's casualty report for the ten days since it had advanced from the Meuse to the Moselle rose to 26,402. German casualties increased to 186,000, including 26,000 dead and 850 tanks destroyed or captured.

During that time, Patton visited the grisly boneyard of Verdun, where the remains of more than 100,000 unknown soldiers are interred, and adjacent Fort Douaumont, which he pointed out "epitomizes the folly of defensive warfare."

Meanwhile, Patton held a press conference for Third Army war correspondents in which he deliberately blued the air with profanity hoping to make himself "unquotable." Referring to the town of Pannes, which he had recently visited, he remarked that it was where he was shot during the Meuse-Argonne campaign of 1918. "I ought to remember it," he said. "I was shot in the ass there." Asked to what he attributed his successful advances Patton responded that his army always arrived at the enemy's defensive line "three days before the Germans thought we would."

Answering a question about the lack of gasoline, Patton told the reporters he could have crossed the Moselle River four days earlier before the Germans got their defenses organized, but added that it didn't make much difference. "I never cared where I killed the bastards," he said.

As to future operations, he told the startled newsmen that he intended to go through the Siegfried Line "like shit through a goose."⁹

* Actually the French took it from the Germans in 1552, but the Germans took it back in 1870.

He continued to put himself in danger with constant visits to the front and he ordered every section of his staff to send someone there each week in order to avoid the scorn of troops who perceived so-called château generals—an allusion to the British high command of World War I who rarely, if ever, visited the front lines and knew little about what their men were going through.

★ ★ ★ ★

ON SEPTEMBER 20, Patton decided to give up capturing Metz, acknowledging it wasn't worth the price in dead and wounded. Then, three days later, he got one of the harshest shocks of his career—Eisenhower was going to take away Patton's XV Corps and one of his armored divisions as well and order him back on defense along the Moselle. Patton was nearly apoplectic but gritted his teeth. After consulting with his remaining corps commanders, he came up with his "rock soup" plan. This involved setting up a defensive front as well as a series of points along the front where he would attack in hopes of breaking through.

The rock soup plan was a Patton invention based on a Depression-era scam that worked roughly as follows. A hobo with a tin can containing several polished stones goes to the back door of a residence and asks the lady of the house if she will give him some water so he can make "rock soup." She complies, but inquires as to the recipe for rock soup. The hobo then asks if she might give him a carrot or two and a potato, then proceeds to light a fire and boil the soup, which he describes as delicious. When she comes back out to see about the soup, the hobo tells her all that is needed is a piece of meat to put in the soup, and so on, until the hobo has acquired from her all the ingredients he needs for a proper soup.

Patton's version of the rock soup plan was to start a battle, and then tell headquarters it looked like a big breakthrough if only he could have reinforcements and supplies. He did just that, and as the battle expanded Patton continued to go back to headquarters with tempting promises and lengthy lists of requests—air strikes, gasoline, ammunition, more men, more guns, and so on. Patton's idea was based in the knowledge that superior officers are naturally reluctant to deny an engaged commander the resources he needs to win a battle.

The Third Army casualty report for the week of September 24 listed 45,130 U.S. troops killed, wounded, or missing, with 4,541 of these dead. German casualties rose to 216,100, with 30,900 killed and 1,200 tanks captured or destroyed. An important difference was that Third Army received 43,566 replacements that week and the German army received none for it was fighting for its life in the east against the Soviets.

Patton interpreted the order to go on the defensive as enabling him to attack across the Moselle and establish secure "defensive" bridgeheads on the other side. These were costly operations that spent lives, but Patton was determined that when the defensive directive was rescinded he would be able to cross the river quickly and in force to get at the enemy at the Siegfried Line.

In the meantime, Patton visited some more of his old haunts from the First World War. He went to Gondrecourt on a mission to find General Marshall's housekeeper but was told the family had moved out of the battle area. He went to Chaumont, which had been AEF headquarters in 1918 when he was running the staff for General Pershing. From there, Patton's party went to Bourg, where his tank brigade headquarters was located.

Patton's opinion of Lorraine, the province where they fought then, as now, was highly disrespectful. It and its neighboring province Alsace had been seized and taken by the Germans in the Franco-Prussian War that ended in 1871. The French had since conducted an almost sacred crusade to have the provinces returned to France.

Now that such a prospect was at hand, however, Patton wrote facetiously to George Marshall in Washington that he hoped, at the conclusion of the war, Alsace-Lorraine would be deeded permanently to the Germans, as all it did there was rain, fog, flood, and freeze, and the most valuable thing any of it citizens owned was the manure piles they kept outside their front doors.

Moving on, Patton was inspecting frontline troops on September 28 when to avoid going over a high mountain in mud on foot he chose to drive down a road that was under direct enemy observation. "They must have practiced on the road," Patton said, because no sooner had they turned down it than the Germans opened up with a salvo of four 150mm shells from their heavy artillery. The first salvo missed widely, the second was "near enough to be uncomfortable," the third threw rocks and mud all over them, and in the fourth a 150mm shell landed two feet from the left running board. Luckily it was a dud, or General Patton's story would have ended there.

Unfazed, Patton decided that during the first week in October he would attack Fort Driant, an early twentieth-century French fortification that was part of the Metz defenses five miles south of the city. He had abandoned one attempt at Metz, but now it became a necessity. Fort Driant was heavily fortified by the Germans and commanded the valley of the Moselle, through which the Third Army would have to pass when the "defensive" order was rescinded. Army Air Force Thunderbolts and other fighter-bombers made the initial attack, but as most of the fort was underground little damage was done. An infantry assault that followed was withdrawn after heavy casualties in hand-to-hand fighting.

In the week to come, several more assaults were made; each was repulsed with many Americans killed or wounded. Disgusted, Patton decided to abandon the attack on Fort Driant since the ammunition supply had also become nearly exhausted and the casualties too high. Instead he would leave a force to contain the fort and bypass it. American casualties for the week rose to 52,698, with 5,131 of these killed.

Patton was appalled that they were now in a vicious war of attrition. He blamed Supreme Headquarters for not supplying his army so that it could go on a mobile offensive, which he insisted would produce far fewer casualties than the present static condition of the battle. Instead, Ike invited Patton to his headquarters in Liège, Belgium, to have lunch with King George VI of England.

When he returned to his headquarters at Nancy, Patton was nearly killed by a huge German railroad gun that emerged from a tunnel and began lobbing 11-inch shells that blew out all the windows in his residence and demolished the house across the street. When Patton heard someone "hollering in French," he dressed and went out to help rescue a husband and wife trapped in debris.

★ ★ ★ ★

On November 2 there was good news. Bradley told Patton that the British and the First Army would be ready for the next attack November 10—which was to take the Siegfried Line some sixty miles to the east. He asked when Patton could go and was told, "Twenty-four hours from when you say go." Afterward he told his diary, "I feel 10 years younger."

The next day, he hosted Marlene Dietrich and her acting troupe for lunch, followed by a show of "Very low comedy, almost an insult to human intelligence."[10]

On November 7, Patton wrote Beatrice, "We jump off in the morning with ten divisions. The weather is so vile we will get no air support." (He'd been promised three hundred bombers to destroy the forts at Metz.) "I know the Lord will help us again," he told his diary. "Either He will give us good weather or the bad weather will hurt the Germans more than it does us." When the artillery barrage opened at 5:15 next morning, Patton described the sensation as "like the slamming of doors in an empty house—very many doors all slamming at once. All the eastern sky glowed and trembled with the flashes of the guns."[11]

At dawn, the skies began to clear and fighter-bombers arrived to take out enemy command posts. The attack rolled forward across the Moselle, which residents told Patton was swollen higher from the rain than at any time in its history (records show it had last been that high in 1919).

Nearly all the first day's objectives were taken, but the flooded countryside made for difficult going; all but one of the bridges they had built over the Moselle and Seille rivers had been either swept away by rushing water or blown up by the Germans. Roads were a sea of stranded trucks tanks, jeeps, ambulances, and other equipment.

After writing Beatrice, "The Lord came across again," Patton celebrated his fifty-ninth birthday, November 11, by going to the forward area "where the dead were still warm." Along one of the roads he went down, the bodies of nearly a thousand Germans, "all neatly piled like cordwood," were waiting to be buried by U.S. Graves Registration Service teams. It being a Sunday, he then went to church "where I heard the worst service yet." Patton sent for the army's chief of chaplains, who had the offender relieved and a new chaplain installed.

Patton's two armored divisions remained stalled in the horrible weather and trench foot among the men was causing more casualties than German fire.* The new attack on Metz also held up the advance and tempers rose among the various corps and division commanders. When asked to surrender, a German general at Metz declared he would fight to the death. "We are trying to satisfy him," Patton remarked.

Third Army battle casualties as of November 15 had risen to 49,606 and nonbattle casualties were 29,857—of which up to a half were the results of trench foot. The Germans had suffered some 290,000 casualties at the hands of Third Army.

Patton then had another go at Metz, and this time he was successful. When it was finally cleared of Germans on November 22 Patton, visiting a hospital, asked a wounded soldier if he knew Metz had been captured. When the soldier nodded yes, Patton took him by the hand, smiled, and said, "Tomorrow, son, the headlines will read 'Patton Took Metz,' which you know is a Goddamn lie. You and your buddies are the ones who actually took Metz."

Patton had the greatest respect for many officers of the German army, whom he saw for the most part as "gallant," but he had little use for members of the SS, Gestapo, or other Nazis. When an SS general was captured following the Battle of Metz, Patton had him brought to his headquarters where he made him stand while berating him at length, accusing him of being a liar, a coward, and "a viper." When the Nazi

---

* Also known as "immersion foot," trench foot, a World War I term, has been a bane of armies since the time of Napoleon. It describes a painful debilitation of the feet caused by water seeping through boot leather. Prolonged exposure causes the feet to swell and begin to decay.

begged to be turned over to the Americans, Patton threatened to throw him to the Free French, which in all likelihood would have been the end of him. Patton later referred to this general as "the most vicious-looking person I've ever seen," adding, "He is the first man I have ever browbeaten, and I must admit I took real pleasure doing it."

Patton next interrogated a German regular army colonel, trying to discern why the German army continued to fight and die when it appeared there was no way it could stand up to the American army. This officer was offered a chair and Patton was extremely solicitous toward him. The officer replied that there were three reasons why the Germans continued. First, there was hope in Hitler's promise of "miracle weapons," such as the V-2 rocket; second was the awful prospect of the Russians, who it was believed would absorb the prostrated country, rape and enslave all the women, and kill all the men; third, Germans are accustomed to following orders and "would not quit until such orders were given." It was a fatal flaw in the Germanic character in more ways than one.

By December 8 the Third Army had driven to the river Saar and the infamous Siegfried Line, or West Wall, guarded by a string of concrete pillboxes and dragon's teeth,* and were poised to break through to the Rhine and the heart of Germany. But in mid-December, because of horrid weather, the advance again bogged down around the city of Saarlautern, where a German counterattack was threatening the timetable. Patton wrote Beatrice that he had never seen such a "hell hole" of a country. "There is about four inches of liquid mud over everything and it rains all the time." He concluded that only divine intervention would break the stalemate and called in the Third Army chaplain for a conversation about composing a prayer, during which the following colloquy took place.

"Chaplain, I'm tired of these soldiers having to fight mud and floods as well as Germans," Patton said. "I want you to publish a prayer for good weather."

---

* Pyramids of reinforced concrete to arrest the advance of enemy tanks and mechanized infantry units.

"Sir, it's going to take a pretty thick rug for that kind of praying," the chaplain responded.

"I don't care if it takes a flying carpet. I want the praying done," Patton told the startled clergyman.

"Yes, sir," said the chaplain, adding as clarification, "May I say, General, that it usually isn't customary among men of my profession to pray for clear weather to kill our fellow men."

"Chaplain," Patton frowned, "are you trying to teach me theology or are you the chaplain of the Third Army? I want a prayer."

"Yes, sir," the chaplain replied, and the next day an entreaty was produced and circulated among Third Army personnel.

> *Almighty and most merciful Father, we humbly beseech Thee, of Thy Great goodness, to restrain these immoderate rains with which we have had to contend. Grant us fair weather for Battle. Graciously harken to us as soldiers who call upon Thee that, armed with Thy power, we may advance from victory to victory, and crush the opposition and wickedness of our enemies, and establish Thy justice among men and nations. Amen.*

The day after the prayer was issued the weather turned crystal clear and remained that way for a week. Patton was exuberant and called in one of his aides. "God Damn! Look at that weather! That was some potent praying. Get that chaplain up here. I want to pin a medal on him."

Patton's headquarters at that point was in the process of moving, but the chaplain was duly produced and Patton awarded him the Bronze Star. "You're the most popular man in this headquarters," Patton told him, shaking his hand. "You sure stand in good with the Lord."[12]

★ ★ ★ ★

LATE IN THE NIGHT OF DECEMBER 16, Bradley's chief of staff phoned Patton that trouble was in the air. The Germans were attacking First Army in great force through the Ardennes Forest, a hundred miles north of

Third Army. This was the great German counteroffensive they had feared. It would become known as the Battle of the Bulge—for the Americans, the deadliest battle of the war and Patton's finest hour.

Patton had suspected something like this was in the making; recent ULTRA intercepts had told Third Army's intelligence that the Germans were amassing men, tanks, and guns from the Eastern Front, but there was no indication of a time or place for an attack. At any rate, having to wheel the Third Army in a different direction to help repel a large enemy counteroffensive had been in the back of Patton's mind. He reacted to Bradley's news by immediately alerting his staff that they might have to head north and that planning should be made along those lines.

Patton groused to his diary next morning that the reason the Germans could have prepared such a large offensive was lack of aggressiveness on the part of Ike, Bradley, and the First Army. "One must never sit still," he wrote. From what he could tell of the German attack, it reminded him of General Ludendorff's last-ditch offensive in 1918, "and I think will have the same results."

Patton ordered his 80th Infantry and Fourth Armored Divisions to prepare immediately for the move north. That night Bradley phoned him saying, "the situation up there is much worse," and that an 11 a.m. conference with General Eisenhower was scheduled at Verdun. The Germans had struck First Army's VIII Corps in the heavily forested and lightly defended area of the Ardennes with 250,000 men and numerous panzer divisions. Most of the American units in that area consisted either of green troops who were still being trained or of outfits that had been in heavy combat and then sent there for rest and recuperation. An embarrassingly large number of U.S. soldiers fell prisoner to the Germans.

At the Verdun conference, Eisenhower told Patton to proceed to Luxembourg, take charge of the luckless VIII Corps and other units that were being gathered, and lead the battle against the German incursion. It was Hitler's intention to thrust through the Allied line for Antwerp, which had fallen to Montgomery in November and was now the Allies' most important shipping port and distribution center for equipment, fuel, and supplies. Its loss would be a tremendous blow and would also split the American and British armies.

Eisenhower told Patton that he wanted him to assemble six divisions to strike at the Germans as soon as possible. "When can you attack?" Ike asked on December 17.

"On December 22, with three divisions," Patton replied calmly, noting that his response "created quite a commotion—some people seemed surprised, others pleased." As Patton's biographer Martin Blumenson notes, "This was the sublime moment of his career."

The reason Patton said he would attack with three instead of six divisions was that the other three "existed only on paper . . . [they] had been virtually wiped out by the Germans." When Eisenhower expressed concern that Patton's force might not be strong enough, Patton argued he'd rather gain the element of surprise by attacking immediately rather than wait to assemble additional divisions.

It was the most daring and audacious operation in Patton's long career. It reflected his supreme confidence in himself and his twin mottos: *De l'audace, encore de l'audace, toujours de l'audace!*, an axiom attributed to the French revolutionary Georges Danton, and "Take not the counsel of your fears," an expression said to have originated with Stonewall Jackson.

It was a vast and complicated undertaking: withdrawing from the fighting front an army of a quarter million men locked in combat with the enemy, wheeling it 90 degrees, and then transporting it with all its accoutrements over icy roads in subfreezing weather more than a hundred miles north to fight a battle against an attacking force. As Blumenson observes, "It was an operation that only a master could think of executing."[13]

As they were leaving, Ike—who had been promoted to four stars right before the Kasserine Pass fiasco and had recently received his fifth star—remarked to Patton, "Every time I get a new star I get attacked." Patton responded, "Yes, and every time you get attacked, I pull you out!"

By that point in the war, Allied airpower had nearly knocked the Luftwaffe out of the fight, but Hitler had evened the odds by making sure the German offensive would begin at a time of bad weather so the Allied planes would also be grounded. As it was, the attack coincided with a time of snow, sleet, and fog that was forecast to outlast the week. Not only had the Germans attacked in force, they had assembled a large unit of English-speaking German soldiers who, dressed as Americans, were creating havoc behind American lines—turning signposts, giving false information, sabotaging, and spreading confusion. To counter this tactic, U.S. MPs installed extraordinary identification measures, including passwords and countersigns that only Americans should know. (General Bradley himself was momentarily caught up in this dragnet when an MP insisted that Chicago—not Springfield, which Bradley had correctly answered—was the capital of Illinois.)

On December 21, the eve of his big counterattack in a snowstorm, Patton wrote Beatrice, "Though this is the shortest day of the year, to me it seems interminable . . . Destiny sent for me in a hurry when things got tight. Perhaps God saved me for this effort." He dismissed the German attack to her this way: "Remember how a tarpon makes one big flop just before he dies? We should get well into the guts of the enemy."

Before daybreak and in the middle of a giant snowstorm, Patton's three-division army hit the German flank along a twenty-mile front and drove it in seven miles. The flashes of 1,296 heavy guns lit the sky with a fiery glow even through the snowstorm. Patton took time to write in his diary, "The men are in good spirits and full of confidence. The situation at Bastogne is grave but not desperate." He was referring to the Germans having surrounded and trapped the 101st Airborne Division in Bastogne, where the Americans were putting up a heroic defense. (When the German general sent a surrender demand under a flag of truce, the 101st's commanding officer Brigadier General Anthony McAuliffe famously replied, "Nuts.")

As the American attack began slowly crowding the Germans out of the salient, or bulge, that they had created in the Allied lines, Patton became a kind of one-man force majeure; he was everywhere—observing, suggesting, urging, cajoling, praising, and pinning on medals. When he passed through part of his 90th Infantry Division moving up to the battle through a raft of ambulances bringing back the bloody wounded, the riflemen—who had been riding all day in open trucks in minus-six-degree weather—stood up and cheered when they identified him by the hood of his jeep famously adorned with the big three stars of a lieutenant general.

On December 25 Patton told his diary, "A clear cold Christmas, lovely weather for killing Germans, which seems a bit queer, seeing Whose birthday it is." But Montgomery, he said, had told Bradley that the army was too weak to attack and should fall back to the Saar-Vosges line or even the Moselle River, a notion that Patton found "disgusting."[14]

The day after Christmas, Patton's Fourth Armored Division broke through and liberated Bastogne, creating a narrow, five-hundred-yard-wide corridor through the German defenses. The Germans counter-attacked, but the corridor remained open. Four days later Patton drove through it in a jeep ("passing quite close to the Germans. Luckily they were not firing") into Bastogne where he decorated General ("Nuts") McAuliffe with the Distinguished Service Cross, the nation's second-highest honor.

The Germans launched continual counterattacks against Bastogne, but all were repulsed with heavy losses. Patton told Beatrice December 29, "This is my biggest battle. I have 16 divisions, but four have strings tied to them"—meaning they were not entirely his.

Asked at a press conference how important the Battle of Bastogne was, Patton compared it to Gettysburg in the Civil War and told the reporters, "I don't care where he fights, we can lick the Germans any place . . . We'll find him and kick his teeth in." Privately, however, he told his diary, "We can still lose this war. The Germans are colder and hungrier than we are but they fight better . . . They are vicious fighters."

On New Year's Day, 1945, Patton issued a general order to the men of his Third Army, congratulating them on their continuing victories and thanking them for his receiving the second oak leaf cluster to his Distinguished Service Medal, "not for what I have done, but for what you have achieved . . . Brave rifles, veterans, you have been baptized in fire and blood and have come out steel."[15]

At about this same time, Luxembourg City was suddenly bombarded "with a peculiar weapon." At first they thought it was rockets, then a long-distance shell, but presently the weapon was captured and it turned out to be a kind of high-pressure pump *(Hochdruckpumpe)* with a two-hundred-plus-foot tube that flung an explosive projectile with fins some thirty-five miles. The thing was wildly inaccurate but one of the explosions killed the captain commanding Patton's Headquarters Company, Third Army, as he stepped from his hotel in the city.

Advanced weapons or not, by the eleventh of January it became clear to Patton that the Germans were withdrawing and he hoped to catch the bulk of them as they tried to cross the Saar. However, the German method of withdrawal was a constant series of deadly counterattacks in which the losses on both sides were horrific. This tactic foreshadowed Hitler's scorched-earth policy in the final days of the war, in which he directed every German to fight to the last man, right before he killed his wife and himself.

For Patton's part, he crowed to anyone who would listen about the stellar role of the Third Army in the fight, and then ordered more attacks—constant attacks because, he said, "If we don't attack first the Germans will." But there was another, selfish reason—if that is the word—that Patton continued to roam for action. Ike's headquarters was forever taking divisions away from him to fight elsewhere and replacing them with green troops. Patton figured out that they wouldn't pull a division away from him if it were locked in combat.

He was incessantly at the front then, morbidly fascinated at times by the grisly sights he encountered on the battlefield. He wrote of a dead German machine gunner instantly frozen at his position of feeding ammunition into the weapon. On another occasion he investigated numerous black objects sticking out of the snow only to find they were the booted toes of dead men. And in his book *War As I Knew It,* he described the phenomenon "resulting from the quick-freezing of men killed in battle—they turn the color of pale claret—a nasty sight."[16]

Third Army's combined casualties for the week ending January 29, which coincided with the end of the Battle of the Bulge, had risen to 99,942, with 14,870 of these killed in action. Nonbattle casualties had risen to 73,011, mostly from frostbite and trench foot. A thousand U.S. tanks had been destroyed or captured. The Germans, as usual, suffered far greater losses, with battle casualties to date tallying 528,500, nearly a hundred thousand of them killed, and material losses of about two thousand tanks and twenty-five hundred pieces of artillery.

Patton wrote this glorifying monograph in his autobiography: "During this operation Third Army moved farther and faster and engaged more divisions in less time than any other army in the history of the

United States—possibly in the history of the world. The results attained were made possible only by the superlative quality of American officers, American men, and American equipment. No country can stand against such an army."[17]

★ ★ ★ ★

THE NEXT STAGE OF THE PROCESS was piercing Hitler's Siegfried Line, or West Wall. But to confirm Patton's "worst fears," higher headquarters (Ike) again began trying to pull divisions away from the First and Third Armies and give them either to the Sixth Army Group, operating south of Patton, or to the Ninth Army, which was under Field Marshal Montgomery in the north. In Patton's view it was "a patent attempt to prevent an attack by the First and Third Armies to give Monty and the British the leading role."

In any event, the normally even-tempered and subservient Bradley blew his stack to Eisenhower's operations chief, telling him, "I want you to understand that the reputation and good will of the American soldiers, the American Army, and its commanders are at stake. If you feel that way about it, then as far as I'm concerned you can take any god-damned division, and/or corps in the 12th Army Group, do with them as you see fit, and those that you leave back will sit on our asses till hell freezes." He concluded by telling the staff officer, "I trust you do not think I am angry, but I want to impress upon you that I am goddamn well incensed."[18]

Patton and other senior officers of the First and Third Armies had been having lunch in Bradley's mess when the call came, so they got an earful of Bradley on the phone. When he was finished, practically every officer in the room stood up and applauded. "We were all very pleased with Bradley's attitude," Patton said, "and we told him so."

The next day, Patton was informed he would lose his 95th Division and as many as six artillery battalions to Ninth Army. He was infuriated, of course, but Bradley had told him the orders came not from Ike but from the Combined Joint Chiefs of Staff headed by

TOP: *George Marshall (left) talks with British prime minister Winston Churchill in 1942.*
BOTTOM: *Marshall (right) discusses strategy with chief of the Allied forces Dwight Eisenhower during the North African campaign in 1943.*

TOP: *George Marshall (left) receives the Distinguished Service Medal from President Truman in 1945.*
BOTTOM: *Marshall as U.S. secretary of state urges Congress to approve his European recovery program—known as the Marshall Plan.*

TOP: *Major General George Patton commands the U.S. First Armored Corps, wearing his "war face," in 1942.*
BOTTOM: *General Patton, wearing his trademark ivory-handled pistols, watches a desert armored attack in Tunisia, North Africa, in 1943.*

TOP: *Patton delivers one of his famous profanity-laced motivational speeches to U.S. troops in Sicily in 1943.*
BOTTOM: *Generals Omar Bradley, Patton, and Eisenhower examine Nazi looted art and other treasures uncovered by Patton's Third Army in Merkers, Germany, in 1945.*

Generals Bradley, Eisenhower, and Patton (left to right) survey damage in Bastogne, Belgium, in 1945.

TOP: *General Douglas MacArthur (left) and his controversial chief of staff Richard K. Sutherland in U.S. underground headquarters on Corregidor Island, Philippines, in 1942*
BOTTOM: *MacArthur (left) at war conference, Pearl Harbor, in 1944 with President Franklin Roosevelt, Admiral Chester Nimitz, and Admiral William Leahy*

MacArthur (center) and staff wade ashore on Leyte, Philippines, 1944, fulfilling his promise: "I shall return."

Japanese general Yoshijiro Umezu signs the surrender documents aboard the USS Missouri in September 1945 while General MacArthur looks on.

MacArthur aboard his command vessel during the U.S. landings at Inchon, Korea, 1950

George Marshall. Orders were for the First and Third Armies to go on the defensive; the main effort to get to the Rhine and the heart of Germany would be made by the British. Patton thought that was foolish. "In my opinion, every division should be attacking," he told his diary. "If such an attack were made, the Germans do not have the resources to stop it."

To cheer himself up Patton went to Spa in Belgium and ordered two expensive shotguns, one for himself and one for his brother-in-law Frederick Ayer. On the way, he passed the wrecked town of Houffalize, which was, in his words, "completely removed." He had seen such destruction in the First World War but not yet in this one, and it inspired him to compose a bit of rhymed doggerel.

> *Oh little town of Houffalize*
> *How still we see thee lie*
> *Above thy steep and battered streets*
> *The aeroplanes sail by.*
> *Yet in the dark streets shineth*
> *Not any Goddamn light*
> *The hopes and fears of all thy years*
> *Were blown to hell last night.*

Incensed, as Bradley had been when the supreme commander began taking away units, Patton decided to attack first and ask questions later. As far as Bradley was concerned, "I shall not tell him," Patton decided. The first attack had been planned as a corps show, but then it expanded in Patton's fertile mind, "like Minerva," and soon developed into what became known as the Palatinate Campaign. He wrote to Freddy Ayer: "I am taking one of the longest chances of my chancy career; in fact, almost disobeying orders in order to attack."

Unfortunately, by February 11 a warm spell had begun thawing the mountains of snow and ice, which "almost obliterated" the roads that were, according to Patton, "literally disintegrating" with the mix of thaw and the tremendous traffic of a mechanized army. By February 13, however, elements of the Third Army had forced their way across the Sauer River, which marked the Siegfried Line, and into Germany. Patton could not wait. He crossed the river, riding in his jeep along its bank, which was studded with hundreds of enemy pillboxes and miles of German barbed wire. "The men were quite surprised to see me," he told his diary, "and the chance of getting hit was small and worth the risk due to the effect it had on the troops."

Because of the weather, the attack had stalled temporarily, and Patton decided to visit Paris, where he ensconced himself in the palatial King George V hotel and visited SHAEF—the Supreme Headquarters Allied Expeditionary Force—at the magnificent palace of Versailles.

Eisenhower was away but his chief of staff Bedell ("Beetle") Smith told Patton that the "high strategy" was to have him resume the attack, and he asked him how many additional divisions he would require. Nearly dumbstruck, Patton responded he would need five divisions and was utterly dumbfounded when Smith said, "I think you should have twelve." For someone who had, in the past, nearly always written insulting things about Smith, Patton now entered into his diary, "I have never known how great he really is."

The two had a roaring time in Gay Paree; Smith took Patton hunting on an elegant preserve once belonging to the king of France where the Third Army commander shot three ducks, a pheasant, and three hares. That night they attended the Folies Bergère, which was "perfectly naked," said Patton, "so much so that no one is interested." They sat in a stylish box and drank champagne, and the manager said for Patton to always make the Folies "his home" when he visited Paris "to rest."

"I can think of no place less conducive to rest," he confided to his diary.

★ ★ ★ ★

WHAT THE RIGHT HAND GIVETH, however, SHAEF would soon seek to take away in the form of what Patton derided as SHAEF's "new toy"—a strategic reserve. Organized in case the Germans tried another Battle of the Bulge–type operation, this was to be made of divisions from all the armies, which were to be pulled out of combat and sent back to rest areas where they could be called upon should trouble break out. Patton's view remained that all the divisions of all the armies should be attacking all at once, so his reaction to the SHAEF directive was predictable. "I wonder if ever before in the history of war a winning general had to plead to keep on winning."

The strategy at this stage was to simply push eastward, shoving the Germans back on themselves, conquering territory, and shutting down the German war manufacturing industry. It seemed clear the enemy did not intend to surrender, which would certainly have been the sensible thing. Instead, he hung on, taking horrendous losses, hoping for a miracle.

The Palatinate in southwest Germany is a region of vineyards and nut groves interspersed with forests and low mountains considered (wrongly, as it turned out) unnavigable for armor. It is bounded by the Rhine River, and Patton's 250,000-man killing machine rumbled across it in nine days, chewing up Germans at an unprecedented rate, crossing the Rhine (which Patton spit in on the way over), gobbling up ancient cities such as Coblenz, Heidelberg, Mainz, and Worms, destroying in the process two German armies and taking 60,000 enemy prisoners.

The Palatinate Campaign was regarded by many, including the Germans, according to Patton's historian and deputy chief of staff Paul Harkins, to be "one of the greatest campaigns of the entire war."[19]

Patton published a congratulatory order filled with phrases such as "The world rings with your praises . . . You have wrested 6484 square miles of territory from the enemy . . . The highest honor I have ever attained is that of having my name coupled with yours in these great events . . . your assault crossing over the Rhine assures you of even greater glory to come . . . This great campaign was only made possible by your disciplined valor, unswerving devotion to duty, etc., etc."[20]

Marshall telegraphed Eisenhower: PLEASE PASS ON MY PERSONAL AND ENTHUSIASTIC CONGRATULATIONS TO PATTON. Eisenhower sent along the telegram in a message satchel, appending it in longhand: "Dear George: To this I add that I continue to have reason to cheer that you came with me to this war. Ike."

★ ★ ★ ★

BY MARCH 26 THIRD ARMY was fairly flying through Germany and had taken Frankfurt. The day before, Patton had ordered one of his corps commanders to send an expedition to the town of Hammelburg to liberate nearly a thousand American officers who had fallen prisoner to the Germans, including Patton's son-in-law Colonel John Waters, who had been captured in Tunisia two years earlier. Patton wrote Beatrice: "Last night I sent an armored column to a place 40 miles east of Frankfurt where John and some 900 prisoners are said to be. I have been nervous as a cat all day because everyone but me thought it was too great a risk. I hope it works."[21]

For five days, there was no word of the relief column, then on March 30 German radio announced that the several hundred American troops going to Hammelburg had been "captured or destroyed." Patton was dismayed. There had been much discussion of the size of the rescue task force. A combat command–size unit, about four thousand men with tanks and heavy weapons, was a potent force that only a large-scale enemy opposition could overcome. That was what Patton had in mind for the operation but Bradley, he told Beatrice, had "talked him out of it." In the end it was agreed to send an armored task force of only two tank companies, which might get in and out fast. Soon, however, remnants of the column returned through the American lines and told what happened.

After bulling its way past several small German units and destroying considerable German matériel, the task force reached the prison camp, where the German commandant decided to surrender. He sent out a delegation consisting of a German captain carrying a white flag and three American officers carrying an American flag—Colonel Waters among them.

As they cleared the gate, however, a German guard suddenly and inexplicably lifted his rifle and shot Waters in the leg, the bullet traveling up to his spine. The two American officers rushed him to the camp hospital, which was run by a Serbian doctor. The relief force then piled as many prisoners as they could on their vehicles and headed back toward Third Army lines.

Unfortunately a German assault gun battalion was also in the area, and this powerful force ambushed the relief column, knocking out the commander's tank and halting its progress. The Americans fought doggedly until they were surrounded and their ammunition and gasoline ran out. Then they lit fire to their vehicles and took to the woods and fields.

One week later, a strong American force recaptured the prison camp and Waters was among the prisoners, recovering from his wound. He was brought back to the Third Army hospital where it was determined that Waters would have to be operated on, and Patton visited him when possible.

There were complaints, however, that Patton had risked and lost an army task force in personal pursuit of rescuing his own son-in-law. Inevitably this grumbling reached the newspapers and another Patton "incident" was created. Patton maintained that he was never sure Waters was in the camp in the first place and that the expedition to rescue the prisoners was part of a "diversion" to mislead the Germans about the direction the army would take next. Eisenhower explained it to Marshall as a "wild goose chase" of Patton's that he hoped would not be inflated by the press. "Patton is a problem child," Ike said, "but he is a great fighting leader in pursuit and exploitation."[22]

Third Army kept grinding across the face of Germany at a terrific pace, but then Eisenhower slowed them down. The reason stated was that Ike wanted all his armies (there were five of them) to proceed across Germany roughly parallel to one another. Patton considered Montgomery to be at the bottom of the new instructions, because he was perpetually falling behind. Patton wrote Beatrice: "We [Third Army] never meet any opposition because the bigger and better Germans fight Monty—he says so. Also, he advertises so much they know where he is coming. I fool them."

"I could join the Russians in a week if they'd let me," he said. "Damn equality."

Patton and several of the other army generals around this time appealed to the visiting Assistant Secretary of War John J. McCloy about the "wanton and unnecessary bombing of German civilian cities." By this point in the war, the Allied strategic bombing campaign was fully fledged. Across Germany, old and historic Teutonic architecture was being blown to rocks and dust by flights of more than a thousand heavy bombers a day. Patton told McCloy, who was also a friend, "We all feel that indiscriminate bombing has no military value and is cruel and wasteful," and recommended the air force concentrate on purely military targets, particularly "on oil."*, 23

On April 7, one of Patton's corps commanders called to say his men had captured the German gold reserve in the city of Merkers. They blew the steel vault door and found in addition to billions in paper marks 4,500 gold bricks weighing 37 pounds apiece and worth approximately $57 million.† On April 12 Patton, accompanied by Bradley and Eisenhower, entered the elevator to an enormous salt mine in Merkers and descended a half mile to the great chamber below, which was heaped with goods looted by the Germans from Jews and other Europeans whose countries they had overrun.

There were, as Patton described it, "suitcases filled with jewelry, silver and gold, watches, utensils, vases, gold-filled teeth, false teeth, etc., in no way labeled, simply valuable metal obtained by bandit methods." Eisenhower joked that he was unable to find a box of diamonds, but they did uncover art treasures, which Patton uncharitably described as

----

* The argument over the strategic bombing campaign in Germany continues to this day. At the time there were those in both the RAF and the U.S. Army Air Forces who argued that the Germans could be bombed into surrender. When it appeared they could not, it was then argued to bomb them into oblivion, which they very nearly did but still the Germans kept on fighting and at last had to be put down by field armies on the ground.

† About $1.23 billion in today's money.

being "worth, in my opinion, about $2.50 and of the type usually seen in bars in America."[24]

★ ★ ★ ★

Rumors of so-called slave labor camps were rife in all the Allied armies but it wasn't until after they visited the mine that they encountered what Patton described as "one of the most appalling sights I have ever seen."

Near the town of Ohrdorf the Germans had constructed one of many "concentration camps" in which the Nazis confined "undesirables"—political enemies, Gypsies, homosexuals, and, principally, Jews. A man wearing the garb of an inmate escorted the Allied generals through the camp. He took them to a gallows where men were hanged for attempting to escape. This was no ordinary gallows but one made to kill in the most painful manner. The drop board was about two feet from the ground and the noose was made not of rope but of piano wire. It was designed so that the toes of the man to be executed would just touch the ground and it would take about fifteen minutes for the wire to strangle him to death.

There was also a whipping table upon which a man was stretched facedown and beaten with a bloody stick the size of a pick handle. Patton noted that their guide was not emaciated as were the rest of the inmates, which Eisenhower also noticed because he asked the man "very pointedly" how he could be so fat. Patton's chief of staff reported that two days later this man was "torn limb from limb" by other prisoners.

Beyond the whipping table was a pile of about forty naked human bodies, shot in the head at close range and lying in a large pool of dried blood. A shed nearby contained another forty bodies in the final stages of emaciation, sprinkled with lime to contain the stench. After the shed had filled to capacity, Patton said, the bodies were removed to a pit about a mile from the camp and buried. This was what the Germans did to prisoners who had grown too weak to work. Patton's party also visited the pit, the bottom of which was filled with arms, legs, and bodies sticking out of scummy green water.

It quickly became clear that, as the American army approached the camp, the Germans had attempted to destroy the evidence. They had some of the prisoners dig up the bodies in the pit and place them on "a mammoth griddle," composed of crisscrossed rail tracks set on brick foundations. They then poured pitch on the bodies and roasted them on a fire of coal and pine.

This method did not cover the crime, however, because the charred bones and skulls of "many hundreds" of inmates were left "on or under the griddle," Patton said. The American commanders ordered their soldiers to visit the scene to "teach our men to look out for the Germans," Patton wrote in his diary. The mayor of the town was also ordered to "confront the spectacle," after which he and his wife went home "and hanged themselves," Patton wrote.[25]

When he returned to his headquarters, Patton called a press conference in which he spoke of "the most horrible sight I have ever seen," and strongly suggested that the reporters visit the camp and tell the world. Two days later leading elements of his army discovered something even worse—Buchenwald.

There, the inmates still living were lying in tiers of bunks like "feebly animated mummies," Patton said. "When we went through they tried to cheer but were too feeble." In a large building with rows of tall smokestacks, luckless inmates were dumped down a chute that delivered them to the basement where the walls were lined with iron meat hooks with piano wire nooses. Two executioners—drawn from the inmate population—lifted the victim up on the hook, where he slowly strangled to death. After a set period of time, anyone showing signs of life was dispatched with a bloody club that looked like "a potato masher."

On the level above were six furnaces resembling "baker's ovens," connected to the basement by an elevator, Patton said. The elevators could accommodate about six bodies at a time to go to the furnace room for disposal.

Patton's chief of staff Brigadier General Hobart R. "Hap" Gay had this observation: "No race and no people other than those who are strictly sadists could commit crimes such as these. To take prisoners . . . and deliberately starve them to death is an atrocity."[26]

Patton ordered inhabitants of towns near these charnel houses taken there to see for themselves what their government was doing. Whatever they had known, whatever rumors they had heard, the German civilians seemed utterly shocked and horrified at seeing the camps in person.

★ ★ ★ ★

ON APRIL 12, PATTON WAS LATE getting to bed and found he'd forgotten to wind his watch. When he turned on the radio to get the time he heard that President Roosevelt had died. "It seems very unfortunate," he told his diary in reference to the new president, Harry S. Truman, "that people are made vice presidents who were never intended, neither by Party, nor by the Lord, to be Presidents."

Three days later, Patton was informed that the Third Army would have a special mission. Bradley had received orders from Eisenhower to turn his army group southeast toward the Bavarian Alps and Austria in search of a Nazi "great National Redoubt," about which army intelligence had been picking up rumors. These rumors stated that Hitler and other high-placed Nazis either had left or would leave Berlin for the hugely fortified and armed redoubt in the mountains where thousands of fanatical Nazis had gathered for a spectacular "last stand."

Patton thought it was nonsense and a wild goose chase but made no objection since attacking in any direction was better than sitting still. "Sometimes I feel I might be nearing the end of this life," he wrote Beatrice. "I have liberated J. [John Waters] and licked the Germans so what else is there to do?" That night he learned from the radio he'd been promoted to full four-star general.

Patton also was informed that his niece and former paramour Jean Gordon, the doughnut girl, was having an affair with a young officer in his headquarters who was resolved to return to his wife and children. Patton had the man transferred to a distant command.[27]

Answering a reporter's question about whether the Germans would continue to resist, Patton said, "I hope they do [but] I don't see what the fools are fighting for . . . I crossed the Danube River today and it wasn't even worth pissing in."

On May 6 Patton got word that some 100,000 misguided White Russians were attempting to surrender. They had been fighting with the Germans against the Red (Communist) Russian army with the notion of somehow "liberating" the Soviet Union of its present form of government. The question arose of whether they were prisoners of war, and Patton said he hoped not, "because if the Russians ever get them they will unquestionably be eliminated." He was right. SHAEF ultimately designated these people POWs and thousands were turned over to the Russians who hanged their leaders and sent the rest to toil in Siberia.[28]

A British sailor whose distasteful job it was to deliver a batch of the unfortunates into the hands of the Soviet army wrote that many of them began to faint and "lose their senses." Having seen many fearful things during the war, the sailor wrote that he had seen nothing "like the fear of those people who were being returned to their native Russia."

Stories like this incited Patton to hate the Russians—"a scurvy race, and simply savages." He thought they would disturb postwar stability, and that Eisenhower's determination to let them take Berlin was a terrible political move. Patton was convinced that a confrontation with the Soviet Union was bound to come to a head, and he knew the American army was at present superior—his Third Army alone contained nearly half a million combat veterans. "We could beat hell out of them," Patton announced.[29]

To a visiting U.S. undersecretary of war Patton strongly recommended that the administration not break up the American army at the conclusion of the war but leave it in place in case the Communists threatened to overrun all of Europe. When the horrified diplomat responded, "You don't realize the strength of these people," Patton scoffed that with the kind of fighting he could give them the Russians might be able to defend themselves up to five days or a week. "After that . . . if you wanted Moscow, I could give it to you."

★ ★ ★ ★

GERMANY SURRENDERED, UNCONDITIONALLY, at a minute past midnight, May 8, 1945. By that date Third Army had inflicted 1,486,000 casualties on the Germans, including 144,500 killed, at a cost to themselves of 136,865 battle casualties, with 21,441 killed in action. According to Colonel Harkins, the Third Army had "gone farther, captured more prisoners, crossed more rivers, liberated more friendly territory, and captured more enemy territory, than any army ever before in American history."[30] George Patton was the man of the hour and the darling of most of the press.

The long nightmare in Europe was over, though another bad dream lay ahead. Hitler was dead by his own hand and the Allies quickly went about gathering up officials of the Nazi regime. Germany was prostrated, its cities in rubble, its manufactories smashed, its people dispirited and unable even to feed themselves. They crawled out of their cellars and hiding places and looked around into a profound silence enveloping the entire nation. Many—probably most of them—were terribly embarrassed and ashamed at what their leaders had put them through but, after all, they had initially voted Hitler and the Nazis into power. It was one of the most horrid mistakes a democracy had ever made and a powerful lesson for today and tomorrow. The Third Reich that Hitler predicted would "last a thousand years" was abolished in little more than a decade, though at terrible cost.

At yet another press conference, Patton was asked whether SS prisoners would be treated differently from other German soldiers and made this reply: "Hell no, SS means no more in Germany than being a Democrat [does] in America—that is not to be quoted." But the remark *was* quoted, and Patton's final self-destruction was set into motion.

CHAPTER THIRTEEN

★ ★ ★ ★

THESE PROCEEDINGS ARE CLOSED

The October 20, 1944, landing had taken the Japanese by surprise, and Douglas MacArthur was holding on to the Philippine island of Leyte by little more than an eyelash, as the enemy fought furiously to prevent the Americans from gaining a stronghold in the islands. The Philippines, after all, were the key to protecting Japan's lifeline to the oil, rubber, rice, copra (from coconut), and mineral resources of Southeast Asia and the southern seas. Since moving south, following the surprise attack on Pearl Harbor, the Japanese had virtually made slaves of the populations of numerous nations and islands and set them to working for the self-defined Greater East Asia Co-Prosperity Sphere, which was, in fact, the Japanese empire.

For several days after the landing, MacArthur's men had fought a bitter inch-by-inch battle to push the Japanese army back from its beachhead, but unbeknownst to the Americans a potential disaster was brewing on the high seas. The Japanese Imperial Navy had summoned its entire naval force—four fleets, one from as far away as Brunei—a mixture of aircraft carriers and heavy surface ships, including the monster "super battleships" *Yamato* and *Musashi* whose 18-inch guns were superior to any warship in the world. What followed would turn out to be the greatest naval battle in history.

The Japanese strategy was to get their heavy ships to the invasion beaches at Leyte, isolate the American troops by destroying the U.S. naval ships there, wreck the supply dumps on the beaches, then pound the U.S. forces into oblivion. The gunfire of just one super battleship could equal the firepower of nine battleships and twenty cruisers in the combined Japanese fleets. To ensure the safe passage of these valuable vessels, to get at the American beachhead, the Japanese avoided being caught in open ocean by timing night passages through two straits—one northern and one southern—that provided passages through the Philippine Islands from the west into the Leyte Gulf and the Philippine Sea.

Still, an enormous obstacle for the Japanese was lack of aircraft and pilots following an ill-advised tangle four months earlier with American naval forces in the Battle of the Philippine Sea or, as it became known, the "Great Marianas Turkey Shoot." In an overwhelming U.S. victory the Japanese lost three fleet carriers and some six hundred warplanes—and their pilots—for all practical purposes putting the Japanese air arm out of business.

On the American side, the U.S. Navy had assigned Admiral Thomas Kincaid's Seventh Fleet to protect MacArthur and facilitate his invasion of Leyte and, in addition, Admiral Bull Halsey's Third Fleet in case the Japanese came in full force with their navy, which they did.

It was Halsey's practice to go after Japanese aircraft carriers whenever and wherever he found them and in the Leyte Gulf battle he found them far to the north of the invasion site. The problem was that the enemy carriers were decoys, because following the Philippine Sea debacle the Japanese navy barely had enough planes and pilots to man a single light carrier. Not realizing this, Halsey took the bait and steamed his fleet out of the action, chasing a phantom enemy carrier force.

The battle began in earnest during the early morning hours of October 25, when the powerful Japanese task force from Brunei entered the San Bernardino Strait near Palawan Island. It was spotted by two

American submarines, USS *Darter* and the USS *Dace*, which shadowed Admiral Takeo Kurita's armada of six battleships, twelve cruisers, and ten destroyers before firing numerous torpedo spreads that sank two cruisers—including Admiral Kurita's flagship *Atago*, which went down so swiftly the admiral had to be fished out of the sea—and knocked still another cruiser out of the fight.

Shaken, Kurita continued on through the strait where he reached the Philippine Sea and steamed southward toward the Leyte beachhead. Because of confusion and some questionable orders by Halsey, the only thing standing in Kurita's way was "Taffy 3," a grab bag of sixteen small, slow, unarmored light escort carriers with several hundred older-model planes and some unarmored destroyers. From a distance, however, Admiral Kurita wrongly perceived that he had encountered Halsey's fleet carriers. The Americans were just as surprised to see the large battleships and cruisers looming ahead of them, but Rear Admiral Thomas Sprague immediately ordered the escort carriers to launch all planes with whatever weapons were on hand. This Taffy 3 did, convincingly, attacking the big enemy battleships and cruisers like a swarm of pesky horseflies—in fact, another of Kurita's cruisers was sunk. Hits were made on both super battleships. When all the American torpedoes were used up, the torpedo bombers made "dummy runs" at the enemy just to keep them feeling threatened.

By all rights, Sprague's weak force should have been destroyed in detail by the heavy guns of Kurita's battleships and cruisers, but Taffy 3 laid down such a heavy smoke screen it simply vanished from sight on the bridges of the enemy ships. The defense of Leyte by Taffy 3 was one of the more heroic events of the naval war in the Pacific. Faced with this startling development, and confused by faulty communications, Kurita retreated back through the San Bernardino Strait, persuaded that he had saved his entire fleet from annihilation.

Meanwhile, further confusion developed on the American side when Halsey sent a message that seemed to indicate he had detached a powerful force of U.S. battleships and cruisers under Admiral Willis "Ching" Lee to guard the approaches to Leyte Gulf, but in fact he had meant to say that he *would* form such a force, if necessary. In any case, it quickly became necessary as reports from scout planes, PT boats, and submarines signaled that several large Japanese task forces were converging on Leyte Gulf. In the south, elements of Kincaid's Seventh Fleet were engaging Japanese warships coming through the Surigao Strait and he sent out a plain-language message: MY SITUATION IS CRITICAL, and requested "fast battleships and air strikes" from Halsey. Matters were made more difficult by the fact that there was no unified command in the battle. MacArthur could *ask* Halsey for help but could not *order* him.

Halsey had located, and was attempting to destroy, the Japanese force that had decoyed him north. Fortunately, however, Kincaid's emergency message soon found its way to the desk of the commander in chief of the Pacific Theater of Operations (CINCPAC), Admiral Chester Nimitz, in Honolulu, three thousand miles away. Nimitz ordered his operations people to get in touch with Halsey and find out what had happened to Ching Lee's task force, which was supposed to be protecting the approaches to the Leyte Gulf.

Halsey, in the midst of a battle of his own, took offense when it seemed that CINCPAC wanted to know where he was and he went into one of his rages when at the end of the message he read the statement THE WORLD WANTS TO KNOW, referring to where he was. What Halsey at the time took for sarcasm is now believed to be "padding" or "wrapping," in which the teletype operator sending secure messages would include nonsense phrases to fool the enemy, should anyone be eavesdropping.

In any case, Halsey was soon steering back south and between him and Kincaid the Japanese took another beating from which they would never fully recover. The Imperial Navy's toll at the end of the Battle of Leyte Gulf was one fleet carrier and two light carriers sunk; three battleships, ten cruisers, and eleven destroyers sunk; three hundred Japanese planes (mostly land based) destroyed; and 12,500 sailors killed. U.S. losses were comparatively negligible. From then on, the Allies had nearly total command of the seas, and at least for the moment Douglas MacArthur and his army were safe.[1]

★ ★ ★ ★

THE RELIEF OVER THE OUTCOME of the Leyte Gulf fracas did not last long. The Japanese army had lots more land-based fighter planes, bombers, and fighter-bombers up on Luzon, the northernmost Philippine island, and no misgivings about using them, especially against MacArthur who, because of the poor conditions of the captured Japanese airfields on Leyte, still required all of his aviation support from the navy. According to MacArthur the Japanese maintained "a continuous, powerful, aerial offensive" against the U.S. landing force never before seen in the Pacific war.

To make matters worse, Leyte saw the introduction of the dangerous and fearsome kamikaze weapon, in which half-trained Japanese suicide pilots made themselves human bombs by personally crashing onto the decks of American warships. To counter this, the U.S. Navy had to keep heavy "air caps" over the fleet hoping to dispatch the kamikazes before they struck, which meant far less air support for MacArthur's ground operations.

Heavy monsoon rains hampered the advance, and the Japanese began sending major reinforcements onto Leyte. Declaring (against his better judgment) that the decisive Battle of the Philippines "will be fought on Leyte," the Japanese commander Lieutenant General Tomoyuki Yamashita—the infamous "Tiger of Malaya"—boasted to reporters, "The only words I spoke to the British commander [Lieutenant General Sir Alfred Percival] during negotiations for the surrender of Singapore were 'All I want to hear from you is yes or no.' I expect to put the same question to MacArthur." For his part, MacArthur said General Yamashita "talked too much."[2]

The Japanese were receiving their supplies and reinforcements through the port of Ormoc on the opposite, or western, side of the island, and they had measured out something known as the "Yamashita Line" constructed of heavy logs and interlocking trenches, at which the Imperial Japanese Army intended to stop the American advance.

After a month of bitter fighting, which included three days of a typhoon, the Allied forces had seemingly stalled. MacArthur, however, in a brilliant strategic move, joined with the navy on December 6 to convoy a full infantry division around the southern tip of Leyte and land it on beaches near Ormoc. Within five days they had seized the city and the port, slamming shut Leyte's "back door," splitting the center of the Yamashita Line, and trapping the Japanese army between the two pincers. As always, the Japanese fought valiantly and viciously and almost to the last man.

On December 18, MacArthur received word that he had been promoted to the five-star rank of general of the army. In his memoirs he wrote, "The old thrill of promotion and decoration was gone. Perhaps I had heard too often the death wail of mangled men—or perhaps the years were beginning to take their inexorable toll." Maybe so, but he was not about to let the occasion pass by without a bit of drama. MacArthur told his aides to collect silver coins from America, Australia, the Netherlands, and the Philippines—representing the forces he commanded—and have a silversmith from Tacloban melt the coins down and fashion the metal into five silver stars shaped into a wreath. These were pinned by his aides on his collar lapels after a ceremony at General Headquarters the day after Christmas 1944.[3]

Meantime MacArthur conducted operations of the South West Pacific Area (SWPA) command in Tacloban from a luxurious two-story estate whose owner, a successful businessman named Walter Price, was murdered by the Japanese after they seized his house for their officers' club. The building soon became the object of a general attack by Japanese aircraft and snipers.

Smoking his oversize corncob pipe, MacArthur could frequently be seen day and night pacing the spacious veranda of the Price house. Some of the younger staff members swore they could tell the general's mood by the way he paced and puffed. When an idea began to germinate in his fertile mind, they said his pace quickened and his pipe smoke resembled that of a choo-choo train. He got little or no exercise other than the pacing but somebody figured out that he paced approximately five miles a day.[4]

People were also stunned by MacArthur's lack of concern during enemy bombing raids. Once as he was briefing senior army and navy people, Japanese planes made a bombing run at the house. Standing at a map with pointer in hand, MacArthur never missed a beat but continued to speak calmly as explosions burst all around them. When he concluded his talk he turned to a subordinate and said, "Better look in the kitchen and outside. That bomb was close and someone may be hurt." At least three people in the kitchen had been wounded by the bomb and one was killed, according to what Eighth Army commander Robert L. Eichelberger told his chief of staff.

Another time, a U.S. antiaircraft shell, apparently aimed at low-flying enemy planes, crashed through the wall and landed on a couch in MacArthur's bedroom. Fortunately it was a dud. MacArthur had it defused and taken to the antiaircraft unit commander with the message, "Bill, ask your gunners to raise their sights just a little bit higher."[5] The Japanese then sent a number of snipers to lurk at the edges of Tacloban waiting for targets of opportunity. MPs and other military units killed a number of these but it is nevertheless astonishing that MacArthur, with all of his public appearances—including the pacing on his veranda or patio—was not a victim.

A month after the original landings, MacArthur was paid a visit by Turner Catledge and A. H. Sulzberger of the *New York Times*. Catledge wrote that MacArthur's quarters were "a principal target," and had been "strafed repeatedly and was pockmarked inside and out with machine-gun bullet holes. My room had a gaping hole in the wall made the week before by a 20-mm. shell."

The two joined MacArthur on his veranda for "one of the most fascinating talks with a public figure that either of us had ever experienced," wrote Catledge. "As he spoke he was variously the military expert, the political figure, the man of destiny. Sulzberger and I later agreed that we had never met a more egotistical man, nor one more aware of his egotism and more able and determined to back it up with his deeds."

Others came away with similar impressions. To a news correspondent, MacArthur began forecasting the future of the world and predicting that "the lands touching the Pacific will determine the course of history for the next ten thousand years." But as usual he wound up his conversations with a blast against "that crowd in Washington," who were by now guilty "of treason and sabotage" for not properly supplying the war in the Pacific.[6]

It was around this time that MacArthur's relationship with his imperious chief of staff Richard Sutherland became severely strained. Sutherland, it seemed, had taken a mistress while in Australia, one Elaine Bessemer-Clarke, daughter of the wealthy Sir Norman Brookes, a two-time Wimbledon tennis champion and his wife, Mabel, a leading Australian socialite. Both Elaine and Sutherland were married with children, but while his marriage was somewhat nondescript she was married to Captain Reginald Bessemer-Clarke, the British heir to the Bessemer steel fortune, who was presently residing in a Japanese prison, having been captured when the Australian unit he was serving with surrendered in Malaya.

The damage to international relations if the affair became public did not seem to factor into Lieutenant General Sutherland's thinking, for he not only took Elaine along when MacArthur moved from Melbourne to Brisbane, he somehow managed to finagle her into the U.S. WACs (Women's Army Corps) as an army captain with no qualifications whatsoever. By most accounts she was an unpleasant, domineering person "much like Sutherland himself" whom—speculates MacArthur biographer Geoffrey Perret—Sutherland fell for because "like other bullies who are cowards at heart, he fell in love with her because she dominated him."[7]

A story about Elaine and Sutherland is told by MacArthur's B-17 pilot Major Henry C. Godman, who some months earlier obtained a jeep for himself that he proudly upholstered in red leather. Elaine coveted the vehicle and one day, when Godman was off flying, she called the motor pool and commandeered it for herself. When Godman returned and found the jeep missing, he discovered the cause and, using his spare keys, quietly liberated it from "Captain Bessemer-Clarke."

Within two days the astonished Godman was standing before Sutherland who told him, "You have been transferred from MacArthur's headquarters. I'm sending you back to combat." Having already flown the required quota of thirty missions, Godman protested, but to no avail. It remains an amazing and revolting example of people who have such little regard for their fellow man that they would put someone's life in jeopardy over a jeep.[8]

In any event, the affair between the WAC captain—with her husband a Japanese prisoner—and the chief of staff of the supreme commander of the South West Pacific Area first came to MacArthur's attention when he discovered Sutherland had moved Elaine to Hollandia, New Guinea, and MacArthur ordered him to send her home.

Imagine MacArthur's astonishment then, and surprise, when he learned that Sutherland had not only defied his order, he had even moved her to Leyte and installed her in a house that he had ordered built by the corps of engineers—right down the road.

An enraged MacArthur stormed into Sutherland's office and began to curse and berate him "using every profanity acquired in a lifetime of military service." He reminded Sutherland in between oaths that he had given him a direct, written order to get rid of the woman and threatened him with arrest. MacArthur's browbeating went on for fifteen minutes without cessation and was so disconcerting that the military sentry at the door was said to have put his fingers in his ears. "That woman will be flown out of Tacloban immediately! And if she is not out of here within 24 hours I will court martial you for disobedience of a direct order!" shouted MacArthur.[9]

This time the dour chief of staff seemed to get the message for, as a staff officer recalled, the speed with which Sutherland had Elaine shipped out of Leyte reminded him of "the stunt in the Barnum & Bailey Circus of the man shot from the mouth of a cannon."

After this incident, it was said that things were never the same between MacArthur and his chief of staff. Why he didn't fire Sutherland is puzzling, but MacArthur did apparently begin to rely on, as a confidant, his intelligence chief Lieutenant Colonel Courtney Whitney. MacArthur had known Whitney as a Manila lawyer before the war and, in time, it was said that Whitney became MacArthur's "alter ego."

★ ★ ★ ★

WITHIN TWO WEEKS AFTER THE LANDING at Ormoc, the American army had killed about 50,000 of the estimated 60,000- to 75,000-man Japanese army and took only 386 prisoners. General Eichelberger stated that his Eighth Army, charged with "mopping up," killed 27,000 more Japanese. The rest are presumed to have escaped north through the jungle, or starved there. (Another 20,000 to 40,000 Japanese soldiers and sailors were thought to have perished in replacement convoys from Japan that were sunk by U.S. Navy planes and submarines.) MacArthur was particularly proud that there were no survivors from the Japanese 16th Division, which had implemented the cruel and disgraceful "Death March" on Bataan. American casualties since the landing at Ormoc were 15,500, with 3,508 killed.[10]

MacArthur also assumed civil duties regarding governance of the Philippines, which was then being run by a Japanese-backed puppet regime in Manila. This put him at odds with the difficult and powerful U.S. secretary of the interior Harold Ickes. Before the invasion of Leyte, Ickes wrote MacArthur that it was his intention to "take charge" of the Philippine government once the country was liberated, a notion MacArthur found unacceptable. "He seemed to think of the islands as another one of his National Parks," MacArthur wrote afterward. "It was his claim that the archipelago [the Philippines had been a U.S.-affiliated commonwealth before the Japanese took over] was a 'possession' of the United States."

After MacArthur made his escape from Corregidor in 1942, and it was clear the country would fall to the Japanese, Philippine president Manuel Quezon, vice president Sergio Osmeña, and other officials made their way to Washington, D.C., to form a government in exile. Upon Quezon's death in 1944, Osmeña became president. MacArthur had him brought back for the invasion with the intention of formally installing him in office once a beachhead was secured.

Ickes violently objected to this plan, assuming that because many Filipinos had cooperated with the Japanese they were a traitorous race undeserving of self-government.* It was evident, MacArthur said, that

---

* Harold Ickes was an avid New Dealer and hatchet man for President Roosevelt. Whenever the press wanted a stinging, acerbic comment about a policy or a person that the White House would find awkward to make, they would seek out Ickes.

Ickes "intended to shoot or hang any Filipino who had anything to do with the puppet government, no matter what reasons they had for cooperating."[11] Because of his service in the islands before the war, MacArthur was familiar with most of the officials who later cooperated with Japan. Many in high administrative positions, MacArthur said, collaborated in order to alleviate the ordeal and suffering imposed on the people by the Japanese.

When the war began, the Roosevelt administration had urged MacArthur to assume control of the Philippine government, but he'd resisted that idea on grounds that the Filipinos were capable of governing themselves. Secretary of War Henry Stimson agreed with MacArthur's plan, which was to restore civil government to each Philippine province as soon as the Japanese were pushed out. As to alleged collaborators or disloyalists, MacArthur promised that they would be brought to a fair trial under terms of the Philippine constitution.

★ ★ ★ ★

MacArthur's next big goal was the island of Luzon and the nation's capital, Manila. Because the soil of Leyte was so marshy, General Kenney and the army engineers were still unable to provide satisfactory runways for his air force, so MacArthur decided to invade the island of Mindoro, to the north, right below Luzon, and establish airfields there. He ran into trouble when Admiral Kincaid balked at the idea of sailing his light, slow, and unarmed escort carriers with the invasion convoy because they would be highly vulnerable to enemy kamikaze attacks.

In fact a single kamikaze could sink an escort carrier and had done so during the Battle of Leyte Gulf. Sometime in the afternoon of November 30, MacArthur cornered Kincaid in his quarters and began trying to persuade him to change his mind. For more than an hour he belabored the admiral, "giving him hell about [his] fear of kamikazes," questioning his loyalty, pacing furiously, waving his hands, sometimes whispering, cajoling, and all the while Kincaid was slumped exhaustedly on a bedpost; when he was finished, said Turner Catledge, who witnessed the episode, MacArthur walked up to Kincaid, put his arms on his shoulders, and said, "But Tommy, I love you still. Let's go to dinner."[12]

Afterward, Admiral Kincaid relented and the invasion got under way on December 12 and landed successfully on December 15. Mindoro was lightly garrisoned, the Japanese were taken completely by surprise, and the operation was successful, although kamikazes smashed through an air cap of P-38s and crashed into two destroyers, three landing ships, and an escort carrier. It was the worst amphibious landing the navy had experienced since a heavy-casualty debacle on Italy's coast at Anzio earlier that year.

By December 23 engineers had established two runways, and a third airfield was near completion. Both MacArthur's Sixth Army under Krueger and Eighth Army under Eichelberger were transferred to Mindoro. This latest invasion also forced Yamashita to cancel a major counterinvasion he had organized because his line of communications had been severed. Landing on Mindoro was a decisive move by MacArthur, without which, the official army history says, MacArthur's Luzon operations would have been "considerably more hazardous and difficult."

The Luzon invasion began with a massive subterfuge. MacArthur had Kenney's air force fly dummy missions over southern Luzon, and bombers bombed targets in the south. Photographic planes flew over southern targets; Kincaid's navy cleared mines in southern harbors; PT boats patrolled southern waters; and guerrilla groups were instructed to harass Japanese operations in the south.

At sunrise on January 9, 1945, nearly a thousand ships lay just offshore in the Lingayen Gulf, a bight in the South China Sea on the northwest coast of Luzon, and the American Sixth Army began landing on the beaches. "No plan ever worked better," MacArthur said.[13]

It was not, however, without travails. As soon as the American convoys were spotted by the Japanese, the kamikazes began their dreadful work. Even though General Kenney had planned to keep an air cap of at least sixty fighters over each U.S. convoy as it came within kamikaze range, some of the suicide planes inevitably broke through. Before it was over, kamikazes had crashed on forty-seven U.S. Navy ships and one Australian cruiser, sinking four and badly damaging the others and leaving more than 2,100 casualties, with 738 men, mostly sailors, dead. The kamikazes seemed to be aiming at the capital ships, which was a relief of sorts to MacArthur who told an aide that if the kamikazes began attacking the troopships they might have to turn back.

As they neared Luzon, MacArthur could often be seen at the rail of his flagship, the cruiser USS *Boise,* watching the action: a sky full of whining warplanes, deafening antiaircraft fire, kamikazes splashing into the sea, ships suddenly engulfed in flame.

When they passed Corregidor in late afternoon, MacArthur became visibly riveted by the sight of Bataan and the entrance to Manila Bay. "I could not leave the rail," he said. "One by one the staff drifted away, and I was alone with my memories. At the sight of those never-to-be forgotten scenes of my family's past, I felt an indescribable sense of loss, of sorrow, of loneliness, and of solemn consecration." As night fell, a Japanese destroyer came barreling out of Manila Bay and was immediately set upon by four American destroyers. Gunfire hit the enemy ship's magazine and she exploded in spectacular fashion, a sight that could be seen clearly from the decks of *Boise.*[14]

From that point on, the convoys were beset by intensified kamikaze attacks and swarms of Japanese midget submarines, looking to MacArthur like "black whales." When the hundreds of American ships finally arrived and anchored at Lingayen, the Japanese sent out seventy small suicide motor craft packed with explosives and instructions to ram as many ships as possible. U.S. destroyers took care of most of them but not before they sank two landing craft and damaged four LSTs (landing ship tanks).

When it was over, MacArthur's battle strategy proved solid and bold. Once Sixth Army established a beachhead and began moving inland toward Manila, Yamashita would undoubtedly move as much of his army as possible northward to stop the Americans. That's when elements of Eichelberger's Eighth Army would land about midway along Luzon's west coast, which by then, according to plan, should be lightly defended. Once ashore, both armies would then "close like a vice on the enemy and destroy him," MacArthur said.[15]

It has been suggested by more recent historians that Yamashita knew all along that MacArthur would land at Lingayen Gulf but was fearful to meet him on the beaches, instead preferring to dig in on the mountains and hills, then hit the Americans in the flank and cut off their drive south. But the Americans, too, suspected that the Japanese thought they would land at Lingayen, for that was where their own General Homma had landed in 1941, and the area contained the best beaches on Luzon. Even if Yamashita planned to strike the Americans hard on their southward march, there is little evidence that he attempted to do so. Also Yamashita must have recognized the futility of attacking across the broad central plain where the American mechanized forces could best employ their superiority in planes, tanks, and self-propelled artillery.

Whatever the Japanese strategy, the men of four divisions of General Krueger had landed to almost no resistance and, despite Krueger's misgivings, headed down Route 3, which ran a hundred miles through the center of Luzon's central plain to the capital city of Manila. Even though MacArthur's SWPA headquarters intelligence section had forecasted that Yamashita's remaining army was 152,000-strong, Krueger's own intelligence people thought he had as many as 250,000.

MacArthur tried to argue that that figure was too high, but Krueger was unpersuaded. In fact, they were both wrong. The Japanese army on Luzon was 275,000-strong but because of the ravagings of Halsey's Third Carrier Fleet the Japanese lines of communication were so disrupted that Yamashita was experiencing major shortages of ammunition and other supplies. As a result, Krueger's army was able to race fifty miles down Route 3 in five days to capture Clark Field and its six airstrips. It had cost the Americans just 250 men killed. The difficulty, however, quickly set in. The Americans soon discovered that the Japanese ensconced in the mountains had the runways under artillery fire and it became necessary for the infantry to assault the mountains and drive the Japanese beyond artillery range so that General Kenney could bring in his P-38s, B-24s, and B-17s.

MacArthur was elated during this period, having traveled in the forefront of the infantry drive, sometimes even getting ahead of it. At one point, riding with his personal physician, Colonel Roger Olaf Egeberg, MacArthur suddenly shouted for his jeep driver to stop. With Japanese artillery peppering the road ahead, he led Egeberg over to an old black muzzle-loading cannon set in concrete with a plaque and told him, "On that spot, Doc, about forty-five years ago, my father's aide-de-camp was killed standing at his side."

Egeberg looked at the cannon, looked at MacArthur, and shouted to the jeep driver, "Let's get the hell out of here!"[16]

Meantime, on January 29, the XI Corps of General Eichelberger's Eighth Army had successfully landed along Luzon's west coast, south of Clark Field, and were pushing inland. Krueger, however, conscious of the numbers of Japanese on the island, was wary of a big counterattack from Yamashita, and the longer he waited for it the warier he got, keeping his army dawdling around Clark Field.

When Krueger balked at pushing on immediately for Manila, fifty miles away, MacArthur prodded him by announcing a race between Sixth and Eighth Armies to see which could first liberate the city. That put some fire into Krueger and he resumed his southward drive.[17]

For his part, Eichelberger planned to have his 11th Airborne Division make an amphibious assault about fifty miles southwest of Manila and march on the city from there. But General Kenney, the airman, made an excellent suggestion—why not have the division make an airborne assault on the airport, barely three miles from the center of the city. It would save all that marching and fighting and, most important, time. The air force chief promised to secure for the 11th Division all the air transport and close air support it needed. Kenney's was a bold idea, but Eichelberger lacked vision. He feared the risks were too great, that his men might parachute into a hoard of Japanese tanks or that the Japanese might have put obstacles on the drop zones, and so forth.

Meantime, MacArthur, unaware of the discussion between Kenney and Eichelberger, had decided that his idea of turning the liberation of Manila into a contest between commanders worked so well that he tried it again with Krueger, who was expecting the crack First Cavalry Division to land at Lingayen on January 27. Why not make it a race between the

37th Division, which was already at Clark Field, and the Cav that was just now hitting the beaches?

To supervise progress and be close to the action, MacArthur moved his headquarters farther south to a sugar plantation hacienda near Tarlac. What he had to observe was three infantry divisions converging on Manila, about 60,000 men. The 11th Airborne had the roughest time of it; the Japanese had thoroughly fortified numerous lines of defense south of the city, including Nielson Field, where Kenney had suggested to Eichelberger that he parachute the division in. For days, intense rivalries were involved—infantry versus cavalry versus airborne; Sixth Army versus Eighth Army.

The cavalry finally won the race. On February 2 the First Cav organized two "flying columns" and tore down Route 5, capturing bridges before the Japanese had a chance to dynamite them. In one case, after the defenders had lit the fuses and fled, brave troopers rushed to extinguish them. At another point, they encountered a convoy of Japanese coming from the direction of Manila and machine-gunned the startled enemy soldiers as the two columns advanced.

By February 3 the lead column was in the northern Manila suburbs and, before dark, inside the city limits. Their first stop was Santo Tomas University, which almost three years earlier had been turned into a prison camp for nearly four thousand American and other Allied civilians. The guards at the gate put up a fight but were quickly overcome and the First Cav freed the miserable prisoners, who were pitifully ragged and emaciated. Next they liberated Malacañang Palace near the center of the city. By February 5 the rest of First Cav was encamped at Grace Park just north of the city.

On February 4 the 37th Division, having overcome numerous obstacles, managed to liberate Old Bilibid Prison containing a mixture of thirteen hundred American military and civilian prisoners. The Japanese guards fled, leaving the victors to assume that enemy resistance would be light.

Around the same time, the 11th Airborne Division, just south of the airport, encountered the redoubtable Genko Line, fortified with mortars and machine guns and artillery, some of it from the heavy guns of ships sunk or damaged in the harbor.

Although the fighting there was ferocious, MacArthur's headquarters on February 6 foolishly sent out a bulletin proclaiming: "Our forces are rapidly clearing the enemy from Manila. Our converging columns entered the city and surrounded the Jap defenders." This elicited congratulatory telegrams from Roosevelt, Stimson, Churchill et al. Moreover, they began planning a big World War I Champs-Élysées-type victory parade through the broad avenues of the city, led by MacArthur in an "army drab" Cadillac convertible.[18]

What nobody knew—including Yamashita, who had pulled his army troops out of Manila after declaring it an "open city" (meaning that it was to be spared fighting over)—was that still lurking within Manila's limits were 20,000 Japanese marines under Admiral Sanji Iwabuchi, a bloodthirsty fanatic who had no intention of surrendering or retreating. Before he would let the Americans conquer the city he determined to reduce it to ashes and its million-plus inhabitants to crow bait.

When the Japanese began destroying the port facilities, a fire spread quickly to shacks in the poorer section of Manila and turned into an enormous conflagration that burned for several days, laying tens of thousands of homes to utter ruin.

On February 7, MacArthur finally entered the city and visited the now free inmates of Old Bilibid Prison who "dragged themselves to some semblance of attention beside their cots." As MacArthur "passed slowly down the scrawny, suffering column, a murmur accompanied me as each man barely speaking above a whisper, said, 'You're back,' or 'You made it,' or 'God bless you.' I could only reply, 'I'm a little late . . .' I passed on out of the barracks compound and looked around at the debris that was no longer important to those inside: the tin cans they had eaten from, the dirty old bottles they had drunk from. It made me ill just to look at them."[19]

It was around this time that word got back from Filipino guerrillas that a large compound of U.S. prisoners were in desperate straits near the town of Cabanatuan. For three years following the Death March, these men had been starved and abused by the Japanese and were dying at an alarming rate. Worse, word had come that the Japanese had begun executing American prisoners if it appeared they would be repatriated.

A pilot who had been a prisoner at the camp on Palawan Island but managed to escape told the horrifying tale of what his Japanese captors did when they saw a U.S. convoy in their area (it was actually headed to Mindoro). They herded all 160 prisoners into a covered air raid trench and poured gasoline over them. Then they set them afire and machine-gunned those who tried to escape (somehow, nine of them did). It was a chilling forewarning of what was to come for the remaining American prisoners as the U.S. Army seized territory from the Japanese.

With a sense of great urgency, a group of rangers from Krueger's Sixth Army developed a daring plan to lead an expedition thirty miles behind Japanese lines and rescue the prisoners. The force consisted of eighty Filipino guerrillas, fourteen Philippine scouts, and one hundred twenty U.S. Army Rangers led by Lieutenant Colonel Henry Mucci, who made a harrowing nighttime march around large Japanese concentrations to fall on the Japanese garrison of the camp.

Armed with Thompson submachine guns, a bazooka team, and a new P-61 "Black Widow" from the 547th Night Fighter Squadron the rescuers arrived in the vicinity of the camp after dark on January 30. The fighter plane pretended to be crippled and on the verge of crashing in order to distract the Japanese guards while the rescue force sneaked up to the main gate and a sergeant shot the padlock off with his .45. Then all hell broke loose. During the ensuing firefight, which lasted half an hour, an estimated five hundred to a thousand Japanese were killed, with very few U.S. casualties.

When a head count was made, 522 emaciated prisoners had been freed, out of an estimated 10,000, the rest having perished or been shipped to slave labor camps in Japan or Manchuria, an activity the Japanese began in 1944 in contemplation of being defeated in the southern islands. The POWs in Cabanatuan, however, were in such wretched condition that some died on the way to freedom, and more than a hundred oxcarts had to be commandeered to get them to safety—though with the slow speed of 2 miles an hour by the Philippine carabao, or ox, the team remained in constant fear of being attacked or overtaken by the furious Japanese.

The success of the raid was celebrated in the United States and raised a terrific storm of indignation and disgust when survivors told their stories of the brutality they had suffered—starved, beaten, shot for little or no reason. The furor added to the public's opinion that the Japanese needed to be fully conquered, in their homeland if necessary, and punished for their behavior.

MacArthur too found himself depressed after seeing the utter degradation of the POW inmates and decided a little time at the front might cheer him up. "Doc," he said to the unenthusiastic Egeberg, "this is getting to me. I want to go forward till we meet some fire." ("He had no respect for sniper fire," Egeberg wrote later.) Earlier that month, at a Japanese roadblock, MacArthur was standing up when an enemy machine gun began to chatter. An infantry lieutenant said, "We're going after those fellers but please get down sir, we're under fire." MacArthur stood his ground and replied. "I'm not under fire. Those bullets are not intended for me."[20]

Emboldened and accompanied by the doctor and two other aides, they rode in a jeep before getting out and walking to the sound of the battle. Rounding a corner, they came upon a scorched Japanese truck filled with the charred corpses of Japanese soldiers "all erect and dead—victims of a flamethrower." They walked through an infantry platoon that was crouching under cover whose members "looked at them as though they were insane."[21]

Presently, with the racket of gunshots reverberating all over the landscape, on the banks of a river they came upon a brewery that happened to be owned by the family of one of MacArthur's aides, Andres Soriano. The workers warned that they were in Japanese territory but, recognizing Soriano, they invited the group inside for a glass of San Miguel beer.[22]

When it became apparent that the Americans would not be "crushed," as ordered, Admiral Iwabuchi was ordered by Yamashita to break out of Manila and join him in the Luzon mountains. The arrival of the First Cav, however, spoiled that plan also and drove the admiral and his marines into the Intramuros, a historic walled city dating back to the 1500s when the Spanish colonialists arrived. The walls of the old fortress, made of giant stone blocks, were estimated to be forty feet thick at the bottom and rose twenty feet above the streets. It was where MacArthur's penthouse apartment was located atop the Manila Hotel, with its vast military library containing perhaps eight thousand volumes, some from the collection of his father.[23]

After their interlude at the beer brewery, MacArthur led his little party forward once more to the wall of the Intramuros, where they could go no farther. Looking up they saw an enemy officer observing them with binoculars. Undaunted, MacArthur assumed "the stance," for which he had become well known—erect, legs spread apart, hands on hips—and stared the Japanese officer down until at last he looked the other way.

As they walked along the wall, MacArthur's party began to attract the attention of enemy snipers who fired no fewer than twenty-eight bullets at them, according to Egeberg, before he stopped counting. An American infantryman under cover warned them about a machine gun ahead that suddenly opened up, prompting MacArthur to at last abandon his excursion and stalk slowly away "showing his contempt for peril."

When Egeberg wanted to know why MacArthur unnecessarily put himself in danger, he was told, "Hell Doc, those weren't real sharpshooters. They were just a scared rear guard. Aiming at me, they were likelier to hit you!"[24]

During the first week of February MacArthur decided to visit his old apartment suite atop the Manila Hotel. He arrived with a patrol from the 37th Division, which was promptly pinned down by Japanese machine gun fire from the hotel itself. As he lay on the ground he watched in astonishment as flames and smoke suddenly shot from the penthouse. The Japanese had set it afire.

Two men with submachine guns accompanied him when the patrol worked its way to the hotel. "Every landing was a fight," MacArthur wrote in his memoirs. Of the penthouse, nothing was left but ashes, and a Japanese colonel lay dead in the threshold, flanked by two large oriental vases presented to MacArthur's father by the former emperor of Japan. Everything was gone, MacArthur agonized, his fine military library, grand piano, silver, and china—the possessions of a lifetime. "It was not a pleasant moment," he said.

★ ★ ★ ★

KENNEY HAD WANTED TO BOMB the Japanese out of Intramuros but MacArthur forbade it. "You would probably kill off the Japs all right," he told the airman, "but there are several thousand Filipino citizens in there who would be killed too. The world would hold up its hands in horror if we did anything like that." Whatever misgivings MacArthur had, he nevertheless lifted his ban on the use of artillery in the city, and soon the big guns filled the air with great booms and dust.

Admiral Iwabuchi's reaction was to send his men on a carnival of boiling vengeance in which rape, robbery, and murder became the order of the day. Nearly a hundred thousand Filipinos were slain by the Japanese in a rampage that overshadowed even the infamous Japanese Rape of Nanking in 1937–38. William Manchester, one of MacArthur's most prominent biographers, describes it this way: "Hospitals were set afire after their patients were strapped to their beds. The corpses of males were mutilated; females of all ages were raped before they were slain, and babies' eyeballs were gouged out and smeared on walls like jelly." The Japanese went on a riot of arson in which a majority of Manila's residential housing, buildings, utilities, and factories were destroyed. The enemy had to be rooted out house to house and room by room as once more the Japanese preferred to die to a man for their emperor.[25]

The Americans accommodated them but at a terrific cost to themselves and the city proper. The artillery MacArthur had permitted didn't do as much damage as the Japanese campaign of arson, but it did its share. In the end, which did not come until March 3, Manila was officially declared a secured city; 16,665 Japanese marines and soldiers, including Admiral Iwabuchi, who committed suicide, were counted dead, as well as 1,010 U.S. soldiers killed in action with 5,565 others wounded.

Because most of the war correspondents assigned to SWPA were on MacArthur's "payroll," so to speak, little news leaked out of the savage Battle of Manila, and after the previous official announcement that Luzon had been taken MacArthur received little or no second-time congratulatory telegrams.

★ ★ ★ ★

BY THE END OF FEBRUARY it had become apparent that Japanese resistance was coming to an end. Meanwhile, U.S. Secretary of the Interior Harold Ickes had been waging a furious war with the White House to overturn MacArthur's scheme to return the Philippines to self-governance and keep the island as a Pacific possession—with Ickes himself as a kind of czar or dictator. In the end, Roosevelt sided with MacArthur. Perhaps it was MacArthur's argument that Ickes's "personality was such as to insure friction" and that he had no experience in the Orient, never even made a visit, that turned the table MacArthur's way.[26] For his part, Ickes from that time on considered MacArthur an archenemy and rarely lost the opportunity to impugn him.

Nevertheless, when the U.S. invasion force had secured its beachhead, MacArthur decided to perform his long-awaited civic duty—to restore the presidency of the Philippines under the old commonwealth constitution. Thus in the early spring of 1945 MacArthur delivered a lengthy address to a gathering of Filipino civilians and his top army brass at the old Malacañang Palace, which had miraculously escaped destruction.

"More than three years have elapsed," he told them, "years of bitterness, struggle, and sacrifice." It was pure MacArthur. He spoke of agonizing over obeying Roosevelt's order for him to withdraw. He painted a picture of prewar Manila with its lovely churches, boulevards, and public and historic buildings and apologized for the damage done. He spoke of democracy and "destroying evil forces that have sought to suppress it by the brutality of the sword." He installed Osmeña, "on behalf of my government," as president of a free Philippine commonwealth and declared Manila "the Citadel of Democracy of the East."

Then his voice suddenly cracked and he choked up; tears filled his eyes and he could not go on for a long, tense moment with everyone looking up at him, their own breath caught up in awe. But he recovered and finished, at the end asking the audience to join him in the Lord's Prayer.

Later MacArthur said of the moment, "To others it may seem like the culmination of a panorama of physical and spiritual disaster. [But] it had killed something inside me to see my men die."

It was too true; whatever his other personal deficiencies, MacArthur cared deeply for the welfare of his soldiers. Any combat general, MacArthur perhaps more than most, realizes that men under his command will die, and he has to do everything he can to keep the cost low. George Patton's method was to keep moving fast and hit hard on the theory that a slow, drawn-out battle will cause more casualties than a swift, fatal strike. MacArthur's approach was different; he liked carefully planned, methodically executed attacks along paths of least resistance to maneuver the enemy where he could best get at him.

He remained dismayed at the navy's style of fighting and shook his head at the terrible casualties taken by the Marine Corps at such places as Guadalcanal, Tarawa, Peleliu, and Saipan, which he felt were out of proportion to the number of troops employed. His own casualties in the battle to retake Luzon were bad enough: more than 10,000 Allied soldiers killed and 37,000 wounded. But MacArthur had two entire armies employed—nearly a quarter million men.

Within two weeks another alarming fact arrived adding to concerns over American men dying in increasing numbers as the Allies neared Japan: the casualty figures for the Battle of Iwo Jima, a tiny island between the Philippines and the southern Japanese mainland. Nearly 7,000 U.S. Marines had been killed out of a total of 70,000 marines employed—a nearly one-man-out-of-ten ratio.

But that number also meant it was time to close in on the Japanese home islands and someone had to command the effort. It had come down to a choice between Admiral Nimitz and General MacArthur and Roosevelt picked MacArthur. Air Corps General Kenney told him about it before the official announcement because he had seen the president on a recent trip to Washington and was asked to "tell Douglas that I expect he will have a lot of work to do North of the Philippines before long."

"I don't believe it," growled MacArthur when Kenney told him he "had heard a rumor that he was going to command the show in Japan."

MacArthur said he had information that Nimitz was to be in charge and that he would be relegated to clean up the Philippines and then move south to the Dutch East Indies. "Who gave you that rumor anyhow?" he asked.

"A man named Franklin Delano Roosevelt," Kenney replied.[27]

Still, it was decided that the next invasion would be to secure airfields on the enemy stronghold of Okinawa in the northern Pacific, only three hundred miles south of Japan. It was shaping up as the worst and biggest battle yet, but MacArthur would not be in it. Nimitz's Central Pacific Command would run that show with a combination of U.S. Marines and U.S. Army divisions. MacArthur, however, had other things to occupy him, namely the arrival of his wife Jean, son Arthur, now seven, and Ah Cheu the *amah,* or nanny. They had been in Australia and MacArthur had not seen them in nearly five months.

★ ★ ★ ★

WHILE THE AMERICANS HAD mostly overtaken the Philippines, Japanese remained almost everywhere in the islands. They still needed to be suppressed, and MacArthur sent Eichelberger's Eighth Army south to do the job while Krueger's Sixth Army on Luzon "mopped up" the remnants of Yamashita's force who had taken to the mountains.

In a phrase that some saw as confusing or contradictory, MacArthur in dispatches or press releases generally referred to the elimination of such concentrations as "mopping up," a term usually understood to mean dealing with an enemy incapable of organized resistance—but in more than one case the Japanese garrisons proved far larger that the SWPA chief predicted.

For instance, MacArthur told Eichelberger he "did not believe there were four thousand Japanese left alive on Mindanao," when in fact there were nearly twenty-four thousand.[28]

Included in the southernmost of these operations were Australian troops under MacArthur's command, which caused the Australian government to balk at the notion of losing more men this close to the end of the war, but MacArthur countered by saying the assaults were in part to secure the rich oil fields of the Dutch Indies in preparation for the invasion of Japan. (Unfortunately and ironically, when Australian troops invaded Borneo they found the oil fields there so smashed up from Allied bombing they could not resume production for over a year.)

Some historians and biographers have criticized MacArthur for initiating these secondary operations because he didn't seek permission from the Joint Chiefs of Staff. But MacArthur evidently did not think he needed permission for what he considered housekeeping. The Japanese were oppressing the people throughout the archipelago and elsewhere and in his view the sooner they were disposed of the better. MacArthur was a sensitive and caring figure when it came to the civilian populations, especially in the Philippines, and he looked on the Filipinos in an almost fatherly way.

Also, MacArthur had secured from Washington a massive $100 million in relief funds to rebuild Manila, much of which had been destroyed between the pyromaniacal urges of the Japanese and the U.S. artillery bombardments during the final battle. His wife Jean was a constant presence during the relief and reconstruction effort, which seemed to subdue some of MacArthur's critics, who had been complaining that no other officer kept his wife and family in the theater of war.

They lived during this period in a fine mansion that had survived the fighting. Casa Blanca was the home of a Mrs. Bachrach, whose husband, the country's wealthiest car dealer, had been killed by the Japanese. It was swank, with a swimming pool, sauna, and lovely gardens. MacArthur had euchred his friend General Kenney out of the home after Kenney—who originally found the house and put in a request for it as his personal quarters—told MacArthur how great it was and, foolishly, *where* it was. MacArthur had been unhappy with the quarters he'd been provided prior to Jean and little Arthur's arrival. It had been a house on the Pasig River that was "dank" and the river "a sewer" in which more than the occasional dead body floated past.[29]

The morning after filing his paperwork for the estate, Kenney went looking for MacArthur but he couldn't find him. Later that day the supreme commander of SWPA informed the astonished Kenney, "George, I did a kind of dirty trick on you. I stole your house."[30]

Kenney eventually one-upped his boss when he found an even swankier home in the neighborhood. Mrs. Bachrach, it seemed, had a sister who was equally rich and who had ordered her builder to construct something "better" than her sister's house.[31]

After moving in, MacArthur used whatever spare time he had doting on little Arthur, instructing him to march in close order drill, reading to him from *Grimms' Fairy Tales* and other children's books. Since all the schools in Manila had been destroyed in the fighting they hired an English tutor for the youngster, who stayed with the MacArthurs throughout the war.

In the meanwhile, MacArthur and his staff were busy planning for the invasion of Japan. Although he denied it later, MacArthur thought it would be necessary to bring the Russians into the war with Japan, "with a hundred divisions in Manchuria."

On April 12 the day Franklin Roosevelt died, MacArthur received a message from George Marshall asking his opinion of how best to end the war against Japan. One school of thought, Marshall said, recommends a blockade and constant aerial bombardment instead of invasion; the other recommends "driving straight into Japan proper." MacArthur favored the latter.

There is nothing on the record as to MacArthur's personal reaction to the president's death but it must have affected him deeply. He'd been on intimate terms with Roosevelt ever since he was appointed chief of staff of the army in 1930. Neither man fully trusted the other but each enjoyed the other's company and respected his talents. Roosevelt, for his part, had favored MacArthur over the navy, which had always wanted to control the war in the Pacific, and the president had named him as commander for the invasion of Japan.

On the other hand, MacArthur was never comfortable serving under anyone else, and probably considered Roosevelt his true boss, bypassing

George Marshall and the chiefs of staff. He was therefore wary of Harry Truman when he assumed the presidency after Roosevelt's passing. Truman was an entity unknown.

No matter who the president, MacArthur believed an invasion of Japan would be relatively easy compared with some of the battles being fought lately. He was appalled by the slaughter at Iwo Jima, and now Okinawa, which was "just awful"—12,520 soldiers and marines had shed their lives and 35,600 were wounded. In his view, the navy's Central Pacific Command continued "needlessly" losing men's lives by insisting on killing the Japanese to the last man.

In less than a week, in all these landings, MacArthur posited, the marines and army forces had secured all the area they needed for airfields and should have gone on the defensive and let the Japanese break themselves on the Allied lines—perhaps forgetting that is exactly what the marines did in 1942 at Guadalcanal where they suffered 7,100 dead of 60,000 engaged, a dreadful killed-to-deployed ratio in which one in every eight men died.

By now, MacArthur said, the Japanese were nearly prostrated. Japan's navy lay at the bottom of the ocean, its air force was decimated, the means of transportation and production were smashed to atoms, and the nation's major cities were firebombed to char.

Japan did, however, possess a large land defense force if home militias were included, filled with conscripted males between the ages of fifteen and sixty and females from seventeen to forty, some equipped only with ancient muskets, spears, bows and arrows, and scythes. All told, on paper the Japanese could field a home army of 34,600,000, but only 2,350,000 of those were regular soldiers. With the war in Europe coming to an end, even without Russia, the Allies could put twelve to fifteen entire armies into the fight, with all their artillery and armor as well as the enormous airpower they possessed.

MacArthur didn't think it would come to that, and said so. He believed the Japanese politicians would ultimately force the army to make a peace—but it wouldn't be easy owing to the Allied insistence on "unconditional surrender" advanced by President Roosevelt at the 1943 Casablanca Conference.

However, by this time, Japanese diplomats were known to be making entreaties to the Soviet Union, which remained officially neutral in the contest, to broker a negotiated peace in which the emperor would continue to rule. The powers in the War Department did not subscribe to this scenario and were making every effort to assemble a powerful force to invade the Japanese mainland and crush the empire for good.

★ ★ ★ ★

WHEN KRUEGER'S SIXTH ARMY had nearly eliminated any threat from the rest of Yamashita's Japanese on Luzon, MacArthur got a hankering for combat again and on June 2 once more cast off aboard *Boise* with a handful of staff members for what Eichelberger cavalierly described as a "grand tour" of the current battlefields. The big cruiser stopped at all of the large islands of the central and southern Philippines where, to the dismay of his staff—especially his personal physician Colonel Egeberg—MacArthur again insisted on going ashore into, and often beyond, the front lines.

Like George Patton, MacArthur seemed drawn to danger that fueled some militant compulsion in his psyche, perhaps needing to prove over and again that he was bulletproof; Patton himself in his letters to Beatrice had compared this sort of syndrome with steeplechasing, in which the expression "riding at breakneck speed" is no mere coin of phrase—in jumping fences and hedges, as in battle, death was always the outrider. June 10 found the cruiser *Boise* lying off Borneo's Brunei Bay so that MacArthur could watch Australian troops hit the beaches to retake Brunei City. On the following day he went ashore and waded through a mile of swamp to waiting jeeps that were to take his entourage to the battlefront.

This "Brass Hat Party," as Kenney characterized it, drove inland "to the accompaniment of an occasional sniper's shot and a burst of machine-gun fire." MacArthur was "enjoying himself hugely," when a firefight broke out just ahead between an Australian tank and enemy snipers hidden in trees. The tank won, and MacArthur and party left the jeeps and walked forward to inspect the scene. Two dead Japanese lay in a ditch. MacArthur remarked that they were probably part of a suicide outfit left to resist to the last. Intensely wary, Kenney and the others were "nodd[ing] nonchalantly (as possible)" when suddenly a photographer standing right next to MacArthur collapsed to the ground with a sniper's bullet in his shoulder.

MacArthur nevertheless wanted to move even farther forward, which was enough for Kenney, one of the few people, if not the *only* person, in SWPA who would stand up to the chief. He told MacArthur it was important to get back to the *Boise* in time for dinner; that as guests of the navy to do otherwise would be discourteous, and that the captain had promised to serve chocolate ice cream (MacArthur's favorite) for dessert.

This caused MacArthur to smile. He said, "All right, George, we'll go back. I wouldn't have you miss that chocolate ice cream for anything."[32]

★ ★ ★ ★

THERE IS AMPLE EVIDENCE that MacArthur favored giving the Soviet Union concessions in the Far East for revoking their treaty and declaring war on Japan, but when he learned of the extent of the compromises agreed to by President Roosevelt at the Yalta Conference he professed to be "shocked."

Neither MacArthur nor other top military commanders were informed of the Manhattan Project, the ultra-top-secret undertaking to build an atomic bomb. They were told of the existence of the bomb only a few days before the first one was dropped on the Japanese city of Hiroshima. Ten days earlier, at a top-level conference at Potsdam, Germany, the Allies had issued an ultimatum for Japan to either surrender or become, as it did in MacArthur's words, "the victim of the most destructive and revolutionary weapon in the long history of warfare."

Two days after the first bomb was dropped the Soviet Union declared war on Japan and the day after that a second U.S. atomic bomb destroyed the Japanese city of Nagasaki. That was enough for the Japanese government, which despite violent internal opposition agreed to the terms of surrender offered by the Allies.

The Truman administration picked MacArthur to preside over the formal surrender ceremonies, which were set for early September 1945. MacArthur's staff was "unutterably opposed" to his plan of flying into Atsugi air base, near Yokohama, which was home to a large renegade band of kamikaze pilots who only days before had revolted against the surrender, stormed the palace grounds, and murdered the commanding general of the emperor's Imperial Guard, among others. With this in mind the Japanese military had entered the air base and removed the propellers from all of the aircraft.

Nevertheless on August 30 MacArthur landed at Atsugi in his C-54 *Bataan* in the shadow of what his military secretary recorded as Japan's "greatest opportunity for a final and climactic act." Taking note of the many antiaircraft batteries surrounding the airfield and Japan's flagrant disregard for "the usual laws of war," Brigadier General Courtney Whitney was genuinely surprised when they were not blown out of the sky, and only after they were safely on the ground did he concede that MacArthur had been right not to worry about treachery. "He knew the basic Japanese character too well to have thus gambled blindly with death."[33]

Smoking his corncob pipe, MacArthur left the plane and met General Eichelberger who had arrived a day earlier. "Well Bob," he said, "from Melbourne to Tokyo is a long way, but this seems to be the end of the road."

They were soon met by what Whitney called a string of "the most decrepit vehicles I have ever seen." It was, however, the best means of transportation the Japanese could assemble for their ride to Yokohama's New Grand Hotel, which would be the Allied headquarters for the time being. All along the tedious fifteen-mile drive past heaps of bombed-out rubble tens of thousands of armed Japanese soldiers stood at attention with their backs to MacArthur in the same "gesture of respect" they showed to their emperor.[34]

That evening, MacArthur was just sitting down to dinner when word came that General Wainwright was in the hotel lobby. Rising immediately, MacArthur strode toward the door when suddenly there was "Skinny" Wainwright, whom MacArthur had left in command at Bataan in 1942 and who had suffered horribly for three years in a Japanese prisoner of war camp. He was shriveled and walked with the aid of a cane.

"He made an effort to smile," MacArthur said, moved to tears, "his hair was snow white and his skin looked like old shoe leather." When MacArthur embraced his old friend, Wainwright began to choke up.

"He'd imagined himself in disgrace for having surrendered Corregidor," said MacArthur, and he believed that he would never hold active command again.

"Why Jim," MacArthur told him, shocked, "your old corps is yours whenever you want it." The emotion that shone on Wainwright's face at that moment haunted MacArthur until the day he died.[35]

★ ★ ★ ★

MacArthur was sent a formal surrender document approved by the highest authorities in Washington, but he was on his own as to what to say. To whom to say it, however, was a different matter—virtually a who's who of the entire Pacific war would be on hand to witness the momentous event, which was held aboard the battleship *Missouri* on September 2, 1945. Besides MacArthur's gang, there were bigwigs from every nation at war with Japan, plus Nimitz and Halsey from the navy, Jimmy Doolittle from the air force, and some chiefs of the services, while nearly every foot of deck space was occupied—even the turrets and long barrels of the 16-inch guns—by jubilant sailors from the fleet.

The Japanese delegation was a woebegone lot; for a nation that made idolization of pride a matter of personal honor these high-ranking militarists and diplomats suffered the uttermost humiliation imaginable. No one would volunteer for the "odious duty" and so selections had to be made, the choice to represent the diplomatic mission falling at last on Foreign Minister Mamoru Shigemitsu and, to stand for the military, General Yoshijiro Umezu, a die-hard militarist who threatened to commit hara-kiri if forced to sign a surrender treaty.

These two men were accompanied by a dozen or so aides, the diplomats dressed somewhat formally in morning clothes with white gloves and incongruous-looking top hats, and appeared before the thronged deck of *Missouri* looking as embarrassed as if they had on no clothes at all. One of their number, a Japanese diplomat named Toshikazu Kase, a graduate of Amherst and Harvard, recorded the following reaction: "We waited for a few minutes standing in the public gaze like penitent boys awaiting the dreaded schoolmaster. Never have I realized that the glance of glaring eyes could hurt so much."

Beneath graying skies MacArthur, flanked by the pitifully thin generals Jonathan Wainwright and Arthur Percival (who had also endured the hardships of Japanese incarceration after the surrender of the British army at Singapore), stepped forward to the forum, which was an old mess table covered in green felt cloth.

"We are gathered here," MacArthur said to a live worldwide radio audience, "representatives of the warring powers, to conclude a solemn agreement whereby peace can be restored." He went on to note that the issues leading into the war had been settled on the battlefields, and that both the victors and the vanquished should put aside "hatreds and distrust" and "rise to that higher dignity" that peace would bring. "It is my earnest hope," he told the audience, "that a better world shall emerge out of the blood and carnage of the past—a world founded on faith and understanding—a world dedicated to the dignity of man and the fulfillment of his most cherished wish—for freedom, tolerance and justice." He then called for the two Japanese delegates to come forward and sign the document of surrender.

Shigemitsu, a peacemaker, clattered across the deck with his cane, limping heavily on his wooden leg, followed by a scowling General Umezu. They put their names on the peace treaty. MacArthur then signed it as Supreme Commander of all the Allied Powers and on behalf of the United States as well, giving Wainwright and Percival each a pen that he had used.* Then representatives of the other warring nations were invited

----

* General Yamashita had held out to the last in the Luzon mountains and surrendered his diminished army to American forces after the emperor's

to sign and MacArthur stepped to the microphone: "Let us pray now that peace be restored to the world and that God will preserve it always. These proceedings are closed."

"At that moment," Kase wrote afterward, "the skies parted and the sun shone brightly through the layers of clouds. There was a steady drone above and now it became a deafening roar and an armada of U.S. airplanes paraded into sight, sweeping over the warships." When the flights of thousands of planes had moved on, MacArthur stepped to the microphone for a final time.

"Today the guns are silent. A great tragedy has ended. A great victory has been won. The skies no longer rain death—the seas bear only commerce—men everywhere walk upright in the sunlight . . . In reporting this to you, the people, I speak for the silent lips forever stilled among the jungles and the beaches and in the deep waters of the Pacific which marked the way . . . We must go forward to preserve in peace what we won in war.

"A new era is upon us," MacArthur continued, his voice rising at its theatrical best. "The destructiveness of the war potential, through progressive advances in scientific discovery, has in fact now reached a point which revises the traditional concept of war . . . We have had our last chance. If we do not now devise some greater and more equitable system, Armageddon will be at our door." MacArthur's voice echoed across the decks of the battleship *Missouri* and into the homes of millions worldwide, dramatic, profound, stirring. It was statesmanlike MacArthur at his very best.

Then he turned to his soldiers' families listening at home, telling them, "Today I report to you that your sons and daughters have served you well and faithfully . . . Their spiritual strength and power has brought us through . . . They are homeward bound—take care of them."

....

broadcast on August 15. He did so in the presence of the Allied generals Wainwright and Percival who had been released from Japanese prison camps and flown to the Philippines for that purpose.

CHAPTER FOURTEEN

★ ★ ★ ★

OLD SOLDIERS NEVER DIE

The Second World War convulsed the earth in seismic proportions. In its wake men wished for peace in our time and a return to normalcy; instead, within a few years, it let loose a world again at war over the ideology of expansive communism and fierce religious animosities.

Enormous China resumed its civil war, which had been postponed during the Japanese occupation between the Communists of Mao Tse-tung and the ruling Nationalist Party of Chiang Kai-shek. In eastern Europe, the Balkans, and in Greece, the Soviet Union began undermining countries prostrated from the war by subversive infil-tration that often instigated civil wars. The Soviets installed puppet Communist governments in Romania, Bulgaria, Poland, and Hungary and were suspected of murdering the foreign minister of the Czech Republic by defenestration before that nation was also absorbed as a Soviet satellite.

In Greece, Soviets backed a Communist guerrilla army against the monarchy and were subverting the shaky governments of Italy and France. In Southeast Asia, the Communist guerrillas of Ho Chi Minh began waging war against the French after they had tried to reclaim their colonies following the Japanese occupation. The Soviets held North

Korea and would eventually attack the democratic South, drawing the United States and the United Nations into war. There were armed Communist insurgencies in Malaya and the Philippines. The African volcano had begun to smoke but had not yet erupted.

The British, French, and Dutch, who were bankrupted by the war, were forced to give up their great colonial empires, adding further unrest and strife: in India Muslims battled Hindus; in the Middle East there was fighting between Arabs and Jews; and in the South Seas a war broke out between the Dutch and their allies against Indonesians who wished for independence.

It was a rocky world and anyone attempting to navigate it was subject to being dashed. So it was with George Marshall, who wanted nothing more than to retire with his wife Katherine to his country home Dodona Manor, in Leesburg, Virginia, where he sometimes puttered in the garden or cleaned leaves from the gutters. He had stayed on as chief of the army's General Staff to preside over the demobilizing of the nine million soldiers under his command. More than two hundred thousand of them had been killed and nearly six hundred thousand wounded. Marshall had sent millions of jeeps and trucks into war surplus and consigned tens of thousands of military fighter planes and bombers to the scrap heap. A few years later during the Berlin blockade crisis when he was told to "give the Russians hell," he would say with no small touch of irony, "My facilities for giving them hell—and I am a soldier and know something about giving hell—were one and one third [infantry] divisions over the entire United States."[1]

Marshall retired from the army on November 18, 1945, and moved from his Quarters Number 1 at Fort Myer to Dodona. The day they arrived, Katherine went upstairs to take a nap and the phone rang. Marshall answered it. Later, when Katherine came downstairs, she found Marshall sitting in the sunroom listening to a newscast and was flabbergasted when it was announced that he had just been named Truman's new special ambassador to China. He would leave immediately.

"That phone call when we came in was from the president," Marshall said. "I could not bear to tell you until you had your rest."[2]

Truman prevailed on Marshall because he had decided the current ambassador was not getting anywhere in settling the fate of the largest country on earth with its half a billion citizens. The U.S. State Department had for some reason concluded that the Communist insurrection was so strong the only solution was to persuade Chiang Kai-shek to include the Communists in his government, and then to convince Mao and his deputy Chou En-lai to accept. Little did Marshall realize the utter impossibility of this approach.

Nearly everybody in the world had heard of the great George Marshall, including the Chinese—both Nationalist and Communist—and they would show him the utmost respect as he shuttled between Nationalist and Communist capitals in China touting the advantages of ending the civil war.

Each side agreed it would be a good thing, but neither side would stop fighting. Marshall continually threatened Chiang with withholding $500 million of U.S. aid, and Chiang would agree to yet another cease-fire. But within a few days the shooting would start once more. Marshall didn't have anything to threaten Mao with. It was maddening.

The Chinese Communists were more or less controlled by Moscow and to have Soviet-style communism in a democratic government was simply unworkable because the two ideologies are polar opposites—like putting a cobra and a mongoose in the same room and expecting them to get along.

But the U.S. State Department did not seem to comprehend that. Its representative appeared to view the Chinese Communists as a band of simple agrarian farmers who were merely seeking a better life. Thus, Marshall's instructions from Washington were to mend the fences between the two warring groups and inspire them with the spirit of cooperation.

He arrived in Shanghai right before Christmas 1945—his first trip back to China since his tour of duty there with the 15th Infantry Regiment in 1927. He was met by his friend Lieutenant General Albert Wedemeyer, the army's top military commander in China, who was generally accepted as an "old China hand."

When Wedemeyer learned of Marshall's mission he informed him it was fantastic, that there was no common ground for a coalition government between Nationalists and Communists, neither of whom trusted the good faith of the other. Marshall jumped down Wedemeyer's throat—"I am going to accomplish my mission and you are going to help me," he snapped.

As each so-call truce broke, Marshall's frustration grew. Chiang stated: "Can it be he has not yet understood the deceptive nature of Communist maneuvers? More and more he is being taken in by the Communists. The Americans tend to be naive and trusting. This is true even with so experienced a man as Marshall."

After a year, Marshall had to admit failure. He summed it up by saying, "I tried to please everyone. The result was that by the time I left nobody trusted me."

In January 1947 he returned to the United States where, as a consolation prize, Truman named him secretary of state. Now, instead of having just China to worry about, Marshall had the world, and it was on fire.

★ ★ ★ ★

THE MOST PRESSING PROBLEMS CONCERNED EUROPE, much of which had been exhausted by the war and was vulnerable to Communist destabilization. Marshall, like many Americans of his day, still was not ready to believe that the Russians could not be trusted. His immediate task was to preside over the U.S. delegation at the Moscow Conference over the future of Germany and Austria.

Two years earlier at the Potsdam Conference, the United States, Great Britain, France, and the Soviet Union split Germany into four zones of occupation. Surrender papers had been signed at the close of the war but now a peace treaty was needed to decide how best to get Germany back on its feet: its continued collapse with virtually no trade in either direction was dragging down its neighbors.

The U.S. position that Marshall argued was to allow Germany slowly to get back into manufacturing in nonmilitary-type goods, and with strict quotas on such military necessities as steel, rubber, glass, etc.* The Soviets rejected this proposal, demanding instead that all remaining German factories be dismantled and sent to the Soviet Union and that Germany be ruled by a strong central government (which could be easily subverted by Communists) and forced to pay the Soviet Union $20 billion in war reparations.†

Marshall patiently tried to explain to the Soviet negotiator, foreign minister Vyacheslav M. Molotov, that Germany was too important a nation in both natural and human resources to be made to lie idle; her recovery was necessary for reviving the fading health of Europe. In this he was flatly turned down by Molotov (of Molotov cocktail fame) who accused the United States and other Allies of trying to resurrect the "trusts and cartels" that caused the war in the first place, and once more he demanded half of the $20 billion reparations immediately, even if German homes and families had to be stripped of their possessions.

Marshall pointed out that if Germany were forced to pay reparations now, the United States would have to provide it aid, which would mean that in effect the reparations would be paid by the American taxpayer. But, like the others, this argument fell on deaf ears.

The talks deadlocked for weeks, and Marshall finally began to come to the conclusion that many had reached some time ago: the Soviets had no intention of cooperating with any plan that might help put capitalist western Europe back on its feet. In fact, the opposite was true; their interests lay in a poverty-stricken Europe all the more vulnerable to Communist entreaties or subversion.

Marshall's naivete vis-à-vis the Russians is difficult to understand. Perhaps the best explanation is that, during the war, the Soviet Union were allies, and as such were relatively easy to work with—even if somewhat demanding and strange. From the Russian Revolution of 1917 until

---

* A widely circulated American proposal formulated by Secretary of the Treasury Henry Morgenthau would have turned Germany into a virtual sheep pasture, with *no* industrial capability whatsoever.

† Nearly $1.5 trillion in today's dollars.

World War II, Communist Russia had been a kind of black hole from which little light had emanated, but it was not known as a particularly expansive or dangerous country.

In fact, it had engaged in a good deal of espionage in the United States through its affiliate Communist Party USA, confirming the age-old maxim that friends do not spy on friends. But after war broke out this same Soviet Union burst upon the world as a victim of Hitler's duplicity (putting aside for a moment the fact that it had only recently signed a mutual nonaggression pact with the Nazi government) and became in the American mind a friend and ally against a wicked foe. It emerged from the war as a major world power but, to the consternation of many, began gobbling up its neighbors and exporting communism at a cosmic rate. It took a while for some to appreciate that—including George C. Marshall.

In those early years following the war, Marshall seemed somehow unable or unwilling to grasp the concept that, far from being allies, the Russians had now become rapacious enemies, and dangerous. He took seriously his change of missions from being America's top military man—who had trained most of his life not only to project power but to use it—to becoming America's top diplomat, who believed that with diplomacy he could sweet-talk the Russians into being reasonable toward their fellow Allies' point of view. Or perhaps he was simply not ready to believe they were a menace.

The final straw was over Austrian reparations. Molotov wanted to strip the country of all its manufacturing, which the Austrians had barely gotten repaired and running again since the war ended. American military administrators in Germany and Austria, who had been dealing with the Soviets on a daily basis for nearly two years, were for taking a hard line with the Russians, but the State Department was inclined to appease them. Marshall felt caught in the middle. He knew and trusted the generals who were governing the former Axis countries but was loath to go against the diplomats who advised giving Russia what she asked.

General Mark Clark, one of Marshall's old friends and the military administrator of Austria, was adamant about not letting the Communists strip the country. They had already pillaged millions of dollars' worth of factories, he said, "then left them to rust away on railroad sidings on the frontiers of the Soviet Union." Moreover, Clark might have been furious at the Communists for having discovered that rooms at the U.S. embassy in Moscow were bugged. He handed Marshall a position paper, which everyone knew the Russians would not agree to. "I've been working with these devils for two years," he told the secretary of state to his face, "and you can no more give in to them than the man in the moon. If you do you will sacrifice all we've been fighting for, what thousands of men have died for."[3]

At the conference that afternoon, as Molotov continued denouncing the United States and Great Britain, Marshall pulled out Clark's position paper and read it. The Soviet minister walked out and the conference ended in a deadlock, the last formal conference the United States would have with the Russians for fifteen years.[4]

★ ★ ★ ★

WHILE HE WAS IN EUROPE, Marshall traveled around and was appalled by what he saw—wrecked homes and buildings, people on the verge of starvation, inflation, recession, black markets, begging in the streets, and black despair. He began to realize that if something were not done to alleviate the situation Europe might fall into the abyss.

By this time, following the death of Franklin Roosevelt, politically, the honeymoon was over for Harry S. Truman. Marshall knew that, in the present air of austerity, Congress was unlikely to make any large appropriations in the president's name to assist the situation in Europe. So on June 5, 1947, at the graduation ceremonies at Harvard where he was receiving an honorary degree, Marshall surprised the world by announcing the need for a European recovery program led by the United States.

It was broad, expansive, and expensive. All European nations were invited to participate, including the Soviet Union and its new satellites, though Marshall added, "Any government that maneuvers to block the recovery of other countries cannot expect help from us."

The Europeans that applied for help, he said, must come up with their own plan, and America would support the program "as far as it may be practical for us to do so."

European reporters had been alerted to the speech and it caused a great stir in the press. One of Truman's advisers suggested to his boss it ought to be named the Truman Plan, but the president was politically savvy enough to know that would be difficult if not impossible to get past the Republicans in Congress. "Call it the Marshall Plan," Truman said.

Marshall testified before the appropriations committee and, shortly afterward, the money was forthcoming. Americans had read of the destitution in Europe and were in the mood to help. In the end, seventeen countries participated to the tune of $17 billion over four years.* The Marshall Plan was credited with speeding the European recovery by perhaps a decade. The Soviet Union declined to participate and refused to let its satellite countries do so, dooming them to even more backwardness than the Communist economic system that held them down. Marshall for the second time became *Time*'s Man of the Year in 1947, and six years later he was awarded the Nobel Peace Prize for his postwar work.

★ ★ ★ ★

THE FOLLOWING YEAR, the British mandate to administer Palestine—stemming from an Allied decision after World War I—was set to expire on May 15, 1948, and the Palestinian Jews were prepared to partition the country and establish a Jewish state. Marshall was staunchly against the idea. He worried about alienating the oil-rich Middle East countries, which might cut the oil supply if the United States supported the Jews. He also worried that the Russians would find ways to exploit Arab unrest, but foremost—and he was vocal about it—he feared that

---

* More than $1 trillion in today's dollars.

a massacre was inevitable given that Jews in Palestine were outnumbered about one hundred to one by Arabs in the region, who also were heavily armed.

"You have Arab states all around you," Marshall told a Jewish leader referring to a map, "and your backs are to the sea." Should the Jews partition, "then war would surely come," he said. Then, Marshall predicted, the United States would probably have to intervene on a humanitarian basis to prevent annihilation, "which had no logic in terms of [American] foreign policy."

Truman, however, facing a tough reelection campaign, believed he needed the Jewish vote in several key states. Against the wishes of his departments of state and defense and the Joint Chiefs of Staff he decided he would recognize Israel, should it apply for membership in the United Nations. Marshall strongly disapproved and said so to the president, who responded, "Well, General, it sounds like even you might vote against me."

"Yes, Mr. President," Marshall replied, "if in the election I was to vote, I would vote against the president."[5]

The next day, Israel declared independence and the United States recognized it—the first nation to do so. Fighting had already begun in the streets of Jerusalem.

★ ★ ★ ★

AT THIS SAME TIME, the Soviet Union spitefully ordered a full blockade of Berlin, threatening starvation for citizens in the western occupied zones. The army administrator General Lucius D. Clay wanted to call the Russians' bluff by sending an armed convoy "to shoot its way in," if necessary, but Marshall turned that plan down. He didn't want the United States to fire the first shots of what might possibly become World War III. The Allies (Russia was semiofficially no longer a part of the group) managed to supply Berlin with an airlift, but the blockade was a major blow. The United States simply did not have the troops immediately available to fight a war.

As the tension reached a high point Marshall visited Bernard Baruch, who had been a close adviser to Roosevelt, and discussed using the atomic bomb against the Soviets, which he had also discussed with the president.

Shortly afterward, Baruch attended a meeting in Washington in which "powerful influences" were in favor of a preventive (atomic) war against the Russians. He asked Marshall's opinion, to which he responded with an Arab proverb that argued against such a notion. The America of this period had assumed the mantle of protector of the free world, and while the idea of using nuclear weapons on such a scale was abhorrent to the secretary of state, if nothing else it remains ironic that—as the nation's top diplomat—he was willing to entertain the idea.

In December, Marshall suddenly entered Walter Reed Hospital for a serious kidney operation that prompted his resignation as secretary of state. After a long but successful recovery, he began serving as president of the American Red Cross, a sinecure almost, when President Truman came calling once again. His secretary of defense, it seemed, had turned out to be a fractious, incompetent political hack that needed replacing. Who else but George C. Marshall was competent enough to do the job?

With his usual misgivings, Marshall dutifully accepted the appointment and was sworn in September 21, 1950, just in time for, of all things, the Korean War.

At the end of World War II, it will be recalled, Korea was divided north and south between the Soviet-backed Communist regime of the original Kim Il Sung and the Democratic South Korean government of Syngman Rhee, backed by the United States. In June 1950, after endless provocations, the North Korean army, directly sponsored by the Soviet and Chinese Communists, invaded the South and pushed the South Korean army into a defensive perimeter near Pusan where it teetered on the verge of collapse.

MacArthur, who remained the supreme commander in the Far East, seemed as surprised as anyone. His Eighth Army, stationed in Japan, was a shell of its former presence during the war. However, MacArthur proved yet again that he was a soldier to be reckoned with.

During this period, Marshall concerned himself primarily with organizing American fighting units and equipment to rush to Korea. He had little contact with MacArthur owing to his long-standing dictum of allowing the commanding officer on the ground to run his campaign as he saw fit.

★ ★ ★ ★

THE ATMOSPHERE IN AMERICA, as the 1950s began, teemed with frustration and mistrust over the Communist menace. China had been "lost" and people were struggling with who or what to blame. In the face of a Communist onslaught, Chiang Kai-shek and his Nationalists had fled to the large island of Formosa, while Mao Tse-tung solidified his grip on the world's largest country and closed out international discourse.

Through the machinations of Soviet spies, the Russians now had the atomic bomb, which terrified everyone; schoolchildren regularly underwent A-bomb drills in which they would hide under their school desks. Tens of thousands of Americans had been killed in the Communist-inspired Korean War with no end in sight. Congressional committees were formed in both houses to investigate "un-American activities." The U.S. State Department came in for special condemnation for allegedly housing disloyal bureaucrats and diplomats. But it came as a great surprise when George C. Marshall was sucked into the Red-scare vortex.

On June 15, 1951, Senator Joseph McCarthy, a Wisconsin Republican, delivered a damning sixty-thousand-word speech to Congress in which he accused Marshall—with Truman and the present secretary of state Dean Acheson as fellow dupes—with what amounted to treason. Specifically Marshall was accused of "losing" China and aiding the Soviets in their international takeovers. The accusations were mostly disparaged in the mainstream press, but it began a controversy that painted Marshall as at best a dupe and, at worst, a traitor. Newspapers variously described the speech as "scurrilous," "a smear marathon," "new outburst of misstatements," "character assassination." Others—respectable publications such as the *Washington Times-Herald*—had this to say: "We will

place a small bet . . . that not one of those who have been calling Joe
McCarthy names since June 15 has actually done the basic homework
job of reading the speech itself . . . The writer of this editorial has read
McCarthy's speech and finds it a challenge that will have to be met and
dealt with, sooner or later."

Marshall was characteristically silent when asked to respond to the
charges. "If I have to explain at this point that I am not a traitor to the
United States," he told the columnist Clayton Fritchie, "I hardly think
it's worth it."

In September 1951, Marshall told President Truman he was resigning
as secretary of defense. Marshall's official biographer Dr. Forrest Pogue
speculates that the China controversy may have prompted Marshall's
decision. Nevertheless, for years afterward it was a cliché among Washington bureaucrats and diplomats looking to fill some office or other to
say, "We need someone like General Marshall; but there *is* no one like
General Marshall."[6]

★ ★ ★ ★

MEANWHILE MARSHALL HAD ACCEPTED Truman's offer to become
chairman of the American Battle Monuments Commission. In 1952 he
and Katherine journeyed on the SS *United States* to Europe to inspect
American monuments in Normandy and elsewhere. There was a poignant moment at Anzio when Katherine laid a dozen red roses on her
son Allen's grave. The next June, Marshall returned overseas heading the
delegation to the coronation of Queen Elizabeth II, whom he had met
with her father, George VI, during the war. As he walked with Omar
Bradley, a fellow delegate, down the famous aisle of Westminster Abbey,
Marshall noted that the bejeweled and bemedaled royalty of the world
had begun standing up, as if a bride were entering the hall. "What are
they rising for?" he whispered.

"You," Bradley told him.[7]

Marshall's remaining years were a mixture of pleasure upon receiving any number of guests at Dodona Manor and illness, which

eventually drove him down. He began using a cane and was in and out of hospitals. In 1959, he entered Walter Reed for the last time and sank into a coma. He died on October 16 at the age of seventy-eight. His body lay in Washington's National Cathedral accompanied by an honor guard from VMI, as well as military representatives from each of the services. Thousands of citizens, great and small, came to pay their respects.

Only family and a few select guests—President Truman and President Eisenhower among them—were invited to the Episcopal funeral service the next day in the Fort Myer chapel.* There was no eulogy at Marshall's request. Burial was at Arlington National Cemetery near the Tomb of the Unknown Soldier. The funeral party remained seated in the chapel when they heard the rifle volley, followed by a bugler's taps. He had come a long way, this boy from Uniontown, Pennsylvania, who had no small hand in changing a world that had evolved beyond almost everyone's wildest imagination.

★ ★ ★ ★

THE END OF THE WAR HIT George Patton hard. Except on those occasions he'd been called on the carpet by Eisenhower, he'd been having the time of his life doing what professional soldiers do—kill the enemy. "Another war has ended," he wrote, "and with it my usefulness to the world. For me, personally, it is a very sad thought."

He tried to inveigle an assignment to fight in the Pacific but instead was sent home for a U.S. War Bonds public relations tour of America. When he arrived at the airport outside Boston, Patton was first off the plane and strode across the runway where Beatrice and the family were waiting. Taking off his helmet, he kissed her and she said to reporters, "When he left me two years and seven months ago, he said he expected to die fighting. It seems like a miracle that he's come back."[8]

* For what it's worth, the author's parents were married there, in 1942.

The whirlwind tour went coast to coast and Patton was mobbed by crowds everywhere—his appearance at the Los Angeles Coliseum drew a hundred thousand people. He "wept, swore, and roared out for the defeat of Japan." He visited many military hospitals to speak to wounded troops. He was well received everywhere and, when the month was out, he returned to Germany.

The change in Patton was noticeable and dramatic, not just his physical appearance—which was older, lined, grayer—but something in his personality. "He was more mature, quieter," said a relative. "I even sensed a new element of grandeur about him."

Before he left Patton, who had always had a clairvoyant, almost supernatural aura surrounding him, had a premonition. He said to his daughters, "Well, goodbye girls, I won't be seeing you again. Take care of [son] George. I'll be seeing your mother, but I won't be seeing you."

One of them reminded him the war was finished, and that he was being foolish.

"No, I mean it," he said. "I have a feeling that my luck has run out at last."[9]

Patton returned to the Third Army in Germany, which was then "the largest army in history," nearly half a million men, some twenty-seven divisions of between 15,000 and 20,000 men each, which was then in the process of redeployment to the United States for a planned invasion of Japan.

But Patton was depressed over the future of Europe, which he believed would go Communist, an ideology he feared would spread to America. "If there ever was a war breeder," he wrote Beatrice, "it is the Europe of today. Russia is just like the French Republic of 1870. Germany is out. The Czechs hate everyone. The French are Communistic. The British are fools. And we, God knows."

It certainly seemed Patton was on to something. The Soviets were a huge armed presence in Germany—menacing and acquisitive—and the United States was pulling out. The German national government was nonexistent, its economy stalled entirely, the cities in ruins, and millions of homeless and displaced persons were on the edge of starvation.

The Russians were shoving in millions of Poles who they wanted out of Poland.

In August, Patton was put in charge of the government of Bavaria, the largest state in Germany. Since Hitler had taken power twelve years earlier nearly every political post large and small had been occupied by a member of the Nazi party or those who acquiesced. But in the summer of 1945 Eisenhower ordered every political and civil office, as well as other positions of importance, purged of Nazi party members by comparing them to a list of some 8.5 million German Nazis. Patton was in the United States at the time and it is unclear whether he saw Ike's directive.* In any case, in an age before computers, this was a stupendous task in itself.

The problem was that de-Nazification created the kind of vacuum in the administration of government services that Patton abhorred. He didn't like Nazis any less than anyone else—witness his treatment of the captured SS general whom he "browbeat with pleasure"—but it became his opinion that aside from the original hard-core members of the party, many small-time, nonpolitical Germans had joined in order to keep their businesses going or because they had been ordered to join by party members.

For them, Patton said, paying dues was akin to "blackmail," and he was disinclined to remove some of these people from public service because of the disruption it would cause. In the autumn of 1945, Patton faced a desperate situation for the Bavarians, as did most of the other U.S. commanders occupying German states. Food was scarce and winter was coming. It was too late to plant. There was no coal stockpiled from the mines and the threat of people freezing to death was very real. Patton had resourcefully ordered German prisoners under his command to cut enough wood from the forests to heat one room in every Bavarian household for the entire winter. This astounding task was completed in time for the first snowfall.

---

* Whether he did or did not, Ike reminded Patton of it in a letter dated September 11.

In between de-Nazifying and other organizational duties, Patton enjoyed himself by reviewing Third Army divisions that were headed back to the States, visiting historic sites, sailing, fishing, and hunting everything under the sun—deer, ducks, geese, Hungarian partridges, pheasant, *auerhahn* (grouse), and chamois (mountain antelope). These expeditions were usually undertaken from the fabulous country estates of German royalty or Junker noblemen and accompanied by guides, beaters, throwers, skinners, gun handlers, and other minions of the wealthy who had not been displaced by the war.

Patton occupied a magnificent house on one of Bavaria's picturesque lakes formerly owned by a Nazi official. It featured a pool, squash and tennis courts, a bowling alley, and magnificent art and Persian carpets, among other amenities. To be a U.S. military officer in Germany during the immediate occupation after the fighting had ended—especially one of Patton's rank and reputation—was about as close to being royalty that any commoner would ever experience.

But, in Patton's own words, "all good things must come to an end." And so came the beginning of that end following a press conference at Third Army headquarters on Saturday morning, September 22, 1945, when a group of reporters asked if they could have a personal meeting with the commanding general. Patton agreed.

During the war, Patton's appearances at press conferences were an enjoyable experience for both him and the reporters. He had developed a certain rapport with those correspondents attached to his command; the Americans were winning the war, moving forward, and Patton always gave them enough stimulating material in colorful language to fill up their columns.

Now, after the surrender, a new type of reporter appeared looking for stories. The reporters did not particularly care whether the stories helped or harmed the U.S. Army; undoubtedly in some cases they were actively hostile to the army and what it stood for.

Four of these newcomers were Raymond Daniell and his wife, Tania, both of the *New York Times;* Carl Levin of the New York *Herald Tribune;* and Edward P. Morgan of the Chicago *Daily News.* They had heard of the upcoming press conference and driven in from Nuremberg the previous evening. These were not regular Third Army reporters and did not have any loyal attachment to the army or to Patton. Quite the opposite, in fact, for they had heard rumors that Patton was not living up to the letter or the spirit of the de-Nazification program.

It is necessary to digress here for a moment to set the stage for what happened later. Patton, by some accounts, was anti-Semitic. Since shortly after the dawn of Christianity, Jews occupied a separate and often secondary place in the Christian world picture, and that included in the minds of most Americans and Europeans of Patton's era. Hitler's Nazism was the ultimate, hideous extension of this unfortunate outlook and it remains a bitter irony that it took that awful level of Nazi persecution to bring about changing attitudes toward the Jews, by society in general, many governments, and a previously, mostly indifferent world.

Patton's anti-Semitism was limited to opinion rather than overt discrimination; in fact, he kept a number of trusted Jewish officers on his staff and was genuinely fond of the educated, refined, and powerful Jews whose paths he crossed, such as Bernard Baruch or Major General Maurice Rose (who commanded the Third Armored Division in First Army and became, unfortunately, the highest-ranking American soldier killed by enemy fire in the European theater).

To Patton's discredit, however, he reserved a flagrant scorn for the pitiful surviving Jewish inmates of the Nazi camps who in his opinion did not recover their humanity as quickly as other groups did. The Jews preferred, Patton said, to live in filth and squalor even though his army had provided them with sanitary facilities, clothing, proper meals, etc. In his diary he compared them with "sub-human animals," and doubted they would ever become fit to rejoin society.

It was ungracious and uncharacteristic of Patton, who was generally a kind person. Perhaps it could be explained as a function of the innate snobbery that stemmed from his wealthy, Episcopal upbringing or related somehow to his compulsive military orderliness. Yet he simply refused to understand how or why people who had been so subjugated and degenerated for years could not snap out of it and return to normalcy once they were liberated. Apparently he considered it a sign of racial or moral weakness, similar, in its way and in his mind, to the slapping incident, a personal opinion that reflected Patton's "bootstrap mentality," the lens through which he saw all matters of war. In any case it was a callous and unbecoming attitude.

But there were other factors at work having to do with his growing hostility toward the Russian Communists and their continued attempts to subvert European governments.

Patton became certain that the United States would one day have to go to war with the Soviet Union and was in favor of getting it over then and there while the forces were present to do so. Because there appeared to him to be a disproportionate number of Jews in Communist groups or "progressive" organizations sympathetic with the worldwide Communist movement, Patton began equating Jews with Communists and using the terms almost interchangeably. His hatred of communism during this period seemed to grow in direct proportion to his frustration in not being able to get Eisenhower or anyone else in power alarmed over the Soviet menace.

It was within this frame of reference that he met with the unfamiliar correspondents from the New York and Chicago newspapers. The press conference was long and boring. Patton didn't speak but let members of his staff do the talking while he sat brooding. Afterward, a number of staff papers were to be read and Patton rose as if to leave but the reporters intercepted him and he agreed to answer a few questions.

Major Ernest Deane, Patton's press officer, recalled that "things went wrong from the start." These reporters, the Daniells, Levin, and Morgan, were utterly unintimidated by Lieutenant General George S. Patton Jr. In fact, they were openly hostile to him, one moving in close so that he deliberately blew smoke in Patton's face. General Hobart "Hap" Gay, Patton's chief of staff, said the reporters "tried to put words in Patton's mouth." Patton's official biographer Martin Blumenson found another witness who stated that the reporters "made use of only partial truths, construed the answers to their questions to their own purposes and . . . tried to bring discredit upon General Patton." Deane added that another correspondent, friendly to the Patton camp, said at breakfast before the press conference that he "overheard three of them . . . plotting to needle the General and make him lose his temper."[10]

Apparently they succeeded, because at one point Patton became so frustrated with the interrogation-like questions of Levin that he responded, "Well, you're so smart you know everything, why ask me?"

The reporters bore in on Patton for retaining Dr. Fritz Schaffer as president-minister of Bavaria because he kept Nazis in his administration. Patton denied knowing anything about that. He told the newsmen that his de-Nazification program was proceeding apace, that in fact he had removed or blocked some forty-seven thousand former Nazis from government work.

The reporters countered that Dr. Schaffer was a "reactionary," who was too right wing to govern the state. (Schaffer, a lawyer by trade, had in fact been imprisoned by the Nazis in the Dachau concentration camp until the end of the war. He went on to hold several high posts in the German national government, including finance minister and minister of justice.)

Patton, who had not appointed Schaffer, denied knowing much about him, then one of the correspondents began ticking off "facts" about Schaffer's fitness to serve. That night Patton told his diary: "The temerity of the newspaper man in suggesting that he knew more about who we should have than I do—although I know nothing—made me mad which I think is what they wanted . . . The more I see of people I regret that I survived the war."

The next day's *New York Times* quoted Patton as saying, "The Nazi thing is just like a Democrat-Republican election fight." Of course the story was wired to every newspaper in the country, causing a great uproar of vituperation against General Patton and General Eisenhower as well. Editorial writers produced stories headlined: "General Patton Should Be Fired." Letters to the editor were published expressing outrage.

Light was shed on this matter a few days later by a highly respected journalist who had been president of the International News Service and a broadcast official at NBC. Frank E. Mason was in Germany on a special mission for former U.S. president Herbert Hoover and, several days after the press conference incident, wrote to Hoover and a few other prominent military and government officials that a number of American newspapers—including those where the Patton press conference correspondents worked—were apparently "trying to run interference for a Red government in Germany." These "radical journalists," Mason wrote, had attacked Patton in "a conspiracy to make sure that only those Germans who were acceptable to the Russians and the German Communists were appointed to local government posts in the American zone."

The clamor in the American newspapers naturally reached Eisenhower's headquarters. Ike phoned Patton and told him to hold another press conference to straighten out the misunderstanding about Democrats and Republicans being like Nazis.

Frank Mason attended this conference in which Patton apologized for any comparison of "so vile a thing as Nazism" with the American Democratic and Republican parties. Calling it an unfortunate analogy, Patton explained that in Germany practically all tradesmen, small businessmen, doctors and lawyers, government workers, and other professionals had been in some way beholden to the Nazi party, "which permitted them to carry on their businesses and professions." He said that if we kick them all out, it would so retard the reorganization of Bavaria "that we will certainly be guilty of death by starvation or freezing of women, children, and old men this winter."

Someone asked him, "General, aren't there some who consider Fritz Schaffer a Nazi?"

Patton again pointed out that Schaffer was picked before he got there, and said there was so far no evidence that he was a Nazi.

The next day the four correspondents—the Daniells, Levin, and Morgan—were in Eisenhower's headquarters a day's drive away, grilling his chief of staff Bedell Smith. "Do you think," Levin demanded, referring to Patton, "that the [de-Nazification] program can be carried out by people who are temperamentally and emotionally in disagreement with it?"

It was a scummy thing to do, but the reporters smelled blood and were determined to keep their stories on the front page. An unsigned memorandum attached to the transcript of the meeting stated: "It was a definite scheme [by the four reporters] to undermine and discredit General Patton. Their method was to sow seeds of doubt as to whether or not General Patton was loyal to General Eisenhower."

Headlines now read: "Patton Belittles de-Nazification Program." Accompanying editorials drew Eisenhower into the controversy, suggesting that he did not have his subordinates under control. Former Nazis, it was implied, were still running the German government in Bavaria.

In response, Eisenhower issued orders reiterating his original instructions—that former Nazis were to hold no positions other than as common laborers. And he sent a telegram to Patton saying, "I simply can't believe that these reports [about opposition to the de-Nazification program] are accurate." He asked Patton to take the first opportunity to fly up and see him for an hour.

Bad weather prevented Patton from going to Eisenhower's headquarters until September 29, when he finally decided to drive. It took seven and a half hours and when he arrived Ike "was quite friendly." But he gave Patton a long lecture on "keeping my mouth shut." Then Ike got around to the reason he had asked his old friend to come.

Eisenhower confided that if there had been some other appropriate command at the time, he would never have given Patton the military governorship of Bavaria. Then he suggested transferring Patton from command of his beloved Third Army to command of the Fifteenth Army, which was essentially a paper organization charged with writing a military history of the war. Patton was stunned; he suggested that Ike might simply relieve (or fire) him, but Eisenhower refused. He didn't want that for his old friend. When Patton argued that he should at least keep command of the Third Army, Ike told him that while he retained complete confidence in him he did not think Patton believed in his (de-Nazification) policies and that it would be best for him to transfer to the Fifteenth. The news correspondents had done their work.

In the moment Patton considered resigning, but he decided "[I] would become a martyr too soon." He took the job.

★ ★ ★ ★

At the Fifteenth Army, Patton's duties were mainly administrative, which gave him much leisure time for his favorite sports and pastimes. He also had been sitting for a majestic-looking oil portrait that was finished October 2. His feelings were hurt over his reassignment, but he got over it—yet he remained bitter about the journalists and continued to hate the Communists. For their part, many American newspapers carried front-page stories of Patton's "punishment" with the headline PATTON FIRED!

Regardless, he wrote his favorite brother-in-law Frederick Ayer to look for a quail-shooting plantation in northern Florida, Georgia, or the Carolinas, and he told Beatrice he was looking forward to sailing when he came home. Upon returning, he hoped to be made president of the Army War College. On October 11, on the occasion of Patton's pending sixtieth birthday, the staff of the Fifteenth Army threw a big party for him.

He wrote Beatrice that he had managed to secure passage across the Atlantic on the battleship USS *New York* and would be home on December 14, in time for Christmas. "I hate to leave the Army," he told her, "but what [else] is there?" He'd planned to shoot pigs that day, but it was too snowy. "I may see you before you see this," he added presciently. It was his final letter to Beatrice.[11]

On the morning of December 9, a Sunday, the day before he was to leave for the United States, Patton and his chief of staff Hap Gay were on the outskirts of Mannheim on their way to some pheasant hunting. They were riding in the rear of a 1938 army Cadillac limousine driven by Private First Class Harold L. Woodring. Woodring had stopped for a train before proceeding when he noticed "two 6 x 6 [two-and-a-half-ton 'deuce-and-a-half'] trucks approaching from the opposite direction." When they came near, Woodring testified, the first truck "just turned into my car."

It struck the Cadillac a sharp blow on its left front fender, knocking it back about ten feet. Gay and Woodring were unhurt, but Patton, sitting in the right rear, was thrown forward and up, striking his head hard on the railing that held the partition glass, which was rolled down at the time.

The blow gashed his forehead to the bone above the eyebrows, partially scalping him and stripping the skin off for three inches. He slumped back across Gay, who was still in his seat. Patton remained conscious "and swore a little," according to Woodring. He bled moderately, but that was not the extent of the damage. He couldn't move anything below his shoulders. He was paralyzed.

MPs arrived within a few minutes and sent for an ambulance that carried Patton to a military hospital near Heidelberg. As they cut off his clothing and began injecting him with plasma, for shock, and antibiotics he raised his head and chuckled, "Relax gentlemen, I'm in no shape to be a terror now." When a chaplain arrived Patton said, "Well, let him get started. I guess I need it."

Several neurosurgeons came in. When they saw Patton's X-rays they understood the gravity of his injury. Two vertebrae had been severely dislocated; there was too much swelling to tell the extent of damage to the spinal cord but it looked bad.

Beatrice left for Germany the day after the accident on a special plane that Eisenhower provided. Also aboard was Colonel Roy Glenwood Spurling, the army's leading specialist in neurosurgery. He had been on leave in the United States, but was summoned back on orders of the adjutant general.

When Spurling looked at the X-rays and consulted with the other doctors he concluded that Patton's condition was "precarious." Patients with that kind of injury seldom lived long. Nevertheless, this was George Patton. When Spurling visited him, Patton asked, "Man to man, what chance do I have to recover?" Spurling replied that he was doing far better than most patients with his type of injury and that it was impossible to tell at that time.

"What chance do I have to ride a horse again?" Patton offered.

"None."

Patton hesitated a moment, then said, "Thank you Colonel, for being honest."

Get-well messages flooded in from around the world, including those from President Truman, Eisenhower, and Winston Churchill. After a day Patton seemed to be getting better, giving the doctors hope that the spinal cord was not as badly damaged as they had feared.

From the beginning, Patton had been held in traction by something called Crutchfield hooks attached to his skull. They tended to slip, so the doctors inserted "large caliber fishhooks" beneath his cheekbones to relieve pressure. By the third day, Spurling said, improvement ceased. The doctors allotted him an ounce and a half a day of scotch whisky, Johnnie Walker Red, brought by a colonel, a friend. Beatrice was concerned about an embolism. He had almost died from one when he broke his leg in the 1930s. On December 20, it happened. X-rays showed an embolism in his right lung, which began to fill with fluid, and he had to use an oxygen mask to breathe.

Beatrice sat beside him that day and the next, as she had since she'd arrived, reading to him from the military histories that he loved—the glories of Rome and Greece. He slept more but was listless and privately told his nurse he was going to die. To Beatrice he said, somewhat incongruously, "I should have done better." Ever since he was a boy he'd always been striving.

On December 21, 1945, the army issued General Orders 685, signed by Patton's close friend General Geoffrey Keyes: "With deep regret, announcement is made of the death of General George S. Patton, Jr." The notion subsequently advanced by some—that Patton was assassinated—is too absurd to contemplate.

"Patton died as he lived," Dr. Spurling said, "bravely." A letter from a friend of Patton's daughter Ruth Ellen summed it up succinctly: "For him I think it is seemly that he rode out on the storm, and escaped the dullness of old age, while he was at the height of his fame."[12]

It was just so. There was a tremendous national outpouring of sympathy in the press and on the air. The old animosities were mostly forgotten, or at least brushed aside, and Patton returned to hero status with glowing praise and recitations of his prowess and feats of martial glory.

The night he died, daughters Bee and Ruth Ellen went to bed knowing only that their father was in grave condition. A little past midnight, which in Washington was the time Patton passed away, Bee's phone rang and a voice from what sounded like an overseas call said, "Little Bee, are you all right?"

"Daddy?" she asked. "Daddy . . ." But the line had gone dead. She called the overseas operator to reconnect but was told no such call had been made to her number.

Right about that same time, Ruth Ellen awoke to see her father lying across a bench in the bay window of her bedroom, in his uniform, with his head propped up on his arm. He gave "his very own smile," she said, and then he was gone. The next morning the two sisters spoke by phone and told each other what had happened. "I guess he's dead then," said Ruth Ellen. "Poor Ma," Bee said.[13]

Beatrice was calmly trying to make arrangements for the body to be shipped to the United States when Spurling, at the behest of General Keyes, took her aside and told her that, upon the orders of General Eisenhower, no deceased American soldier had been sent home since the war began.

"Of course he must be buried here," Beatrice cried. "Why didn't I think of it? I know George would like to lie beside the men of his Army."[14]

An Episcopal service of the Burial of the Dead was held in Heidelberg, after which the casket was put aboard a train for Hamm, Luxembourg, and its great American military cemetery. There, in a pouring rain, George S. Patton Jr. was buried on Christmas Eve among the graves of so many of his Third Army soldiers, beneath a simple white cross bearing only his name, rank, and serial number.*

In the years afterward Beatrice wrote to her "Georgie" on a regular basis, putting the letters in a desk drawer. Outwardly she was upbeat as usual but once wrote, "I cry from the back of my eyes." She kept up with the things she and Patton used to love—sailing, shooting, even foxhunting, which had always frightened her. "What I live from now on is extra," she said, "and if I get hurt it won't hurt anyone else."[15]

---

* In 1948 the grave would be moved to a more open space to accommodate the thousands of people who came to visit the site.

In 1953, on a crisp autumn day while riding in a foxhunt near her Massachusetts estate Green Meadows, Beatrice suddenly tumbled from her horse as the result of an aneurysm and died. She was cremated, at her wish, in order to be buried in the Luxembourg cemetery with her husband.

The army, however, did not allow civilians to be buried in its overseas military cemeteries, and so Beatrice's ashes were placed beneath a tree at Green Meadows until, several years later, son George,* Ruth Ellen, and her sixteen-year-old son around sundown visited the Luxembourg gravesite. Just as it became dark, Ruth Ellen removed a large brown envelope from her purse "and poured a stream of crumbly ashes into her palm." These she sifted through her fingers onto the grass on Patton's grave, recalling the verse from 2 Samuel that says: "In their death they were not divided: they were swifter than eagles, they were stronger than lions."[16]

★ ★ ★ ★

FOLLOWING THE JAPANESE SURRENDER ceremony aboard the battleship *Missouri,* Douglas MacArthur set up headquarters on the top floor of the six-story Dai-ichi Mutual Life Insurance building, which was one of the few structures in Tokyo still standing—likely because of its close proximity to the Royal Palace that MacArthur had forbidden the air force to bomb. From its windows he could look into the palace gardens, where Tokyo Rose had promised MacArthur would one day be hanged.

The task that lay before him was both Herculean and Solomonic. MacArthur would have absolute authority over a nation of 80 million souls whose cities, like Germany's, had been bombed to oblivion, and whose people were desperate and starving. But unlike Germany,

----

* George Patton IV graduated from West Point and became a great leader and hero in his father's footsteps during the wars in Korea and Vietnam, winning two Distinguished Service Crosses and retiring as a major general. He died in 2004.

Japan's people had "more nearly a feudal society," MacArthur said, "of the type discarded by Western nations four centuries ago"—a kind of theocracy in which the emperor was a divine being whose word was law. "There was no such thing as civil rights," he said. "There were not even human rights."[17] Anything could be taken away at any time—including your life.

After the war, the Japanese were jaded, apathetic, and tired. Not only was there no will to fight, there was no will to work. From one end of the island chain to the other, the country stagnated. The people were suffering from "national shell-shock," as General Kenney put it. "No one smiled. The people were not hostile to the occupying forces, they were just sullen. You got the idea that the people were waiting for something, but that they did not know what they were waiting for."[18]

The first two things MacArthur did were to liberate the Allied POW camps and round up and try Japanese war criminals. The most egregious of these—General Tojo, for instance, convicted of initiating the Pearl Harbor attack, and General Yamashita, whom MacArthur wrongly blamed for the destruction and wanton killing in Manila—were hanged. General Homma, of Bataan Death March infamy, was shot at his own request by firing squad. Some twenty-five major war criminals were put to death in this manner. Others received long prison sentences, and thousands of so-called militarists and their followers were, like the German Nazis, purged from government work, schools, and other responsible employment.

Some four million Japanese soldiers were brought home from China and the far-flung islands of what had been the Imperial Japanese Empire and demobilized. The army was disarmed and dispersed on MacArthur's order and the means for making war destroyed. Likewise, the Kempeitai, or "thought police," the Japanese equivalent of the Gestapo, were disbanded; Japanese military secret societies that had wielded extraordinary political powers were abolished. The people were told they were free to think or say anything they wished.

Shinto, or worship of the emperor as a state religion, was abolished without a peep from the people. MacArthur ignored a clamor from some quarters—notably the Soviet Union—to try the emperor with a mind toward hanging him. Members of MacArthur's staff urged him to call on the emperor "as a show of power," but this MacArthur declined. He was certain that in time the emperor would come to visit him.

He was right. One day the emperor appeared, wearing of all things a cutaway, striped pants, and a silk top hat. MacArthur broke the ice by reminding him that he, himself, as a young army lieutenant, had been received by the emperor's father when he and his own father paid a visit to Japan in 1906 at the close of the Russo-Japanese War. The emperor, to MacArthur's astonishment, said that he had come "to bear sole responsibility for every political and military action taken by my people in the conduct of war." He was in fact offering himself up as the top war criminal.

"A tremendous impression swept me," MacArthur wrote afterward. "This courageous assumption of a responsibility implicit with death . . . moved me to the very marrow of my bones. In that instant I knew I faced the First Gentleman of Japan in his own right."[19]

On New Year's Day, 1946, Emperor Hirohito made a national radio speech declaring that he was not divine and that the Japanese "should not consider themselves a superior race with a mission to dominate the world." Kenney pointed out, somewhat snidely, that most Japanese had privately reached that conclusion on August 14, 1945 (the day of Japan's unconditional surrender to the Allies).[20]

Having thus cleaned house, MacArthur embarked on the task of rebuilding and rejuvenating the country in an image he felt would be peaceful and prosperous among the community of nations. He was well aware of the ill-fated history of conquerors occupying foreign lands— including the blunders of Caesar and Napoleon—and was determined to allow the Japanese as much leeway as possible as quickly as possible to generate an economy.

In the back of every Japanese mind was the notion that Americans were a rapacious robbing, raping, murdering class of thugs, a propaganda theme that had been drummed into them since the war began. Thus, early upon his arrival, MacArthur issued a public statement: "[America] is not concerned about how to keep Japan down, but how to get her on her feet again."

Baron Kijuro Shidehara, a respected diplomat, was appointed prime minister and a governing arrangement was contemplated along the lines of the British parliamentary system. To initiate reforms, MacArthur instructed Shidehara to get with his people and draw up a constitution— actually a revision of an existing constitution—similar in nature to the Constitution of the United States. But, as many people have pointed out, it was one that belied the heavy hand of MacArthur himself in its language. It was astonishingly liberal from the Japanese point of view, for the people had been under the relentless thumb of the military for as long as anyone could remember.

Women, for example, for the first time were given the right to vote. People were for the first time granted rights similar to those in the U.S. Bill of Rights—freedom of speech, thought, assembly, and religion. The Japanese press, which had long been constrained by total censorship, was now unleashed.

The big Japanese family financial and industrial clans were broken up—Mitsubishi, Toyoda, etc.—as were the feudal landowning families. The peasant farmer class was given small ownership allotments of land, thus turning them into instant capitalists. In addition, MacArthur ordered the school curriculum liberalized, encouraged labor unions, and abolished child labor practices.

Soon Japan began to come alive. Its heavy industry was destroyed but it began making toys and china pottery to sell abroad. These items started to appear in U.S. five-and-dime stores marked "Made in Occupied Japan."

The Russians and British had been pushing to divide Japan into three zones of occupation, as had been done in Germany, but MacArthur refused to allow it on grounds of the disappointing mess that dividing Germany had continued to cause. The Russians were persistent, but after the Potsdam Conference had turned out in favor of the Soviets, MacArthur was determined not to let the Russians "have any part in the control of Japan."

Prime Minister Shidehara sought an audience with MacArthur to test a novel idea. When the new constitution was finalized, he said, the framers would like to include a clause that actually abolished war. MacArthur was in full concurrence.

"For years," he told the prime minister, "I have believed that war should be abolished as a means of resolving disputes between nations. Probably no living man has seen as much of war and destruction than I have. I have fought with or against the soldiers of practically every country and my abhorrence reached its height with the perfection of the atomic bomb." Shidehara was so overcome by MacArthur's answer that he had to leave the office. Tears rushed down his face, and he turned and said, "The world will laugh and mock us as impractical visionaries, but a hundred years from now we will be called prophets."[21]

A general election was held on April 10, 1946. Thirteen million women registered to vote for the first time, which "changed the whole complexion of Japanese political life," MacArthur said. "Farmers, teachers, laboring men and doctors now sat in the house once dominated by lawyers and industrialists."

The day after the results were announced, however, MacArthur received a call from an extremely dignified but distraught Japanese legislator. "I regret to say that something terrible has happened," the man said. "A prostitute, Your Excellency, has been elected to the House of Representatives."

"How many votes did she receive?" MacArthur inquired.

"Two hundred and fifty-six thousand," came the embarrassed answer.

"Then I should say there must be more than her dubious occupation involved," MacArthur told the chagrined politician.[22]

The inclusion of women in the electorate boded for larger reforms. There had been no coeducation of women in Japan but women now sought equality of education and got it, as well as maternity leave, abolition of contract marriages, and the end of "concubinage."

Because the agricultural and transportation systems had completely broken down, MacArthur in the first year of occupation had to import some three and a half million tons of food from the United States to keep the people from starvation. The financial system had also disintegrated, and the national debt was astronomical. MacArthur decided to start over, beginning with a more equitable revision of the income tax laws.

MacArthur's promotion of labor unions got off to a sensational start. By 1947 there were approximately twenty-five thousand unions in Japan, divided into leftist and rightest groups—the former often infiltrated by Communists who continued to give MacArthur trouble. The unions often went on strike, with occasional bemusing results. In a theatrical union, a chorus line went on half-strike by kicking only half as high as they usually did. A railroad union broadcast its disapproval by blowing the whistle on all the trains in Japan at the same time for a full minute.

★ ★ ★ ★

In 1948, the Republic of Korea, a capitalist democracy, was proclaimed south of the 38th parallel, with Syngman Rhee as its president. Its status as an independent nation was recognized by the new United Nations, of which it became a member. But in neighboring China events were not proceeding as well. Chiang Kai-shek continued to battle the Communists who, MacArthur said sarcastically, were still known to the U.S. State Department as "agrarian reformers." Slowly Chiang's troops had given way, until at last, in 1949, they were forced onto the large island of Formosa (Taiwan) more than a hundred miles off the Chinese coast.

MacArthur railed publicly and privately that the entire U.S. mission in the Far East had been compromised. He pointed out that since November 26, 1941, the fundamental policy of the U.S. government was the independence of China, and that this (among other policy statements) led directly to the Japanese attack on Pearl Harbor. He lamented the reversal of that policy to a strategy of appeasement of the Red Chinese and predicted that "its consequences will be felt for centuries and its disastrous effects on the fortunes of the free world are yet to be unfolded."[23]

In the dark early morning of June 25, 1950, MacArthur answered the phone in his quarters to be told by the duty office that hordes of North Korean troops, spearheaded by a legion of Soviet-made tanks, had crashed through the border at the 38th parallel. They were sweeping aside South Korean defenses and overwhelming all opposition. MacArthur, who recalled a similar dead-of-night phone call a decade before in Manila, was furious—and not just at the Communists.

His Eighth Army occupying Japan was only a shell of a complete army prepared for combat. His intelligence section had for months been warning of an intense buildup of North Korean troops (Korean People's Army or KPA) at South Korea's border. It fell on deaf ears at the American State Department and White House. Five years earlier, America was by far the strongest country in the world militarily, a virtual arsenal of democracy, that had now, according to MacArthur, "been frittered away in a bankruptcy of courageous leadership."

South Korea had four infantry divisions but, at the behest of the U.S. State Department, they were lightly equipped with no tanks, artillery, air force, or navy—to keep them from attacking the North Koreans. This, MacArthur said, of course encouraged the North Koreans, and now the South was reaping the whirlwind. The United Nations—with Russia unable to veto because it was boycotting the UN in protest of its recognition of China's national government—voted to help South Korea resist aggression. President Truman interpreted this to mean immediate military assistance by United States naval and air forces.

MacArthur was tasked with the job.

On June 28 he climbed aboard the *Bataan* and flew to Korea, landing thirty miles south of Seoul, the capital, which could be seen burning in the distance. In a commandeered jeep, he then headed toward the scene of battle, arriving at the Han River to encounter the last vestiges of the defeated and disorganized South Korean army, preceded by tens of thousands of refugees, who clogged the roads in a great "writhing, dust-shrouded mass of humanity."

MacArthur telegraphed Washington that, given the force and power of the North Korean thrust, only the inclusion of U.S. ground forces could stop the enemy advance. The next day Truman authorized it, and America went to war on the policy statement of a president, with no congressional debate or approval.

MacArthur's only chance was more a tactic than a strategy: to commit his army piecemeal as fast as he could from Japan to Korea. The Eighth Army contained four divisions, each understrength by about one-third, with light, not heavy, tanks and light, not heavy, artillery. The 24th Division was landed in Korea first. Without adequate antitank and heavy weapons to match the two hundred Russian tanks the North Koreans employed, they fought a running delaying action southward and lost nearly five thousand men killed, wounded, or captured. They managed to form and hold a defensive perimeter at Pusan, in the far southern part of Korea, a foothold from which MacArthur could conduct future operations. For the moment, MacArthur's orders for the perimeter were "to stand or die." The remainder of South Korea, meanwhile, was conceded to the Communists.

All the while, MacArthur was studying ways to expel the North Koreans from the country. The demilitarization of the military under Truman had been so severe that there wasn't enough shipping to deploy the kinds of forces needed, nor were there adequate forces themselves. He conceived a scheme to land a combination of marines, U.S. soldiers, and South Korean units at the port of Inchon, close to Seoul, that would trap the Communist forces between themselves and the Pusan defenders. It was a daring stratagem that was at first turned down by those in Washington as too risky.

MacArthur begged for and got a conference in Tokyo consisting of the highest-ranking army, navy, marine, and air force representatives. The navy men argued that Inchon's twenty- to thirty-foot tides created enormous, unnavigable mudflats that jutted out two miles from shore. On the target date for the landing in September, the navy said, the first high tide was reached at 6:59 a.m. and the evening tide at 7:19 p.m. Two hours after each high tide the mudflats would reappear. Thus the first assault wave would have to get ashore, push inland, secure a beachhead, and withstand counterattacks for twelve hours before more troops could be landed on the next high tide. If anything went wrong, the troops in the assault boats would be sitting ducks for enemy artillery.

The navy representative concluded, "If every possible geographic and naval handicap were listed—Inchon has 'em all." The army chief of staff didn't like the plan either. He called it too far to the enemy's rear to be effective and warned that the landing force might meet with overwhelming enemy resistance and be destroyed.

Then MacArthur arose and made his argument. He said that the very objections given to abandon the idea were the ones that would make it work—namely, the element of surprise. Because of all the difficulties of an Inchon landing, he said, the North Koreans would not be expecting it. He cited in detail the capture of Quebec in the French and Indian War, in which the British won a stunning victory on the Plains of Abraham by surprising the French.

MacArthur said that by landing at Inchon he could cut the enemy's supply line and roll him up in detail. The speech was so effective that it changed the minds of both the army and the navy representatives. On August 29 the Joint Chiefs of Staff gave MacArthur the go-ahead.

Planning and preparation proceeded apace until a week before D-day, when the Joint Chiefs got cold feet and told MacArthur they didn't think the landing would be successful. Skeptics were calling for another Dunkirk, but MacArthur silenced them with a reply of such overwhelming confidence that they again approved the operation.

On September 12, MacArthur boarded the USS *Mount McKinley,* a specially designed amphibious forces command ship, for the three-day trip to the waters off of Inchon. There, in the inky darkness of the blacked-out ship, MacArthur paced the decks at 2 a.m. absorbing the tension that had been building among the 40,000-man landing party scarcely five hours from its mission. "I alone was responsible for tomorrow," he proclaimed theatrically. "If I failed, the dreadful results would rest on judgment day against my soul."[24]

★ ★ ★ ★

THE INCHON LANDINGS WERE a complete success and perhaps MacArthur's most brilliant accomplishment as a soldier. Total surprise was achieved. The marines quickly overcame initial opposition and the beachhead was secured. The remainder of the assault force landed at the Seoul airport, and then the city itself—or what was left of it—was captured.

At the same time, several hundred miles south, the First Cavalry Division and various support units broke out of the Pusan Perimeter and began an advance northward, pushing the surprised North Korean army before it. Now MacArthur stood astride the tenuous supply lines between North Korea and the KPA. At Osan, thirty miles south of Seoul, the First Cavalry linked up with the Seventh Infantry Division, which had landed at Inchon and marched south. The two American divisions then threatened to trap the main Communist force in South Korea, which was being heavily damaged by U.S. air raids.

Rather than regroup for an orderly withdrawal beyond the 38th parallel, the KPA simply disintegrated; tens of thousands were captured and a mere thirty thousand managed to make their way northward. In Moscow, Joseph Stalin was furious because he had assigned Soviet military advisers to the North Korean effort.

MacArthur's army followed, attacking and taking prisoners. It was his intention, he stated, not to simply drive the North Koreans beyond the 38th parallel but to destroy their army and reunite the two Koreas as a democracy.

On September 27, Truman sent a message telling MacArthur that he was not authorized to go north of the 38th parallel if Chinese or Russian forces had come into North Korea, or if they publicly threatened such a move. But two days later, then Secretary of Defense George Marshall told MacArthur he was authorized to proceed with "unhampered" operations beyond the dividing line.

The following day the Chinese warned they would go to war if the United States crossed the 38th parallel. Nevertheless, on October 7, with sanction from the United Nations, MacArthur crossed the parallel into North Korea. Stalin secretly asked the Chinese to join the fight.

With Stalin's blessing, Mao Tse-tung ordered a 200,000-man Red Chinese army to prepare for an invasion of Korea. This army moved to the Manchurian–North Korea border by night to avoid detection.

On October 15, MacArthur flew to Wake Island for a conference during which he assured President Truman there was little chance the Chinese would intervene in Korea. By then the United States and the South Koreans had been joined by troops from Great Britain and Turkey. Truman insisted on calling it a United Nations "police action."

When he returned, MacArthur's intelligence section informed him that thousands of Red Chinese "volunteers" were infiltrating North Korea by way of the Yalu River. He asked his superiors in Washington for permission to destroy the Yalu bridges from the air, but this was denied for fear of provoking a Chinese intervention. After protesting the decision MacArthur was told he could bomb the southern part of the bridges but not the half attached to Red China. He protested further that he had never figured out how to bomb "half a bridge."

After managing to cross the Yalu River without detection, the Red Chinese on October 25 launched an overwhelming assault on United Nations forces, driving them back toward the 38th parallel. They were assisted by Soviet air cover, the first time U.S. pilots had tangled with Russian-made MIG fighter planes.

The Communist attacks continued to drive the UN forces southward utilizing their superior troop strength to encircle UN positions. A combined U.S. Army–Marines force of 20,000 was nearly wiped out at the Battle of Chosin Reservoir, but escaped with nearly 15,000 casualties. On December 16, 1950, Truman declared a national emergency and young men began receiving draft notices under the Conscription Act. MacArthur considered using nuclear weapons against the Communist onslaught, insisting that it should be his prerogative, not the president's, which naturally infuriated Truman. He also considered a scheme to dump a belt of atomic waste in the Yalu River to prevent the Chinese from resupplying themselves.

After the commanding general of Eighth Army was killed, General Matthew Ridgway was put in command. He managed to restore confidence, stabilizing the army and abandoning the retreat. The Red Chinese continued to attack but their tactics were extremely costly. The action, bloody and ferocious, settled around the 38th parallel.

★ ★ ★ ★

TRUMAN DEVELOPED A SORT of inferiority complex after he was suddenly pitchforked into the presidency; he felt inadequate replacing such a man as Franklin Delano Roosevelt and was touchy about people not giving him proper respect. Truman had not liked MacArthur even while he was vice president, complaining privately about MacArthur's imperial demeanor, especially vis-à-vis the president of the United States. Roosevelt knew how to handle MacArthur, but Truman was sensitive and picked fights; MacArthur gave him ample cause.

Truman became particularly incensed when a photograph appeared in newspapers showing MacArthur in Formosa kissing the hand of Madame Chiang after it had become official State Department policy to distance the United States from the Nationalist Chinese. (This was to keep from losing face should they be overrun by the Chinese Communists.) MacArthur told a State Department official he didn't care if Chiang "had horns and a tail so long as he fought against the Communists." Next, MacArthur issued a statement to the American Legion assailing American foreign policy in the Far East, which made Truman's blood boil.

At the Wake Island conference, Truman had confided his private feelings to his diary: "Gen. MacArthur was at the airport with his shirt unbuttoned, wearing a greasy ham and eggs cap that evidently had been in use for twenty years." Not long after that meeting Truman became almost apoplectic when MacArthur gave an interview to *U.S. News & World Report* in which he criticized the military restrictions placed upon him by those in Washington. In response, Truman issued a gag order that forbade high military or civilian officials from making a public statement without first clearing it with their department.[25]

With the war seemingly stalemated, Ridgway's Eighth Army scored a convincing victory over the Red Chinese. Truman was contemplating calling for a truce and holding peace talks when MacArthur, seemingly out of the blue, issued a public statement to the Chinese threatening to invade their port cities and take other destructive action against them unless they capitulated immediately. To Truman that was sheer insubordination and he used the occasion to relieve MacArthur of his command on April 11, 1951.

When Bradley got wind of the firing he awakened Truman to tell him that if word reached MacArthur before Truman's order did MacArthur would likely resign. "The son of a bitch isn't going to resign on me. I want him fired," the president said. A 1 a.m. press conference was held that night at the White House to announce MacArthur's relief. In Tokyo, one of MacArthur's staff heard the news on the radio and hurried to tell Jean. She informed the general, who calmly told her, "Jeannie, we're going home at last."[26]

★ ★ ★ ★

WHEN MACARTHUR LEFT TOKYO the following day, a quarter million Japanese lined his route to the airport. He was incensed over Truman's dismissing him without first letting him know, but he never addressed the issue publicly; he was soldier enough to know that the president has a right to fire anybody.

He was immediately invited to address a joint session of Congress, and he wrote his speech in flight. When he reached San Francisco late at night, half a million people were waiting for his plane chanting, "MacArthur for president!" In Washington, George Marshall, Omar Bradley, and a dozen three- and four-star generals were there to welcome him.

His address to Congress has been called "an epic moment" in the early years of television. It "left a grainy, if indelible, impression among millions of Americans of what a living legend and walking myth looked like in the flesh."[27]

In almost direct contravention to the foreign policies of Truman and his State Department, MacArthur spoke for more than an hour, frequently interrupted by wild ovations. He spoke about Asia, about the impoverishment and suffering of its people, and also about the dangers inherent in the rise of Red China. He criticized the lack of reinforcements for the army fighting in Korea and the restrictions placed upon him that he claimed kept him from winning a complete victory.

"It has been said that I am a warmonger," he said, his words ringing throughout the congressional chamber. "Nothing could be further from the truth. I know war as few men now living know it, and nothing to me is more revolting. I have long advocated its complete abolition . . . But once war is forced on us there is no alternative than to apply every available means to bring it to a swift end. War's very object is victory— not prolonged indecision," he said. "In war, indeed, there can be no substitute for victory."

He ended his speech with perhaps the most stirring closing remarks ever spoken in the halls of Congress. "When I joined the Army even before the turn of the century, it was the fulfillment of all my boyish hopes and dreams. The world has turned over several times since I took the oath on the Plain at West Point, and the hopes and dreams have long since vanished. But I still remember the refrain of one of the most popular barrack ballads of that day which proclaimed most proudly that—'Old soldiers never die, they just fade away.' And like the old soldier of that ballad, I now close my military career and just fade away—an old soldier who tried to do his duty as God gave him the light to see that duty—Goodbye."

It not only brought down the house, it nearly caused a riot. There were cries of "No! No!" Men wept and stamped their feet and beat upon their thighs with their fists; many jumped up and waved their arms wildly in the air, shouting MacArthur's name. The Speaker of the House had never seen such an outburst during his fifty years in politics. He told a friend, "There wasn't a dry eye on the Democratic side of the House . . . nor a dry seat among the Republicans!"[28]

Truman denounced the speech as "One hundred percent bullshit."[29]

The next day, MacArthur went to New York City for a spectacular ticker-tape parade that an estimated seven million people attended. His speech was followed by lengthy congressional hearings on the conduct of the war, in which MacArthur charged that his recommendations on how to proceed were accepted by the Joint Chiefs of Staff but torpedoed by the Truman administration. To contradict this allegation, the Democrats put George C. Marshall under oath, creating the sorry spectacle of two senior statesmen of the army accusing each other of lying. This episode was what prompted Senator Joe McCarthy's three-hour "treason" screed in Congress against Marshall.

In the summer of 1951 the MacArthurs took a large apartment on the thirty-seventh floor in the Waldorf Astoria Towers on New York's East Side. The spacious rooms were filled with an opulence of Oriental art and mementos, and MacArthur resumed his eternal pacing, stopping only to sleep, watch sports on TV—especially football—or attend Broadway plays.

A friend of the author's recalled an occasion when legendary football coach Paul "Bear" Bryant, who had recently won the first of his many national championships at the University of Alabama, was a guest at the Waldorf during the Heisman Trophy awards ceremony. Bryant had assembled a number of his fellow coaches—including such luminaries as Darrell Royal, Woody Hayes, Ara Parseghian, and Duffy Daughtery—for a cocktail party in his suite. He had instructed a former player who served as an assistant coach not to let anyone from the press disturb the party.

At some point there was a knock at the door and the assistant answered it to find an elderly gentleman inquiring whether this were Coach Bryant's suite. The assistant acknowledged it was, and the man asked if he could see the coach. "Coach Bryant is busy at the moment," the assistant answered and asked for the man's name.

"Douglas MacArthur," came the reply.

The assistant was so flabbergasted he simply stared, dumbstruck, but Bryant had noticed the incident and intervened, inviting MacArthur in. He had stayed only a short while when there was another knock and Mrs. MacArthur appeared in the doorway. "It is time for the general to go to bed," she said.

In 1960, at the age of eighty, MacArthur agreed to write his memoirs for Time Inc.'s Henry Luce for $900,000—the equivalent of more than $7 million today.

Two years later, with his health deteriorating, he accepted West Point's prestigious Sylvanus Thayer Award and journeyed up the Hudson to give his final speech at the United States Military Academy. After reviewing the corps at parade on the Plain, MacArthur had lunch in the dining hall with the cadets, then gave perhaps his most inspiring oration ever.

Its theme was the West Point motto: "Duty, Honor, Country," and in spine-tingling prose MacArthur reached back across the years for meaningful examples.

"From your ranks come the great captains who hold the nation's destiny in their hands the moment the war tocsin sounds. The long gray line has never failed us. Were you to do so, a million ghosts in olive drab, in brown khaki, in blue and gray, would rise from their white crosses, thundering those magic words: duty, honor, country . . .

"The soldier, above all other people," he said, "prays for peace, for he must suffer and bear the deepest wounds and scars of war. But always in our ears ring the ominous words of Plato . . . 'Only the dead have seen the end of war.'"

In conclusion, MacArthur said in a now quavering but still strong, gravelly, baritone voice: "The shadows are lengthening for me. The twilight is here . . . I listen, then, but with thirsty ear, for the witching melody of faint bugles blowing reveille, of far drums beating the long roll.

"In my dreams I hear again the crash of guns, the rattle of musketry, the strange, mournful mutter of the battlefield. But in the evening of my memory I come back to West Point. Always there echoes and re-echoes: duty, honor, country.

"Today marks my final roll call with you. But I want you to know that when I cross the river, my last conscious thoughts will be of the corps, and the corps, and the corps.

"I bid you farewell."[30]

There was an instantaneous outburst of cheering and a long standing ovation, during which it was said that "grown men fumbled with their handkerchiefs and blew their noses in a vain attempt to hide their tears."

Two years later, almost to the day, MacArthur died in Walter Reed Hospital of complications from surgery. He was eighty-four years old. He wanted to be buried not at West Point nor at Arlington but in Norfolk, Virginia, his mother's hometown. There they had promised him an entire city square, including the remodeled old courthouse, in which to house the MacArthur Memorial, including the MacArthur archives, a theater, and nine museum galleries containing his mementos.

The day after he died, MacArthur's body was taken to the U.S. Capitol where it lay in state by order of President Lyndon Johnson. The military caisson and flag-draped coffin were accompanied there by Black Jack, the horse that had accompanied the body of slain President John F. Kennedy to Arlington not five months previous. Some 150,000 people visited MacArthur's casket before it was taken by train to Norfolk.

In the large domed rotunda of the MacArthur Memorial his black tombstone lies in the center of a circular sarcophagus, and Jean lies next to him, having died in the year 2000. Around the top and inside of the rotunda are carved in marble the names of all the battles MacArthur fought, from the Philippine Insurrection Campaign, to World Wars I and II, and finally Korea. It is an impressive sight, of which MacArthur would be justly proud.

★ ★ ★ ★

THESE THREE MEN COULD HARDLY have been more different. Patton and MacArthur were the killers—but while one abhorred war, the other was an inveterate war lover. Marshall spent much of his career keeping the two of them, with their outsize egos, from self-imploding. In the end he had to preside over the demise of both their careers, which—in the greatest irony of all—seemed not to tarnish their reputations but to vastly enhance them.

MacArthur and Patton were seriously intellectual and each had a grasp of history that equaled or exceeded that of a university professor, while Marshall was a brilliant thinker who spurned the intuition-based choices of the other two and engineered a total victory in World War II.

They had been born into the age of horses and buggies and lived to the age of nuclear weapons and—in MacArthur's case—the spectacle of men in outer space. At times they were revered by their peers and by the multitudes as gods, but they weren't, of course. They were exceptionally good soldiers, and great captains, brave as lions, bold as bulls, audacious, and inventive, marshaling huge victorious armies. With all their quirks and foibles and mistakes they were still fine men who served their country with distinction, and when they died their memory enriched the national trust.

★ ★ ★ ★

NOTES

Chapter One: First Captain, VMI

1   George C. Marshall. *Interviews and Reminiscences* (Lexington, Va.: George C. Marshall Research Foundation, 1996). To avoid endless *ibid.* in these notes, this recollection and all of those that follow unless otherwise noted are taken from this collection of transcripts taped by Marshall in 1956–57 in response to written questions sent him by his official historian Forrest C. Pogue. In nearly 650 pages of interviews Marshall vividly recounts his life story from his earliest recollections until roughly two years before his death in 1959.

2   Forrest C. Pogue. *George C. Marshall: Education of a General 1880–1939* (New York: Viking, 1963).

3   Ibid.

4   Marshall, *Interviews and Reminiscences.*

5   William Frye. *Marshall: Citizen Soldier* (Indianapolis, New York: Bobbs-Merrill, 1947).

6   Ibid.

7   Pogue, *Education of a General.*

8   Frye, *Citizen Soldier.*

9   Ibid.

10 Pogue, *Education of a General.*

11 Frye, *Citizen Soldier.*

12 Ibid.

13 Ibid.

Chapter Two: Master of the Sword

1   Carlo D'Este. *Patton: A Genius for War* (New York: HarperCollins, 1995).

2   Ruth Ellen Patton Totten. *The Button Box: A Daughter's Loving Memoir of Mrs. George S. Patton* (Columbia: University of Missouri Press, 2005).

3   Martin Blumenson. *The Patton Papers: 1885–1940* (Boston: Houghton Mifflin, 1972).

4   D'Este, *Patton*.

5   Ladislas Farago. *Patton: Ordeal and Triumph* (New York: Ivan Obolensky, 1964).

6   Ibid.

7   Robert H. Patton. *The Pattons: A Personal History of an American Family* (New York: Crown, 1994).

8   D'Este, *Patton*.

9   Ruth Ellen Patton Totten, *The Button Box*.

10   Ibid.

11   D'Este, *Patton*.

12   Ibid.

13   Ibid.

14   Robert H. Patton, *The Pattons*.

15   Fred Ayer, Jr. *Before the Colors Fade: Portrait of a Soldier: George S. Patton, Jr.* (Boston: Houghton Mifflin, 1964).

16   D'Este, *Patton*.

17   Robert H. Patton, *The Pattons*.

18   Ibid.

19   Ibid.

20   Blumenson, *Patton Papers: 1885–1940*.

21   Ibid.

22   Ibid.

23   Ibid.

24   Robert H. Patton, *The Pattons*.

25   Ibid.

26   Ibid.

27   Blumenson, *Patton Papers: 1885–1940*.

28   Ayer, *Before the Colors Fade*.

29   D'Este, *Patton*.

30   Blumenson, *Patton Papers: 1885–1940.*

31   Ruth Ellen Patton Totten, *The Button Box.*

32   Blumenson, *Patton Papers: 1885–1940.*

33   Robert H. Patton, *The Pattons.*

34   D'Este, *Patton.*

35   Ruth Ellen Patton Totten, *The Button Box.*

36   Ibid.

37   Blumenson, *Patton Papers: 1885–1940.*

38   Ruth Ellen Patton Totten, *The Button Box.*

Chapter Three: The Champion of Vera Cruz

1   Douglas MacArthur. *Reminiscences: General of the Army* (New York: McGraw-Hill, 1964).

2   William Manchester. *American Caesar: Douglas MacArthur 1880–1964* (Boston: Little, Brown, 1978).

3   William Forbes Skene. *The Highlanders of Scotland* (Stirling, Scotland: Eneas Mackay, 1902).

4   D. Clayton James. *The Years of MacArthur Volume I, 1880–1941* (Boston: Houghton Mifflin, 1970).

5   Ibid.

6   Ibid.

7   Ibid.

8   MacArthur, *Reminiscences.*

9   Ibid.

10   James, *Years of MacArthur Volume I.*

11   Manchester, *American Caesar.*

12   Jules Archer. *Front-Line General: Douglas MacArthur* (New York: Julian Messner, 1963); MacArthur, *Reminiscences.*

13   MacArthur, *Reminiscences.*

14   Ibid.

15   Manchester, *American Caesar.*

16   Ibid. (citing the *Ohio Historical Quarterly*).

17   Frazier Hunt. *The Untold Story of Douglas MacArthur* (New York: Devin-Adair, 1954).

18   Ibid.

19   Robert Considine. *General Douglas MacArthur* (Greenwich, Conn.: Fawcett, 1964); Thomas J. Fleming. *West Point* (New York: William Morrow, 1969).

20   MacArthur, *Reminiscences;* Archer, *Front-Line General.*

21   MacArthur, *Reminiscences.*

22   Ibid.

23   Geoffrey Perret. *Old Soldiers Never Die: The Life of Douglas MacArthur* (Holbrook, Mass.: Adams Media Corp., 1996).

24   Ibid.

25   Ibid. (from the MacArthur Memorial and Archives).

26   Ibid.

27   Ibid.

Chapter Four: "Some Damned Foolishness in the Balkans"

1   George C. Marshall. *Memoirs of My Services in the World War 1917–1918* (Boston: Houghton Mifflin, 1976).

2   Martin Blumenson. *The Patton Papers: 1885–1940* (Boston: Houghton Mifflin, 1972).

3   Ibid.

4   Ibid. Quoted from Frank Vandiver. *Black Jack: The Life and Times of John J. Pershing, Volume II* (College Station: Texas A&M University Press, 1977).

5   Fred Ayer, Jr. *Before the Colors Fade: Portrait of a Soldier: George S. Patton, Jr.* (Boston: Houghton Mifflin, 1964).

6   Harry H. Semmes. *Portrait of Patton* (New York: Appleton, 1955).

7   Blumenson, *Patton Papers: 1885–1940.*

8   Douglas MacArthur. *Reminiscences: General of the Army* (New York: McGraw-Hill, 1964).

9   D. Clayton James. *The Years of MacArthur Volume I, 1880–1941* (Boston: Houghton Mifflin, 1970).

10   MacArthur, *Reminiscences.*

11   Blumenson, *Patton Papers: 1885–1940.*

12   Forrest C. Pogue. *George C. Marshall: Education of a General 1880–1939* (New York: Viking, 1963).

13   Ibid.

14   George C. Marshall. *Interviews and Reminiscences* (Lexington, Va.: George C. Marshall Research Foundation, 1996).

15   Ibid.

16   Ibid.

17   Ibid.

18   Blumenson, *Patton Papers: 1885–1940.*

19   Ibid.

20   Ibid.

21   Carlo D'Este. *Patton: A Genius for War* (New York: HarperCollins, 1995); Blumenson, *Patton Papers: 1885–1940.*

22   Martin Blumenson. *Patton: The Man Behind the Legend, 1885–1945* (New York: William Morrow, 1985).

23   James, *Years of MacArthur Volume I.*

24   MacArthur, *Reminiscences;* Francis P. Duffy. *Father Duffy's Story: A Tale of Humor and Heroism, of Life and Death with the Fighting Sixty-Ninth* (New York: Doran, 1919).

25   MacArthur, *Reminiscences.*

26   James, *Years of MacArthur Volume I.*

27   Blumenson, *Patton Papers: 1885–1940.*

28   Ibid.

29   Ibid.

30   Ibid.

31   Blumenson, *Patton.*

32   Ibid.

33   Blumenson, *Patton Papers: 1885–1940.*

34   Marshall, *Memoirs of My Services.*

35   Winston Churchill. *The World Crisis 1911–1918, vol. III* (London: Thornton Butterworth, Ltd., 1927).

36   Pogue, *Education of a General.*

37   Ibid.

38   Frazier Hunt. *The Untold Story of Douglas MacArthur* (New York: Devin-Adair, 1954).

39   James, *Years of MacArthur Volume I.*

40   Jules Archer. *Front-Line General: Douglas MacArthur* (New York: Julian Messner, 1963).

41   Duffy, *Father Duffy's Story.*

42   Hunt, *The Untold Story of Douglas MacArthur.*

Chapter Five: Courage Was the Rule

1   Martin Blumenson. *The Patton Papers: 1885–1940* (Boston: Houghton Mifflin, 1972).

2   Martin Blumenson. *Patton: The Man Behind the Legend, 1885–1945* (New York: William Morrow, 1985).

3   Harry H. Semmes. *Portrait of Patton* (New York: Appleton, 1955); Blumenson, *Patton Papers: 1885–1940.*

4   Douglas MacArthur. *Reminiscences: General of the Army* (New York: McGraw-Hill, 1964).

5   Ed Cray. *General of the Army: George C. Marshall, Soldier and Statesman* (New York: Cooper Square Press, 1990).

6   George C. Marshall. *Interviews and Reminiscences* (Lexington, Va.: George C. Marshall Research Foundation, 1996).

7   MacArthur, *Reminiscences.*

8   Blumenson, *Patton Papers: 1885–1940.*

9   William Henry Amerine. *Alabama's Own in France* (New York: Eaton and Gettinger, 1919); Lt. John H. Taber. *The Story of the 168th Infantry* (Iowa City: State Historical Society of Iowa, 1925).

10 MacArthur, *Reminiscences.*

11 D. Clayton James. *The Years of MacArthur Volume I, 1880–1941* (Boston: Houghton Mifflin, 1970); MacArthur, *Reminiscences.*

12 MacArthur, *Reminiscences.*

13 Blumenson, *Patton Papers: 1885–1940.*

14 Ibid.

15 George C. Marshall. *Memoirs of My Services in the World War 1917–1918* (Boston: Houghton Mifflin, 1976).

16 Forrest C. Pogue. *George C. Marshall: Education of a General 1880–1939* (New York: Viking, 1963).

17 Geoffrey Perret. *Old Soldiers Never Die: The Life of Douglas MacArthur.* (Holbrook, Mass.: Adams Media Corp., 1996).

18 Frazier Hunt. *The Untold Story of Douglas MacArthur* (New York: Devin-Adair, 1954).

19 Amerine, *Alabama's Own in France.*

20 Ibid.

21 Ibid.

22 Perret, *Old Soldiers Never Die.*

23 Hunt, *The Untold Story of Douglas MacArthur.*

Chapter Six: The Sad, Great Heap of *Fleurs Blanches*

1   Forrest C. Pogue. *George C. Marshall: Education of a General 1880–1939* (New York: Viking, 1963).

2   George C. Marshall. *Interviews and Reminiscences* (Lexington, Va.: George C. Marshall Research Foundation, 1996). (The descriptions of Marshall's visit to England are contained in his diary located in the appendix.)

3   George C. Marshall. *Memoirs of My Services in the World War 1917–1918* (Boston: Houghton Mifflin, 1976).

4   Ibid. (Again, it is Marshall's diary in the appendix that provides these descriptions.)

5   Winston Groom. *A Storm in Flanders: Tragedy and Triumph on the Western Front* (New York: Atlantic Monthly Press, 2002).

6   Marshall, *Memoirs of My Services.*

7   Marshall, *Interviews and Reminiscences.*

8   Ruth Ellen Patton Totten. *The Button Box: A Daughter's Loving Memoir of Mrs. George S. Patton* (Columbia: University of Missouri Press, 2005); Carlo D'Este. *Patton: A Genius for War* (New York: HarperCollins, 1995).

9   Ruth Ellen Patton Totten, *The Button Box.*

10 Ibid.

11 D'Este, *Patton.*

12 Ruth Ellen Patton Totten, *The Button Box.*

13 Stephen Ambrose. *Eisenhower: Soldier, General of the Army, President-Elect, 1890–1952* (New York: Simon and Schuster, 1983).

14 D'Este, *Patton.*

15 Martin Blumenson. *The Patton Papers: 1885–1940* (Boston: Houghton Mifflin, 1972).

16 Marshall, *Interviews and Reminiscences.*

17 Ruth Ellen Patton Totten, *The Button Box.*

18 Ibid.

19 D. Clayton James. *The Years of MacArthur Volume I, 1880–1941* (Boston: Houghton Mifflin, 1970); Douglas MacArthur. *Reminiscences: General of the Army* (New York: McGraw-Hill, 1964).

20 MacArthur, *Reminiscences.*

21 William Addleman Ganoe. *MacArthur Close-Up* (New York: Vantage Press, 1962).

22 James, *Years of MacArthur Volume I.*

23 MacArthur, *Reminiscences.*

24 William Manchester. *American Caesar: Douglas MacArthur 1880–1964* (Boston: Little, Brown, 1978).

25 Ibid.

26 Ed Cray. *General of the Army: George C. Marshall, Soldier and Statesman* (New York: Cooper Square Press, 1990).

27 William Frye. *Marshall: Citizen Soldier* (Indianapolis, New York: Bobbs-Merrill, 1947).

28 Cray, *General of the Army.*

29 Ibid.

30 Mary Sutton Skutt. *George C. Marshall: Reporting for Duty* (Lexington, Va.: Blue Valley Books, 2001).

31 Ibid.

32 Ibid.

33 Pogue, *Education of a General.*

34 Cray, *General of the Army.*

35 Pogue, *Education of a General.*

36 Ibid.

37 Cray, *General of the Army.*

38 Pogue, *Education of a General.*

39 Skutt, *George C. Marshall.*

40 Cray, *General of the Army.*

41 Pogue, *Education of a General.* (The story of Katherine Brown comes almost entirely from Pogue, who recorded interviews with her in the 1960s, which are available from the George Marshall Foundation in Lexington, Virginia.)

42 Blumenson, *Patton Papers: 1885–1940.*

43 Ruth Ellen Patton Totten, *The Button Box.*

44 D'Este, *Patton.*

45 Ruth Ellen Patton Totten, *The Button Box.*

46 Blumenson, *Patton Papers: 1885–1940.*

47 D'Este, *Patton.*

48 Ruth Ellen Patton Totten, *The Button Box.*

49 Blumenson, *Patton Papers: 1885–1940.*

50 MacArthur, *Reminiscences;* Manchester, *American Caesar* (Boston: Little, Brown, 1978).

51 Manchester, *American Caesar.*

52 MacArthur, *Reminiscences.*

53   Ibid.

54   Manchester, *American Caesar.*

55   Ibid.

56   James, *Years of MacArthur Volume I.*

57   Ibid.

58   Manchester, *American Caesar.*

59   MacArthur, *Reminiscences.*

Chapter Seven: "I Am All He Has"

1   Mary Sutton Skutt. *George C. Marshall: Reporting for Duty* (Lexington, Va.: Blue Valley Books, 2001).

2   Ed Cray. *General of the Army: George C. Marshall, Soldier and Statesman* (New York: Cooper Square Press, 1990).

3   Carlo D'Este. *Patton: A Genius for War* (New York: HarperCollins, 1995); Ruth Ellen Patton Totten. *The Button Box: A Daughter's Loving Memoir of Mrs. George S. Patton* (Columbia: University of Missouri Press, 2005).

4   Ibid.

5   Ibid.

6   D'Este, *Patton.*

7   Robert H. Patton. *The Pattons: A Personal History of an American Family* (New York: Crown, 1994); D'Este, *Patton;* Ruth Ellen Patton Totten, *The Button Box.*

8   Ruth Ellen Patton Totten, *The Button Box.*

9   William Manchester. *American Caesar: Douglas MacArthur 1880–1964* (Boston: Little, Brown, 1978).

10   Ibid.

11   William Frye. *Marshall: Citizen Soldier* (Indianapolis, New York: Bobbs-Merrill, 1947).

12   Winston Groom. *1942: The Year That Tried Men's Souls* (New York: Atlantic Monthly Press, 2005). The World War II background is taken largely from this book.

13   John Costello. *The Pacific War 1941–1945* (New York: Rawson, Wade, 1981).

14   Fleet Admiral William F. Halsey and Lt. Commander J. Bryan III. *Admiral Halsey's Story* (New York: Whittlesey House, 1947).

15 Martin Blumenson. *The Patton Papers: 1885–1940* (Boston: Houghton Mifflin, 1972).

16 D'Este, *Patton.*

17 Ibid.

18 General George C. Kenney. *The MacArthur I Know* (New York: Duell, Sloan and Pearce, 1951).

Chapter Eight: This Means War

1 John Toland. *The Rising Sun: The Decline and Fall of the Japanese Empire* (New York: Random House, 1970).

2 Winston Churchill. *The Second World War, vol. II* (Boston: Houghton Mifflin, 1948).

3 Lewis H. Brereton. *The Brereton Diaries* (New York: William Morrow, 1946).

4 Ibid.

5 William Manchester. *American Caesar: Douglas MacArthur 1880–1964* (Boston: Little, Brown, 1978).

6 Ruth Ellen Patton Totten. *The Button Box: A Daughter's Loving Memoir of Mrs. George S. Patton* (Columbia: University of Missouri Press, 2005). The entire episode regarding Ruth Ellen's marriage to James Totten is recorded in this excellent book.

7 Martin Blumenson. *The Patton Papers: 1885–1940* (Boston: Houghton Mifflin, 1972).

8 Ibid.

Chapter Nine: There Will Be a Big Tank Battle in the Morning

1 Martin Blumenson. *The Patton Papers: 1940–1945* (Boston: Houghton Mifflin, 1974).

2 Winston Groom. *1942: The Year That Tried Men's Souls* (New York: Atlantic Monthly Press, 2005).

3 Ibid.

4 Blumenson, *Patton Papers: 1940–1945.*

5 General George S. Patton Jr. *War As I Knew It* (Boston: Houghton Mifflin, 1947, 1995). (The diaries, letters, and other documents quoted regarding Patton's adventures in North Africa and Sicily unless otherwise noted are contained in this book and in Blumenson, *Patton Papers: 1940–1945,* and in order to avoid the repeated *ibid.* they will not be further annotated.)

6 Carlo D'Este. *Patton: A Genius for War* (New York: HarperCollins, 1995).

7 Winston Groom. *1942: The Year That Tried Men's Souls* (New York: Atlantic Monthly Press, 2005).

8 Ernie Pyle. *Here Is Your War* (New York: Henry Holt, 1943).

9 Omar N. Bradley and Clay Blair. *A General's Life* (New York: Simon and Schuster, 1983).

10 Omar N. Bradley. *A Soldier's Story* (New York: Henry Holt, 1951).

11 D'Este, *Patton.*

12 Ibid. (quoting Albert N. Garland and Howard M. Smyth. *Sicily and the Surrender of Italy* [Washington, D.C.: GPO, 1965]).

13 Ibid.

14 Carlo D'Este. *Bitter Victory: The Battle for Sicily* (New York: Penguin Putnam, 1992).

15 Bradley and Blair, *A General's Life.*

16 Ibid.; D'Este, *Bitter Victory.*

17 Ibid.

18 Bradley and Blair, *A General's Life.*

19 Blumenson, *Patton Papers: 1940–1945.*

20 Winston Groom. *The Aviators: Eddie Rickenbacker, Jimmy Doolittle, Charles Lindbergh, and the Epic Age of Flight* (Washington, D.C.: National Geographic, 2013).

Chapter Ten: "I Shall Return"

1 Jonathan M. Wainwright. *General Wainwright's Story* (New York: Doubleday, 1945).

2 Douglas MacArthur. *Reminiscences: General of the Army* (New York: McGraw-Hill, 1964).

3 Ibid.

4 Winston Groom. *1942: The Year That Tried Men's Souls* (New York: Atlantic Monthly Press, 2005).

5 MacArthur, *Reminiscences.*

6 Ibid.

7 Brigadier General Steve Mellnik. *Philippine Diary 1939–1945* (New York: Van Nostrand Reinhold, 1969).

8 Donald Knox. *Death March: The Survivors of Bataan* (New York: Harcourt, 1981).

9 Abie Abraham. *Oh, God, Where Are You?* (New York: Vantage Press, 1997).

10 Knox, *Death March.*

11 Ibid.

12 John Costello. *The Pacific War 1941–1945* (New York: Rawson, Wade, 1981).

13 Robert L. Eichelberger. *Our Jungle Road to Tokyo* (New York: Viking, 1950).

14 Ibid.

15 MacArthur, *Reminiscences.*

16 Ibid.

17 General George C. Kenney. *The MacArthur I Know* (New York: Duell, Sloan and Pearce, 1951).

18 Allen Phelps Julian. *MacArthur: The Life of a General* (New York: Duell, Sloan and Pearce, 1963).

19 Ibid.

20 Col. Charles H. MacDonald. "Lindbergh in Battle," *Colliers,* June 6, 1946.

21 Julian, *MacArthur.*

22 MacArthur, *Reminiscences.*

23 Samuel I. Rosenman. *Working with Roosevelt* (New York: Harper and Brothers, 1952), quoted in D. Clayton James, *The Years of MacArthur Volume II* (Boston: Houghton Mifflin, 1975).

24 James, *Years of MacArthur Volume II.*

25 MacArthur, *Reminiscences.*

26 Ibid.

27 Ibid.

28 William Manchester. *American Caesar: Douglas MacArthur 1880–1964* (Boston: Little, Brown, 1978).

29 Ibid.

Chapter Eleven: Overlord

1 William Frye. *Marshall: Citizen Soldier* (Indianapolis, New York: Bobbs-Merrill, 1947).

2 Ibid.

3 Ibid.

4 George C. Marshall. *Interviews and Reminiscences* (Lexington, Va.: George C. Marshall Research Foundation, 1996).

5 Ibid.

6 Ibid.

7 Martin Blumenson. *The Patton Papers: 1940–1945* (Boston: Houghton Mifflin, 1974).

8 Ibid.

9 Forrest C. Pogue. *George C. Marshall: Organizer of Victory 1943–1945* (New York: Viking, 1973).

10 Blumenson, *Patton Papers: 1940–1945*. (All of the following Patton letters and diary inserts come from this source.)

11 Carlo D'Este. *Patton: A Genius for War* (New York: HarperCollins, 1995).

12 Pogue, *Organizer of Victory.*

13 Ibid.

14 Ibid.

Chapter Twelve: Let's Win It All

1 General George S. Patton Jr. *War As I Knew It* (Boston: Houghton Mifflin, 1947, 1995).

2 Alan Axelrod. *Patton's Drive: The Making of America's Greatest General* (Guilford, Conn.: Lyons Press, 2009).

3 Omar N. Bradley and Clay Blair. *A General's Life* (New York: Simon and Schuster, 1983).

4 Dwight Eisenhower. *Crusade in Europe* (New York: Doubleday, 1948).

5 Axelrod, *Patton's Drive.*

6 Terry Brighton. *Patton, Montgomery, Rommel: Masters of War* (New York: Crown, 2008).

7 Martin Blumenson. *The Patton Papers: 1940–1945* (Boston: Houghton Mifflin, 1974).

8 Ibid.

9 Patton, *War As I Knew It.*

10 Blumenson, *Patton Papers: 1940–1945.*

11 Ibid.

12 Colonel Paul D. Harkins, Patton's deputy chief of staff, as told in Patton, *War As I Knew It.*

13 Blumenson, *Patton Papers: 1940–1945.*

14 Ibid.

15 Patton, *War As I Knew It.*

16 Ibid.

17 Ibid.

18 Blumenson, *Patton Papers: 1940–1945*.

19 Colonel Paul D. Harkins, cited in Patton, *War As I Knew It*.

20 Patton, *War As I Knew It*.

21 Blumenson, *Patton Papers: 1940–1945*.

22 Ibid.

23 Ibid.

24 Patton, *War As I Knew It*.

25 Blumenson, *Patton Papers: 1940–1945*.

26 Hobart R. Gay, cited in Blumenson, *Patton Papers: 1940–1945*.

27 Martin Blumenson. *Patton: The Man Behind the Legend, 1885–1945* (New York: William Morrow, 1985).

28 Lt. Gen. Wladyslaw Anders. *Russian Volunteers in the German Army in World War II* (1997), accessed 2015. Feldgrau.com (German military history website).

29 Blumenson, *Patton*.

30 Colonel Paul D. Harkins, cited in Patton, *War As I Knew It*.

Chapter Thirteen: These Proceedings Are Closed

1 Samuel Eliot Morison. *History of United States Naval Operations in World War II. Vol. XII: Leyte, June 1944–January 1945* (Boston: Little, Brown, 1961); J.F.C. Fuller. *The Decisive Battles of the Western World II* (London: Eyre and Spottiswoode, 1955). The short account of the Battle of Leyte Gulf comes principally from these two sources.

2 Douglas MacArthur. *Reminiscences: General of the Army* (New York: McGraw-Hill, 1964).

3 D. Clayton James. *The Years of MacArthur Volume II* (Boston: Houghton Mifflin, 1975).

4 Ibid.

5 Ibid.

6 Ibid.

7 Geoffrey Perret. *Old Soldiers Never Die: The Life of Douglas MacArthur.* (Holbrook, Mass.: Adams Media Corp., 1996).

8 Henry C. Godman. *Supreme Commander* (Harrison, Ark.: New Leaf Press, 1980).

9 Perret, *Old Soldiers Never Die*.

10 MacArthur, *Reminiscences.*

11 Ibid.

12 James, *Years of MacArthur Volume II;* Perret, *Old Soldiers Never Die.*

13 MacArthur, *Reminiscences.*

14 James, *Years of MacArthur Volume II.*

15 MacArthur, *Reminiscences.*

16 Roger Olaf Egeberg. *The General: MacArthur and the Man He Called "Doc"* (New York: Hippocrene, 1983).

17 Perret, *Old Soldiers Never Die.*

18 James, *Years of MacArthur Volume II.*

19 MacArthur, *Reminiscences.*

20 Egeberg, *The General.*

21 William Manchester. *American Caesar: Douglas MacArthur 1880–1964* (Boston: Little, Brown, 1978).

22 Egeberg, *The General.*

23 James, *Years of MacArthur Volume II.*

24 Ibid.; Manchester, *American Caesar.*

25 Manchester, *American Caesar.*

26 MacArthur, *Reminiscences.*

27 George C. Kenney. *General Kenney Reports* (New York: Duell, Sloan and Pearce, 1949).

28 James, *Years of MacArthur Volume II.*

29 Kenney, *General Kenney Reports.*

30 Ibid.

31 Ibid.

32 Ibid.

33 MacArthur, *Reminiscences.*

34 Ibid.

35 Ibid.

Chapter Fourteen: Old Soldiers Never Die

1   Ed Cray. *General of the Army: George C. Marshall, Soldier and Statesman* (New York: Cooper Square Press, 1990).

2   Katherine Marshall. *Together* (New York: Tupper & Love, 1946).

3   Leonard Mosley. *Marshall: Hero for Our Times* (New York: Hearst Books, 1982).

4   Ibid.

5   Cray, *General of the Army.*

6   Forrest C. Pogue. *George C. Marshall: Statesman 1949–1959* (New York: Viking, 1987); Cray, *General of the Army.*

7   Mosley, *Marshall.*

8   Martin Blumenson. *The Patton Papers: 1940–1945* (Boston: Houghton Mifflin, 1974).

9   Ibid.

10   Ibid.

11   Ibid.

12   Ibid.

13   Robert H. Patton. *The Pattons: A Personal History of an American Family* (New York: Crown, 1994).

14   Blumenson, *Patton Papers: 1940–1945.*

15   Robert H. Patton, *The Pattons.*

16   Ibid.

17   Douglas MacArthur. *Reminiscences: General of the Army* (New York: McGraw-Hill, 1964).

18   General George C. Kenney. *The MacArthur I Know* (New York: Duell, Sloan and Pearce, 1951).

19   MacArthur, *Reminiscences.*

20   Kenney, *The MacArthur I Know.*

21   MacArthur, *Reminiscences.*

22   Ibid.

23   Ibid.

24   Ibid.

25   Geoffrey Perret. *Old Soldiers Never Die: The Life of Douglas MacArthur.* (Holbrook, Mass.: Adams Media Corp., 1996).

26   Ibid.

27   Ibid.

28   Ibid.

29   William Manchester. *American Caesar: Douglas MacArthur 1880–1964* (Boston: Little, Brown, 1978).

30   William Safire, ed. *Lend Me Your Ears: Great Speeches in History* (New York: W. W. Norton, 2004).

★ ★ ★ ★

NOTES ON SOURCES
AND ACKNOWLEDGMENTS

T his is my tenth book of history. I always begin by acknowledging "those dogged biographers and historians who have gone before," and I see no reason to abandon the practice now. They are the ones who, before files and indeed huge documents could be ordered over the Internet, would spend countless hours in libraries and archives throughout the country—and in some cases the world—digging into records, squinting into microfilm viewers, copying material by hand, or relentlessly standing at the Xerox machine. To each and every one of you my hat is off.

As with my previous book *The Aviators,* this is not a full-blown biography of the three army generals; such a book that examines every orifice would likely be several thousand pages long. But nor are the three intertwined stories merely sketches. As my editor once observed, I have actually written three books here. It is nice being able to "cherry-pick," but I find it lamentable that there was so much richness in these characters' lives that I wasn't able to include for fear of sawing down entire forests for the printing paper.

As in *The Aviators,* the three subjects of *The Generals* either wrote their own autobiographies or memoirs (MacArthur's *Reminiscences;* Patton's *War As I Knew It*) or in George Marshall's case did extensive interviews with his early biographer that are available to the public. Some argue that memoirs or other autobiographic material are self-serving, which is probably true, but one could argue the same thing about what the subject says to an interviewer. I find them useful, but the collected papers are more so. Biographer Martin Blumenson put together a fascinating three-volume collection of nearly every letter, scrap of paper, or military order associated with George S. Patton that I find superior as a research tool. Dr. Forrest Pogue's four-volume biography of Marshall is accompanied by a 641-page collection of interviews and reminiscences in which the author submitted questions to the general, who was near the end of his life, that he would answer speaking into a Dictaphone. There are some very good biographies of MacArthur, beginning with the three-volume study by Clayton James entitled *The Years of MacArthur.* The much-heralded *American Caesar* by William Manchester is a good read, but a more reliable biography is *Old Soldiers Never Die* by Geoffrey Perret.

For MacArthur's experiences in World War I, I relied heavily on the 42nd Infantry "Rainbow" Division's official history, *Americans All,* published in 1936; the 1919 history of the 167th Infantry Regiment; and Nimrod Frazer's *Send the Alabamians,* which relates unknown details of the Battle of Croix Rouge Farm. For general information on the issues and causes of both world wars, I depended largely on my own works *A Storm in Flanders* and *1942: The Year That Tried Men's Souls* and on my knowledge of the subject.

For insightful and delightful peeks into the lively private life of George Patton, several books by family members are must-reads: *The Button Box* by Patton's daughter Ruth Ellen; *Before the Colors Fade* by brother-in-law Fred Ayer Jr.; and *The Pattons: A Personal History of an American Family* by Patton's grandson Robert H. Patton.

The Internet offers a wealth of information these days provided you select it carefully and discriminately. Significant newspapers and periodicals are available online—either subscribe or pay an individual fee and all the news the *New York Times* sees fit to print is at your fingertips.

The usual suspects (mostly) provided, variously: support, comfort, encouragement, research, and/or money to see the project through. My editor at the Geographic, Lisa Thomas, who is now editor in chief there, has been a saint, as has associate editor Anne Smyth, who is seeing the book to its conclusion. Ann Day of publicity has been available night and day. Though I didn't have my magic line editor Andrew Carlson this time, stepping into his shoes is the highly talented editor Phil Marino, who has managed to make sense of the mess I sent him. My longtime copy editor Don Kennison has once more saved me from myself. My faithful executive assistant Dr. Wren Murphy has again organized all of my research with graciousness and skill. And literary agent (and author) Keith Korman read every word of this book as it was produced, chapter by chapter, offering keen suggestions (and making snide, incisive comments). To these and all the others too numerous to mention I owe an undying debt of gratitude.

Winston Groom
Point Clear, Alabama
April 5, 2015

P.S. Thanks to my friend Tommy Moore of Tuscaloosa, Alabama, for the delightful story of MacArthur and the football coach at the Waldorf.

★ ★ ★ ★

BIBLIOGRAPHY

Abraham, Abie. *Oh, God, Where Are You?* New York: Vantage Press, 1997.

Adler, Selig. *The Isolationist Impulse: Its Twentieth-Century Reaction.* London and New York: Abelard-Schuman, 1957.

Ambrose, Stephen E. *The Supreme Commander: The War Years of Dwight D. Eisenhower.* New York: Anchor Books, 1969, 1979, 2012.

———. *Eisenhower: Soldier, General of the Army, President-Elect, 1890–1952.* New York: Simon and Schuster, 1983.

Amerine, William Henry. *Alabama's Own in France* (Primary Source Edition). New York: Eaton and Gettinger, 1919.

Archer, Jules. *Front-Line General: Douglas MacArthur.* New York: Julian Messner, 1963.

Axelrod, Alan. *Patton's Drive: The Making of America's Greatest General.* Guilford, Conn.: Lyons Press, 2009.

Ayer, Fred, Jr. *Before the Colors Fade: Portrait of a Soldier. George S. Patton, Jr.* Boston: Houghton Mifflin, 1964.

Baldwin, Hanson. *Battles Lost and Won: Great Campaigns of World War II.* New York: Harper and Row, 1966.

Beal, John Robinson. *Marshall in China.* New York: Doubleday, 1970.

Belote, James H., and William M. Belote. *Corregidor: The Saga of a Fortress.* New York: Harper and Row, 1967.

Blumenson, Martin. *The Patton Papers: 1885–1940*. Boston: Houghton Mifflin, 1972.

———. *The Patton Papers: 1940–1945*. Boston: Houghton Mifflin, 1974.

———. *Patton: The Man Behind the Legend, 1885–1945*. New York: William Morrow, 1985.

Borneman, Walter R. *The Admirals: Nimitz, Halsey, Leahy, and King—The Five-Star Admirals Who Won the War at Sea*. New York: Little, Brown, 2012.

Bradley, Omar N. *A Soldier's Story*. New York: Henry Holt, 1951.

Bradley, Omar N., and Clay Blair. *A General's Life*. New York: Simon and Schuster, 1983.

Brereton, Lt. Gen. Lewis H. *The Brereton Diaries*. New York: William Morrow, 1946.

Brighton, Terry. *Patton, Montgomery, Rommel: Masters of War*. New York: Crown, 2008.

Carmichael, Thomas N. *The Ninety Days*. Old Saybrook, Conn.: Konecky, 1971.

Churchill, Winston. *The World Crisis* (5 vols.). London: Thornton Butterworth, Ltd., 1923–1931.

———. *The Second World War* (6 vols.). Boston: Houghton Mifflin, 1948–1953.

Clayton, Tim, and Phil Craig. *The End of the Beginning*. New York: Free Press, 2007.

Considine, Robert. *General Douglas MacArthur*. Greenwich, Conn.: Fawcett, 1964.

Costello, John. *The Pacific War 1941–1945*. New York: Rawson, Wade, 1981.

Cray, Ed. *General of the Army: George C. Marshall, Soldier and Statesman*. New York: Cooper Square Press, 1990.

D'Este, Carlo. *Bitter Victory: The Battle for Sicily*. New York: Penguin Putnam, 1992.

———. *Patton: A Genius for War*. New York: HarperCollins, 1995.

Drea, Edward. *MacArthur's ULTRA: Codebreaking and the War Against Japan*. Lawrence: University Press of Kansas, 1992.

Duffy, Francis P. *Father Duffy's Story: A Tale of Humor and Heroism, of Life and Death with the Fighting Sixty-Ninth*. New York: Doran, 1919.

Dyess, Lt. Col. William E. *Bataan Death March: A Survivor's Account.* Toronto: Longmans, Green, 1944.

Edmonds, Brig. Gen. Sir James E., ed. *History of the Great War Based on Official Documents* (28 vols.). London: Macmillan, 1920–1961.

Egeberg, Roger Olaf. *The General: MacArthur and the Man He Called "Doc."* New York: Hippocrene, 1983.

Eichelberger, Lt. Gen. Robert L. *Our Jungle Road to Tokyo.* New York: Viking, 1950.

Eisenhower, Dwight D. *Crusade in Europe.* New York: Doubleday, 1948.

Farago, Ladislas. *Patton: Ordeal and Triumph.* New York: Ivan Obolensky, 1964.

———. *The Last Days of Patton.* New York: McGraw-Hill, 1981.

Ferrell, Robert. *The Question of MacArthur's Reputation: Côte De Châtillon, October 14–16, 1918.* Columbia: University of Missouri Press, 2008.

Fleming, Thomas J. *West Point: The Men and Times of the United States Military Academy.* New York: William Morrow, 1969.

Frazer, Nimrod T. *Send the Alabamians: World War I Fighters in the Rainbow Division.* Tuscaloosa: University of Alabama Press, 2014.

Freeman, Roger. *B-17 Fortress at War.* New York: Charles Scribner's Sons, 1977.

Friend, Theodore. *Between Two Empires.* New Haven: Yale University Press, 1965.

Frye, William. *Marshall: Citizen Soldier.* Indianapolis, New York: Bobbs-Merrill, 1947.

Fuchida, Mitsuo, and Masatake Okumiya. *Midway: The Battle That Doomed Japan.* Annapolis: United States Naval Institute, 1955.

Fuller, J.F.C. *The Decisive Battles of the Western World II.* London: Eyre and Spottiswoode, 1955.

Ganoe, William Addleman. *MacArthur Close-Up.* New York: Vantage Press, 1962.

Garland Albert N., and Howard M. Smyth. *Sicily and the Surrender of Italy.* Washington, D.C.: GPO, 1965.

Gilbert, Sir Martin. *The First World War.* New York: Henry Holt, 1994.

Godman, Henry C. *Supreme Commander.* Harrison, Ark.: New Leaf Press, 1980.

Groom, Winston. *A Storm in Flanders: Tragedy and Triumph on the Western Front.* New York: Atlantic Monthly Press, 2002.

————. *1942: The Year That Tried Men's Souls.* New York: Atlantic Monthly Press, 2005.

————. *The Aviators: Eddie Rickenbacker, Jimmy Doolittle, Charles Lindbergh, and the Epic Age of Flight.* Washington, D.C.: National Geographic, 2013.

Halsey, Fleet Admiral William F., and Lt. Commander J. Bryan III. *Admiral Halsey's Story.* New York: Whittlesey House, 1947.

Hart, Sir Basil Henry Liddell. *Liddell Hart's History of the First World War 1914–1918.* London: Faber & Faber, 1930.

————. *History of the Second World War.* New York: Putnam, 1971.

Hibbs, Ralph Emerson. *Tell MacArthur to Wait.* New York: Carlton Press, 1987.

Hobbs, Joseph P. *Dear General: Eisenhower's Wartime Letters to Marshall.* Baltimore: Johns Hopkins University Press, 1971.

Hunt, Frazier. *The Untold Story of Douglas MacArthur.* New York: Devin-Adair, 1954.

Jablonski, Edward. *Air War* (4 vols.). New York: Doubleday, 1971.

James, D. Clayton. *The Years of MacArthur Volume I, 1880–1941.* Boston: Houghton Mifflin, 1970.

————. *The Years of MacArthur Volume II, 1941–1945.* Boston: Houghton Mifflin, 1975.

————. *Triumph and Disaster: The Years of MacArthur Volume III, 1945–1964.* Boston: Houghton Mifflin, 1985.

Jones, Charles T. *The Wit and Wisdom of General George S. Patton: Laws of Leadership Series,* vol. VI. Mechanicsburg, Penn.: Executive Books, 2007.

Julian, Allen Phelps. *MacArthur: The Life of a General.* New York: Duell, Sloan and Pearce, 1963.

Kagan, Donald. *On the Origins of War: And the Preservation of Peace.* New York: Doubleday, 1995.

Kennan, George F. *Memoirs.* Boston: Little, Brown, 1967.

Kenney, General George C. *General Kenney Reports.* New York: Duell, Sloan and Pearce, 1949.

————. *The MacArthur I Know.* New York: Duell, Sloan and Pearce, 1951.

Knox, Donald. *Death March: The Survivors of Bataan.* New York: Harcourt, 1981.

Lloyd, Nick. *Hundred Days: The Campaign That Ended World War I.* New York: Basic Books, 2014.

MacArthur, Douglas. *Reminiscences: General of the Army.* New York: McGraw-Hill, 1964.

———. *MacArthur. Duty. Honor. Country: A Pictorial Autobiography.* New York: McGraw-Hill, 1965.

Manchester, William. *American Caesar: Douglas MacArthur 1880–1964.* Boston: Little, Brown, 1978.

Marshall, George C. *Selected Speeches and Statements of General of the Army George C. Marshall,* ed. H. A. DeWeerd. New York: Da Capo, 1973.

———. *Memoirs of My Services in the World War 1917–1918.* Boston: Houghton Mifflin, 1976.

———. *Interviews and Reminiscences for Forrest C. Pogue,* ed. Larry I. Bland. Lexington, Va.: George C. Marshall Research Foundation, 1996.

Marshall, Katherine. *Together.* New York: Tupper & Love, 1946.

McCarthy, Senator Joseph R. *America's Retreat from Victory: The Story of George Catlett Marshall.* New York: Devin-Adair, 1951.

McCartney, William F. *The Jungleers: A History of the 41st Infantry Division.* Washington, D.C.: Infantry Journal Press, 1948.

Mellnik, Brigadier General Steve. *Philippine Diary 1939–1945.* New York: Van Nostrand Reinhold, 1969.

Milner, Samuel. *Victory in Papua.* Washington, D.C.: Center of Military History, United States Army, 1989.

Morison, Dr. Samuel Eliot. *The Rising Sun in the Pacific: 1931–April 1942,* vol. III. Boston: Little, Brown, 1948.

———. *History of United States Naval Operations in World War II Volume XII: Leyte, June 1944–January 1945.* Boston: Little, Brown, 1961.

———. *The Two-Ocean War: A Short History of the United States Navy in the Second World War.* Boston: Little, Brown, 1963.

Mosley, Leonard. *Marshall: Hero for Our Times.* New York: Hearst Books,1982.

Munch, Lieutenant Colonel Paul G. *General George C. Marshall and the Army Staff: A Study in Effective Staff Leadership.* Washington, D.C.: United States Army, 1992.

New Yorker Magazine, Inc. *The New Yorker Book of War Pieces: London 1939–Hiroshima 1945.* New York: Reynal & Hitchcock, 1947.

Parrish, Thomas. *Roosevelt and Marshall. Partners in Politics and War: The Personal Story.* New York: William Morrow, 1989.

Patton, General George S., Jr. *War As I Knew It.* Boston: Houghton Mifflin, 1947, 1995.

Patton, Robert H. *The Pattons: A Personal History of an American Family.* New York: Crown, 1994.

Perret, Geoffrey. *Old Soldiers Never Die: The Life of Douglas MacArthur.* Holbrook, Mass.: Adams Media Corp., 1996.

Perry, Mark. *Partners in Command: George Marshall and Dwight Eisenhower in War and Peace.* New York: Penguin, 2007.

Pogue, Forrest C. *George C. Marshall: Education of a General 1880–1939.* New York: Viking, 1963.

———. *George C. Marshall: Ordeal and Hope 1939–1942.* New York: Viking, 1965.

———. *George C. Marshall: Organizer of Victory 1943–1945.* New York: Viking, 1973.

———. *George C. Marshall: Statesman 1949–1959.* New York: Viking, 1987.

Prang, Gordon W. *At Dawn We Slept: The Untold Story of Pearl Harbor.* New York: Penguin Books, 1982.

Pyle, Ernie. *Here Is Your War.* New York: Henry Holt, 1943.

Reilly, Brigadier General O.R.C. Henry J. *Americans All: The Rainbow at War. Official History of the 42nd Rainbow Division in the World War.* Columbus, Ohio: F. J. Heer Printing Co., 1936.

Ricks, Thomas E. *The Generals: American Military Command from World War II to Today.* New York: Penguin, 2012.

Semmes, Harry H. *Portrait of Patton.* New York: Appleton, 1955.

Sherwood, Midge. *Days of Vintage, Years of Vision,* vol. I. San Marino, Calif.: Orizaba Publications, 1982.

———. *Days of Vintage, Years of Vision,* vol. II. San Marino, Calif.: Orizaba Publications, 1987.

Sherwood, Robert E. *Roosevelt and Hopkins: An Intimate History.* New York: Harper, 1948.

Skene, William Forbes. *The Highlanders of Scotland*. Stirling, Scotland: Eneas Mackay, 1902.

Skutt, Mary Sutton. *George C. Marshall: Reporting for Duty*. Lexington, Va.: Blue Valley Books, 2001.

———. *George C. Marshall: Man Behind the Plan (Statesman and Retirement Years, 1945–1959)*. Lexington, Va.: News-Gazette Print Shop, 2004.

Spector, Ronald H. *Eagle Against the Sun: The American War with Japan*. New York: Vintage, 1985.

Stoler, Mark A. *George C. Marshall: Soldier-Statesman of the American Century*. New York: Twayne, 1989.

Taaffe, Stephen R. *Marshall and His Generals: U.S. Army Commanders in World War II*. Lawrence: University Press of Kansas, 2011.

Taber, Lieutenant John H. *The Story of the 168th Infantry*. Iowa City: State Historical Society of Iowa, 1925.

Terraine, John. *The Great War*. London: Hutchinson, 1965.

Thomas, Ed. *As I Remember: The Death March of Bataan*. Sonoita, Ariz.: 1990.

Toland, John. *But Not in Shame*. New York: Random House, 1961.

———. *The Rising Sun: The Decline and Fall of the Japanese Empire*. New York: Random House, 1970.

Totten, Ruth Ellen Patton. *The Button Box: A Daughter's Loving Memoir of Mrs. George S. Patton*, ed. James Patton Totten. Columbia: University of Missouri Press, 2005.

Wainwright, General Jonathan M. *General Wainwright's Story*. New York: Doubleday, 1945.

Whitney, Courtney. *MacArthur: His Rendezvous with History*. New York: Knopf, 1956.

Wilcox, Robert K. *Target: Patton. The Plot to Assassinate General George S. Patton*. Washington, D.C.: Regnery, 2008.

Yeide, Harry. *Fighting Patton: George S. Patton, Jr. Through the Eyes of His Enemies*. Minneapolis: Zenith Press, 2011.

★ ★ ★ ★
INDEX

Index

INDEX

INDEX

INDEX

ILLUSTRATIONS CREDITS

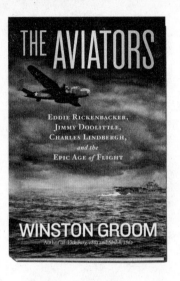

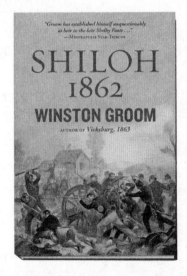